INSIGHT GUIDE
EAST ASIA

D1550780

APA PUBLICATIONS

Part of the Langenscheidt Publishing Group

ABOUT THIS BOOK

Editorial
Project Editor
Heidi Sopinka
Managing Editor
Tom Le Bas
Editorial Director
Brian Bell

Distribution

UK & Ireland
GeoCenter International Ltd
The Viables Centre , Harrow Way
Basingstoke, Hants RG22 4BJ
Fax: (44) 1256-817988

United States
Langenscheidt Publishers, Inc.
46–35 54th Road, Maspeth, NY 11378
Fax: (718) 784-0640

Canada
Prologue Inc.
1650 Lionel Bertrand Blvd., Boisbriand
Québec, Canada J7H 1N7
Tel: (450) 434-0306. Fax: (450) 434-2627

Australia & New Zealand
Hema Maps Pty. Ltd.
24 Allgas Street, Slacks Creek 4127
Brisbane, Australia
Tel: (61) 7 3290 0322. Fax: (61) 7 3290 0478

Worldwide
Apa Publications GmbH & Co.
Verlag KG (Singapore branch)
38 Joo Koon Road, Singapore 628990
Tel: (65) 865-1600. Fax: (65) 861-6438

Printing

Insight Print Services (Pte) Ltd
38 Joo Koon Road, Singapore 628990
Tel: (65) 865-1600. Fax: (65) 861-6438

©1999 Apa Publications GmbH & Co.
Verlag KG (Singapore branch)
All Rights Reserved
First Edition 1989
New Edition 1999

CONTACTING THE EDITORS
Although every effort is made to
provide accurate information, we
live in a fast-changing world and
would appreciate it if readers
would call our attention to any
errors or outdated information
that may occur by writing to us:
Insight Guides, P.O. Box 7910,
London SE1 8WE, England.
Fax: (44 171) 403-0290.
insight@apaguide.demon.co.uk

This guidebook combines the interests and enthusiasms of two of the world's best known information providers: Insight Guides, whose titles have set the standard for visual travel guides since 1970, and Discovery Channel, the world's premier source of nonfiction television programming.

The editors of Insight Guides provide both practical advice and general understanding about a destination's history, culture, institutions and people. Discovery Channel and its Web site, www.discovery.com, help millions of viewers explore their world from the comfort of their own home and also encourage them to explore it first hand.

This fully updated edition of *Insight: East Asia* is carefully structured to convey an understanding of the region and its varied cultures as well as to guide readers through its major sights and activities:

◆ The **Features** sections, indicated by a yellow bar at the top of each page, covers the history and culture of the four countries in a series of informative essays.

◆ The **Places** sections, indicated by a blue bar, provide a full run-down on the capital cities and other exciting destinations. Places of special interest are coordinated by number with the maps.

◆ At the back of the book, the **Travel Tips** listings for each country are indicated by an orange bar and provide a handy point of reference for information on travel, hotels, shops, cultural sights and more.

EXPLORE YOUR WORLD
Discovery
CHANNEL

The contributors

This latest edition of *Insight: East Asia* was supervised by managing editor **Tom Le Bas** at Insight's editorial office in London. Enlisted to distil the work of many Insight Guide writers for this book was **Heidi Sopinka**, a Canada-based editor. The book has been completely updated with the invaluable help of a number of contributors based in Asia.

CHINA: **Hilary Smith** updated the Beijing, Xi'an and Shanghai chapters, **Ed Peters** and **Annie Galpin** revised Hong Kong and Macau while **Benjack Phillips** covered Guilin and Guangzhou. Contributors whose work from previous editions appears include **Manfred Morgenstern, Tim Larimer, Leslie Burgoine, Ellen Sheng, Sharon Owyang, Lily Tung, Bill Smith, Jim Goodman, Angie Ching Yuan, Ron Glotzer, Helmut Forster-Latsch, Marie-Luise Latsch,** Marie-Luise Beppler-Lie, Karl Grobe-Hagel, Eva Klapproth, Elke Wandel and **Tom Ots**.

TAIWAN: The Places chapters and the Travel Tips were updated by **Lise Lingo**. The pictorial essay on Traditional Medicine was written and researched by **Clare Griffiths**. Original contributors include **Bernd Hans-Gerd Helms** and his wife **Linda Chih-Ling Hsu, John Gottberg Anderson, Keith Stevens, Paul Zach** and **Andy Unger**.

KOREA: The Features, Places and Travel Tips sections for this edition were revised by **Ed Peters**. The original text was compiled by **Michael Breen, John Gustaveson, Leonard Lueras, Nedra Chung, James Wade, Barbara Mintz, Norman Thorpe, Jon Carter Covell, Gary Clay Rector, Laurel Kendall, Norman Sibley, Gertrude Ferrar, Michael E. Macmillan, Tom Coyner** and **Ken Kaliher**.

JAPAN: The text was updated by **Scott Rutherford, Hugh Paxton, Mason Florence** and **Ed Peters**. Contributors whose work from previous editions appears include **Malcolm Davis, Bill Williams, Matsutani Yuko, Kim Schuefftan, Steve Usdin, John Carroll, Alex Kerr, Davis Barrager, Mark Schreiber, David Benjamin, Anthony J. Bryant, Bruce Leigh, Rich Blumm, Peter Ujlaki, Peter Hadfield, Arturo Silva, Gail Feldman, Evelyn Corbett, Wayne Graczyk, Robert McLeod** and **Otani Eiho**.

Photographers for this edition include **Catherine Karnow, Jack Hollingsworth, Bill Wassman, Dan Rocovits** and **Dave Houser**.

Thanks also go to **Pam Barrett** for her marshalling of the Travel Tips and to **Penny Phenix** for proofreading and indexing.

Map Legend

▬ ▬ ‥ ▬	International Boundary
‒ ‒ ‒ ‒	Province State/ Boundary
⊖	Border Crossing
▬ • ▬ • ▬	National Park/Reserve
‒ ‒ ‒ ‒	Ferry Route
Ⓜ	Metro
✈ ✦	Airport: International/ Regional
🚌	Bus Station
🅿	Parking
❶	Tourist Information
✉	Post Office
† ✝	Church/Ruins
†	Monastery
☾	Mosque
✡	Synagogue
♜ ⌂	Castle/Ruins
∴	Archaeological Site
∩	Cave
𝟏	Statue/Monument
★	Place of Interest

The main places of interest in the Places section are coordinated by number with a full-colour map (e.g. ❶), and a symbol at the top of every right-hand page tells you where to find the map.

CONTENTS

Maps

The bright lights of
downtown Shanghai

Insight on ...

South Korea

Japan

WHERE THE PAST MEETS THE FUTURE

East Asia is a region where ancient traditions thrive against a backdrop of rapid economic and urban growth

To arrive in the region is to descend into abstractions. The Western mind, steeped in Aristotelian logic and preconceptions, can knit itself into a knot of pure bewilderment trying to recognize the undercurrents of East Asia. Foreign armies, armadas and adventurers have done so countless times. (One hopes that the days of invading armies, from outside and from within, are over.)

Why does someone nowadays make the trek to East Asia? It's a long haul for the traveller coming from Europe or the Americas to Beijing, Hong Kong, Taipei, or Seoul, and an expensive prospect if the destination is Tokyo. Visitors generally fall into one of two categories: the pragmatist, who comes for business or education; and the romantic, drawn to fulfil a dream or satisfy a wanderlust.

The pragmatist comes because Asia is where the 21st century is likely to be defined, and where much of the world's economic engine will be fuelled. The new century, pundits predict, belongs to Asia, just as the 19th century was dominated by Europe, and the 20th century by America. Two of the world's largest three economies are Asian – China and Japan. China's share of the world's output exceeds 6 percent and is growing, yet in economic terms the country has just begun to rub the sleep from its eyes. With more than 1 billion people, it is the world's largest consumer market, and if it is seeking an economic model, it has only to gaze towards its neighbours, Japan, Korea and the island of Taiwan (which it regards as part of China).

Most paths in East Asia lead to China, whether in art, architecture, language, writing, philosophy. The Korean peninsula and Japanese archipelago have nurtured ancient Chinese culture into rich and unique civilizations of their own – although the Japanese are not keen to remember their Chinese or especially their Korean heritage.

The historical and political dynamics of East Asia are complex, changing, and usually subtle. These countries have at times been isolationist, resisting not only interference from outside the region but also from their neighbours.

In recent years Japan has cast the biggest shadow across East Asia, if not all of Asia, representing a possible economic paradigm for other Asian peoples. But beneath the envy and admiration for Japan's trading success – and the *schadenfreude* when it stumbled economically in the 1990s – is a lingering bitterness about the country's brutal domination of Asia during World War II. The Koreans certainly have a strong memory of those times; many Japanese

PRECEDING PAGES: Sani woman in Yunnan, China; bamboo grove in Kamakura, Japan; buddhas at Chikji-sa, South Korea; Ami harvest dance, Hualien, Taiwan.
LEFT: the painted mask is critical in Chinese opera.

things are outlawed in Korea. On the other hand, many Japanese today seemed convinced that Japan was the principal victim of World War II. Other Asian countries will probably resist Japan's efforts to obtain a permanent seat on the Security Council at the United Nations, at least until the Japanese acknowledge that the economic high ground does not carry with it the moral high ground. So close in geography and yet so distant.

Hong Kong, that aberrant, fussy and vibrant city, spins on the pressured time of business and politics. Yanked from China in 19th-century colonial land grabs, Hong Kong has been a borrowed place on borrowed time, to borrow a phrase from the novelist Han Su-yin. In many ways, it still is, despite its return to China in 1997. The 1989 pro-democracy movement in China and subsequent government crackdown eroded any confidence Hong Kong might have had in the possibility of an enlightened Beijing. Nearby Macau, the Portuguese outpost, reverts on better terms.

Perhaps Taiwan, that other detached limb of the Chinese dragon, may do likewise one day. Despite expulsion from the United Nations, of which it was a founding member, and the severing of diplomatic ties with most Western nations, Taiwan has transformed itself into a modern industrial state, America's fifth largest trading partner. Despite the lack of diplomatic recognition, the Taiwanese are the best-fed people in East Asia, and have more urban living space than the Japanese.

Neither Beijing nor Taipei disputes that Taiwan is an integral province of China. It's a question of perspective – and pride. Mainland China calls its capital city Beijing, which means northern capital. The Taiwanese call the same city Peiping, which means northern peace. The inference? Beijing is not the capital of China, at least at the moment.

However, Asian units of time are patience and fate, not ticks of the clock. China, after all, is nearly 50 centuries old. Its written language has been around since long before the collapse of the Pharaonic dynasties in Egypt. Another year – or 50 – is little more than a blink in time and history.

A note on spelling

For much of the 20th century, the most common way to romanise Chinese was the Wade-Giles method. Increasingly, however, *pinyin* is the modern standard, and it is the official system used within the People's Republic. Taiwan, on the other hand, uses the Wade-Giles system. In this book we have therefore used the pinyin system for China and Wade-Giles for Taiwan.

It is worth pointing out that travellers will encounter both forms in Asia, and so must make certain linguistic leaps of recognition at times. China's capital was Peking the old way, Beijing in pinyin. Nanking has become Nanjing. The founder of the Communist Party, Mao Tse-tung, is now known as Mao Zedong. The goddess of mercy is Kuan Yin in Taiwan, Guanyin in China. And the Ch'in dynasty is now the Qin dynasty. The city of Foochow is now Fuzhou, Tsingtao is Qingdao, while the province of Kwangtung becomes Guangdong.

Pinyin transliterations liable to induce indigestion are *q* (pronounced as a hard *ch*), *x* (pronounced *sh*) and *zh* (pronounced something like a soft *j*). ❏

RIGHT: morning walk on Shiretoko Peninsula, northeast Hokkaido, Japan.

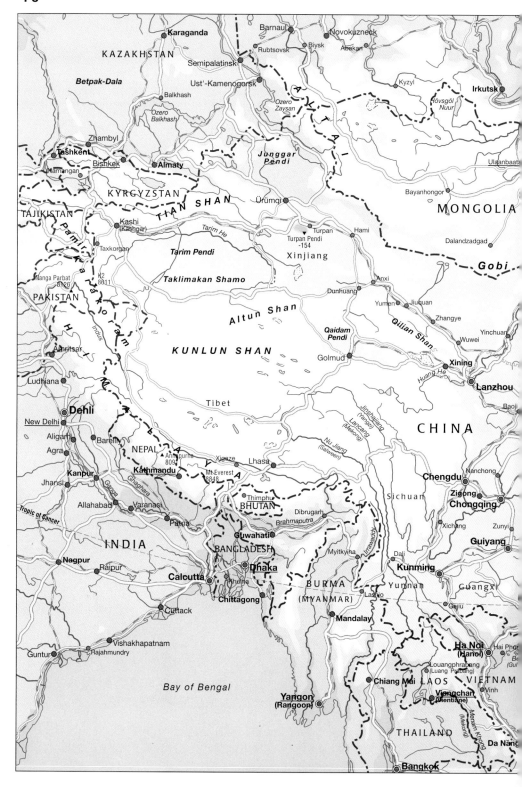

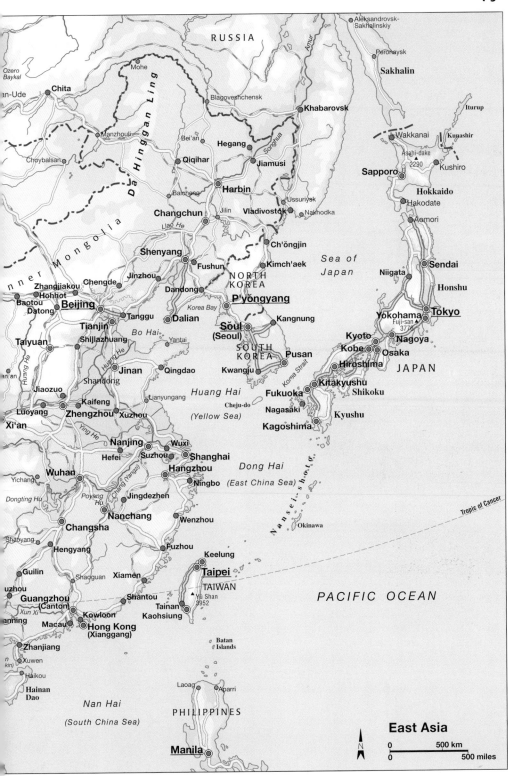

East Asia

雍和門

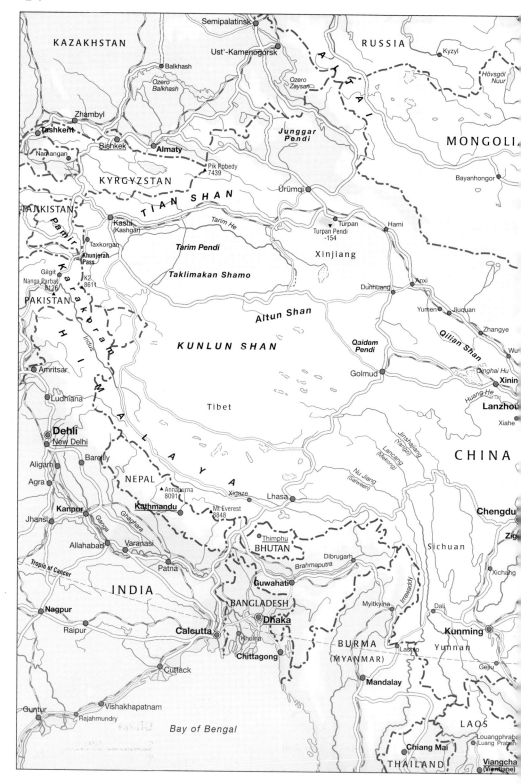

KAZAKHSTAN

Semipalatinsk

Ust'-Kamenogorsk

RUSSIA

Kyzyl

Hövsgöl Nuur

Balkhash

Ozero Balkhash

Ozero Zaysan

A L T A I

MONGOLI

Zhambyl

Tashkent

Bishkek

Almaty

Junggar Pendi

Bayanhongor

Namangan

KYRGYZSTAN

Pik Pobedy 7439

TIAN SHAN

Ürümqi

TAJIKISTAN

Pamir

Kashi (Kashgar)

Tarim He

Turpan

Turpan Pendi -154

Hami

Xinjiang

Taxkorgan

Khunjerab Pass

Tarim Pendi

Gilgit

Nanga Parbat 8126

K2 8611

Karakoram

Taklimakan Shamo

Dunhuang

Anxi

Yumen

Jiuquan

Qilian Shan

Zhangye

Wu

Altun Shan

PAKISTAN

Indus

KUNLUN SHAN

Qaidam Pendi

Qinghai Hu

Xinin

Amritsar

H

Golmud

Lanzhou

Ludhiana

I

M

Tibet

Huang He

Xiahe

A

Dehli

New Delhi

L

Jinshajiang (Yangzi)

CHINA

Aligarh

Bareilly

A

Lancang (Mekong)

Agra

NEPAL

Y

Annapurna 8091

Xigaze

Lhasa

Nu Jiang (Salween)

Chengdu

Jhansi

Kanpur

Ganga

Ghaghara

Kathmandu

Mt Everest 8848

Zig

Allahabad

Varanasi

Thimphu

Dibrugarh

Sichuan

Patna

BHUTAN

Brahmaputra

Xichang

Tropic of Cancer

INDIA

Guwahati

Nagpur

BANGLADESH

Myitkyina

Irrawaddy

Dali

Raipur

Dhaka

Kunming

Calcutta

Khulna

BURMA

Lashio

Yunnan

Cuttack

Chittagong

(MYANMAR)

Geju

Mandalay

Guntur

Vishakhapatnam

Rajahmundry

LAOS

Bay of Bengal

Louangphrab (Luang Praban)

Chiang Mai

Viangcha (Vientiane)

THAILAND

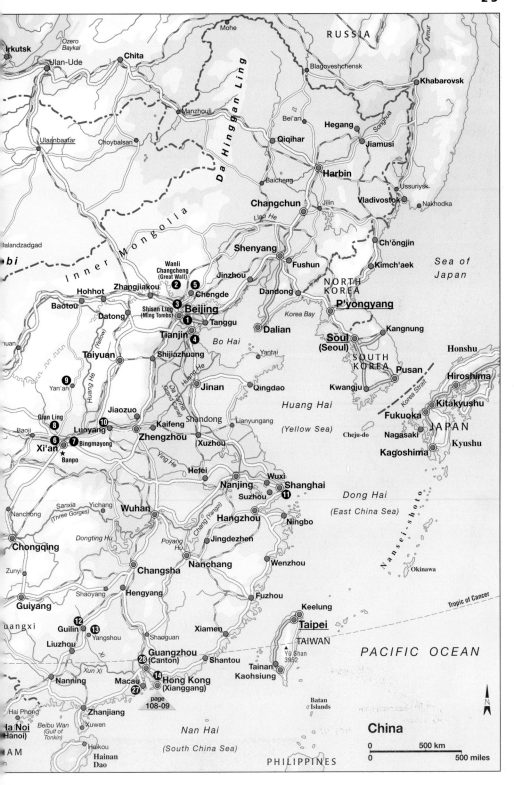

China

PACIFIC OCEAN

Tropic of Cancer

| 0 | | 500 km |
| 0 | | 500 miles |

CHINA

After 40 centuries of looking inward, China is set to play an increasingly important role in the world's future

Zhonghua Renmin Gongheguo is the official name of the People's Republic of China, but in everyday language it is simply Zhongguo – the Middle Kingdom. In the Temple of Heaven in Beijing, a marble altar signifies the center of the world, a place that only the Emperor was allowed to enter in order to communicate with heaven. According to the cosmological view of the world held in ancient Chinese cultures, the Middle Kingdom lay precisely below the centre of the firmament. The peoples living on the dark peripheries of the earth's disk were regarded as barbarians. Perhaps they still are.

Westerners have for centuries regarded China as an empire at the edge of the world. The ancient Greeks wrote about the Serers, which means the "bearers of silk", and for more than a millennium there was only one link between Europe and China: the hazardous land route via the ancient Silk Road. Knowledge of China was not gained easily, or quickly.

The variations of China's contours are as expansive as its vast territory, and deserve a book to themselves (which they have in *Insight Guide: China*). Nevertheless, a book on the region must pay its dues to China, the origin of everything East Asian. In *Insight Guide: East Asia* we'll introduce you to three of mainland China's most important cities, Beijing, Shanghai and Guangzhou, and one its most ancient cities and capitals, Xi'an. Beijing, Shanghai and Guangzhou (often known in the West as Canton) are thoroughly Chinese and thus thoroughly different, not only in latitude and appearance, but in cuisine, dialect, and attitude. Hong Kong and Macau, now reverted to Chinese sovereignty, are also included, as is Guilin with its wonderful, quintessentially Chinese landscapes.

The foundations of modern China are probably the world's most complex and have the deepest roots anywhere. Yet even recent events give breadth and depth to its people and personality. The 19th century was a period of humiliation for China as the powers of industrialized Europe pushed it into a marginal existence, dividing up its territory and injuring its self-esteem. From this situation arose national and revolutionary forces working towards a strong China, a self-centred independence, often keeping itself at a long arm's length from the outside. The Chinese learn, always, never forgetting a lesson.

While you're walking the streets of a Chinese city, don't forget an old Chinese proverb – "Seeing is easy, learning is hard". Or putting it another way, again through an old Chinese proverb, "None are as blind as those who don't want to see".   ❑

PRECEDING PAGES: view from Huang Shan, Anhui Province; Yonghe Gong, Beijing.
LEFT: *mahjong*, a national pastime in China.

Decisive Dates

THE EARLY EMPIRE

circa 21st–16th centuries BC Xia dynasty. Some scholars question whether this dynasty existed.
circa 16th–11th centuries BC Shang dynasty, the first recorded dynasty. Ancestor worship is ritualised.
circa 11th cent.–256 BC Zhou dynasty. Capital established at Chang'an (now Xi'an), later at Luoyang.
770–476 BC Spring and Autumn Period. Consolidation of aristocratic family-states. Confucius (551–479 BC) stresses moral responsibility of ruler.
403–221 BC Warring States period.

QIN DYNASTY (221–206 BC)

221 BC Qin Shi Huangdi unifies China to found the first imperial dynasty. Weights and measures, currency, and writing are standardised. Qin Shi Huangdi builds a vast underground tomb, including an army of thousands of terracotta warriors.

HAN DYNASTY (206 BC–AD 220)

206 BC Han dynasty founded; capital in Chang'an.
180 BC Eunuchs appear at the imperial court to look after the emperor's wives and concubines.
165 BC Civil service examinations instituted.
AD 25 Capital moved to Luoyang.
AD 105 Traditional date for the invention of paper. Paper may have already been in use for two centuries. Commerce between China and Asia/Europe thrives.
2nd century The first Buddhist establishments are founded in China.
AD 220 Abdication of the last Han emperor. Wei, Jin, and Northern and Southern dynasties divide China.

SUI DYNASTY (581–618)

581 Following nearly four centuries of division, Sui dynasty reunifies China. New legal code established.
589–610 Repairs of early parts of the Great Wall. Construction of a system of Grand Canals linking northern and southern China.

TANG DYNASTY (618–907)

618 Sui dynasty collapses, Tang dynasty proclaimed. Government increasingly bureaucratised. Buddhism influences all sectors of society. Chang'an (Xi'an) grows into one of the world's largest cities by the end of the Tang dynasty.
690–705 Empress Wu (627–705) governs China as its first female ruler. Writing of poetry becomes a requisite in civil service examinations.
907–960 Fall of Tang dynasty. Five Dynasties and Ten Kingdoms partition China. Anarchy in much of China.

SONG DYNASTY (960–1279)

960 Northern Song dynasty reunites China, capital established at Kaifeng.
1040 Invention of movable type, but not as efficient for printing pages of Chinese characters as wood-block printing. Development of Neo-Confucianism during 11th and 12th centuries.
1127 Beginning of the Southern Song dynasty, as invaders take over northern China and the Song capital is moved to Hangzhou, near Shanghai.

YUAN DYNASTY (1279–1368)

1279 After nearly half a century of trying, Mongols led by Kublai Khan, grandson of Ghengis Khan, rout the Song court. Tibet is added to the empire. Trade along the Silk Road flourishes. Beijing is made the capital.

MING DYNASTY (1368–1644)

1368 Founding of the Ming dynasty after Han Chinese overthrow the Mongols.
1405–33 During the reign of Emperor Yongle, Muslim eunuch Zheng He (1371–circa 1433) commands seven overseas expeditions to Southeast Asia, India, Persia, and East Africa.

1514 The first Portuguese ships set anchor off Guangzhou (Canton).
1553 Macau becomes a Portuguese trading port, and the first European settlement in China.

QING DYNASTY (1644–1912)

1644 A non-Han Chinese people from Manchuria, the Manchu, seize Beijing, to initiate the Qing dynasty.
1661–1722 Reign of Emperor Kangxi.
1736–96 Reign of Emperor Qianlong.
1800 First edict prohibiting the importation and local production of opium.
1838 Lin Zexu, a court official, suspends all trade in opium. The following year, the Qing court terminates all trade between England and China.
1839–42 English forces gather off China's coast. Fighting begins in 1841 in what has been called the First Opium War.
1842 Treaty of Nanjing signed. More Chinese ports are forced open to foreign trade, and Hong Kong island is surrendered to Great Britain "in perpetuity".
1851–64 Taiping Rebellion.
1855–75 Muslim rebellions.
1858 Conflicts arise between European powers, mainly France and England, and China. Treaty of Tianjin signed, opening more ports to foreigners.
1860 British and French troops burn the Summer Palace in Beijing; Kowloon Peninsula ceded to Britain.
1894–95 Sino-Japanese War, which China loses.
1900 Boxer Rebellion seeks to remove foreign influences from China.
1905 Abolishment of the civil service examinations.
1911 Republican Revolution: Sun Yatsen is chosen president, but soon steps down.
1912 Abdication of the last emperor, Puyi.

POST-IMPERIAL CHINA

1916–28 President of the republic, Yuan Shikai, considers declaring himself emperor. Several provinces declare independence, Yuan dies, and China falls apart. Civil war amongst various warlords.
1919 On 4 May in Beijing, a large demonstration demands measures to restore China's sovereignty, thus beginning a nationalist movement.
1921 Founding of the Communist Party in Shanghai.
1925 Sun Yatsen dies, disappointed with the anarchy of China's civil war.
1934–36 The Long March: Communists forced by Nationalists to abandon their stronghold in southern China. 30,000 of the original 100,000 who

LEFT: Emperor Kangxi reigned from 1661 to 1722.
RIGHT: Mao Zedong surrounded by Red Guards.

began the march arrive at the Communists' northern base in Yan'an, west of Beijing.
1937 Marco Polo Bridge Incident instigates full-scale war against Japan. Communists and Nationalists unite to fight the Japanese.
1945 Japan defeated in World War II; full-scale civil war ensues in China.

PEOPLE'S REPUBLIC OF CHINA

1949 Mao Zedong declares People's Republic in Beijing on 1 October; Nationalist army flees to Taiwan.
1950–53 Chinese troops support North Korea.
1958–61 Great Leap Forward results in a mass famine that kills upwards of 30 million Chinese.

1960 Split between China and the Soviet Union.
1964 China explodes an atomic bomb.
1966 Beginning of Cultural Revolution.
1976 Zhou Enlai and Mao Zedong die, Cultural Revolution ends. Demonstrations in Tiananmen Square.
1978 Deng Xiaoping becomes leader, instituting a policy of economic reform and opening to the West.
1979 The United States recognises China.
1989 Tiananmen Square demonstrations; military crackdown ends with hundreds of deaths.
1992 Deng restarts economic reforms.
1997 Deng Xiaoping dies in February; Hong Kong reverts to Chinese sovereignty on July 1.
1999 Anti-NATO demonstrations after the accidental bombing of the Chinese embassy in Belgrade. ❏

THE CHINESE

Over 1.2 billion people – almost a fifth of the planet's population – live in China,
yet they occupy only one-fifth of the country's land area

The Chinese consider themselves descendants of the Han dynasty that was a pivotal period in Chinese history. Although over 90 percent of Chinese are ethnically Han, the distinction between Han and other racial groups is not clear cut. The notion of being Chinese – Han Chinese – is to some degree a cultural concept, an acceptance of Chinese values. The Han Chinese are, of course, derived from a distinctive racial background, but over the many centuries, the Han have absorbed numerous racial minorities.

The Han Chinese have traditionally populated the eastern part of the country, leaving the empty spaces to the west and north, at least up until modern times, to the minority ethnic groups. Within China, only in Tibet is a minority group actually the majority, with Tibetans making up 98 percent of the population.

Population headaches

Ninety percent of China's population lives on just one-fifth of China's land, mostly in the east and south. In contrast, the vast empty areas in the north and west are sparsely populated and often hardly habitable.

China's population was counted for the first time about 2,000 years ago, in AD 4. By AD 742, during the Tang dynasty, China's population was just over 50 million people. At around the same time as the invasion of Genghis Khan and the Mongols, around AD 1250, the 100 million mark was probably exceeded for the first time. By the middle of the 18th century, the number had doubled; a century later, in 1850, a population of 400 million had been reached.

Shortly after World War II, there were half a billion people in China. Between the mid 1960s and the early 1980s, China's population grew by over 300 million, more than the total population of either the United States or the former Soviet Union. China now has more than 1.2 billion people, nearly a fifth of the world's total. Recently, the population has increased by about 15 million annually. The governing and administrative challenges of such an immense population are mind-boggling. Gathering statistics for over a billion people, much less analysing it, defies the imagination.

The government, in 1978, began a one-child-per-family programme. Opportunities and incentives for those who have only one child are considerable. In urban areas, the program has been mostly successful. In the countryside, where traditions die hard and larger families are needed for farming, the one-child policy has had limited success.

Skewing all population statistics, however, is the preference for male heirs. In China, family lines are passed on through the male child. Partly because of this, and because male offspring are more likely to support ageing parents, especially in rural areas, sons are preferred to daughters. Female infants in the countryside

LEFT: long-time companions in Wenzhou, south China.
RIGHT: department store pitch in Shenzen, one of the early special economic zones.

have fallen victim to infanticide. From 1953 through 1964, the sex ratios at birth were a little under 105 males for every 100 female infants. Ultrasound scanners, which allow the determination of the sex of fetuses, were first introduced to China in 1979. As their use became widespread, especially amongst the middle and upper classes, the ratio climbed. Doctors are officially banned from disclosing the results of ultrasound scans, but they can usually be persuaded to tell. Also, private businessmen now offer the service.

China's population is increasingly more difficult for the nation to sustain. Most Chinese

experts have said China can comfortably support a population of only 800 million, a major reason for the great emphasis China has placed on birth control.

Thirty percent of births are not planned, despite widespread use of condoms. The State Family Planning Commission, a government agency, suggests several reasons. First, attitudes have not changed in rural areas. To a farmer, sons still provide the only security for old age. Second, sex education is still a taboo topic, especially in conservative rural areas where the grandmother educates her grandchildren according to her own beliefs. In the cities, on the other hand, families actually prefer to have

one child, as living space is restricted. Considering that living space in Shanghai or Beijing averages 3.5 sq. metres (38 sq. ft), population-control measures are accepted.

Given the diverging sex ratio, many males will find themselves without female partners. The government has predicted that, if the current trend continues, there will soon be a 50- to 70-million-strong army of bachelors.

Traditional family values

With so many hopes riding on them, particularly if they are male, children with no siblings are usually spoiled by doting parents and even more by grandparents. These kids have been dubbed "little emperors".

The demographic shift to single-child families may have had profound influences on Chinese society. Parents, who grew up during the Cultural Revolution, excessively dote on their children amidst a limbo in clear social values. Still, despite despotic little emperors dominating family life, the family – and traditional Confucian values – remains Chinese society's most important unit.

Land, that icon of family wealth, was passed on equally to a family's sons by the father. Over generations, the amount of land being passed on to each individual grew less and less, until family plots became exceedingly small. Average family wealth decreased. At the turn of the century, and for the decades until the Communists took control in 1949, conditions for rural families were dismal, with scarce food, minimal health care, and a continuing civil war. Rural conditions stabilised after 1949, with the quality of life gradually improving.

Although increasingly a rare occurrence in the cities, in a rural family three generations may be living together, with responsibility for elders falling to the sons. Daughters, on the other hand, become members of their husbands' families after marriage. Families in the cities, however, are increasingly small and self-contained, like most urban families worldwide.

"Women hold up half the sky," proclaimed Mao, but even under his rule, women rarely achieved high positions. The years since have seen further official affirmations of sexual equality, but surveys comparing the real status of women in the world rank China in the bottom third of the rankings. Age-old beliefs are largely to blame. According to Confucius, a woman without talent is virtuous. Besides regarding women as problematic and less innovative, employers are also concerned that if a woman becomes pregnant, she will be entitled to nine months' maternity leave. Adding to the woes of working women is the fact that they are victims of increasing sexual harassment.

Social life

As their rich and varied cuisine reflects, the Chinese love to eat, and China's rise in living standards is apparent at meal times. City

FOOD WASTE

By one estimate, the Chinese waste enough food, especially at official banquets, each year to adequately feed 100 million people.

include delicacies such as exotic fungi or, sadly and illegally, endangered wildlife such as tiger.

Until recently, dinner was the chief evening event. It may remain so for many people, who, after eating, leave claustrophobic homes for the street outside to meet neighbours or read under street lights. With little privacy at home, young couples head for parks in search of romance. While there are still arranged marriages in China, single people are increasingly free to marry as they please, particularly in urban areas.

residents, to whom even pork was once special, now regularly consume beef, fish, and shrimp. While meals in the home may be relatively simple affairs with a small selection of dishes from which to choose, restaurant meals can be veritable banquets.

This is especially the case if the meal is charged to entertainment expenses, or is being paid for by a businessman who wants to impress; the Chinese do not usually split the tab. For a banquet to really impress, it should

---

LEFT: rural unemployed fill urban centres, such as here in Guangzhou.
ABOVE: home life in Xiamen.

China's national and regional television stations are improving, but even though they feature foreign as well as domestic programmes, their efforts rarely grip viewers. However, increasing numbers of people are no longer limited to watching domestic stations. The masses may be officially banned from receiving foreign satellite television with its Western influences, but state-run factories have been enthusiastically producing the satellite dishes which now dot city rooftops.

Outside of Hong Kong, domestically produced films are rare, since, like television, the movie industry is stymied by ideologues. Even so, the Chinese film industry, with directors such as Zhang Yimou, is gaining greater international respect, not to mention audiences.

Karaoke, that vain Japanese-invented singalong addiction, has swept China as elsewhere in Asia, joining the discos, bars, and other social venues. Karaoke bars range from the modestly priced to those that are costly even by Western standards. A few establishments are fronts for prostitution and risk the ire of the authorities, who may close them down to "eliminate the social evils and purify the air of society".

> ### BUYING SALVATION
>
> In 1978, Deng Xiaoping announced to the people of China that "to get rich is glorious". And try they did.

meant the farm; urban life, the factory or office. Two-thirds of China's people live in rural areas. Yet they are not all farmers. Increasingly, light industries are peppering the countryside, owned and operated by villages and towns in what the *Washington Post* newspaper called an industrial revolution more profound than that in the coastal urban areas.

Typically called township-and-village enterprises, these small industries blend private-style management with government ownership. For a decade and a half, annual growth rates of

Working life

Despite increases in urban wages, China's current income levels are still very low compared to those of the West. The figures are, however, deceptive. This is partly because rents for most workers are still heavily subsidised, with apartments costing perhaps the equivalent of just a few dollars per month. The cost of living, too, is invariably lower in comparison with the West. Urban life is rapidly becoming expensive, however, in Beijing, Shanghai, and Guangzhou, and it always has been in Hong Kong.

There was a time – until recently, in fact – when the distinction between rural and urban workers was quite clear and obvious. Rural life

these enterprises has exceeded 20 percent, twice as high as China's economic growth. Employing over 100 million people, more than in the notoriously inefficient state-owned industries, town-and-village enterprises are helping to ease the problem of rural people migrating to the cities in search of work.

Many of these enterprises began as workshops in the commune system established in the 1960s. After Deng Xiaoping took power in 1978 and liberalised both agriculture and industry, rural incomes rapidly increased, as did buying power. These communal leftovers, at least those that survived, shifted to meet demand. Some are sweatshops, to be sure, and there is a conflict of interest for local governments, who are both owners and regulators of the enterprises.

While these township-and-village enterprises have offered new opportunities for the rural population and thus lessened the burden on cities somewhat, migrant workers seeking employment in the cities remains a city planner's headache. The problem is especially acute in the south. In Guangzhou, a quarter of the population are migrant workers, the "floating population". It is estimated by the official press that China's floating population may exceed 100 million, nearly equivalent to the popula-

unresponsive to China's increasing demand for commodities and services. China has moved to stem the losses, cutting hundreds of thousands of jobs in state-run companies during the early 1990s, and privatising most of those companies in the late 1990s. But the job cuts have met with resistance; sacked workers have assaulted managers and demonstrated in Sichuan and elsewhere. By contrast, the flourishing private sector is characterised by vitality and vigour.

Nationalities

There are over 50 officially recognised minority groups in China, including those in Tibet

tion of Japan and greater than that of France. What drives the floating population are urban incomes that are twice that to be found in the countryside.

The "iron rice bowl", as the system of permanent jobs and guaranteed wages was once called, has proved over the years to be ineffectual, whether in industry or the civil service (which is the world's largest at nearly 40 million bureaucrats). Not surprisingly, most state-run firms have proved to be uneconomical and

and Xinjiang. Most minority groups live along China's strategic, sometimes troubled and usually sparsely populated international borders.

Thus, when one of the minority groups needles Beijing, such as happens with Tibetans, the central government takes such deviations quite seriously. The minorities have often maintained close relationships with those of their group living on the other side of those borders. As a result, the central government cannot retain absolute control over some frontier peoples.

The defining elements of a minority are language, homeland, and social values. Around 8 percent of China's population is part of a

LEFT: elderly men enjoying an outdoor performance of Beijing opera.
ABOVE: tradition makes female babies less desirable.

minority group, with the largest being the 12-million-strong Zhuang, in southwestern China.

Out of China's population of 1.2 billion, more than 70 million people are non-Han Chinese. The constitution guarantees them certain national rights and privileges.

One of the most important is the right to use their own language. To grant these minorities the right to live according to their own beliefs and traditions is, in the eyes of the Chinese, a sign of goodwill, and the renunciation of the expansionism of the old regime.

However, spoken and written fluency in standard Mandarin is the only way to become

educated and improve social status. Schools for members of national minorities are not found everywhere, and universities teaching a minority language hardly exist. This reflects an ancient concept, based on historical experience, that there is no other developed culture apart from the Chinese.

In reality, the slow expansion of the Chinese nation from the original area on the Huang He, or Yellow River, and its tributaries up to the South China Sea is linked to an equally slow assimilation of non-Chinese peoples into the Han Chinese society, considered culturally and technically more advanced than the surrounding cultures.

The small minorities that continue to live in less accessible areas (known as "areas one flees to") have resisted the attraction of Chinese culture and civilisation, and so have paid the price of slow progress within their own cultures. At the same time, over the past century, Han Chinese have moved to the outlying regions in great numbers, lured by government financial incentives. The Han usually end up becoming the majority group in the main urban centres of these regions.

In the autonomous region of Xinjiang, Uighurs remain the largest existing ethnic group, but these days make up only 45 percent of the population. Only when grouped together with the Kazakhs, Kirghiz, and others do Uighurs constitute an Islamic, Turkic-speaking majority. Forty years ago, 80 percent of the population fulfilled these criteria. But now, all the large cities have a clear majority of Han Chinese (with the exception of Kashi). Urümqi, a city with over one million people and the capital of Xinjiang, is made up of 80 percent Han Chinese.

The Muslim Hui make up only one-third of the population in their autonomous region of Ningxia, and they usually live in the economically less-privileged parts of the country in the south. Regarding Islam, most Hui can only satisfy the criteria used to classify a Hui (Chinese-speaking Muslim) with great difficulty. One often encounters a Hui to whom the city of Mecca means nothing.

In Inner Mongolia, the Han have predominated for decades and now represent 80 percent of the population. On the other hand, more Mongols live in this region than in the neighbouring country to the north, Mongolia. It is mainly the nomadic population who are Mongolians; almost all settled farmers and people living in towns are Han Chinese whose families immigrated from eastern China.

Although the Zhuang have given their name and the status of an autonomous region to Guangxi, they are nevertheless a minority. In fact, they represent the largest non-Han nationality within modern China today. Nowadays the Zhuang are also more assimilated within mainstream Han society than any of the other minority groups. ❑

LEFT: a woman of the Kazakh minority, Xinjiang.
RIGHT: Hong Kong resident and prized canine.

BELIEFS AND RELIGION

As diverse as the land and people, the beliefs and philosophies found in China reflect an historical depth and breadth unparalleled elsewhere

For centuries before the Communists took power, several religious and philosophical beliefs were prominent in China. Two systems that originated in China, Taoism and Confucianism, were not so much religions as ethical and pragmatic standards of behaviour, especially for the educated classes. Buddhism was imported from India in the first century AD.

When the Communists came into power, religion was deemed incompatible with Communism. In recent years, however, religious beliefs have gained wider acceptance, or at least are now more openly tolerated. Confucianism, Taoism, and Buddhism are practised with varying amounts of mixing amongst them. Islam is also practiced, especially in the western parts of China, and there is also a small Christian minority. But no matter what the politics or theology, there are the age-old traditions of lucky numbers, fortune-telling, and geomancy.

Feng shui and lucky numbers

The idea of fate started in the feudal society, when it was believed that "the god" – the emperor – decided one's destiny. However, when the Yin dynasty was overthrown by rebellions, the myth that the emperor was invulnerable was broken. Thereafter, people worshipped horses and cows, and realised that the different physical features of animals – such as shape, hair and skin colour – decided their capability, temper and how long they lived. They gradually applied this observation to people.

Feng shui (wind and water) is a set of traditional spiritual laws, or geomancy, used to attract the best luck and prevent bad fortune. Those who take *feng shui* seriously consult a geomancer – a master of *feng shui* – to advise on designs of buildings, dates of important decisions, and layout of one's home and office.

Most *feng shui* experts tell fortunes by reading faces and palms, or doing complicated calculations based on a person's name or the

LEFT: temple guardian deities, Datong.
RIGHT: incense offering.

time and date of birth. The system of 12 animal signs – rat, bull, tiger, rabbit, dragon, snake, horse, goat, monkey, chicken, dog and pig – was created during the Han dynasty (206 BC–AD 220) by a Chinese philosopher. The theory divides people into the 12 categories according to the year they are born, and also

tells their fortune and future by combining philosophy and numbers. Usually, the number two stands for easy, three for living or giving birth, six for longevity, eight for prosperity, and nine for perpetuity or eternity. But it is the combinations of numbers that make a big difference. For example, 163 means "live forever" or "give birth nonstop". The superstition over numbers also applies to street and telephone numbers, not to mention lottery numbers.

Ancestor worship

The ancestor worship of the Chinese is based upon the assumption that a person has two souls. One of them is created at the time of conception, and when the person has died, the soul stays in the grave with the corpse and lives on the sacrificial offerings. As the corpse decomposes, the strength of the soul dwindles, until it eventually leads a shadow existence by the Yellow Springs in the underworld. However, it will return to earth as an ill-willed spirit and create damage if no more sacrifices are offered. The second soul only emerges at birth. During its heavenly voyage, it is threatened by evil forces, and is also dependent upon the

CHOICE STOREY

An apartment on the 18th storey is greatly preferable to one on the 14th. In Cantonese, 14 means "definitely dies", while 18 means "definitely prospers".

Taoism

A central concept of Taoism is the *tao*, which basically means way or path, but it also has a secondary meaning of method and principle. Another important premise is *wuwei*, which is sometimes simply defined as passivity, or "swimming with the stream". The concept of *te* (virtue) is closely linked to this, not in the sense of moral honesty, but as a virtue that manifests itself in daily life when tao is put into practice. The course of events in the world is

sacrifices and prayers of the living descendants. If the sacrifices cease, then this soul, too, turns into an evil spirit. But if the descendants continue to make sacrificial offerings and look into the maintenance of graves, the soul of the deceased ancestor may offer them help and protection.

Originally, ancestor worship had been exclusive to the king. Only later did peasants too begin to honour their ancestors. The original religion of the people actually focused on the worship of natural forces. Later, the people began to worship the Jade Emperor, a figure from Taoism who became the highest god in the popular religion after the 14th century.

determined by the forces yang and yin. The masculine, brightness, activity and heaven are considered to be yang forces; the feminine, weak, dark and passive elements are seen as yin forces.

Laozi, born in a village in the province of Henan in 604 BC, was the founder of Taoism. He lived at a time of crises and upheavals. The Taoists were opposed to feudal society, yet they did not fight actively for a new social structure, preferring instead to live in a pre-feudalistic tribal society. Experts today are still arguing about Laozi's historical existence. Since the second century, many legends have been told about the figure of Laozi. One of them, for instance, says that he was conceived by a beam of light, and that his mother was pregnant with him for 72 years and then gave birth through her left armpit. His hair was white when he was born; he prolonged his life with magic.

Ordinary people were not particularly attracted by the abstract concepts and metaphysical reflections of Taoism. Even at the beginning of the Han period (206 BC–AD 220), there were signs of both a popular and religious Taoism. As Buddhism also became more and more popular, it borrowed ideas from Taoism, and vice versa, to the point where one might speak of a fusion between the two.

The Taoists and Buddhists both believed that

him, too, tao and te were central concepts. For more than 2,000 years, the ideas of Confucius (551–479 BC) have influenced Chinese culture, which in turn sculpted the world-view of neighbouring lands such as Korea, Japan and Southeast Asia. It is debatable whether Confucianism is a religion in the strictest sense. But Confucius was worshiped as a deity, although he was only officially made equal to the heavenly god by an imperial edict in 1906. (Up until 1927, many Chinese offered him sacrifices.)

Confucius came from an impoverished family of the nobility who lived in the state of Lu (near the village of Qufu, in the west of Shan-

the great paradise was in the far west of China, hence the name, Western Paradise. It was believed to be governed by the queen mother of the West, Xiwangmu, and her husband, the royal count of the East, Dongwanggong. And without making any changes to it, the Taoists also took over the idea of hell from Buddhism.

Confucianism

While Laozi was active in the south of China, Confucius lived in the north of the country. For

LEFT: old photograph depicting ancestor worship.
ABOVE: fortune-tellers are ubiquitous; lucky license numbers aren't.

dong Province). For years, Confucius – or Kong Fuzi (Master Kong) as he is known to the Chinese – tried to gain office with many of the feudal lords, but he was perpetually dismissed. So he travelled around with his disciples and instructed them in his ideas. He is said to have had 3,000 disciples, 72 of them highly-gifted ones who are still worshiped today.

Confucianism is, in a sense, a religion of law and order. Just as the universe is dictated by the world order, and the sun, moon and stars move according to the laws of nature, so a person, too, should live within the framework of world order. This idea, in turn, is based upon the assumption that people can be educated.

Ethical principles were turned into central issues. Confucius believed that he would create an ideal social order if he reinstated the culture of the early Zhou period (11th century–256 BC). Humanity (*ren*) was a central concept at the time, its basis being the love of children and brotherly love. Accordingly, the rulers would only be successful in their efforts if they could govern the whole of society according to these principles. Confucius defined the social positions and hierarchies very clearly and precisely. Only if and when every member of society took full responsibility for his or her position would society as a whole function smoothly.

Family and social ties – and hierarchy – were considered to be of fundamental importance: between father and son (the son has to obey the father without reservations); man and woman; older brother and younger brother; and a ruler and subject.

Buddhism

The Chinese initially encountered Buddhism at the beginning of the first century, when merchants and monks came to China along the Silk Road. There were two aspects that were particularly attractive to the Chinese: the teachings of *karma* provided a better explanation for individual misfortune, and there was a hopeful promise for existence after death. Nevertheless, there was considerable opposition to Buddhism, which contrasted sharply with Confucian ethics and ancestor worship.

Buddhism was most influential in Chinese history during the Tang dynasty (618–907). Several emperors officially supported the religion; the Tang empress Wu Zetian, in particular, surrounded herself with Buddhist advisors. For three years late in the dynasty, however, Chinese Buddhists experienced the most severe persecutions in their entire history: a total of 40,000 temples and monasteries were destroyed, and Buddhism was blamed for the dynasty's economic decline and moral decay.

Since the seventh century, the ascetic bodhisattva has been a popular female figure in China. She is called Guanyin, a goddess of mercy who represents a central deity for the ordinary people. Guanyin means "the one who listens to complaints".

In Chinese Buddhism, the centre of religious attention is the Sakyamuni Buddha, the founder of the religion, who was forced into the background in the 6th century by the Maitreya Buddha (who was called Milefo in China, or redeemer of the world). In Chinese monasteries, Sakyamuni greets the faithful as a laughing Buddha in the entrance hall. Since the 14th century, the Amitabha school had dominated the life and culture of the Chinese people.

In the 7th century AD, another type of Buddhism, known as Tantric Buddhism or Lamaism, was introduced into Tibet from India. With the influence of the monk Padmasambhava, it replaced the indigenous religion, while at the same time taking over some of the elements of this naturalist religion.

In 1949, the year the People's Republic of China was founded, there were approximately 500,000 Buddhist monks and nuns, and 50,000 temples and monasteries. A number of well-known Buddhist temples were classified as historical monuments. By the beginning of the Cultural Revolution in 1966, it seemed as if the Red Guards were intent on completely eradicating Buddhism. Autonomous Tibet was hard-hit by these excesses. Only a few important monasteries and cultural objects could be protected and preserved. ❑

LEFT: ink drawing of Kong Fuzi, or Confucius.
RIGHT: altar at Man Mo Temple, Hong Kong island.

ARTS AND CRAFTS

With its long history and inward-looking propensities, China has had the patience
to develop and refine a resplendent catalogue of fine arts and exquisite crafts

From very early times, Chinese artisans dazzled the world with technical brilliance and innovation, and today, Chinese arts and crafts are renowned the world over. Since the 1950s, China has attempted to revive the traditional and native arts. Research institutes were established in craft centres to continue the tradition of the crafts, as well as to make further technical advancements. Promising young talent is recruited from around the country for training in specialised schools.

Painting

There has always been a close connection between Chinese painting and calligraphy. As a rule, classical Chinese painters have extensive training in calligraphy, while calligraphers have experience in painting. Both forms are created with the same brushes and are often present together in one piece of work.

Both calligraphy and painting are considered scholarly pursuits and have grand and esteemed traditions, but calligraphy has been held in higher regard. Literati painters, for example, judged works by their combination of painting, poetry, and calligraphy. Success in all three areas deemed paintings to be art. Under such standards, paintings and other art forms that lacked calligraphy were simply crafts, regardless of their level of technical brilliance.

For the Chinese, the written word is the carrier of culture, and the difficulty of learning written Chinese ensured the high social status of the scholar-gentry class. Mastery of writing and calligraphy was highly esteemed.

Furthermore, despite the numerous spoken dialects in China, Chinese writing has maintained its single standard and style. This nationwide unifying and historically continuous script was therefore always more important than the spoken language.

Painting is learned in much the same way as writing: by copying old masters or textbooks.

LEFT: glazed porcelain from the Song dynasty.
RIGHT: a calligrapher at work.

Once developed, a particular painting style is rarely lost or abandoned, and is preserved in the painting canon. Classical Chinese paintings can be grouped into six general categories: landscapes, portraits, flowers and birds, bamboo and stone, animals, and palaces or other buildings. Art connoisseurs later added four

more groups: religious paintings, barbarians and foreign tribes, dragons and fish, and vegetables and fruits.

One of the most favoured painting forms in China since the Tang dynasty (618–907) is landscape painting. Called "mountain water paintings" in Chinese, this style features mountains and water most prominently, accented with clouds, mist and trees. By contrast, human figures are small specks in the landscape and lack the detail lavished on the vegetation, water and mountain. These proportions reflect Chinese philosophies on the relationship between individuals and the outside world.

Chinese paintings are abstract and do not aim

for realism. Chinese painting values quick execution. Indeed, the nature of the materials and brush techniques do not allow for careful sketching or repainting; mistakes cannot be concealed or painted over.

Silk

Calligraphy, painting, poetry, and music are regarded in China as noble arts, the knowledge of which was required of any scholar. By contrast, applied arts such as silk and carving are considered merely honourable crafts.

such knowledge was acquired only in the 6th century AD. The Chinese had long prohibited the export of silkworm eggs and the dissemination of knowledge of their cultivation, but a monk is said to have succeeded in smuggling – an offence punishable by death – some silkworm eggs to the West.

Today's major centres of silk production are in Zhejiang Province around Hangzhou, Suzhou and Wuxi, where silk can be bought at a lower price. Hangzhou has the largest silk industry in the People's Republic, while in Suzhou silk embroidery has been refined to the highest artistic level.

Porcelain

The Chinese invented porcelain sometime in the 7th century. The history of Chinese ceramics, however, goes back to neolithic times. Along the Huang He (Yellow River) and Chang Jiang (Yangzi), 7,000- to 8,000-year-old ceramic vessels – red and even black clay with comb and rope patterns – have been found.

The Yangshao and Longshan cultures of the 5th to 2nd millennium BC developed new types of vessels in a diversity of patterns in red, black, and brown. Quasi-human masks, stylised fish, and hard, thin-walled stoneware, with kaolin and lime feldspar glazes, were created.

Later, light-grey stoneware with green glazes, known as *yue* ware – named after the kilns of the town of Yuezhou – were designs of the Han period (206 BC–AD 220). During the Tang dynasty, Chinese porcelain was known in Europe and the Middle East.

The most widespread form of ancient Chinese porcelain was celadon, a product of a blending of iron oxide with the glaze that resulted, during firing, in a green tone. *Sancai* ceramics, with three-colour glazes from the Tang dynasty, became world-famous. The colours were mostly strong green, yellow, and brown. Sancai ceramics were also found among the tomb figurines of the Tang period in the shape of horses, camels, guardians in animal or human form, ladies of the court, and officials.

The Song-period celadons – ranging in colour from pale or moss green, pale blue or pale grey to brown tones – were also technically excellent. As early as the Yuan period, a technique from the Near East was used for

The cultivation of the silkworm is said to date back to the 3rd century BC. The planting of mulberry trees and raising of silkworms is credited to Fuxi, a legendary figure of prehistoric China. For centuries, silk held the place of currency: civil servants and officers as well as foreign envoys were frequently paid or presented with bales of silk. The precious material was transported to the Middle East and the Roman empire, mostly overland via the various strands of the Silk Road.

The Chinese maintained a monopoly on silk until about 200 BC, when the secret of its manufacture became known in Korea and Japan. In the West – in this case the Byzantine empire –

underglaze painting in cobalt blue, commonly known as Ming porcelain. Some common themes seen throughout the Ming period were figures, landscapes, and theatrical scenes. At the beginning of the Qing dynasty, blue-and-white porcelain attained its highest level of quality.

Once patronised by the imperial courts, Jingdezhen has been the centre of porcelain manufacture since the 14th century. Today, however, relatively inexpensive porcelain can be bought throughout China. Nevertheless, antique pieces are still hard to come by as the sale of articles predating the Opium Wars is prohibited by the Chinese government.

Ivory

The carving of ivory can be traced as far back as the Shang dynasty (16th to 11th centuries BC), during which time elephants were not uncommon in China. Once artisans began to regard elephant tusks as a desirable material with which to make jewellery and containers, the once-large herds of elephants in the south of China eventually shrank to a small remnant, and soon ivory had to be imported. Ming-dynasty carvings exemplified excellent skills, and during Qing times, ivory carving was even further refined, though it was probably not until the 19th century that intricate carvings such as intertwined balls were created.

Today's centres for ivory carving are Beijing, Guangzhou, and Shanghai. All the ivory is imported from Thailand and several African countries. When considering buying ivory in China, keep in mind that the import of ivory is prohibited in many countries.

Jade

Jade is China's most precious stone and one of the earliest art forms to reach a superior level of achievement. According to a Chinese creation myth, when the god Pan Gu died, his breath became the wind and clouds, his muscles became soil, and the marrow of his bones jade and pearls. Chinese valued the stone for its beauty as well as for attributed magical powers. In early times, jade was used for ritual and religious purposes, but later it came to be used for ornamentation and other aesthetic purposes.

The oldest jades so far discovered come from the neolithic Hemadu culture about 7,000 years ago. Jade was believed to have preserving powers and, consequently, burial suits were made with the precious stone.

Jade is not a precise mineralogical entity, but rather comprises two minerals, jadeite and nephrite. Jadeite is more valuable because of its translucence and hardness, as well as its rarity. Nephrite is similar to jadeite, but not quite as hard. Colours vary from white to green, but can also be black, brown or red. The Chinese value a clear, emerald-green stone most highly.

Famous among the jade workshops today are

those in Qingtian (in Zhejiang Province), Shoushan (Fujian), and Luoyang (Henan).

Lacquerware

The oldest finds of lacquered objects date back to the Warring States period (403–221 BC). At that time, lacquerware was used as an every-day item: bowls, tins, boxes, vases, and furniture made of various materials (wood, bamboo, wicker etc) were often coated with a skin of lacquer, which is strong and lightweight as well as attractive. Emperor Qianlong (1735–1796) had a special liking for carved lacquerware; he was buried in a coffin carved and preserved using this technique. ❑

LEFT: porcelain jar from the Qing dynasty.
RIGHT: modern brushes.

ARCHITECTURE

Chinese architecture and the basic layout of imperial palaces and surrounding environs were dictated by the cosmology defining Heaven and Earth

Traditional Chinese architecture follows a plan that reflects philosophies of order and authority. Careful layout applies not only to residences and ceremonial buildings, but to entire cities as well. Buildings are preferably oriented on a north–south axis, with the most important structures facing south. Chinese households traditionally centre around courtyards; the higher the rank, the greater the number of courtyards. Therefore, an important official might live in a large residence along with numerous relatives and servants. The home of the head family is situated to the north of the compound and faces south. The side buildings facing the central courtyard might belong to sisters and brothers, while more distant relatives might live around courtyards further south. In more modest homes, a similar layout prevails, with parents living in the main northern quarters facing south and children occupying side quarters facing the courtyard.

Surrounding and enclosing the residence is a wall. Walls are very important to Chinese landscapes, whether as part of a home, palace, temple, town, village, or city. Walls not only provided protection and privacy, but symbolised containment and a group mentality that is an important aspect of Chinese society. Indeed, the longest wall of all, the Great Wall, which once formed the northern boundary of the country, reflects this concept.

The Imperial Palace and the surrounding city layout of Beijing are fine examples of classical Chinese architecture and planning. Designed during the Ming dynasty, the architectural planning reflects the centred power of the emperor from the heart of the capital, which was the cultural and political heart of the country. Clusters of buildings within the complex reflect the organisation and intricacy of political power. From the central imperial complex, the city radiates outward in orderly

fashion and is enclosed by city walls flanked with gates and towers. Today, the walls are no longer in place, but much of the original plan is still apparent. The palace rests close to the exact centre of the city with the various highways and expressway ring roads radiating outward in concentric squares.

The design and construction of the imperial complex are in line with classical Chinese planning, only on a very grand and opulent scale. Three basic building types – the hall, tower and pavilion – are unified by common elements in their tile roofs, stone floors, and bays made of wooden posts.

One approaches the imperial complex from the south. Large buildings in the front part of the palace rise from a terrace. As the most important building of the entire complex, Taihe Dian (Hall of Supreme Harmony) has the largest and most splendid terrace in the whole of the palace grounds. In three raised levels, the entire terrace is framed by a marble balustrade.

LEFT: print of the Longhua Pagoda, Shanghai.
RIGHT: golden roofs and eves at the Imperial Palace, Beijing.

Through symmetry and balance, the numerous buildings of the Imperial Palace complex create a pattern according to their function and importance. Their organisation thus symbolised the harmony of the universe maintained by the emperor, the Son of Heaven.

Architecture and superstition

Very conspicuous on palace roofs are ridge decorations: mythological beasts at the ends of the ridge to protect the building from evil spirits. The animals include a lion, dragon, phoenix, flying horse, and unicorn, amongst others. One can also spot a man riding a hen – intended to

protect the building and occupants against disaster. Legend has it that this represents a tyrannical prince from the state of Qi (3rd century BC). After his defeat and death, the inhabitants of Qi are said to have fixed replicas of him riding on a hen to their roofs in order to keep away disaster. The belief is that the evil tyrant on the hen cannot leave the roof because the hen cannot carry him in flight.

Traditional beliefs are often reflected in Chinese architecture. The so-called ghost wall, for example, was usually put up behind the entrance of all apartments and palaces to bar the entry of evil spirits, believed to be able to move in a straight path only and not around

corners. In large palaces, *Jiulongbi*, the splendid Nine Dragons Wall, fulfilled this function.

Pagodas

Majestic and ornate, pagodas have inspired many an imagination and are integral to images associated with the Far East. In fact, pagodas are not indigenous to China and are rather a good example of foreign influence on Chinese architecture. Through many centuries, Chinese pagodas have evolved from an imported concept to one that has incorporated and reflects traditional architectural styles, construction methods, and developments.

Pagodas provide scenic focal points in a landscape, but they are also parts of a whole, segments of a larger harmonious design. In India, where they originated, pagodas were made of brick and used to enshrine sacred objects. During the early centuries AD, Buddhist missionaries spread the teachings of Buddha to China. Many Chinese monks later travelled the same route back to India. In this way, reports of burial rites, religious art, and the impressive monastic and temple architecture filtered into China. In China, however, pagodas slowly lost much of their religious associations and became largely decorative.

The secularism of Chinese society (and architecture) is also reflected in the temple design of various religious sects. Buddhist temples, for example, have the same architectural design as Taoist and Confucian temples and are built and designed by the same craftsmen as those who build homes and palaces.

The first pagoda structures found in China go back to the third and fifth century AD and were presumably constructed in timber; none of these survive. Songyue Pagoda, the oldest surviving pagoda, is found in the district of Dengfeng, near the old imperial city of Luoyang and close to the famous Shaolin monastery. This 40-metre-high (130-ft), 12-sided pagoda was built in AD 523. For over 1,400 years, it has withstood the ravages of weather, natural disasters, and revolutions, from the Mongol invasion to the Cultural Revolution.

At the nearby Shaolin monastery, there is

LEFT: mythical animals on palace roofs are believed to protect the building from evil spirits.
RIGHT: Bai Ta (the White Dagoba) in Beijing
FAR RIGHT: Great Wild Goose Pagoda, Xi'an.

another rare sight: Talin, the Forest of Pagodas, a cemetery with more than 200 stone funerary pagodas and the last resting place of monks. These pagodas are only a few metres high and have a square core with attached memorial tablets or small recesses for offerings. Function and symbolism correspond to the original Indian stupas, but not their architectural style.

Best known for its Imperial Palace complex, Beijing also contains many fine examples of Buddhist-inspired architecture. In Beihai Park, Bai Ta or the White Dagoba rises majestically to the west of the Imperial Palace and above the old imperial city. The white, massive bell-shaped structure is set on a square base in the style of a Tibetan *chorten*. It was built in 1651 by Emperor Shun Zhi to commemorate the first visit of the Dalai Lama to Beijing.

Other ancient structures include what are possibly the best-known pagodas in China: the two Wild Goose pagodas in Xi'an. Dayan Ta, the Great Wild Goose Pagoda, was built at the proposal of and to the design of the monk Xuan Zang, who, in the 7th century AD, undertook an adventurous years-long journey to northern India. His travels are known to today's Chinese as a legend from the literary masterpiece, *Journey to the West*. After his return to China, he

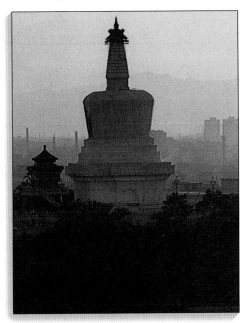

GARDENS OF PHILOSOPHY AND EMPIRES

Chinese gardens strive for a delicate balance between natural and artificial elements, reflecting Taoist principles of harmony with nature. Philosophical concepts such as *yin-yang* as well as literary and artistic subjects were bases of design.

The art of gardens flourished in China during the Ming and Qing dynasties. Emperors – and the rich and powerful of the times – invested huge amounts of money and labour to build elaborate, private gardens and retreats.

Two main types of gardens dominate: the imperial park and the scholar-official's private retreat. The best-known gardens of the first type are the Summer Palace and Yuanming Yuan, the old summer palace, as well as Chengde (Jehol). Imperial parks were meant to suggest the riches and diversity of the empire. Chengde, the massive imperial park built by Emperor Qianlong, contains Buddhist-inspired architecture of Tibet that was meant to assert the diversity of China.

The southern cities of Suzhou and Hangzhou, outside of the Shanghai metropolitan area, offer numerous examples of the scholar-officials private garden hideaways, which sought to stir emotions by creating an intense microcosm of the natural world.

had a pagoda constructed to store the manuscripts he brought back with him.

The curious name of this pagoda goes back to a legend supposedly brought from northern India by Xuan Zang. It is said that a large, wild goose fell out of the sky in response to the prayers of starving Buddhist monks. But instead of eating the goose, the monks buried it to show their gratitude. The pagoda in Xi'an is believed to be named after one in India of the same name.

The smaller Xiaoyan Ta, or Little Wild Goose Pagoda, originally had another name but was simply renamed, in the course of time, because of its striking similarity to the Great

Wild Goose Pagoda. It is of approximately similar age but appears – because of its slender form and gently-curved topmost point – more graceful than the monumental and somewhat clumsy Great Wild Goose Pagoda.

Chinese construction

From the earliest days, the Chinese favoured timber as a building material. Wood was not only easily transported, but was also more practical. Residences were meant to be rebuilt, not to be permanent monuments.

Brick and stone were used, however, for construction of important structures intended to withstand the elements for a long time, such as imperial tombs and ceremonial buildings, and, occasionally, bridges. As a result of the widespread use of wood, few original ancient remnants remain.

Chinese craftsmen developed timber-frame construction into its ultimate form. Traditional Chinese buildings rest on a floor made of beaten earth, brick, or stone. Posts and beams satisfy structural requirements and are built without the aid of glue or nails. Heavy columns set in stone bases carried the roof and could also be carved for decoration and embellishment.

Raising the roof

Roof construction in China differs greatly from that in the West. A Chinese roof is made of beams placed one atop another, gradually diminishing in length. This type of construction made it natural to curve the roof, but might also have been done for aesthetic reasons. Finally, the roof is covered in semicircular tiles.

Colour and construction material varied according to the significance of the building, and social status of the owner. Yellow tiles, for example, were used for imperial buildings, as seen in the sea of golden roofs at the Imperial Palace in Beijing. In addition, different roof shapes were used to denote the importance of a building. The most important buildings had hipped roofs, while unimportant ones had simple gabled roofs.

The roofs of Chinese buildings lend to them an air of weightlessness. The overhanging, up-turned eaves cast a shadow upon the walls and appear to float in midair. Yet aesthetic as this may be, the overhanging eaves also serve a very practical purpose: keeping out rain as well as controlling the amount of light entering the building, and keeping out the sun during summer but letting it in during winter.

Traditional Chinese construction provides much flexibility. Partitioning the interior were walls made of light materials that could easily be built up or removed. The function of the walls was not to support the roof, but to separate living space. In summer, the infill panels between the load-bearing columns of simple houses can be easily removed. Windows and doors can be made and changed without any change to the main structure of the building. ❑

LEFT: Temple of Heaven dome, Beijing.
RIGHT: ornate ceiling in the Summer Palace.

CUISINES OF CHINA

If there's a truly global cuisine, then the nomination of Chinese food is not to be underestimated. Indeed, where in the world can't one buy a Chinese meal?

Few people in the world have a more passionate relationship with food than the Chinese. Food shortages over the many centuries have forced the Chinese to be creative in order to utilise and conserve their food supplies. In addition, the elite have long used food as a way to display wealth and status, boasting numerous cooks and elaborate dishes. China's great geographical variety offers a wealth of different produce and spices.

The Chinese preoccupation with food is reflected in China's philosophy and literature. Indeed, as depicted in numerous historical, literary, and philosophical writings, scholars were also gourmands more often than not. Laozi, the founder of Taoism, said, "Handle a large country with as gentle a touch as you would cook a small fish." Another famous philosopher, Zhuang Zi, wrote a poem in which he advises an emperor to watch his cook: "A good cook needs a new chopper once a year – he cuts. A bad cook needs a new one every month – he hacks." Few will dispute the old saying that "appetite for food and sex is nature." A strong tradition recognising and encouraging the importance of food has helped nurture cuisines that are among the world's best.

Preparing the food

It is said that the four essentials in a Chinese kitchen are a cutting board, knife, wok, and spoon. Periodic fuel shortages made a reduced cooking time an early priority, and the proper cutting of ingredients is an important first step in this. Rapid, even cutting is a required trademark of any good cook. Faithful students of Confucius recorded that "he would not eat meat that was not cut properly, nor that which was served without its proper sauce." His apparent pickiness made sense, since meat and vegetables cut to varying proportions result in unevenly cooked food.

The most common method of cooking is stir-frying in a wok over very high heat. Not only does this save fuel, but it results in a crisp texture and maximum vitamin retention. Deep-frying, steaming, and braising are also popular, whereas slowly roasted or baked meats are usually produced only in restaurant kitchens.

Chinese cuisines seek a balance of textures, flavours and colours within a meal. Few Chinese dishes feature any one ingredient exclusively. Harmonious blending of ingredients and balance in seasoning is important. The common seasonings are soy sauce, ginger, garlic, vinegar, sesame oil, soybean paste, and scallions.

Ingredients

Rice is the staple food for most Chinese, although those living in the north traditionally eat food created from wheat flour, including noodles, dumplings, and various steamed, deep-fried or griddle-fried breads. Soybean curd,

LEFT: even the simplest urban meal can be diverse in its dishes.
RIGHT: sidewalk noodle-maker.

both fresh and dried in either sheets or twists, provides important protein in a country where the majority of arable land is given over to agriculture rather than grazing.

Large animals – cows and sheep, for example – requiring pasture lands are not as common as poultry and the ubiquitous pig. Without doubt, pork is the most popular meat. In addition, both fresh- and saltwater fish are highly prized and usually well prepared.

Vegetables are of supreme importance, but are rarely eaten raw. This stems partly from hygienic considerations, as the typical fertiliser was human waste. The range of vegetables cul-

tivated in China is vast, particularly in the warmer south, and includes not only those known in the West, but other delights such as a huge range of leafy greens, bamboo shoots, water chestnuts, taro, and lotus root. Some common vegetables such as cabbage and white radish are also salted or dried and used as seasoning, especially during the frigid winter months in the cold north.

The use of monosodium glutamate (MSG) has had a significant effect on 20th-century Chinese cooking. Called *wei jing* in Chinese, this miracle powder was introduced by the Japanese in the 1940s. Cooks discovered that it instantly added a meaty sweetness to the food, which could otherwise only be achieved by simmering stock for hours. After its mass production, cost was no longer prohibitive and a small revolution in Chinese cooking came about.

Regional differences

Being such a vast land, China encompasses a wide range of terrain, climate and agricultural produce. Here one can find snow-capped mountains and harsh deserts, mountain gorges slashed by mighty rivers, fertile rice paddies, rich coastal plains and seas teeming with fish. With such climatic and geographic differences, it is hardly surprising that different regional cuisines have developed.

Experts argue endlessly over just how many regional cuisines exist, but it is generally agreed that there are four major styles. These include Cantonese, the food found in the southern province of Guangdong (and in neighbouring Hong Kong); Sichuan, the pungent food of the western region of China, particularly of the cities of Chengdu and Chongqing; Huaiyang, which includes the eastern Chinese cuisines of Shanghai, Jiangsu, and Zhejiang; and Northern cuisine, centred in Beijing but largely inspired by the neighbouring province of Shandong, whose chefs monopolised Beijing's restaurant business in the 19th century.

Cantonese cuisine

Thanks to the large-scale emigration of Chinese from the southern province of Guangdong to elsewhere in the world, this is China's best-known cuisine. Many claim that it is also the finest, and there's no doubt that the fertile south benefits from a benign climate and the widest selection of fresh produce anywhere in China.

Cantonese food is characterised by its great variety, and its delicate seasoning and freshness of ingredients. Cantonese chefs are renowned for their creativity and willingness to incorporate foreign ingredients. Chefs make abundant use of fruit and many types of vegetables, as well as seafood such as prawn, abalone, squid, and crab.

Cantonese cooking methods are lacquer roasting, very quick stir-frying, and steaming. Cantonese roasted chicken and pork are justifiably renowned. Seafood is typically seasoned first and stir-fried in hot oil, or else steamed.

The famous Cantonese array of tidbits known as *dim sum* (or, in Mandarin, *dian xin*) is often served as brunch or a snack. Dim sum portions are usually dainty. Amongst the great variety of treats are dumplings of pork or seafood wrapped in transparent rice-dough wrappers; stuffed mushrooms or chilli peppers; deep-fried yam balls; and tiny spring rolls. Self-serve trolleys arranged with small plates are wheeled through restaurants and teahouses. Although the Chinese do not normally eat dessert, two common offerings at a dim sum spread are custard tarts and cubes of almond-milk jelly.

> ### SOUTHERN COOKING
>
> Southerners joke that they will eat anything with four legs but a table, anything that flies but a kite or plane.

"pepper" (the dried berry of the prickly ash or fagara), garlic, ginger, and fermented soybean. Some writers claim that the Sichuan love of spicy, pungent food can be attributed to the highly variable climate, which is characterised by humidity throughout much of the year, and to its freezing winters.

There are many excellent Sichuan dishes, including duck smoked over a mixture of camphor and tea leaves, then deep-fried, and beancurd scrambled with minced pork and spicy seasonings. One of the best

Sichuan cuisine

After Cantonese, the cuisine of the central province of Sichuan (sometimes spelled as Szechuan) is perhaps the best known to Westerners. The food from this province is the most emphatically-flavoured in all of China.

Much of this emphasis comes from chillies, which appear in many guises: dried and fried in chunks, together with other ingredients; ground into a paste with a touch of added oil; as chilli oil; and crushed to a powder. Other ingredients important to Sichuanese cuisine are Sichuan

---

LEFT: filled dumplings, or *jiaozi*, are popular snacks.
ABOVE: clear oxtail soup.

known Chinese dishes in the world, *mapo tofu* (or *doufu*), comes from Sichuan. Translated as "the pockmarked woman's tofu," this dish originated in the 19th century, so the story has been passed along over the years, when Mrs. Chen, the pockmarked woman, created a spicy beancurd dish in a family-owned Sichuan tavern that she owned with her husband.

A typical Sichuan eating experience is hot pot, or *huo guo*. Diners sit around a table with a pot of seasoned broth heated by a gas fire (charcoal was used in the past). Each diner adds bits and pieces of prepared vegetable, meat, fish, and beancurd. The food cooks very quickly and can be fished out of the broth using chopsticks or a special strainer, then dipped in sesame oil, peanut sauce, or a beaten egg.

Huaiyang cuisine

The cuisine of the lower reaches of Chang Jiang (Yangzi River), especially around Huaian and Yangzhou, gave rise to the term *huaiyang* to describe the food of China's eastern seaboard. A fertile area of fish and rice, this region has a wide range of agricultural products, as well as abundant fish, prawns, crab, and eel.

For the most part, the cooking of Shanghai, Jiangsu, and Zhejiang is usually regarded as being part of Huaiyang cuisine. The distin-

ing meat in stock with soy sauce, star anise, and other flavourings) and heavy use of peanut oil and lard are characteristic.

Northern cuisine

The cuisine of the north tends to be a rustic, home-style cooking that makes abundant use of onions and garlic, but lacks the variety of vegetables of China's more fertile regions. Most northern cuisine stems from Shandong Province, but with some influences from Mongolian and Hebei cooking. Braised meat and poultry in brown sauce, which forms the base of much northern cuisine, are common dishes.

guishing feature of Huaiyang food is the wide variety of quality freshwater and saltwater fish and shellfish; crabs from this region are especially famed. Aquatic foods are cooked simply, bringing out natural flavours. Huaiyang cooks often steam or gently simmer their food, rather than using the faster deep-frying style. Signature dishes include pork steamed in lotus leaves, Duck with Eight Ingredients, and Lion's Head Meatballs, all of which should be found in any good restaurant around Shanghai.

Huaiyang cuisine places emphasis on soups, which come with every meal. A great many wonderful and imaginative soups originated in this region. In addition, "red cooking" (stew-

ETIQUETTE PRIMER

The Chinese slurp their soup (in order to cool it off on the way to the mouth), keep their elbows on the table, and lift their bowls. The proper way to eat a bowl of rice is to hold the bowl up with one hand and shovel the rice in with chopsticks. Similarly, soup bowls can be held in one hand and the soup either sipped directly from the bowl or with a soup spoon. A word of warning: don't stick the chopsticks upright into a bowl of rice. This is taken as a very inauspicious sign, and quite rude – it resembles incense sticks burned for funerals or at shrines.

Northerners eat wheat-based foods as a staple, not the rice found elsewhere in China and Asia. Indeed, one can find a wide variety of noodles: dumplings that are steamed, pan-fried or boiled; breads (once again, fried or steamed); and deep-fried lengths of dough, excellent with a bowl of sweet or salty soybean milk.

Although the indigenous food is relatively simple, Beijing benefitted from the years when it was the imperial capital, attracting people from throughout China. The emperors sought out the best chefs in the land, and the first among them could count on being given the rank of minister.

After the duck is slaughtered, air is pumped between the skin and the flesh of the duck, and then the skin painted with a mixture of honey, water and vinegar. The duck is dried, and then roasted in a special oven. The succulent, crisp skin is tucked into fine wheat-flour pancakes, painted with sweet black-sauce and enlivened with spring onions. After this course, diners might enjoy the meat of the duck and complete the experience with a finale of duck soup.

The language of food

For all the attention and significance lavished on food by the Chinese, it is not surprising that

It was during these days that the most refined and complex dishes such as Peking Duck, Mandarin Fish, Phoenix in the Nest, and Thousand-Layer Cake were created. Today, the ordinary citizen of Beijing (and, of course, visiting foreigners) can sample these palace dishes in special, but often expensive, restaurants.

No visitor should leave without a meal of Peking Duck. Proper Peking Duck (or Beijing Duck, if one goes by the *pinyin* transliteration of the Chinese capital) is made from specially-bred ducks.

LEFT: China has its share of upmarket restaurants.
ABOVE: casual lunch in an old-style *hutong*, Beijing.

Chinese food "language" developed to a level probably unparalleled by any other cuisine. Food can be endowed with symbolic meaning, and special occasions such as holidays or birthdays are observed with specific foods.

Chinese New Year is a particularly significant food event. As the most important holiday of the year, much care, planning, and money is spent on celebrating this event with as sumptuous a feast as possible. Oranges and tangerines keep the sweetness of life, ducks represent fidelity and joy, and fish represent prosperity, wealth, and regeneration.

Birthdays are often observed by the serving of noodles, because the lengthy strands are said to represent long life. Another birthday food is steamed buns shaped and coloured to look like peaches, as peaches also represent longevity. Probably the most conspicuous custom of the mid-autumn festival, also known as the Moon Festival, is the eating of heavy, round-shaped pastries called mooncakes. Shaped much like the full moon that can be seen during the festival, these cakes are usually filled with sweet paste and sometimes an egg yolk in the centre.

During the dragon-boat festival, people eat fragrant sticky rice wrapped in bamboo leaves or reeds, a treat called *zong zi*. The story behind this tradition dates to the time of Confucius,

when a disgraced imperial official drowned himself. Townspeople, faithful to his memory, threw *zong zi* into the river to feed the fish so that the fish would not eat the official's body.

Healthy eating

For centuries, Chinese have regarded food as curative or preventative medicine. Indeed, at times the relationship between food and medicine can seem quite blurred. In fact, the word for recipe, *fang*, is the same for prescription.

When planning a menu, the chef will want to consider the physical conditions of the diners and external conditions such as the weather. One of the most basic theories behind a bal-

anced Chinese diet is that of "hot" and "cool" foods. Certain foods are believed to be either *yin* (cooling) or *yang* (warming); the ideal is to seek a balance between the two.

Internal heat is caused by eating "hot" foods such as coffee, meat, and spicy food. Excess internal heat can cause unpleasant symptoms such as heartburn, rashes, cold sores, and bad breath. Not surprisingly, "hot" foods are popular in cold weather. Snake meat, for example, is considered to be fortifying and is therefore a popular winter dish. On the other hand, "cooling" foods combat excess internal heat. Low-calorie, bland vegetables such as watercress, bitter melon, and white radish, as well as most fruits, are considered "cooling."

Practical matters

Everyday meals are simple affairs. Breakfast might consist of a bowl of *zhou* (rice porridge) with pickled vegetables and bits of meat. For lunch, a noodle soup or a plate of rice with some meat and vegetable is common. A proper family dinner will normally consist of the staple rice or noodles, soup, and three or four freshly-prepared hot dishes. The soup is generally served at the end of a meal, except in Guangdong, where it is sipped throughout the meal. Desserts are not usually served, and when they are, the choices are fairly limited.

If fortunate enough to be invited to a meal in a Chinese home or to an official function, be well advised to bring a small gift for the hosts, such as alcohol or cigarettes, or even a gift from your home country. The number of dishes served will depend on the formality of the occasion. A formal meal commences with several cold appetisers. Pace yourself, as you can be sure that there may be another six or seven courses to follow, including meat, poultry, vegetables, and soup. No one leaves hungry.

One by one, the prepared dishes of food are placed in the centre of the table. Diners help themselves with either a serving spoon, if provided, or with their own chopsticks. It is considered polite to place choice morsels on your neighbour's plate, but be sure to help yourself only to what is nearest you, rather than reaching across the table. ❑

LEFT: mooncakes are enjoyed at the mid-autumn festival.

RIGHT: Oriental restaurant in Hong Kong.

CHINESE OPERA

The emphasis in Chinese opera is on Confucian ethics and morality. Stories invariably have endings in which goodness is upheld and evil is punished.

Although Chinese theatre in the form of skits, vaudeville, puppet shows, and shadow plays has existed since the Tang dynasty (618–907), formal music-drama had its origins in the Yuan dynasty (1279–1368), when scholars who were displaced from their government positions by the foreign Mongols turned to writing dramas in which songs often alternated with dialogue. Since then, opera has become one of the most popular forms of mass entertainment in China.

Today, there are more than 300 different styles of Chinese opera. Although rarely performed now, the classical *kunqu* had its origins in the 16th century and was considered by its primary audience, the scholarly gentry, to be too genteel and esoteric for the masses. The flute is the primary instrument and its melodies are wide-ranging. Other styles of regional opera include *chaozhou* (Teochew) opera, the puppet operas of Fujian, and the *bangzi xi* (clapper operas), which are popular in Shaanxi and the northern part of China, and which featured as its main accompaniment a datewood clapper struck with a stick.

By far the most popular Chinese opera, however, is the highly stylised *jingxi* (Beijing or Peking opera), which dates from the 1800s. Beijing opera is a composite of different forms: literature, song, dance, mime, and martial arts. Time is marked with the aid of a redwood clapper that produces a high-pitched clicking sound when struck. The accompanying musical instrument in Beijing opera is usually the *huqin,* a Chinese fiddle, although cymbals are sometimes, if not usually, employed in action scenes.

While there are endless variations among the different opera styles, all of them share some general characteristics that are associated with Chinese opera. Plots are based on historical stories or folklore with which audiences are already familiar.

△ **COLOURS OF THE FACE**
Red make-up on a male character indicates bravery and loyalty, while white denotes a powerful villain. Clowns have their own special make-up, often with a white patch on the tip of the nose to indicate wit or playfulness.

▷ **WORDS UNDERSTOOD**
Whether in soliloquys, spoken verse, songs, or dialogue, the words used in any Chinese opera performance are almost always colloquial. The opera was meant to be watched by the common people. Audiences are usually noisy but appreciative.

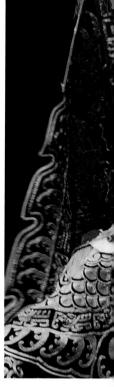

△ **SOCIALIST OPERA**
During the Cultural Revolution, traditional operas were replaced with ideological pieces upholding the values of socialism.

◁ **HELP NEEDED**
It is not uncommon for musicians and assistants to remain on stage throughout the performance to help with prop changes.

THE ART FORM OF OPERA TRAINING

Chinese opera is considered one of the most conventionalised forms of theatre to be found anywhere, requiring years of training to master.

Actors often undergo seven years of training as children, after which they are selected for specific roles such as the male, female, warrior, or clown. Prior to the 1930s, all the roles were required to be played by men.

Mastery of singing, of course, is essential for the male and female roles, while clowns are often required to demonstrate acrobatic prowess. All actors must hone the fine body movements that are the opera's style. An actor's training includes applying the elaborate make-up that identifies the character.

> **PROPS AND SYMBOLS**
Changes in time and place are evoked through speech, action, and ritualised use of props. Walking in a circle is symbolic of a journey, while circling the stage with a whip indicates riding a horse.

SLEEVE ACTING
The long flowing sleeves in certain costumes can be manipulated in more than 100 movements.

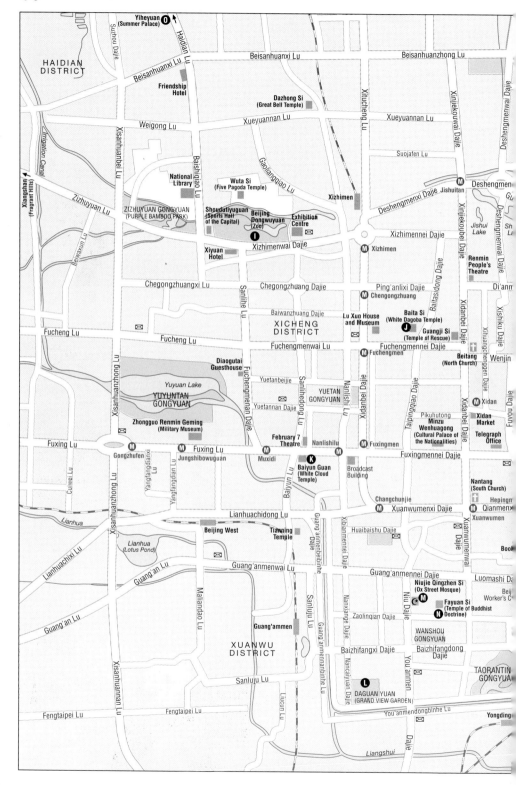

Yiheyuan (Summer Palace)

Suzhou Dajie

Haidian Lu

Beisanhuanxi Lu

Beisanhuanzhong Lu

HAIDIAN DISTRICT

Beisanhuanxi Lu

Friendship Hotel

Xitucheng Lu

Xinjiekouwai Dajie

Deshengmenwai Dajie

Dazhong Si (Great Bell Temple)

Weigong Lu

Xueyuannan Lu

Xueyuannan Lu

Suojafen Lu

Irrigation Canal

Xisanhuanbei Lu

Baishiqiao Lu

Gaoliangqiao Lu

Deshengmen

Gu

National Library

Wuta Si (Five Pagoda Temple)

Xizhimen

Deshengmenxi Dajie Jishuitan

Jishui Lake

Sh
La

Xiangshan (Fragrant Hills)

Zizhuyuan Lu

ZIZHUYUAN GONGYUAN (PURPLE BAMBOO PARK)

Shoudutiyuguan (Sports Hall of the Capital)

Beijing Dongwuyuan (Zoo)

Exhibition Centre

Xizhimennei Dajie

Xinjiekoubei Dajie

Renmin People's Theatre

Beiwazun Lu

Xizhimen

Xiyuan Hotel

I

Xizhimenwai Dajie

Xizhimen

Di'ann

Baitasidong Dajie

Chegongzhuangxi Lu

Sanlihe Lu

Chegongzhuang Dajie

Ping'anlixi Lu

Chengongzhuang

Fucheng Lu

Baiwanzhuang Dajie

Lu Xun House and Museum

Baita Si (White Dagoba Temple)

Xidanbei Dajie

Xishiku Dajie

Fucheng Lu

XICHENG DISTRICT

Guangji Si (Temple of Rescue)

J

Xihuangchengen Dajie

Wenjin

Fucheng Lu

Fuchengmenwai Lu

Fuchengmennei Dajie

Beitang (North Church)

Fuchengmen

Fuvou Lu

Diaogutai Guesthouse

Fuchengmenan Dajie

Yuetanbeijie

Yuyuan Lake

YUYUNTAN GONGYUAN

Sanlihedong Lu

YUETAN GONGYUAN

Nanlishi Lu

Xidanbei Dajie

Taipingqiao Dajie

Pikuhutong

Xidan

Xidan Market

Xisanhuanzhong Lu

Yuetannan Dajie

Zhongguo Renmin Geming (Military Museum)

February 7 Theatre

Nanlishilu

Minzu Wenhuagong (Cultural Palace of the Nationalities)

Fuxingmen

Telegraph Office

Fuxing Lu

Gongzhufen

Fuxing Lu

Jungshibowuguan

Muxidi

Baiyun Lu

K Baiyun Guan (White Cloud Temple)

Broadcast Building

Fuxingmennei Dajie

Cuiwei Lu

Yangfangdianxi Lu

Yangfangdian Lu

Xisanhuannan Lu

Yangfangdian Lu

Lianhua

Changchunjie

Nantang (South Church)

Hepingm

Xuanwumenxi Dajie

Qianmenx

Lianhuachidong Lu

Guang'anmenbeibinhe Dajie

Xuanwumen

Lianhua (Lotus Pond)

Beijing West

Tianning Temple

Xibianmennei Dajie

Huaibaishu Dajie

Xuanwumenwai Dajie

Bool

Lianhuachixi Lu

Guang'an Lu

Guang'anmenwai Lu

Guang'anmennei Dajie

Luomashi Da

Guang'an Lu

Niujie Qingzhen Si (Ox Street Mosque)

Beiji
Worker's C

Mallandao Lu

Niu Dajie

Guang'anmennanbinhe Lu

Zaolinqian Dajie

Fayuan Si (Temple of Buddhist Doctrine)

N

Guang'ammen

Namxiange Dajie

Nancaiyuan Lu

You'anmen

WANSHOU GONGYUAN

XUANWU DISTRICT

Baizhifangxi Dajie

Baizhifangdong Dajie

**TAORANTIN
GONGYUA**

Sanluju Lu

Liucun Lu

L

DAGUAN YUAN (GRAND VIEW GARDEN)

You'anmendongbinhe Lu

Fengtaipei Lu

Fengtaipei Lu

You'anmen

Yongding

Dajie

Liangshui

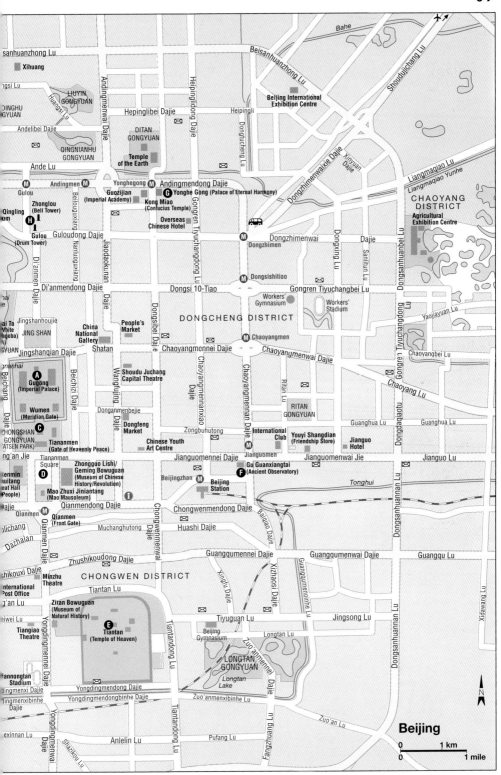

Beijing

BEIJING

Laid out in a grid according to ancient feng shui principles, the Northern Capital, once the centre of the world, is still anchored by the immense and spectacular Imperial Palace

Maps:
Area 24
City 66

Beijing

As the primary residence for three major dynasties for most of the past 1,000 years, **Beijing** ❶ has a prominent place in Chinese history. Under the rule of Kublai Khan in the 13th century, the city was known as Khanbaliq – the City of the Khan, and was a magnificent winter residence for the Yuan dynasty emperor. During the Ming dynasty, which replaced the Yuan, Beijing gained the layout that survives today. The Qing emperors lived in the palace until the dynasty collapsed in 1912.

In traditional Chinese thought, the world was not the Ptolemaic disc of the West, but rather a square. It was believed that a city, especially a capital city, should reflect this cosmic order and adhere to its geometrical definition, with a north–south and east–west orientation of roads and buildings. In no other Chinese city was this idea fulfiled as completely as in ancient Beijing. But the history of the area around the capital goes back much further: the discovery of the skull of *Sinanthropus pekinensis* (Peking Man), southwest of Beijing, proved that prehistoric humans settled here more than half a million years ago.

PRECEDING PAGES: the Great Wall. **LEFT:** guardian lion, Imperial Palace. **BELOW:** Imperial Palace gateway.

Geomantic design

The third Ming emperor, Yongle, is credited with the planning of the capital. In 1421, he moved his government from Nanjing to Beiping (Northern Peace) and renamed it Beijing (Northern Capital). The plans of Yongle followed the principles of geomancy, the traditional doctrine of *feng shui* (wind and water), that strives to attain harmony between human life and nature.

Screened from the north by a semicircle of hills topped by the Great Wall, Beijing lies on a plain that opens to the south, an auspicious direction, as it was towards the south that the generosity and warmth of *yang* was thought to reside. All important buildings in the old city face south, protected from harmful influences from the north – whether Siberian winds or enemies from the steppes. South-facing Qianmen – the Front Gate of the city – was the largest, most beautiful, and most sacred gate.

A north–south axis centred on the Imperial Palace divides the city; important buildings and city features were laid out as mirror images on either side. Equally complementary were Xidan and Dongdan, the eastern and western business quarters, which are still two of the capital's main shopping streets. Some of the most notable landmarks of old Beijing lie on the north–south axis itself, lined up like pearls on a string. In the middle of this chain is the heart of ancient China, the Dragon Throne, from which the emperor governed as the ritual mediator between heaven and earth. This was considered the centre of the physical

For the Chinese, dragons are friendly creatures with a protective function, and are linked to the east – where the sun rises and rains originate. Since the Han dynasty, dragons have symbolised emperors.

world, perceived, like the city, as a gigantic grid. The throne remains embedded in a majestic palace, which is also square and surrounded by high red walls on all sides – the so-called Forbidden City. Outside was the imperial city, also square, and crowded around it was a sea of mainly single-storey houses.

In the Qing dynasty (1644–1912), the inner city was the domain of the ruling Manchu, the outer city to the south for the Han Chinese. Today, the area south of Qianmen remains livelier than other parts of the city. A bustling street running west from the top of Qianmen is **Dazhalan**, a narrow and crowded alley filled with old established shops and businesses of excellent reputation. Dazhalan still attracts crowds from the Beijing suburbs as well as the provinces. Not far away is **Liulichang**, a shopping street restored to its original style for tourists, selling almost everything that China can offer in antiques, art, and kitsch. The busiest shopping districts are Xidan and Wangfujing, both lined with fashionable boutiques and fast-food restaurants.

The imperial city of Ming and Qing times was also a place where the great religions of China, with their impressive sacred buildings, competed spiritually. Unfortunately, many of the Taoist, Buddhist, and Lamaist shrines and temples, as well as mosques and churches, were damaged or destroyed during the Cultural Revolution of the late 1960s, or had already been turned into factories, barracks or schools after 1949.

Imperial Palace

BELOW: palace doorways were built to last.

Five hundred years ago, in the early mornings when the fourth guard watch of the night was proclaimed by powerful beats from Gulou – the Drum Tower – the mandarins in the imperial city would push aside their silk bed curtains, wash and

Map on pages 66–7

dress, then step into the litters in which porters carried them to their morning audience with the emperor in **Gugong**, the **Imperial Palace** Ⓐ (open daily, summer 8.30am–4.30pm, winter 8.30am–3.30pm; entrance fee). A eunuch would show them to their places, arranged according to rank. In silence, the mandarins listened to the emperor.

In 1421, after 17 years of construction, the Ming emperor Yongle moved into the new palace. Up to the founding of the republic in 1911, the palace was the imperial residence and centre of the Middle Kingdom during the reign of 24 emperors, from the Ming dynasty (1368–1644) until Puyi, the last emperor of the Qing dynasty, and of China. It has 8,706 rooms in which an estimated 8,000–10,000 people lived, including 3,000 eunuchs, as well as maids and concubines, all within an area of 70 hectares (170 acres). The entire palace complex can be divided into two large areas: **Waichao**, the Outer Court, in the south, and in the rear, **Neiting**, the Inner Residence.

Approaching from the south through 35-metre (117-ft) high **Wumen** (Meridian Gate), one encounters the three great halls and courtyards of the outer area. **Taihe Dian** (Hall of Supreme Harmony), the largest building in the palace, is the first and most impressive of these. In its centre is the ornately carved and golden **Dragon Throne**, from which the emperor ruled. The outside courtyard could hold 90,000 spectators. Behind Taihe Dian are **Zhonghe Dian** (Hall of Complete Harmony) and **Baohe Dian** (Hall of Preserving Harmony), completing a trinity that reflects the Three Buddhas and the Three Pure Ones of Taoism. To the east of Baohe Dian is the magnificent **Jiulongbi** (Nine Dragons Screen).

On the other side of the Outer Court, separated by Qianqingmen (Gate of Heavenly Purity), lies a labyrinth of gates, doors, pavilions, gardens and palaces. This is **Qianqing Gong** (Palace of Heavenly Purity), residence of the imperial family – almost all female, as the emperor and eunuchs were the only men permitted to enter.

Across the street from **Shenwumen** (Gate of Divine Prowess), the north gate of the Imperial Palace, is **Jing Shan** (Coal Hill) (open daily, 6am–9pm; entrance fee), the best place from which to view the palace complex. This artificial hill was built with the earth dug from the palace moats in the early 15th century. Five pavilions crown the hill. The Drum and Bell Towers stand out to the north, and the White Dagoba dominates the west.

To the immediate west of Jing Shan, in the grounds of today's **Beihai Gongyuan** (North Lake Park) (open daily, 6am–9pm; entrance fee), was the winter residence of the Mongol emperor Kublai Khan. Only legends remain of his former palace on Qinghuadao (Jade Island), the site of **Bai Ta** (White Dagoba) Ⓑ, 35 metres (115 ft) high, and a Buddhist shrine from 1651, built in Tibetan style to commemorate the first visit to Beijing by a Dalai Lama.

South and east of the Imperial Palace

Nestling closely against the southern walls of the palace, to the west between Wumen and Tiananmen, **Zhongshan Gongyuan** (Sun Yatsen Park) Ⓒ (open daily, 6.30am–8pm; entrance fee) retains impressive

BELOW: Golden Water River, Imperial Palace.

The focus of China's national emblem is Beijing's Tiananmen, the gate from which Mao Zedong proclaimed the creation of the People's Republic of China.

BELOW: Qinian Dian, Tiantan.

imperial architecture and landscaping. The park occupies the site of an old temple honouring the gods of the earth and of fertility. It was renamed after Sun Yatsen (1866–1925), one of the founders of the Chinese republican movement, was buried here.

To the east of Tiananmen is the former shrine of the imperial ancestors, now called **Laodong Renmin Wenhua Gong** (Working People's Cultural Palace) (open daily, 6am–9pm; entrance fee) and functioning as a college for continuing education and a venue for concerts and art exhibitions. The shrine dates from the Ming dynasty and housed the ancestral tablets of the imperial forebears, which the emperor was required to honour.

On 1 October 1949, Mao Zedong, chairman of the Communist Party, proclaimed the founding of the People's Republic of China from the balcony of **Tiananmen** (Gate of Heavenly Peace) (open daily, 8.30am–4.30pm; entrance fee to climb the tower). Today, Mao gazes south from a huge portrait on the south side of the gate onto **Tiananmen Square ⓓ**, south of the expansive ceremonial boulevard Chang'an Jie, due to re-open for the 50th anniversary of the PRC on 1 October 1999, after being closed for renovation.

The square was quadrupled in size during the 1950s so that it could hold up to a million people. Rallies of Red Guards took place here during the Cultural Revolution; so did the 1989 student demonstrations, which ended when the government used the army to oust the demonstrators, resulting in numerous deaths. In the centre of the square is an obelisk, unveiled in 1958 as a monument to the heroes of the nation and a perfect example of the socialist realist style.

The massive façades of the **Zhongguo Lishi Bowuguan** (Museum of Chinese History) (open Tues–Sun, 8.30am–3.30pm; entrance fee) and **Zhongguo Geming Bowuguan** (Museum of the Chinese Revolution) (open Tues–Sun, 8.30am–5pm; entrance fee) border the square to the east. The former covers the entire history of China, and has many ancient cultural relics from across the country. The latter displays photographs, paintings, documents, and relics representing the leading events and personalities that brought communism to China. In 1977, one year after Mao's death, the **Mao Zhuxi Jiniantang**, or **Mao Mausoleum** was completed at the southern end of Tiananmen Square. Even today, when the teachings of the Little Red Book of Mao quotations have long gone out of fashion (except amongst tourists who buy them as souvenirs), people from all over China visit his mausoleum, filing respectfully past his embalmed body in its rose-hued, glass enclosure. The Mausoleum was closed for renovation work in 1999.

Tiantan

Twice a year in imperial times, the emperor and a magnificent procession of 1,000 eunuchs, courtiers and ministers left Gugong, the Imperial Palace, for **Tiantan** (Temple of Heaven) **ⓔ** (open daily, 8am–5pm; park open 6am–9pm; entrance fee), 3 km (2 miles) south of the palace. Each time he would spend a night of fasting and celibacy in **Zhai Gong** (Palace of Abstinence) prior to the sacrificial rites the next morning. At the winter solstice he expressed thanks for the last harvest and on the 15th day of the first month of the lunar year he begged the gods who controlled the elements to bless the harvest to come.

Set in the middle of a park of 270 hectares (670 acres), Tiantan is an outstanding example of religious architecture, dating from the Ming dynasty. Destroyed several times (once by lightning) it was last rebuilt in 1890. An exquisite example of Chinese wooden buildings, constructed without the use of a single nail, is the round, 40-metre (130-ft) high **Qinian Dian** (Hall of Prayer for Good Harvests), its three levels covered with deep blue tiles that symbolise heaven. The roof is supported by 28 pillars: the four largest in the centre represent the four seasons, the double ring of 12 pillars represents the 12 months, and the traditional divisions of the Chinese day comprise two hours.

To the south of the park lies a white, circular marble terrace, **Tianqiutan** (Altar of Heaven), and the **Echo Wall**, famous for its acoustics.

Head east from Tiananmen along Jianguomennei Dajie to reach **Gu Guanxiangtai** (Ancient Observatory) ❻ (open daily, 8.30am–5.30pm; entrance fee). Chinese emperors, known as "sons of heaven", were keen patrons of astronomy. An observatory was first built here in 1422, on what was then a tower in the city wall of the imperial capital. Its name changed several times: in the Yuan period it was the Terrace to Bring Down the Heavens, perhaps reflecting the Mongols inclination to conquer. In Ming times it was the Terrace for Watching the Stars; 17th-century astronomical instruments are displayed on the roof of the tower.

North of the Palace

The most elaborately-restored sacred building in Beijing is **Yonghe Gong** (Palace of Eternal Harmony) ❼ (open Tues–Sun, 9am–4pm; entrance fee), a

Map on pages 66–7

BELOW: dusk on Tiananmen Square and Qianmen.

Stone sculpture of Kong Fuzi, known to Westerners as Confucius.

BELOW:
Yonghe Gong.

Lamaist temple in the northeast of the old city. From the Ancient Observatory, head west along Jianguomennei Dajie, then north for about 5 km (3 miles) along Dongdanbei Dajie until it becomes Dongsibei Dajie and eventually Yonghe Gong Dajie. Originally the private residence of Prince Yong, Yonghe Gong was turned into a monastery when Yong became emperor in 1723. According to ancient Chinese custom, the former residence of a Son of Heaven had to be dedicated to religious purposes once he left. The temple belongs to the Yellow Hat sect, whose spiritual leader is the Dalai Lama. In the three-storied central section of Wanfuge (Pavilion of Ten Thousand Happiness) is a statue of the Maitreya Buddha, 23 metres (75 ft) high, and carved from a single piece of sandalwood.

Opposite Yonghe Gong, across Yonghegong Dajie, are **Kong Miao** (Temple of Confucius) and **Guozijian** (Imperial Academy) (open daily, 8.30am–5.30pm; entrance fee), tranquil and now largely ignored former centres of scholarship. In its glorious past, Kong Miao was where emperors came to offer sacrifices to Confucius for guidance in ruling the empire. Built in 1306 during the Yuan dynasty, the temple's prize possession is a collection of 190 steles inscribed with records of ancient civil service examinations. It is the second-largest Confucian temple in China, after one in Confucius's home town, Qufu.

To the west of Kong Miao, **Zhonglou** (Bell Tower) and **Gulou** (Drum Tower) ❶ (open daily, 8.30am–4pm; entrance fee) date from the Yuan dynasty rule of Kublai Khan. They once marked the northern edge of Beijing, but were in the centre of the Yuan dynasty city. Last rebuilt in 1747, the Bell Tower stands 33 metres (108 ft) high. The Drum Tower once held 24 giant drums that were struck to mark the closing of the city gates and the passing of the night watches.

Today, one of the chief attractions of the Drum Tower is the view from the top over the surrounding area of traditional *siheyuan* courtyard houses.

Map on pages 66–7

West of the Palace

Beijing Dongwuyuan (Beijing Zoo) ❶ (open daily, 7.30am–5.30pm; entrance fee) is 7 km (4 miles) west of the Drum Tower, near the Beijing Exhibition Centre. The zoo was known as Wanshengyuan (Ten Thousand Animals Garden) when it was the personal menagerie of Empress Dowager Cixi. Standards for the animals' space and living conditions are not as good as those in some Western zoos, but the pandas remain as popular as ever.

    Baita Si (White Dagoba Temple) ❶ (open daily, 8.30am–5.30pm; entrance fee) lies 3 km (2 miles) to the southeast. The temple was established in 1096 and extensively rebuilt in Lamaist style in 1271. The white dagoba here is a Tibetan shrine similar to the one in Beihai Park (see page 71). The temple holds an exhibition showing the layout of the Yuan dynasty city of Dadu, as Beijing was known, and the social and political systems under Mongol rule.

    Southwest of Baita Si, not far from the showpiece Beijing West Railway Station, lies the serene **Baiyun Guan** (White Cloud Temple) ❻ (open daily, 8.30am–4.30pm; entrance fee), once the greatest Taoist centre of northern China. This former imperial palace was given by Genghis Khan as the head-quarters of Qui Chang Chun, a Taoist leader who had promised that "if the conqueror respects Taoism, the Chinese will submit". Today, a small group of monks lives here, but because of the repression of religion during the Cultural Revolution, they are either very old or very young, with an age gap corresponding to that period of upheaval.

BELOW: procession in the Taoist temple of Baiyun Guan.

*The area around the
Ox Street Mosque
has a number of
excellent Muslim
restaurants.*

At the southwest corner of the old city moat, 3 kms (2 miles) south of Baiyun Guan, **Daguan Yuan** (Grand View Garden) ❶ (open daily, 8.45am–4.30pm; entrance fee) was constructed in 1984 as the incarnation of the idyllic garden in the novel *Dream of the Red Mansion*, by Cao Xueqin. It is a beautiful example of a classical Chinese landscaped garden, and visitors will see elaborate rockeries, lotus ponds, covered walkways, bridges, and pavilions.

Islam reached China during the Tang dynasty (618–907), and the **Niujie Qingzhen Si** (Ox Street Mosque) ⓜ (open daily, 9am–9pm; entrance fee), a 10-minute walk northeast of Daguan Yuan, was built in 966. It has the features common to all mosques – minaret, prayer hall facing Mecca, Arabic inscriptions – but in distinctly Chinese-style buildings. The surrounding area has one of the main concentrations of Hui Muslims in the capital.

A further five-minute walk east is **Fayuan Si** (Temple of the Source of Buddhist Doctrine) ⓝ (open daily, 8.30–11am and 1.30–3pm; entrance fee), completed in 696 during the Tang dynasty to honour soldiers killed in battle. It is the oldest surviving temple in the city, though the current buildings are all from the 18th century. Today, the temple houses the Buddhist Academy, formed in 1956 and devoted to teaching Buddhist novices, who are then sent to monasteries across China. The academy has a library of more than 100,000 precious texts and an exhibition of Buddhist sculpture, some dating from the Han dynasty.

Summer palaces

The great aesthete Emperor Qianlong, who ruled from 1736–95, had a masterpiece of landscaping and architecture created 16 km (10 miles) northwest of the city centre: **Yuanming Yuan** (open daily, 7am–7pm; entrance fee), now better

BELOW: Mao
memorabilia at the
flea market, Beijing.

known to Westerners as the **Old Summer Palace**. Construction followed the most lavish European styles, according to plans by the Italian Jesuit missionary and artist Guiseppe Castiglione and based upon models such as the palace at Versailles. During the Second Opium War (1856–60), the Western powers, led by British and French troops, pillaged the palace and reduced it to rubble. Amidst the rubble today is a restored brick maze with a central pavilion.

The Qing dynasty built a replacement for the devastated Yuanming Yuan nearby, in the grounds laid out by Qianlong as a place of retirement for his mother. This new summer residence took on special interest for the notorious Empress Dowager Cixi, who fulfilled a wonderful, if rather expensive, dream in 1888. Using money intended for the building of a naval fleet, she constructed **Yiheyuan** (Garden of Cultivated Harmony) **O**, and the **Summer Palace** (open daily, 6.30am–6pm; entrance fee), west of the Old Summer Palace. Originally a concubine of the third rank, Cixi had placed herself on the Dragon Throne after the death of the emperor and ruled in an unscrupulous manner for 50 years.

Empress Dowager Cixi found the Summer Palace a pleasant enough place to house her ego.

As in every classical Chinese garden, water and mountains (usually represented by rocks) determine the landscape of Yiheyuan. **Kunming Lake** covers three-quarters of the total area of over 30 sq. km (10 sq. miles); on its shore is **Wanshou Shan** (Hill of Longevity). Accessible via a series of bridges, stairs, gates and halls is the massive **Foxiangge** (Pagoda of the Incense of Buddha), which crowns the top of Wanshou Shan. In the eastern corner is a jewel of classical Chinese garden design, **Xiequ Yuan** (Garden of Joy and Harmony), a picturesque copy of a lotus pool from the old city of Wuxi.

To make it more difficult for strangers to spy into the grounds, **Renshou Dian** (Hall of Benevolence and Longevity) was built right next to the eastern

BELOW: Foxiangge, Summer Palace.

Map on pages 66–7

gate, **Dongmen**, now the main gate. Behind it lay the private apartments of Cixi, which today also house a theatrical museum. Here, Cixi used to enjoy operatic performances by her 384-strong ensemble of eunuchs.

OUTSIDE BEIJING

In the area surrounding Beijing there are some interesting sites which are well known and which attract visitors hoping to get away from the daily chaos of the capital. Transport by train or bus is readily available and convenient, although for the shorter and most popular trips, such as the Great Wall and Ming Tombs, a hired car may be the easiest way to get around. Travel agents can arrange tours for short trips outside Beijing.

Most people clambering along the Great Wall remember that it is one of the few places on earth that can be identified from the moon.

Wanli Changcheng (Great Wall)

Wanli Changcheng ❷, the Great Wall, winds its way like an endless slender dragon from the Huang Hai (Yellow Sea) through five provinces, two autonomous regions, and up into the Gobi Desert. Towers are located at strategic points. The very earliest stages of the building of the wall were in the 5th century BC, but the present course was basically determined around 220 BC by Qin Shi Huangdi, the first Chinese emperor and founder of the empire. He had smaller, previously constructed sections linked and extended north to ward off attacks by horse-riding nomads. But the most impressive portions we can see today were built during the Ming dynasty. Soldiers and peasants from all over the country were conscripted, forced to spend several years of their lives building this "ten thousand *li* wall" – *wanli changcheng*. (*Wan*, the Chinese character for 10,000, is a synonym for unimaginable hugeness.) Blocks of rock

BELOW: the Great Wall loops its way across the Western Hills (Xishan).

weighing several hundred kilograms had to be heaved up the steep slopes, and an unknown number of people paid with their lives for this project.

Several Great Wall sites are accessible from Beijing, each fulfilling a different role. From 10am until 3pm, **Badaling**, the section of the wall that is most accessible from Beijing, turns into a true tourist carnival. The avalanche of visitors streams past countless stalls selling tacky souvenirs promoting this great symbol of Chinese civilisation. Then it moves in two different directions, attempting to conquer the steep climb. From the high points are views of the breathtaking scenery, where the mighty wall climbs and descends in a fascinating mountain landscape.

The scenery at **Mutianyu** is also imposing. This part of the wall, some 120 km (75 miles) north of Beijing, was restored in recent years and is less busy than Badaling. Small parts of the wall here remain as they were – it has not been rebuilt – so you can get a better sense of its antiquity. The walk is difficult but not dangerous. Cable cars take visitors from the bottom of the hills nearly to the wall itself.

Simitai is 100 km (60 miles) northeast of Beijing. A cable car starts its ascent at the east side of the reservoir. The hike at this site is difficult, as the renovated section quickly turns into steep, dilapidated climbs. However, this area makes for great hiking and camping, with panoramic mountain views. **Jinshanlin**, which has been restored, is a bit kinder and easier to climb.

This part is located west of Simitai. **Huanghua Cheng**, 25 km (15 miles) west of Mutianyu, makes for good vigorous hiking. The climb up to the remains of the wall is the most difficult part, but be careful when you are hiking on the wall as well, as it can be a little crumbly underfoot.

Map on pages 24–5

Defending the wall: the top part of the Great Wall was designed so that five or six horsemen could ride side by side. Fortified towers, signal beacon towers, and garrisons completed the defences.

Map on pages 24–5

Ming tombs

A visit to the Great Wall is usually combined with a trip to the **Shisan Ling** ❸, the Ming Tombs (open daily, 8am–5.30pm; entrance fee). Protected by an auspicious range of hills to the north, east and west, the tombs of 13 of the 16 Ming emperors lie in this geomantically-favourable spot. Entry from the south on the valley floor passes through numerous gates of honour along **Shendao** (Soul Path), flanked by the stone guardians of the tombs. The guard of honour of twelve human figures represents civil and military dignitaries and officials; there are also lions, horses, camels, elephants, and mythical creatures.

Two of the 13 tombs here are most often visited. **Chang Ling** is the final resting place of Emperor Yongle (died 1424), the third emperor of the Ming dynasty. Yongle made significant adjustments to the institutional forms of the state established by his father, the founder of the Ming dynasty. The founder's chosen successor was Yongle's nephew, but Yongle usurped power from him, and moved the capital city from Nanjing to Beijing after reconstructing the city.

He was also the one to choose the spot of the present-day Ming Tombs on which to build his own. As he was the first to be buried there, his tomb is the largest and also the most centrally located. Moreover, this has served as the model for the other tombs that followed. The mound of the tomb has not been excavated, and the emperor and the empress still lie within the underground vaults today. Above are the magnificent courtyards and ceremonial halls.

Ding Ling, the tomb of the 13th emperor Zhu Yijun (died 1620), was opened to the public in 1959. It is the only Ming Tomb to have been excavated. The emperor's primary wife and one concubine were buried with him. The underground palace was sealed with a specially designed lock. The locking stone, which is still on display inside the entrance, fell automatically into place inside the vault when the doors were closed, making it nearly impossible to open them again. But, of course, grave robbers will always find a way. When the tombs were finally opened, it was discovered that the vaults were nearly empty. The underground palace consists of three main halls. Two exhibition rooms above the vaults are a showcase for rare relics belonging to the royals.

Longer excursions

Tianjin ❹ has a population of 7 million and is one of China's major cities. Some 140 km (90 miles) south-east of Beijing, it is noted for its busy port and its carpet manufacture. Eight large factories produce the renowned carpets, although many of them are still made, at least partially, by hand. A leisurely walk around Tianjin will tell much about its history. And if some of the city's architecture and its layout seem similar to that of Shanghai, this is because Tianjin was home to a prosperous international community during the late 1800s.

Five hours northeast of Beijing is **Chengde** ❺ formerly known as Jehol. This was both the summer residence of the Qing emperors and a politically important meeting place for the leaders of ethnic minorities. The "palace for escaping from the heat" is surrounded by a magnificent park.

BELOW: stone guardian on the Soul Path, Ming tombs.
RIGHT: the temple at Xumifushou.

XI'AN

Over 7,000 terracotta warriors found in the tomb of Qin Shi Huangdi, the first Chinese emperor, lure travellers to Xi'an. Beyond is Yan'an, where Mao Zedong consolidated the Communist Party

Maps:
Area 24
City 83

Chinese civilisation is anchored at the bend of the **Huang He**, or **Yellow River**, in the central provinces of Shaanxi and Henan. Here, in the fertile valleys of the loess-covered landscape, the ancient ancestors of the Han Chinese settled in the 3rd century BC. The rich soil encouraged settlements, with the river irrigating the land. The erratic personality of the river – flooding and changing course with regularity – forced people to work in close cooperation. Eventually, the first and strongest states of China developed in this region.

Xi'an **❻**, capital of Shaanxi Province, lies in the protected valley of the river Wei, a few dozen miles west of the Wei's confluence with the Huang He. From this valley, the emperor Qin Shi Huangdi first unified China. During the Tang dynasty (618–907), Xi'an was the largest city in the world. Chang'an (Heavenly Peace), as it was called, was linked to many central Asian regions and Europe via the Silk Road, with thousands of foreign traders living here. For more than 1,000 years Xi'an served as the capital for a dozen imperial dynasties, but following the demise of the Tang dynasty Xi'an's importance began to evaporate. Today the city has a population of around 5 million.

LEFT: each terracotta warrior has unique facial features.

Old imperial centre

In its earlier days, the metropolis was surrounded by a large wall. The city itself stretched over 9 km (6 miles) from east to west, and nearly 8 km (5 miles) north to south. All roads in the town itself were laid out in a classic Chinese grid pattern, running straight north– south and east–west, meeting at right angles. While the grid layout remains today, the layout of the ancient city is not quite identical with the modern one. Although the walls built during the Tang dynasty no longer exist, 14 km (9 miles) of the wall from the Ming dynasty still surround the centre. The city has been rebuilding the 12-metre (40-ft) thick walls, and the moat outside the wall has also been reconstructed and integrated within a park. In certain places it is possible to climb on top of the walls for a nominal fee.

In the city centre where the city's two main roads intersect, is **Zhonglou** (Bell Tower) **❶** (open daily, 8am–7pm; entrance fee). This renovated 36-metre (118-ft) tower dating from 1384 was moved to its present site in 1582, and is now encircled by the shopping and

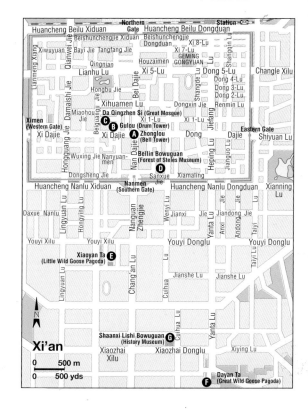

The pagoda of Dayan Ta (Great Wild Goose Pagoda).

BELOW: the sun rises on the terracotta warriors.

commercial centre. East from Zhonglou runs Dong Dajie, with many shops and restaurants. Dong Dajie intersects with Jiefang Lu, which runs to the north and to the railway station.

A few minutes' walk northwest from Zhonglu is **Gulou** (Drum Tower) **Ⓑ** (open daily, 8am–6pm; entrance fee). Resembling the Bell Tower and dating from the 18th century, it was rebuilt after the 1949 communist revolution. More than 60,000 Hui Muslims live in Xi'an, and the Drum Tower highlights the Muslim quarter to the west. Lined with shops selling souvenirs, peasant paintings, and other local artefacts, alleys winding through the Hui neighbourhoods lead to **Da Qingzhen Si** (Great Mosque) **Ⓒ** (open daily, 8am–7pm). The mosque dates back to the Ming period and has been renovated several times. With its inner courtyards, it bears a resemblance to a Chinese temple. The main prayer hall is accessible only to Muslims. The area around the mosque is one of the most fascinating and diverse quarters of the city: wander down an alley to get a sense of how the Hui Muslims live, and try the delicious food at one of the many stalls.

Near the south gate of the city wall, **Nanmen**, and in a former Confucian temple is the **Beilin Bowuguan** (Forest of Steles Museum) **Ⓓ** (open daily, 8.30am–5.30pm; entrance fee), formerly Xi'an's provincial museum, with exhibits in three main buildings. The first building has a chronologically arranged exhibition of ancient Buddhist images from the early period of the Silk Road to the end of the Tang dynasty. The second building, the museum's centrepiece, features a "forest" of steles, around 1,100 stone tablets on which ancient Chinese classical texts, including those of Confucius and Mencius, are engraved. In the early days when printing was still too expensive, this was a way

Map on page 83

of recording the classic texts for posterity and for the many scholars who came from far and wide. The third section of the museum houses animal sculptures in stone, Tang-dynasty stone friezes, bronzes, and jewels.

Outside the city walls and about one kilometre from Nanmen, the 43-metre (141-ft) high **Xiaoyan Ta** (Little Wild Goose Pagoda; open daily, 8am–6.30pm; entrance fee) **E** was built in the 8th century. It was severely damaged during an earthquake eight centuries later, but was repaired in the late 1970s, only to be damaged again in the early 1990s. It has still not been fully restored.

More noteworthy is the 64-metre (210-ft) high, seven-storey **Dayan Ta** **F** (Great Wild Goose Pagoda; open daily, 8am–6.30pm; entrance fee), anchoring the southwest end of Yanta Lu. It was built at the beginning of the Tang dynasty, in 652, by Crown Prince Li Zhi as a memorial to his deceased mother. A noted monk, Xuanzang, went on a pilgrimage to India in 629, returning in 645 with many Buddhist scriptures, which were stored in the pagoda at that time and translated into Chinese. The pagoda was originally part of a Buddhist temple complex. Although only a few buildings remain of the original temple complex of 13 courtyards and over 300 rooms, a few monks have returned, and the temple itself is now a popular place for locals to come and pray. None of the scriptures remain in the pagoda, having long since been removed to various museums and institutions around the country.

Near that pagoda, in the south of the city, is a true gem: the **Shaanxi Lishi Bowuguan** (History Museum) **G** (open daily, 8.30am–5.30pm; entrance fee). Opened in 1991, the modern museum is housed in a handsome Chinese-style building with clear and attractive displays arranged in chronological order and labelled in English. Included are terracotta horses and soldiers, Ming and Qing

Since some of the terracotta warriors were exhibited in the West they have become a hugely popular tourist attraction, so expect crowds.

pottery, and bronze cooking vessels that sit on tripods from the Shang and Zhou dynasties, as well as tools and pottery from the Palaeolithic and Neolithic ages.

Terracotta warriors

Hu fu, a tiger figure of the Qin dynasty uncovered in the Xi'an area.

Museums in the city proper offer but a glimpse of Xi'an's greatest and most important attraction: **Bingmayong** ❼, the underground army of **terracotta warriors** (open daily, 8am–5.30pm; entrance fee). This vast treasure lies 35 km (20 miles) east of Xi'an, at the foot of Li Shan. In 1974, peasants digging a well uncovered these life-size figures of horses and warriors. The terracotta army is only part of a grand tomb, **Qin Shihuang Ling**, built by the first Chinese emperor, Qin Shi Huangdi. What is believed to be the main tomb of the emperor is about 1.5 km (1 mile) to the west of the terracotta warriors. According to historic surveys, a splendid necropolis apparently depicting the whole of China in miniature is centred under the 47-metre (154-ft) high mound. The necropolis itself is said to be immense in size.

According to old records, the ceiling is studded with jewels depicting the sky, and mercury was pumped in mechanically to create images of flowing rivers. Trial digs have revealed high contents of mercury in the soil. However, the official entrance to the tomb has yet to be found. Several hundred thousand workers spent 36 years building the tomb, which the emperor, at the age of 13, ordered to be constructed after he ascended the throne. It is said that workers and supervisors involved in its design and construction were buried alive within the tomb. Some speculation has it that the emperor was so superstitious and fearful that he had the necropolis built as a decoy and is, in fact, buried somewhere else.

Outside Xi'an

On the way back to the city from Bingmayong is **Huaqing Chi** (Hot Springs of Huaqing), in use for over 3,000 years. There are baths and pavilions in the park area, which would be pleasant enough if it were not for the throngs of tourists. During the Tang dynasty, this is where the most famous concubine in China, Yang Guifei, bathed. Farther up in the mountain is the place where Chiang Kaishek was recaptured by two of his own generals during an escape attempt, taken prisoner in 1936, and persuaded to join with the communists against the Japanese.

A visit to the neolithic settlement of **Banpo** (open daily, 8am–6.30pm), 10 km (6 miles) to the east of Xi'an, is also interesting. Some relics, including ceramics, weapons, and even infant burial jars from the Yangshao culture, are exhibited. The excavated village shows the outlines of houses and cooking areas, and is part of the museum. The community living here 6,000 years ago was matriarchal.

Farther afield, about 50 km (30 miles) northwest of Xi'an, is **Xianyang**, which served as the capital during the reign of Qin Shi Huangdi. Xi'an's airport is located here today. Few traces are left of the palaces said to have been built here. There is a museum in a former Confucian temple that contains more than 3,000 artefacts from the time of the Warring States

Map on pages 24–5

era and the Han and Qin dynasties. The collection of miniature terracotta horses and soldiers from the Han dynasty – each about 50 cm (20 in) high – is impressive.

About 85 km (53 miles) to the northwest of Xi'an is **Qian Ling** ❽, the joint burial place of the Tang emperor Gaozong and his wife, the empress Wu Zetian. The tomb itself has not been opened. The approach to the tomb is guarded by a "ghost avenue" of large stone sculptures of animals and dignitaries. There is also a group of 61 stone sculptures, with their heads missing, apparently representing foreign dignitaries. The peasants of the time are said to have knocked the heads off during a famine, believed to have been caused by the presence of these foreigners. The tombs contain exquisite frescoes from the Tang dynasty.

Yan'an

Mao Zedong's Long March during the civil war with the Nationalists ended in Wuqi, in 1936. The leaders then established their base in **Yan'an** ❾ and stayed for a decade. This small market town of just under 60,000 people is 270 km (170 miles) to the north of Xi'an, where a river cuts through the dry mountains.

During the Cultural Revolution, and until the 1970s, Yan'an was the national centre of pilgrimage, as well known to cadres as the Imperial Palace in Beijing. The headquarters of the military commission of the Chinese Communist Party, along with the houses of the communist leaders Mao Zedong and Zhu De, are still preserved in the Fenghuang mountains north of Yan'an. The **Museum of the Revolution** contains over 2,000 documents and objects from the Yan'an period, which is still praised by many older functionaries of the Chinese Communist Party as the "golden revolutionary era".

Around Yan'an it is still possible to see the caves which are typical of this central loess landscape, and which were used for shelter and protection during World War II by the leaders of the Communist Party and the Red Army.

Luoyang

Five hours by train from Xi'an is **Luoyang** ❿, known primarily for its spectacular Buddhist caves. The emperors of the Eastern Han dynasty (AD 25–220) moved the capital here from Xi'an and the city flourished during the Tang and Song periods.

The famous **Longmen Shiku** (Dragon Gate Caves; open daily, 8am–5pm; entrance fee), are 13 km (8 miles) south of town. These Buddhist caves were created between the 5th and 7th centuries, with most of the figures and grottoes sponsored by noblemen of the time. There are over 1,300 grottoes and 700 niches containing 40 pagodas, 2,780 inscriptions and more than 100,000 statues and images. Many of the most beautiful sculptures were stolen or beheaded around the start of the 20th century and are now in museums in the West. Despite this, the Longmen caves provide a record of Buddhist art, reflecting different styles from the northern Wei dynasty to the Tang dynasty.

The biggest statue is more than 17 metres (56 ft) tall, and the smallest one is less than 2 cm (⅘-inch). The most striking part of the site is **Fengxian Si** (Temple for Worshipping Ancestors), with an exposed 17-metre-tall (56-ft) central Buddha statue. ❏

BELOW: Longmen Shiku, Luoyang.

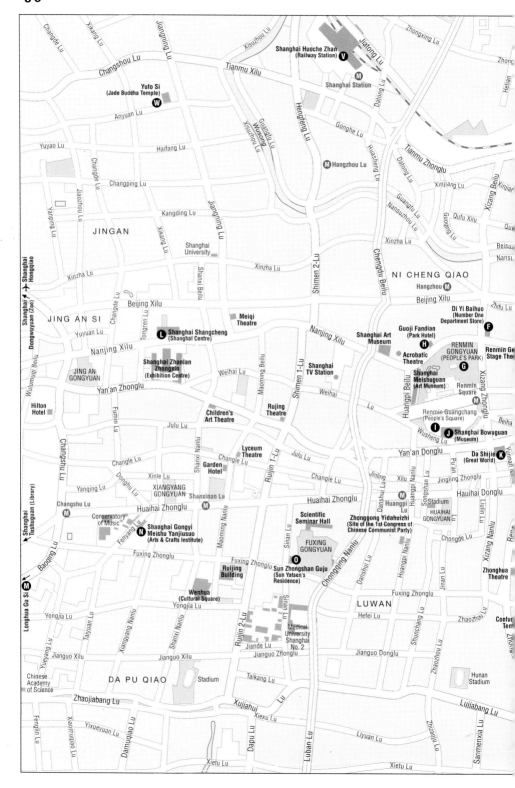

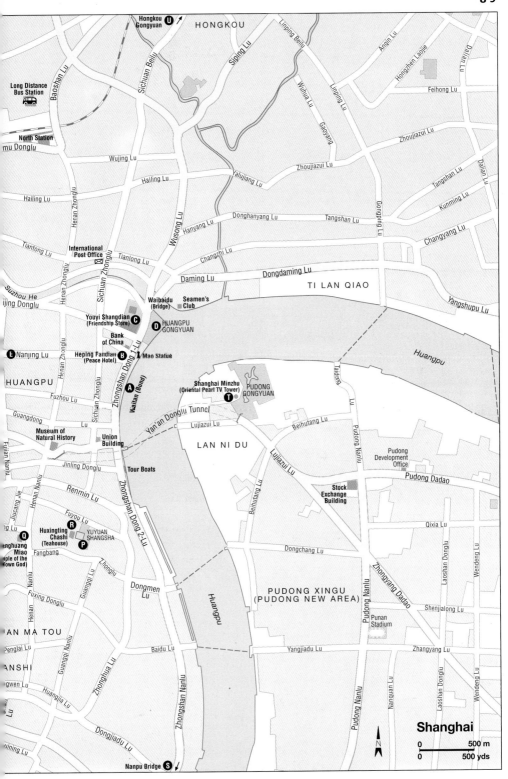

HONGKOU

Hongkou Gongyuan **U**

Linong Beilu

Siping Lu

Angin Lu

Hongzhen Laojie

Dalian Lu

Baoshan Lu

Sichuan Beilu

Wuhua Lu

Gaoyang

Linping Lu

Feihong Lu

Long Distance Bus Station

Zhoujiazui Lu

North Station

mu Dongtu

Wujing Lu

Yalujiang Lu

Zhoujiazui Lu

Tangshan Lu

Dalian Lu

Hailing Lu

Hanyang Lu

Donghanyang Lu

Kunming Lu

Hailing Lu

Henan Zhonglu

Wusong Lu

Tiantong Lu

Changyang Lu

Tianlong Lu

Changzhi Lu

International Post Office

Sichuan Zhonglu

Daming Lu

Dongdaming Lu

TI LAN QIAO

Suzhou He

ijing Donglu

Henan Zhonglu

Gongping Lu

Taidong

Yangshupu Lu

Youyi Shangdian (Friendship Store) **C**

Waibaidu (Bridge)

Seamen's Club

Huangpu

E Nanjing Lu

Heping Fandian (Peace Hotel) **B**

Bank of China

HUANGPU GONGYUAN **D**

Mao Statue

HUANGPU

Fuzhou Lu

Sichuan Zhonglu

Zhongshan Dong 1-Lu

Waitan (Bund) **A**

Shanghai Minzhu (Oriental Pearl TV Tower)

PUDONG GONGYUAN **T**

Guangdong Lu

Yan'an Donglu Tunnel

Lujiazui Lu

Beihutang Lu

Pudong Nanlu

Pudong Development Office

Museum of Natural History

Union Building

Jinling Donglu

LAN NI DU

Lujiazui Lu

Pudong Dadao

Tour Boats

Henan Nanlu

Renmin Lu

Zhongshan Dong 2-Lu

Beihutang Lu

Stock Exchange Building

Qixia Lu

Jiucang Jie

Fuyou Lu

Laoshan Donglu

Wendeng Lu

ng Lu **Q**

Huxingting Chashi (Teahouse) **R**

YUYUAN SHANGSHA

Zhonglu

Dongchang Lu

Zhongyang Dadao

Shenjialong Lu

anghuang Miao ple of the own God)

P

Fangbang

Guangqi Lu

Dongmen Lu

PUDONG XINGU (PUDONG NEW AREA)

Pudong Nanlu

Punan Stadium

Fuxing Donglu

Huangpu

Zhangyang Lu

Henan

AN MA TOU

Guangqi Nanlu

Baidu Lu

Yangjiadu Lu

Nanquan Lu

Laoshan Donglu

Wendeng Lu

englai Lu

Zhonghua Lu

Zhangyang Lu

ANSHI

gwen Lu

Huangjia Lu

Zhongshan Nanlu

Pudong Nanlu

uining Lu

Dongjiadu Lu

Nanpu Bridge **S**

Shanghai

0   500 m
0   500 yds

SHANGHAI

*Back in its glamorous colonial heyday, Shanghai was called the
Paris of the East. Today, the government intends it to be
the heir to Hong Kong, whatever the cost*

Maps:
Area 24
City 88

Shanghai sits on the **Huangpu Jiang**, an 80-km (50-mile) tributary of Chang Jiang, locally also known as the Yangzi, and which provides Shanghai (literally, upriver to the sea) with ocean access. Once a muddy fishing village, **Shanghai ⓫** today is undergoing an impressive transformation that leaves one breathless. Where there were once neighbourhoods of small houses, there are now high-rises. Where there were once handsome colonial-era buildings, there are now glitzy hotels. To visit Shanghai today is to visit a giant public-works project: new highways, new ports, new bridges, new office towers. In fact, in the late 1990s, Shanghai required so many construction cranes that there was a regional shortage of cranes in Asia.

The intent of all this urban revamping is nothing less than to make Shanghai a world-class regional centre of banking and finance. China's former leader Deng Xiaoping himself chose Shanghai as the country's economic spearhead, one that is intended to surpass Hong Kong by 2010. Land that was rice paddies and farmland just a few years ago is suddenly dominated by skyscrapers and instant communities. Marking this ambition is the Shanghai World Financial Centre, which will be the world's tallest building at 459 metres (1,506 ft) high when it is completed around 2001.

Administratively, Shanghai is a metropolis without a province, made up of surrounding rural districts and a dozen city districts. But locals and outsiders agree on one thing: *ren tai duo* – there are too many people in China's largest city. The greater metropolitan area has more than 14 million inhabitants. The city proper covers 375 sq. kms (145 sq. miles) and has 8 million inhabitants. Whatever the exact number, the density of Shanghai is among the highest in the world. China's most worldly, fashionable and open people are very individualistic, speaking a dialect that nobody else understands, eating a different cuisine, and generally considering themselves to be light-years ahead of their nearest competitor, Beijing. Indeed, Shanghai's higher living standard, pulsating night life, and cosmopolitan air make Beijing seem a bit dowdy in comparison.

For getting away from the central district, the bus routes are somewhat Byzantine, and the buses themselves an exercise in chaos. It's always better to take cabs, which are plentiful and easy to hail. Shanghai recently built an elevated ring road that circles the city, but traffic can still be maddening. However, the ever-expanding subway system is superb.

A cosmopolitan history

Distinctly a city of commerce, the region was already a trading centre in AD 960, flourishing for centuries and becoming an important trading port. Japanese

LEFT: the Bund at night.
BELOW: the Brave New World of Pudong.

Oriental Pearl TV Tower, in the Pudong area.

BELOW:
Huangpu Jiang.

pirates were attracted by this wealth, and after numerous attacks Shanghai built a protective wall in the 16th century. The wall surrounded the old city centre until 1912, just south of the Bund in a circular area defined by the Renmin Lu and Zhonghua Lu roads. While the wall eventually humbled the Japanese pirates, it failed to impede Western colonial intrusions.

As a result of the Opium Wars in the 1840s, the British imposed upon China the Treaty of Nanjing, which, among many things, opened up Shanghai to Westerners. Foreign concession areas took up most of what is now central Shanghai, save for the old walled Chinese part of the city. Soon Shanghai became the place to be – a city with the best culture, most opulent dance halls, largest volume of business, the tallest buildings. It became a mix of cultures that was always to define its internationalism, even up to the present.

New ideas also allowed for radicalism, a Shanghai tradition. The Communist Party was founded in the city in 1921, and the Cultural Revolution of the 1960s not only began here, but had its headquarters in Shanghai. But despite the enthusiasm of the Red Guards to demolish everything not defined as Socialist Realism – and that included anything foreign, Buddhist, or simply old – many buildings from colonial times have survived in the city. Unfortunately, however, many may not survive China's push to modernise.

On the waterfront

One gets a fine view of this modernisation along Zhongshan Dong Lu, which parallels the western bank of the Huangpu Jiang. Most foreigners know this road as the **Bund** (Waitan) **Ⓐ**. During Shanghai's heyday, the Bund was occupied by the European, American, and Japanese banks, trading houses, clubs,

consulates, and hotels. After liberation, the Communist Party took over the structures for their own use. Today, these neo-classical buildings have been renovated by the government as a sightseeing showcase and are beautifully illuminated at night by floodlights. Opposite is a waterfront promenade extending for over a kilometre and packed with locals and tourists, hustlers and hawkers. In early morning along the Bund, directly opposite the Peace Hotel, the Shanghai day starts before dawn, with crowds of people practising *ta'i chi chuan* and other exercises.

Where Nanjing Lu meets the Bund and river is the **Heping Fandian** (Peace Hotel) ❸, known as the glamorous Cathay Hotel in the old days, and Shanghai's most treasured colonial building, with a 1930s atmosphere. Views of the Bund and Shanghai skyline are excellent from its eighth floor. Have breakfast or dinner on old silver plates and meditate on the transforming waterfront. After dinner, have a drink in the first-floor German pub to the sounds of the famous Old Peace Hotel Jazz Band, which has been performing jazz in the city since the early 1920s.

At the northern extent of the Bund, near the **Youyi Shangdian** (Friendship Store) ❻ – a favourite of tourists shopping for arts and crafts, and silk products – and **Huangpu Gongyuan** (Huangpu Park) ❼, the boulevard crosses **Suzhou He** (also called Wusong), a canal that cuts east–west across the city and empties into the river. Huangpu Gongyuan is said to have once had signs prohibiting "dogs and Chinese" from entering the park, although this is unsubstantiated. The old bridge across the canal, **Waibaidu**, has been somewhat overshadowed by a newer parallel structure. Formerly called Garden Bridge, Waibaidu connected the American and British districts until, in 1863, both merged into the Interna-

Map on pages 88–9

BELOW: bird fancier on his way.

TIP

Daily river cruises
offer views of the
Bund and the industry
and scenery along the
banks of the Huangpu.
The one-hour and
half-day trips travel
from the Bund (the
dock is at Jinling Lu)
to Wusong and back.

tional Settlement (Shanghai Zujie), which stretched west and east, with Yan'an Lu its southern border. From 1937 onwards, the bridge defined the border with the Japanese-occupied territory north of the Suzhou. Just at the northern end of the Waibaidu are some examples of old Shanghai architecture, including the Shanghai Mansions hotel, Shanghai Stock Exchange, and the blue-walled consulate of the Russians, the only foreigners who have succeeded in retaining their original consulate building.

Central Shanghai

The heart of the city is mostly in Huangpu and Jingan districts, which make up much of what was the International Settlement of old Shanghai. **Nanjing Lu** **E**, Shanghai's main thoroughfare, crosses east–west through these two districts. At night, neon signs light up the street until the wee morning hours, and in the day, hordes of pedestrians, bicycles, and cars make it what some have called the busiest street in the world. It is often said that Shanghai is nothing but a consumer's paradise, bereft of culture. Street activity along the Bund and Nanjing Lu would certainly enforce the city's reputation as a shopper's paradise – not limited to clothes, silk, or electronic goods, but also traditional theatre props and musical instruments, art, and even collectors' stamps. Old state-owned food stores run alongside the glitzy commercialism of new department stores and the chic fashion of Burberry's, Esprit, and Christian Dior.

Halfway down the street from the Bund at the corner of Xizang Lu is the store that sells everything – the state-owned **Di Yi Baihuo** (Number One Department Store) **F**, a typical experience in Chinese domestic shopping. Further west, wedged between Fuzhou Lu to the south and Nanjing Lu to the north, is

BELOW:
Nanjing Lu at night.

Renmin Gongyuan (People's Park) **G**. A race course of the powerful *taipan* before 1949, it is now the largest, but most unremarkable, park in the city. The **Shanghai Meishuguan** (Shanghai Art Museum, open daily, 9am–5pm; entrance fee) is currently at 425 Nanjing Lu. It is due to move a short distance east along the street into the former racecourse club, until recently the Shanghai Library.

North of the park on Nanjing Lu is yet more colonial history. The art deco **Guoji Fandian** (Park Hotel) **H** was once the tallest hotel in Asia and almost as glamorous as the venerable Peace Hotel on the Bund. South of Renmin Gongyuan is **Renmin Guangchang** (People's Square) **I**, a social centre for the locals, and often crowded with families flying kites, kids rollerskating, and people ballroom dancing and practising martial arts.

The new and impressive **Shanghai Bowuguan J** (Shanghai Museum, open daily, 9am–5pm; entrance fee) is also found here at the south end of the park. This modern and elegant facility, opened in 1996, offers a spectacular collection in a superb setting. Its 11 state-of-the-art galleries house China's first international-standard exhibit of paintings, bronzes, sculpture, ceramics, calligraphy, jade, Ming and Qing dynasty furniture, coins, seals, and minority art. The bronze collection is reputedly the best in the world. Information is well presented in English, and the highly informative audio guide is also excellent. This is one socialist project that got it right.

Just south of Renmin Guangchang on Xizang Lu is the **Da Shijie** (Great World) **K**, Old Shanghai's notorious den of gambling, cabaret, drugs, and prostitution. It has been restored and turned into an entertainment centre offering everything from acrobatic shows to fantasy rides, and even a *Guinness Book of World Records* hall.

Map
on pages
88–9

Early morning ta'i chi in a city park

BELOW: Renmin Guangchang, with the Shanghai Museum in the background.

All regional varieties of Chinese cuisine are represented in Shanghai's restaurants.

Continuing west on Nanjing Lu, Shanghai's commercialisation continues 4 km (2½ miles) to the western extent of the street. The Soviet-built **Shanghai Zhanlan Zhongxin** (Shanghai Exhibition Centre) is at Xikang Lu. Across the street is a foreign business, travel, and social centre, the **Shanghai Shangcheng** (Shanghai Centre) **L**. This huge complex houses the Portman Shangri-la Hotel, two residential towers, a multinational office building, and a shopping area that includes major airline offices, Western stores, and chain restaurants such as the Hard Rock Café.

To the south

In the south of the city is the **Longhua Gu Si M**, on a road of the same name, a temple and pagoda built in 242 and since destroyed and rebuilt several times. The temple site consists of seven halls that, after the turmoil of the Cultural Revolution, are once again being used for religious purposes. Adjoining the temple, the Longhua Hotel was designed especially for Buddhist travellers and includes a vegetarian restaurant, but it welcomes all visitors.

Considerably closer to central Shanghai, the former French Concession has kept its own charming character with French-inspired architecture and avenues. Founded in the 1840s it is set in the southern part of downtown, south of Yan'an Lu. Its main road, Huaihai Lu, is perhaps the more pleasant choice for shopping or just strolling. It offers a more relaxed, upscale atmosphere, with many shops, designer boutiques and cafés, but still reflects French and Russian influence. Two hotels – the Jinjiang Hotel (Lao Jinjiang Fandian) and the Garden Hotel (Huayuan Fandian) – on Changle Lu at Maoming Lu (one block north of Huaihai) feature some of old Shanghai's most luxurious architecture.

BELOW:
Longhua Gu Si.

South of Huaihai on Fenyang Lu is the old French mansion that houses the **Shanghai Gongyi Meishu Yanjiusuo** (Shanghai Arts and Crafts Research Institute, open daily, 9am–5pm) **N**. Visitors can watch artisans working and purchase a variety of traditional Chinese work. The new **Shanghai Tushuguan** (Shanghai Library, open daily, 9am–5pm), one of the largest in the world, is located further west on Huaihai Lu. Opened in 1996, the library features the most up-to-date informational technology. Many foreign consulates are also located in the vicinity.

Sun Zhongshan Guju (Sun Yatsen's Residence) **O** (open daily, 9am–4.30pm; entrance fee) is on Xiangshan Lu at Sinan Lu, just south of Huaihai, near Fuxing Gongyuan (Fuxing Park). Mao Zedong and Zhou Enlai also lived and worked in this area. At Xingye Lu and Huangpi Lu is the site of the First National Congress of the Communist Party of China (Zhonggong Yidahuizhi). You can enter the room where the first delegates founded the Party. It remains in its original form, complete with a table set for 13 people at tea.

The Old City

From the north, paralleling Sichuan Lu, Henan Lu intercepts Renmin Lu, which together with Zhonghua Lu defines a circle outlining the edge of the Old City. The city walls paralleled this small ring road until

1912, when they were knocked down; then the moats were filled in, and the two streets were laid down.

Before 1949, the Old City remained under Chinese law and administration while the rest of central Shanghai was carved up by foreign powers. Most of the residents of these old back alleys were Chinese. Eventually it became notorious as a gangster-and-opium slum. Today, the vices are gone, but the tiny lanes, crowded but quaint neighbourhoods and small houses still exist.

At the heart of the Old City is **Yuyuan** (Yuyuan Gardens) **P** (open daily, 8.30am–4.30pm) and **Chenghuang Miao** (Temple of the Town God), **Q**. Yuyuan Gardens is one of the few old tourist sights left in the city – and touristy it certainly is. Since the 18th century, the complex, with traditional red walls and upturned tile roofs, has been a market place and social centre. The bazaar has been recently renovated, complete with chrome and shiny glass. As befits a bazaar, here one can find both schlock and traditional Chinese trinkets. There is also a basement antique market. Don't be put off by the exterior of the various restaurants. The best one is certainly the **Huxingting Chashi** (Huxingting Tea-house) **R**, the city's oldest teahouse, set in the middle of a small lake whose famous zigzag bridge leads directly to Yuyuan. The second floor of the teahouse serves some of the best tea in town and is one of the only places in Shanghai that offers a truly tranquil break from the city's chaos. A bit of old China is preserved here, and musicians meet here nightly to play traditional Chinese music.

Legend has it that Yuyuan's gardens were built in the 16th century by the eccentric and gifted landscape architect Zhang Nanyang, who was commissioned by the Pan family of the Ming court. The traditional rock-and-tree garden is filled with artificial hills, carp-filled ponds, dragon-lined walls, and

Map on pages 88–9

BELOW: Yuyuan, in the heart of the old Chinese city.

*Modern architecture
in the city centre.*

pavilions connected by zigzagging bridges. One can well imagine this park serving as the home base for the rebels of the Society of Small Swords during the Taiping rebellion. Today, an exhibition about this secret society is located in their former headquarters, the Spring Hall.

Just west of Yuyuan, at Henan Lu, is the Fuyou Lu Sunday antique market. Hawkers come here as early as 4am to set up their goods, usually directly on the ground. The tiny lane is bustling with people by mid morning, by which time the best goods are usually already sold. You'll find an eclectic collection of antiques, including old maps of Shanghai, baskets and boxes, porcelain, and old watches, plus some scattered modern goods and Mao paraphernalia.

On the east side

Shanghai harbour is the fourth-largest in the world and an important factor in making Shanghai China's most important industrial base. Across the river from the Bund, on the eastern side, is the special economic zone of **Pudong Xinqu**, or the **Pudong New Area**. But this is not just another urban development project. Pudong is a massive US$40 billion undertaking that is significantly redefining Shanghai. It will have a new container port, an international airport timed for completion by the millennium, and acres of new high-rises and sky-scrapers, including the future home of the Shanghai Stock Exchange. But, as work progressed, many analysts were beginning to wonder if the Chinese had been too ambitious with Pudong, as many of the high-rises were lacking tenants, and the regional economy was increasingly stagnant.

BELOW: colonial ambiance in a restaurant.

The **Nanpu Bridge ❺** connects Pudong to western Shanghai. An underwater tunnel for vehicles links the Bund with Pudong, and several more tunnels are

Map
on pages
88–9

planned. (It is hoped that the civil engineers working on the project have studied Shanghai's subterranean history, because since 1920, when the problem of subsidence was first noticed, Shanghai has sunk several metres.)

If for some reason you are unable to locate Pudong from your perch on the Bund, look once more across the river for the impossible-to-miss **Shanghai Minzhu** (Oriental Pearl TV Tower, open daily, 8am–9.45pm) ❶, the huge space-ship-like observation and broadcast spire on the other side of the river, with globes lit up in bright colours at night. High-speed elevators to the top bring visitors to a 360-degree, bird's-eye view of the city. Asia's largest department store can also be found in Pudong. The 10-storey mega-mall Yaohan Department Store (Ba Bai Ban) on Zhangyang Lu sells everything from clothing to cars.

The business-minded may want to look further into Pudong to witness its special economic areas – the central financial area of Lujiazui, the Waigaoqiao bonded zone, and the Jinqiao industrial zone. There is a rather unspectacular beach at the eastern edge of Pudong that touches the East China Sea.

North of Suzhou He

From Suzhou He, Sichuan Lu leads northward into Hongkou District, which has retained some of its old southern Chinese charm. As in much of the Old City and the former international and French settlements, laundry is draped from balconies on bamboo canes, and in the side streets, elderly people sit outside on stools to chat, chop vegetables, play cards, or guard the bedding airing out in the street. An evening walk through the streets of Hongkou can be enlightening, although the black, murky canals emit a terrible smell in summer.

BELOW: street food.

Map on pages 88–9

Novelist Lu Xun.

BELOW: Jade Buddha, Yufo Si.
RIGHT: Nanpu Bridge to Pudong.

At the edge of the northern part of Sichuan Lu is **Hongkou Gongyuan** ❶, one of the loveliest parks in Shanghai. Within the park is a museum and the grave of Lu Xun, the most famous Chinese novelist of the 20th century. He lived in Shanghai from 1933 until his death some three years later, and his former home on Dalu Xincun, a side alley of Shangyin Lu, is just a few minutes' walk east of the park.

Hongkou was already in Japanese hands before the occupation of 1937 and had the nickname of Little Tokyo. In fact, a large percentage of Shanghai's resident 30,000 Japanese lived here. Ironically, despite Japan's alliance with Nazi Germany, Little Tokyo became a haven for Jewish refugees from Europe. Until 1941, China was one of the last countries open to immigrants, requiring neither entry visa nor proof of financial means. Although these conditions were tightened after 1939, the Jewish community – considered a valuable asset in Shanghai – gave others assistance with money and job opportunities. By 1939, 14,000 refugees had reached Shanghai. In 1943, more than 20,000 Jewish refugees lived in the Hongkou ghetto, when the Japanese, meeting demands from their Nazi allies, forced them into the "Designated Area for Stateless Refugees".

Today, the **Moxi Huitang** (Ohel Moshe Synagogue), built in 1927 by Hongkou's Jewish residents, still stands on Changyang Lu and now houses a small museum dedicated to Shanghai's Jewish community.

Due west a few kilometres is the **Shanghai Huoche Zhan** (Shanghai Railway Station) ❷, which lies in Zhabei District. Here, the day begins even earlier than in the parks, with crowds of migrants from all over China camping out, either about to leave or having just arrived. The train station has the reputation of being the dingiest and roughest part of town, but the authorities have recently begun efforts to build up the area by constructing nice hotels and apartment buildings, along with classy Western shopping malls and commercial centres.

To the west

West of the station, on the south side of Suzhou He on Anyuan Lu, is **Yufo Si** (Jade Buddha Temple) ❸ (open daily except Chinese New Year). The temple is famous for its two Buddha statues made of white jade, brought back to China from Burma (Myanmar) by the monk Huigen in 1882. The statues were brought to Shanghai in 1918, when the temple was completed. One of the statues, of the Sleeping Buddha, representing his entry into nirvana, is a special rarity, but the other white-jade statue of the Seated Buddha – 2 metres (6 ft) tall, decorated with jewels and weighing 1,000 kg (2,200 lbs) – is the more famous. About 70 monks are in residence here, overseeing religious and tourist activities, and running a restaurant.

To the southwest is the special commercial zone of **Hongqiao**, with a large concentration of Western hotels, office buildings, and exhibition centres. The **Shanghai Hongqiao International Airport** (Shanghai Hongqiao Feijichang) lies at the western end of Hongqiao Lu. The thoroughfare was once an elite colonial road lined with glamorous country villas of old Shanghai's expatriate residents, some of which are still standing. ❑

GUILIN AND ENVIRONS

Map on pages 24–5

Picture-perfect is how artists and photographers have described the landscape near Guilin – limestone spires rising above a smooth river at one of China's most beautiful destinations

"The river is like a green silk belt, and the hills are like turquoise jade hairpins". So wrote the Tang dynasty scholar and writer Han Yu (768–94), becoming the first prominent voice to immortalise this bizarre landscape. Ever since, artists have joined the chorus of eulogies in poems and paintings. Nowadays, photographers from all over the world have taken up the aesthetic challenge, aiming for the most evocative possible image. Together with Beijing, Shanghai, and Xi'an, Guilin has become one of China's foremost destinations.

The Guilin area owes its exquisite beauty to geological disruptions over 300 million years ago. Limestone formations pushed through an ancient sea bed, then the wind and rain eroded the hills and peaks into innumerable shapes, leaving behind labyrinthine caves and grottos within them. With some peaks rounded, and some sharply pointed, with perpendicular cliffs and trees that sprout from the cracks to bend skyward, this is the surreal landscape geographers call *karst*, which lures travellers to Guilin.

Guilin is in the northeastern area of Guangxi Zhuangzu Zizhiqu, an autonomous region lying in the southern, subtropical part of China, bordering Vietnam to the south. The long summers are hot and humid, and winters often wet, so the best times to visit are spring and autumn. The Zhuang minority is the largest ethnic minority in China, comprising a third of Guangxi's 40 million inhabitants and dominating its eastern half. Another five percent belong to 10 other minorities, such as the Yao, Miao, Dong, and Yi, living primarily in the western and northern mountains. The Han Chinese are the predominant group in the urban areas and in the western part of Guangxi.

Because they are far from Beijing, Guilin and Guangxi have a tradition of sheltering refugees. In 1647, the fleeing Ming court established a temporary residence here in their flight from the Manchus. Three centuries later, as the Japanese army swept into China, hundreds of thousands of northerners sought safety here. In 1949, it was one of the last Kuomintang (Nationalist) strongholds to fall to the communists.

Until the end of the 1970s, this area along the **Li Jiang** (Li River) was a remote and quiet place. But with the development of tourism and the establishment of flight connections with the major cities of China, the city of Guilin has grown up.

Guilin

Guilin ⑫ literally means "cassia tree forest", named for the local cassia trees, whose scent wafts through the city in autumn. Historical records put Guilin's founding at 214 BC, during the reign of Qin Shi Huangdi, the first emperor of a united China, when he ordered the construction of the Ling canal to connect

LEFT: Li Jiang and limestone spires.
BELOW: cormorant fishing.

Fishing with cormorants is mostly performed for the tourists nowadays.

BELOW: Ludiyan, or Reed Flute Cave.

the central plain of China with the south and with Southeast Asia, via the Yangzi, Li and Zhu rivers. The canal still exists and can be easily seen at Xing'an, 65 km (40 miles) northwest of Guilin.

The plains around Guilin are still mostly agricultural, though the cultivated areas are constantly interrupted by hills and occasional clumps of bamboo. Labour is often done by hand, with water buffaloes the beasts of burden. Rice is the main crop. Sugar cane and *jujube* (the Chinese date), are also grown, as well as peppers, which go into the piquant local sauce known as *guilinjiang*.

Guilin, with over half a million residents, has no old town left because the city was razed by the Japanese in 1944. A construction boom only began with the blooming of the tourist business. The city now has the usual characteristics of a modern metropolis – heavy traffic, shopping centres and boutiques, plus the usual scam artists, souvenir stalls and ticket booths that are a part of any popular tourist spot. The most imposing buildings are the fancy new hotels. But it's a clean city with a charming waterfront and ever-changing moods. Hills and parks mottle the urban landscape. A few sights, like Xiangbi Shan (Elephant Trunk Hill), Fubo Shan, and the port area, are illuminated at night. And the many small restaurants offer Li Jiang cuisine, such as fish, eel, frog, turtle, snail, shrimp, and snake.

North of the centrally-located Lijiang Hotel (on Jianwu Bei Lu) stands **Duxiu Feng**, the Peak of Solitary Beauty. Three hundred steps lead to the top of this 150-metre (500-ft) hill, from which one has a splendid panorama of the city. Just below it is **Wang Cheng**, briefly the former capital of the Ming court. Its buildings now house the Guilin Teachers' College. To the east, at the corner of Binjiang Lu and Fengbei Lu, **Fubo Shan** sits on the bank of the Li. This hill

MAGICAL ORIGINS

The local inhabitants of the Guilin area have a pleasingly fanciful explanation for the landscape's contours, which has nothing to do with such prosaic things as geological formations. They believe that the hills were herded into the region by the King of All under Heaven, wielding a magic whip made from the hairs left in the hair brush of a goddess, and carefully woven together. The goddess, it is said, had temporarily assumed the disguise of an old lady (as goddesses are wont to do), leaving the whip in the hands of her workers.

But the King of All under Heaven, presumably believing he had as much right to a magic whip as he had to anything else, had confiscated it and was intent on driving the hills towards the South Sea in a desperate attempt to fill up the oceanic realm of his rival, the Dragon King.

Unfortunately for him, Shark Girl, a loyal helper of the Dragon King, contrived to steal the whip, and the King of All under Heaven, powerless to move mountains without it, had to give up his scheme when it was only half completed. Ever since then, the hills have remained where they stood when the project was abandoned, enchanting countless generations. Sometimes, it seems, a lust for power can have an unexpectedly beneficial outcome.

bears the nickname of a Han dynasty general – Restraining the Waves – who saved Guilin from a rebel army. At the foot of Fubo Shan is a two-ton bronze bell, while nearby a huge cooking pot, said to have served 1,000 people, is encased in cement. Underneath the hill is Returned Pearl Cave, where a dragon used to live, using a magnificent pearl to light his cave. A boy once stole it, but his mother persuaded him to return it to the owner, and the grateful dragon richly rewarded them.

At the riverside exit of the cave's tunnel is **Qianfo Yan** (Thousand Buddha Rock), where Tang and Song dynasty devotees have carved hundreds of Buddhist sculptures and left prayers inscribed on plaques. Farther north lies **Diecai Shan** (Piled Brocades Hill), at 220 metres (720 ft) in height, the tallest in the city, with changing hues on the slopes, caves with Buddhist sculptures and calligraphy, and a grand view from the summit.

On the eastern bank of the Li, just across Jiefang Bridge, lies **Qixing Gongyuan** (Seven Stars Park). It acquired its name from the positions of its seven hills, which suggest the pattern of the Big Dipper constellation. Caves here are also part of the sights, especially Yinlongyan (Hidden Dragon Cave), with its ancient inscriptions. In the park's centre rises Luotou Shan (Camel Hill) and it needs little imagination to notice the almost startling resemblance. Nearby are a bonsai garden and a small zoo.

In the northwest corner of the city, 6 km (4 miles) from the centre, is **Ludiyan** (Reed Flute Cave), which takes its name from the reeds, which were fashioned into flutes, that once grew at the mouth of the cave. Nowadays, a ticket booth and concrete stairway mark the entrance, where guides meet visitors to take them on an illuminated tour 250 metres (800 ft) into the mountain's interior.

Map on pages 24–5

Cave temple near Yangshuo.

BELOW: Yangshuo.

Map on pages 24–5

menu at a Yangshuo restaurant; the town is popular with Western backpackers.

BELOW: traditional village.
RIGHT: agriculture is the mainstay of the region's economy.

The trip passes numerous stalactites and stalagmites in ever-changing shapes, suggesting pagodas, mushrooms, lions, waterfalls and chandeliers. The highlight of the descent is the impressive Crystal Palace of the Dragon King, said to be able to hold 1,000 people. Most enchanting of all is the subterranean pond at the far end, where the rocks, bathed in soft lights, are reflected in the water.

Li Jiang

The boat excursion on the placid waters of the Li Jiang from Guilin to Yangshuo is an essential part of any visit. The armada of boats leaves in the morning from the port area between Jiefang Bridge and Xiangbi Shan (Elephant Trunk Hill). The cruise takes 4–5 hours to reach Yangshuo, 60 km (40 miles) south, and costs over US$50. Much cheaper rides can be arranged from Yangshuo, either north to Yangdi (halfway back to Guilin), or east to Fuli, which are some of the best parts of the river. In drier months the river is too shallow around Guilin, so boats start at Yangdi. The cruise passes through karst landscape, with fascinating spires, many with near-vertical cliffs that shoot up eerily from the flat plains. Along the way, fishermen pole their narrow, three-bamboo rafts along the waters in the evenings, sometimes with a group of cormorants on board for fishing.

Yangshuo ⓭ lies within a half-circle of steep hills on the west bank of the Li. A small developed town in which tourism is the main business, Yangshuo fills up in the afternoons when visitors disembark from the Guilin boats. It mainly caters to low-budget travellers, with a long street lined with restaurants and handicrafts stalls. Among the visitors who come here, the most popular pastime is renting bicycles for excursions. In Yangshuo, the eerie landscapes are closer at hand and superb views can be had from the hilltop pavilion in the city park, from the port area and from the bridge just south of the settled area. Minibuses take visitors back to Guilin, a two-hour journey past similar plains studded with odd-looking hills.

Beyond Guilin

To the northwest of Guilin are the counties of **Longsheng** and **Sanjiang**. The former is home to the Dong, Miao and Yao minorities, the latter to the Dong people. Traditional architecture, terraced hills, and ethnic costumes make this an excellent introduction to the lifestyles of southwest China's minorities. Some Yao and all Miao groups are famous for their embroidery skills. Dong architecture features the multi-tiered drum towers, before which important assemblies are held, and the triple-towered, covered "wind and rain bridges", the most outstanding of which is the Chengyang Qiao (165 metres/540 ft long) in Sanjiang.

To Guilin's southwest is the industrial heartland of Guangxi. **Liuzhou**, a city of over half a million residents in the province's centre, has a picturesque river and scattered hill parks, the best at **Dule Yan**, 10 km (6 miles) to the west, also with karst caves.

Wuzhou, 250 km (160 miles) southeast of Liuzhou, lies at the confluence of the Guijiang and Xijiang rivers. This city has been an important trading town since the 18th century. There is a fast jetfoil service from here to Guangzhou and Hong Kong.

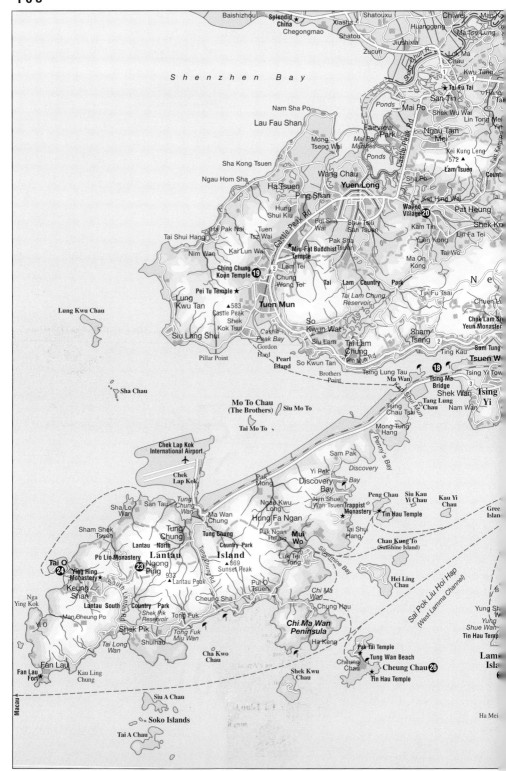

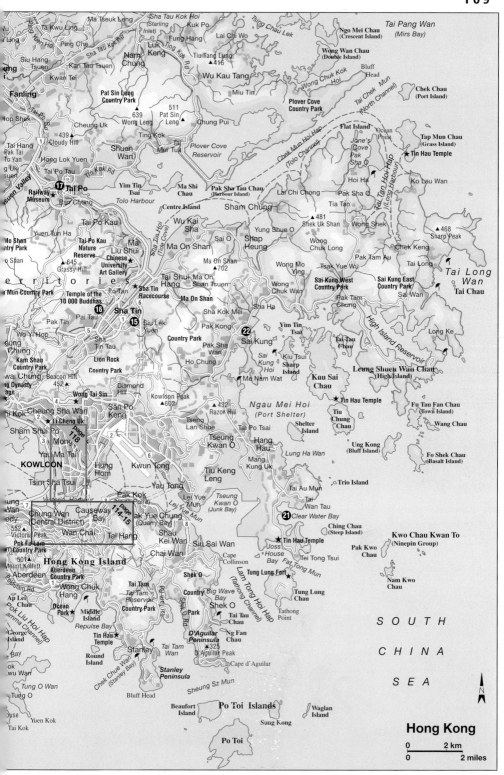

Ma Tseuk Leng
Sha Tau Kok Hoi
(Starling
Inlet)
Kuk Po
Sha Tau Kok Hoi
Tsing Chau Lek
Tai Pang Wan
(Mirs Bay)
Ngo Mei Chau
(Crescent Island)
Wong Wan Chau
(Double Island)

Ta Kwu Ling
Fung Hang
Lai Chi Wo

Ping Che
Luk
Keng
Tiu Tang Lung

Wong Chuk Kok
Hoi
Bluff
Head

Kan Tau Tsuen
Nam
Chung
Wu Kau Tang
Miu Tin

Tai Chek Mun
(North Channel)
Chek Chau
(Port Island)

Kwan Tei

Fanling
Pat Sin Leng
Country Park
Plover Cove
Country Park

511
Pat Sin
Leng
Chung Pui
Flat Island
Ocean
Point
Tap Mun Chau
(Grass Island)

639
Wong Leng
Tin Hau Temple

Cheung Uk
Ting Kok
Plover Cove
Reservoir
Chek Mun Hoi Hap
(Tolo Channel)
Jane's
Cove
Pak
Sha O

439
Cloudy Hill
Shuen
Wan
Mei Tuk
Hoi Ha
Ko Lau Wan

Hong Lok Yuen
Tai Po Tau
Ma Shi
Chau
Pak Sha Tau Chau
(Harbour Island)
Lai Chi Chong
Pak Sha O

Railway
Museum
Tai Po
Yim Tin
Tsai
Centre Island
Sham Chung
Tia Tan
Wong Shek

Pan Cheng
Tolo Harbour
Wu Kai
Sha
481
Shek Uk Shan
Sharp Peak
468

Tai Po Kau
Sai O
Yung Shue O
Wong
Chuk Long
Chek Keng

Yuen Tun Ha
Shap
Heung
Pak Tam Au
Tai Long

Tai Po Kau
Nature
Reserve
Ma
Liu Shui
Ma On Shan
702
Wong Mo To
Tsak Yue Wu
**Tai Long
Wan**

645
Grassy Hill
Chinese
University
Country Park
Tai Shui
Hang
Ma On
Shan Tsuen
Wong
Chuk Wan
Sai Kung West
Country Park
Sai Kung East
Country Park
Tai Chau

Po Tan
Sha Tin
Racecourse
Ma On Shan
Sha Ha
Pak Tam
Chung

Temple of the
10 000 Buddhas
Sha Tin
Sha Kok Mei

Pak Tin
Pai Tau
Siu Lek
Yuen
Pak Kong
Yim Tin
Tsai
Long Ke

Wo Yi Hop
Sha
Tin Tau
Country Park
Pak Sha
Wan
Sai Kung
Tai Tau
Chau
High Island Reservoir

Kam Shan
Country Park
Lion Rock
Country Park
Ho Chung
Sai
Kung
Hoi
Kiu Tsui
Sharp
Island
Leung Shuen Wan Chau
(High Island)

Beacon Hill
452
Diamond
Hill
Kowloon Peak
602
Ma Nam Wat
Kau Sai
Chau
Tin Hau Temple
Fu Tau Fan Chau
(Town Island)

Wong Tai Sin
San Po
Kong
432
Razor Hill
Ngau Mei Hoi
(Port Shelter)
Tiu
Chung
Chau
Wang Chau

Cheung Sha Wan
Tseng
Lan Shue
Shelter
Island
Ung Kong
(Bluff Island)
Fo Shek Chau
(Basalt Island)

Li Cheng Uk
Tseung
Kwan O
Tai Po Tsai
KOWLOON
Hung
Hom
Kwun Tong
Hang
Hau
Lung Ha Wan

Sham Shui Po
Mong
Yau Ma Tei
Tsim Sha Tsui
Yau Tong
Tiu Keng
Leng
Mang
Kung Uk
Trio Island

Victoria Harbour
Pak Kok
(Point)
Tseung
Kwan O
(Junk Bay)
Tai Au Mun
Tai
Wan Tau

**Chung Wan
(Central District)**
**Causeway
Bay**
Lei Yue
Mun
Lei Yue Mun
Clear Water Bay
Ching Chau
(Steep Island)
Kwo Chau Kwan To
(Ninepin Group)

Wan Chai
Tai Hang
Yau Chung
(Quarry Bay)
Shau
Kei Wan
Tin Hau Temple
Pak Kwo
Chau

Victoria Peak
Pok Fu Lam
Country Park
Chai Wan
Siu Sai Wan
Cape
Collinson
Joss
House
Bay
Tei Tong Tsui
Nam Kwo
Chau

501
Mount Kellett
Hong Kong Island
Shek O
Tung Lung Fort
Fat Tong Mun

Aberdeen
Aberdeen
Country Park
Wong Chuk
Hang
Tai Tam
Country Park
Big Wave
Bay
Shek O
Country
Park
Tung Lung
Chau

Ap Lei
Chau
Ocean
Park
Middle
Island
Tai Tam
Reservoir
Tai Tau
Chau
Tathong
Point

Repulse Bay
Tin Hau
Temple
Tai Tam
Wan
D'Aguilar
Peninsula
Ng Fan
Chau

Round
Island
Stanley
325
D'Aguilar Peak

Chek Chue Wan
(Stanley Bay)
Tai Tam
Wan
Cape d'Aguilar

**Stanley
Peninsula**
Sheung Sz Mun

Bluff Head

Beaufort
Island
Po Toi Islands
Waglan
Island

Sung Kong

Po Toi

**SOUTH

CHINA

SEA**

Hong Kong

0   2 km
0   2 miles

HONG KONG

*From "barren rock" to thriving commercial entrepôt, Hong Kong's
vibrant brand of East-meets-West atmosphere lives on
after its return to the motherland*

Maps:
Area 108
City 114

Archaeological evidence shows Hong Kong has been inhabited since the
Stone Age. Han Chinese people began settling here in the Song dynasty
(960–1279), but it remained a relatively obscure corner of Guangdong
province until British opium merchants recognised the advantages of "annex-
ing" 45 sq. km (17 sq. miles) of the best deep-water harbour in the region. In this
they proved more far-sighted than their monarch. "Albert," tutted the Queen, "is
so much amused by my having got the island of Hong Kong, and we think Victoria ought to be called Princess of Hong Kong in addition to Princess Royal."
And foreign secretary Lord Palmerston has gone down in history as calling it "a
barren island with hardly a house upon it".

The former British colony of **Hong Kong ⑭** can be divided into three parts:
Hong Kong Island, Kowloon, and the New Territories (incorporating the outlying islands). The Island, as it's popularly known, is 80 sq. km (31 sq. miles)
of topsy-turvy real estate. The earliest British settlements were established here,
and the "barren island" is now dominated by great banks and financial houses,
enormous futuristic buildings, opulent hotels, splendid residences on Victoria
Peak, beach resorts, and some of the oldest Chinese communities.

Across Victoria Harbour – 5 minutes by the underwater Mass Transit Railway,
8 minutes by the Star Ferry and less than 10 minutes
by car on a clear run through the three tunnels – is
the city of Kowloon, a commercial complex packed
into 46 sq. km (18 sq. miles). Kowloon and Stone-
cutters' Island were ceded to the British in 1860, for
better defence of the harbour. Most tourists see only
the tip of Kowloon, the Tsim Sha Tsui district and its
many hotels, bars, and shopping centres. North of
Tsim Sha Tsui, along Nathan Road, are the Yau Ma
Tei and Mong Kok districts. Boundary Street marks
the demarcation line between the old colony, granted
to the British "in perpetuity", and the New Territories, which were leased in 1898 for a 99-year period.
All reverted to Chinese sovereignty in July 1997.

Along with the New Territories, England leased 233
outlying islands, only four of which are inhabited by
sizeable communities. One of these, Lantau, over
twice the size of the Island, is now home to the state-
of-the-art international airport. Together with Lamma,
Cheung Chau and Peng Chau it serves as a "dormi-
tory" for professionals wanting to escape the rat race.

LEFT: Hong Kong's
Central District and
the Star Ferry.
BELOW:
water transport
the old way.

Hong Kong island

Hong Kong's **Central District** is dominated by its
legislative offices, but real power here is held by the
banks. Dominating Central is the gleaming 370-metre
(1,200-ft) **Bank of China Tower ⓐ**, designed by the
famous Chinese-American architect I. M. Pei. The

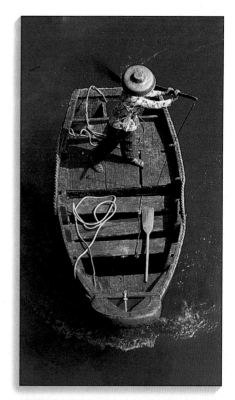

tower's sharp angles point directly at the other banks, which makes for bad (or good, depending which side you're on) *feng shui*. The Hongkong Bank (HSBC) headquarters, designed by British architect Sir Norman Foster, and one of the most expensive buildings in the world, is another Central landmark.

The best place to begin a Central tour is at the **Star Ferry Pier ⓑ**. The green-and-white Star Ferries have been shunting passengers across the harbour between the Island and Kowloon since 1898. Right of the terminal is **Jardine House ⓒ**, whose distinctive round windows have inspired the Chinese to nickname it the House of a Thousand Orifices. Close by are the shiny towers of Exchange Square, one of the most modern office complexes in the world and the home of the Hong Kong Stock Exchange. The International Finance Centre is also a towering presence in this area.

The colonial **Supreme Court Building** houses the Legislative Council. On the other side of Queen's Road, is **Government House**, home of the former colonial governors. Behind it lies the **Zoological and Botanical Gardens** (open daily, 6am–7pm; free), which includes a large number of red-cheeked gibbons, and a good botanical collection. **Hong Kong Park** includes the Flagstaff Museum of Teaware (open Tues–Sun, 10am–5pm; free), and some interesting aviaries. The Victorian-Gothic **St John's Cathedral ⓓ**, dating from 1849, is the city's oldest Anglican church.

Victoria Peak ⓕ is Hong Kong's most visited tourist attraction and a prime residential area. Before the opening in 1888 of the funicular railway called the **Peak Tramway** (operates daily, 7am–midnight), sedan chairs transported privileged colonials to the top. The best way to see the Peak is by walking around Lugard Road, which begins just opposite the Peak Tram's upper terminus at

Low-tech trams still trundle along the north coast of Hong Kong island. For the best views and a cooling breeze, try to secure a seat at the front of the top deck.

BELOW:
handover ambiance, Central District.

400 metres (1,300 ft) above sea level. At the top of the Peak, on a clear day, are some of the world's finest vistas, all the way to Guangdong and Macau.

Map on pages 114–5

Western District

As its name suggests, the **Western District** is located to the west of Central, but, although there has been much recent redevelopment here, it is still worlds apart from the ultra-modern financial district, offering a rare glimpse of the more traditionally Chinese Hong Kong. Western is the last refuge of the Hong Kong Chinese artisan, unseen by most visitors, where there are mahjong-makers, herbalists and craftsmen. The area begins at Possession Street and sprawls west to Kennedy Town, but its atmosphere begins to emerge around the purpose-built fresh-food **Central Market**. The Central-Mid-Levels Escalator, the world's longest, stretches up to the old city of Victoria. Built in 1993, it runs downhill from 6–10.10am, uphill from 10.20am to midnight. Take it to the **Man Mo Temple ᴳ** (open daily, 7am–5pm), built around 1840 on what was a dirt track leading up from Central. Tourists regularly throng through Man Mo, but this doesn't inhibit the temple's regular worshippers from creating thick and redolent clouds with their burning joss offerings. Near the altar are three sedan chairs encased in glass. Years ago, the icons of the gods Man and Mo were paraded through Western on festival days seated on these chairs.

TIP

Bargain hunters will love the area around Man Mo Temple. It's where you'll find the main antique shops, as well as the lively Cat Street flea market.

Wan Chai

East of Central are the island's liveliest districts for eating, drinking and, of course, shopping. Wan Chai and Causeway Bay are among the territory's most crowded and active districts, revealing the authentic flavour of modern Hong

LEFT: Wan Chai on the night of the handover, 1997.
BELOW: local millionairess.

Wednesday evening at Happy Valley racecourse. The total amount wagered every season is the highest of any racing establishment in the world.

Kong. **Wan Chai G** is the nightlife centre of Hong Kong immortalised in the 1960 film *The World of Suzie Wong*, about a Chinese prostitute with a heart of gold. By day, however, Wan Chai has a completely different personality.

Close to the Wan Chai waterfront is the **Academy for Performing Arts** and the **Hong Kong Arts Centre**, two of the most popular venues for theatrical and cultural performances. Right on the harbour is the futuristic **Hong Kong Convention and Exhibition Centre Extension**, completed just in time to host the official hand-over ceremony in 1997. Nearby is the **Central Plaza** office tower, Hong Kong's tallest building. Elevated walkways lead south from the convention centre to Lockhart Road, one of the busiest streets in the centre of Wan Chai's nightlife district. The western end of Lockhart Road is a lively neighbourhood of bars, restaurants, and old office buildings. To the south of Lockhart Road is a far more Chinese part of town, in the side streets off Queen's Road East which traces Wan Chai's original waterfront. The **Hung Shing** (Tai Wong) Temple (1860) and the old **Wan Chai Post Office** (1912) are both on Queens Road East, and the **Pak Tai Temple** is nearby in Stone Nullah Lane.

Inland is **Happy Valley H**, home of the Hong Kong Jockey Club's Happy Valley Racecourse. During the October to May racing season, it attracts up to 75,000 punters a week on Wednesday race nights. The **Hong Kong Racing Museum** (open 10am–5pm, 10am–12.30pm on race days, closed Mon; entrance fee) is at the Happy Valley Stand. Opposite are the Colonial and Parsi cemeteries. **Aw Boon Haw Gardens I** (open daily, 9.30am–4pm; free), formerly known as the Tiger Balm Gardens, on the other side of the causeway, is actually an amusement park, resembling an hallucinogenic vision of a Chinese Disneyland. Recently sold, the gardens may soon be redeveloped.

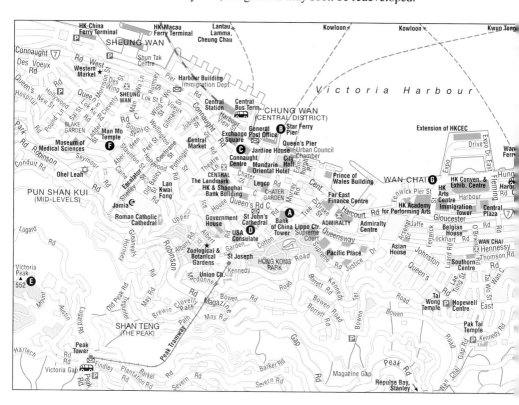

Causeway Bay

This actually was a bay until the 1950s, when it disappeared in a land recla-mation project. The present-day "bay" is occupied by the Royal Hong Kong Yacht Club on Kellett Island (which also was once a real island before land reclamation), and the Typhoon Shelter. Causeway Bay is best known as a busy shopping district, featuring large department stores, mostly Japanese.

Nobody is sure why the **Noon-Day Gun** is fired at noon every day. One story has it that the tradition began in the mid-1800s when one of the Jardine opium boats sailed into the harbour and a willing minion gave the boat a 21-gun salute. The Hong Kong governor, incensed that a mere purveyor of "foreign mud" (as the Chinese called opium) should receive the same greeting as an official figure, ordered the gun to be fired at noon every day in perpetuity.

Victoria Park, named after Queen Victoria, is one of the few public areas in Hong Kong likely to have its name changed. The decision has not yet been made, but a favoured alternative is to call it Central Park.

South Island

Unlike the northern part of Hong Kong island, the rocky coastline of the south side has changed very little. Fishing villages, beaches, and mountain scenery make this a particularly popular area for visitors. **Aberdeen** has a character unlike any other town in Hong Kong, and is famous for its bustling harbour, a natural typhoon shelter crowded with fishing trawlers, houseboats, pleasure junks and tiny sampans, rounded off by three rather theatrical floating seafood restaurants. The old sampan ladies keep an eye out for tourists and are always happy to negotiate a fee for a quick and sometimes rather hair-raising spin. A

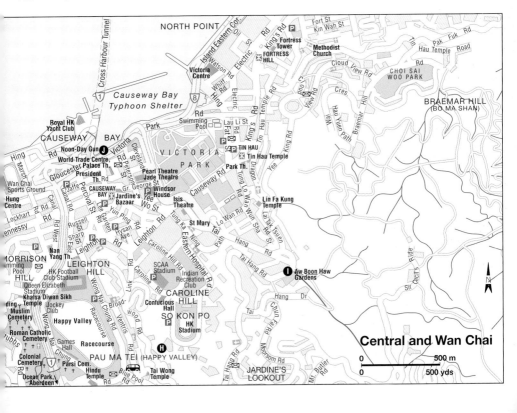

Central and Wan Chai

quick bus or taxi ride away is **Ocean Park** (open daily, 10am–6pm; entrance fee), one of Hong Kong's biggest tourist attractions. Offerings include a spectacular cable car ride overlooking the South China Sea, a 3,500-seat marine-mammal theatre, the world's largest reef aquarium, adventure rides, and Middle Kingdom, a recreation of life in ancient China.

Repulse Bay, widened to several times its original size, can get very crowded at weekends. The bay was named after the battleship *HMS Repulse*, which helped to thwart pirates in the early days of settlement in the territory. **Stanley** was the site of the largest indigenous settlement in Hong Kong when the British first set foot here in 1841. The main attraction is **Stanley Market**, which draws thousands in search of the perfect souvenir or clothing bargain.

The Repulse Bay apartment block; the hole allows the heavenly dragon passage from the mountains to the sea.

Kowloon

Kowloon Peninsula starts at **Tsim Sha Tsui**. When exploring, start at the **Star Ferry Pier ⓚ**. The waterfront promenade from Star Ferry to Tsim Sha Tsui East offers spectacular views of the harbour and Hong Kong island. The **Railway Clock Tower**, erected in 1915 next to the ferry terminal, is the final vestige of the historic Kowloon–Canton Railway Station, the Asian terminus of the old Orient Express to London.

Across Salisbury Road is the venerable **Peninsula Hotel ⓛ**, built in 1928, where people used to stay before boarding the Orient Express. In addition to luxurious hotels, Tsim Sha Tsui has a series of run-down mansion blocks, the most infamous being **Chungking Mansions**, a labyrinth of guest houses, curry messes, sweat-shops, and sari stores. For budget travellers, the cheap guest houses of Chungking are about the only options left in a city of spiralling rents.

BELOW: Aberdeen.

The **Hong Kong Cultural Centre** , between the peninsula and the water-front, is a minimalist structure with an impressive concave roof spoilt by ugly tiles. It caused a great deal of controversy in 1984, as it was designed without windows on the prime harbour site in the territory. The centre stages local and international opera, classical music, theatre and dance. This complex also houses the **Hong Kong Space Museum** (open Mon, Wed–Fri, 1–9pm, Sat–Sun, 10am–9pm, closed Tues & some holidays; tel: 2734 2722; entrance fee), with daily showings of Omnimax movies on space travel and exhibitions of Chinese astronomical inventions. The **Hong Kong Museum of Art** (open Mon–Sat, 10am–6pm, Sun, 1-6pm, closed Thurs; tel: 2734 2167; entrance fee) displays traditional and contemporary calligraphy and painting, and historic photographs and artefacts of Hong Kong and Macau. Other major museums include the **Hong Kong Museum of History** (open Mon–Thurs & Sat, 10am–8pm, Sun, 1–8pm; tel: 2724 9042; entrance fee) in Chatham Road South; and in Science Museum Road, the **Hong Kong Science Museum** (open Tues–Fri, 1–9pm, Sat–Sun, 10am–9pm; tel: 2732 3232; entrance fee except Wed).

At the bottom of **Nathan Road** — the start of Hong Kong's famous Golden Mile tourist belt — hundreds of small shops are crammed together: tailors' shops, jewellers and camera and electronics stores. Less than a kilometre north on Nathan Road, in the southeastern corner of Kowloon Park, is the **Kowloon Mosque**, whose four minarets and large white marble dome gracefully stand out. Built in 1984, it serves the territory's 50,000 Muslims. The previous mosque was built 90 years earlier for the British army's Muslim troops from India.

Continue north on Nathan Road and left onto Kansu Street, where the **Jade Market** (open daily, 10am–3.30pm) is packed with stalls selling jade orna-

Maps on pages 114–5 / 118

At the south end of the Repulse Bay beach a bizarre medley of colourful Taoist and Buddhist statues decorate the Life Guard club.

BELOW: crowded Tsim Sha Tsui street, and the Railway Clock Tower.

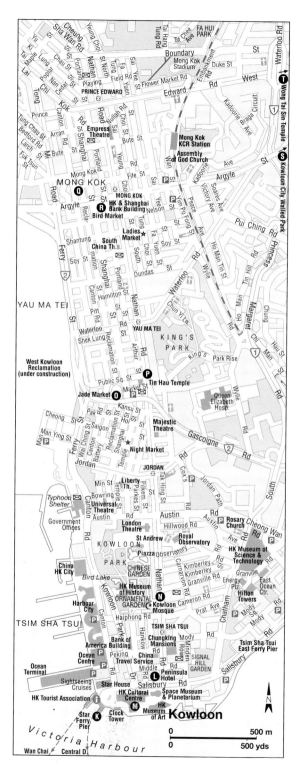

ments and jewellery. Dealers offer jade in every sculptable form – from large blocks of the raw material to tiny, ornately-carved chips. Remember that not everything on offer is genuine.

North from here is **Yau Ma Tei**, Temple Street, originally famous for its temples but now renowned for the **Temple Street Night Market** (open daily 2pm, but doesn't really get going until 7pm). Here, between Jordan Road and Kansu Street, fake Rolexes, mandarin hats, and other tacky souvenirs are hawked.

The **Tin Hau Temple** complex ⓟ (open daily, 8am–6pm) stands in Public Square Street, where old men play Chinese chess and cards. Built over 100 years ago this is one of the oldest and most interesting temples, dedicated to the protector of fisherfolk and seafarers, as befitted its original waterfront location before the days of land reclamation. The second temple on the left was built to honour the local city god and the Ten Judges of the Underworld, depicted with human torsos and animal heads.

If Hong Kong is the most densely populated place on earth, **Mong Kok** ⓠ is certainly one of the most crowded, noisy, and lively districts in the territory. In the early days of British rule, *gweilos* (foreign devils) seldom ventured past Yau Ma Tei, and even today Mong Kok is notorious for triads, illegal gambling dens, and sleaze. It is known for several colourful street markets: the **Ladies Market** (open noon–10.30pm) sells a mixture of clothes and souvenirs; the **Goldfish Market** (open 10am–6pm) is self-explanatory; and there are fashion bargains galore in the factory outlet shops on Fa Yuen Street. Further north is Hong Kong's premier **Flower Market** (open 10am–6pm) at the end of which you will find the Yuen Po Street **Bird Market** ⓡ (open 7am–8pm), with hundreds of songbirds and beautiful birdcages for sale.

Situated in what's commonly called **New Kowloon**, on the east side of the peninsula and near the old Kai Tak Airport, Kowloon City and Kowloon Tong are two of the districts that have so far evaded redevelopment. Along Junction

Road you'll find the tiny **Hau Wong Temple** (open daily, 8am–5pm) with traditional roof tiles and incense spirals hanging from the rafters. Built in 1730, the temple is dedicated to Yang Liang Jie, a loyal and courageous general of the exiled Song dynasty's (960–1279) boy emperor, Ping.

Maps:
Area 108
City 118

Continue east past the temple for 15 minutes towards **Kowloon City Walled Park ⑨**. Before the British arrived in 1841, the old Walled City was already governed by a Manchu magistrate, and therefore was excluded from the treaty that granted Britain the New Territories on a 99-year lease. At first, Qing dynasty officials continued to be posted in the city, but in 1899 British forces invaded the city, and the Qing officials and troops were expelled.

Due north, one of Kowloon's most colourful and popular places of worship, the **Wong Tai Sin Temple ❼** (open daily, 7am–5.30pm) on Lung Cheung Road, sits opposite an MTR station bearing the same name. Wong Tai Sin, the Taoist god of healing, is said to have discovered the secret of transforming cinnabar (vermillion, a red mercuric sulphide) into an immortal elixir. Backed by the formidable Lion Rock a kilometre away and facing the sea, geomancers agreed that this new site had favourable *feng shui*. Since Wong Tai Sin is also the god of good fortune, the Chinese, who are too cautious to rely solely on luck, flock to the temple to ask him for advice on all matters, including horseracing.

Tin Hau, the ubiquitous goddess of the sea.

New Territories

Sha Tin ⑮ is one of Hong Kong's fastest growing New Towns, with massive housing projects occupying what were once rice paddies. Sha Tin, directly north of Kowloon, has several places of worship. The **Temple of 10,000 Buddhas ⑯** (open daily, 9am–5pm) is reached by climbing 431 steps up the hillside above

BELOW: seductive shopping lights, Tsim Sha Tsui.

BELOW: Buddha, Po Lin Monastery.

the Sha Tin station. A main altar room has 12,800 small Buddha statues on its walls, and the temple is guarded by huge, fierce-looking statues of various gods.

A further 69 steps up the hill is the shrine to the monastery's founder. Called Yuet Kai, he was a monk who spent a lifetime studying Buddhism and living a meditative life. His greatest concern was to achieve immortality. After his death he was buried, but according to Chinese custom his body was later exhumed to be reburied in its final resting place. However, the body was found to be perfectly preserved and radiating a ghostly yellow glow. Since there was obviously something supernatural about Yuet Kai, it was decided to preserve his body in gold leaf. North of Sha Tin is **Tai Po ⑰**, meaning "buying place": once a small market community, this is now a booming New Town. Two sites worth visiting here are the 19th-century **Man Mo Temple** and the picturesque **Hong Kong Railway Museum** (open daily, 9am–5pm).

On the western side of the Kowloon Peninsula, huge reclamation and construction projects are changing the map almost daily for the road and rail links to the new airport on Lantau. The most striking new arrival is the **Tsing Ma Bridge ⑱**, the world's longest road and rail suspension bridge, linking Lantau Island to the Kowloon Peninsula. Over 2 km (1 mile) long, its 200-metre (650-ft) twin towers are visible along much of the highway that leads out to Kwai Chung. The **Tsing Ma Bridge Visitors' Centre and Viewing Platform** (open daily, except Wed, 10am–5pm) offers a fascinating experience.

Near 580-metre (1,900-ft) **Castle Peak**, adjacent to the light-railway station, is a temple called **Ching Chung Koon ⑲** which serves as a repository for many Chinese art treasures, including 200-year-old lanterns and a jade seal over 1,000 years old. The library, which holds 4,000 books, documents Tao history.

Just outside of Yuen Long are the **walled villages of Kam Tin 20**. The most popular for visitors is the Kat Hing Wai village, which stands rather incongruously across the road from a supermarket. There are 400 people living here, all with the same surname: Tang. Built in the 1600s, it is a fortified village with walls 6 metres (19 ft) thick, guard-houses on its four corners, slits for the arrows used in fighting off attackers, and a moat.

The eastern edge of the New Territories is arguably the most attractive area. In summer, **Clear Water Bay 21** is dotted with revellers on corporate junks, and the beach is jam-packed with sunbathers. Branching off Clear Water Bay Road, the highway leads down to **Sai Kung 22**, a bustling seaside town known for its Chinese seafood restaurants, and a kicking-off point for exploring the natural beauty of **Sai Kung Country Park**.

Outlying Islands

Despite the presence of the new airport at **Chek Lap Kok** (another masterpiece by Sir Norman Foster), the large island of **Lantau** has managed to retain its predominantly rural character. Up on the mountainous central spine is the best-known attraction, the brightly painted red, orange and gold **Po Lin Monastery 23**. The world's largest outdoor bronze statue of Buddha (24 metres/79 ft high) was completed here in 1990. Po Lin's resident monks serve a hearty vegetarian lunch to visitors. West of Po Lin, in the direction of Tung Chung on Lantau's north coast, is an excellent walking path that traverses mountain ridges and small canyons en route to Lantau's **Yin Hing Monastery**, a haven rich with traditional Buddhist paintings and statues.

Offshore from **Tai O 24**, on the west coast, the island's Tanka boat people have become semi-land dwellers, with some of their larger junks now three-storey permanent living structures. They have also built rickety homes on stilts over parts of a creek, where waters rise during tide changes.

Lantau is also popular for its many long, smooth, and often empty beaches. The finest sandy sweeps are on the southeast coastline that arcs from Cheung Sha south of Silvermine Bay to Tong Fuk. The most popular and crowded beach (probably because it is the easiest one to reach) is **Silver Mine Bay Beach**.

The third largest of the outlying islands, and somehow less well-known both to visitors and local people, is **Lamma 25**, associated with some of the earliest settlements in Hong Kong. Although it is just over 13 sq. km (5 sq. miles) in area, Lamma is rich in green hills and beautiful bays, and is renowned for its seafood restaurants.

Cheung Chau 26, much smaller than Lantau, is urbanised in a pleasing "Old China" way. This dumbbell-shaped isle, with hills at either end and a village nestled in a connecting rod of land, is so narrow you can walk from Cheung Chau Harbour on the west side to Tung Wan Harbour on the east in just a few minutes. Cheung Chau is a fishing island, its curving harbour filled with boats of all sizes, shapes, and colours, including Chinese junks and sampans. They compete for space with the ubiquitous *kaido*, the small boats used as motorised water taxis. ❏

Map on pages 108–9

The Hakka are Hong Kong's oldest landowners, arriving from central and southern China centuries ago

BELOW: stilt houses at Tai O, Lantau.

Map on pages 24–5

MACAU AND GUANGZHOU

Colonial atmosphere and the roll of the dice are to Macau what the Pearl River and exquisite dim sum are to Guangzhou – elements that make up a very unique Asian face

Macau, established in 1557, was both the first Western colony on China's shore and also the last. On 21 December 1999, **Macau ㉗** reverted back to the sovereignty of China under a one-country, two-systems policy that guarantees its freedom for 50 years.

The best place to start any foray into this fascinating hybrid of Far East and Mediterranean is at **Largo do Senado Square**, the old city's main plaza. The pride of the square is the **Leal Senado** (Loyal Senate) building, regarded by most as the best example of Portuguese architecture in the territory. The Leal Senado was dedicated in 1784 and its façade completed in 1876.

From the main road, Avenida de Almeida Riberio, the square runs up to **São Domingos** (St Dominic's Church); the church building, in Christian-Oriental motif, stands as one of the oldest and most famous of Macau's many churches. It's said that there are more churches per square kilometre here than in Vatican City. St Dominic's dates from the 17th century, but the Spanish Dominicans had a chapel and convent here as early as 1588.

Leaving St Dominic's, follow the curving pavement on to the ruins of **São Paulo** (St Paul's Church). Historians often cite it as the finest monument to Christianity in the Far East. In 1835, a fire destroyed the building, leaving just the towering façade and impressive grand staircase which form one of the most striking of all Macau's sights. Restoration work took place in the early 1990s.

Overlooking the façade of St Paul's are the massive stone walls of the **Fortaleza do Monte**, simply called **Monte Fort**, built in the early 1620s. When Dutch ships attacked Macau in 1622, the then half-completed fortress was defended by clerics and African slaves. A lucky cannon shot by an Italian Jesuit hit the powder magazine of the Dutch flagship and saved the city. The new **Museum of Macau** here (open Tues–Sun, 10am–6pm; entrance fee) showcases Macau's colourful history, popular arts and traditions.

The historic **Hotel Bela Vista** ("beautiful view") was closed in early 1999 in order to convert it into the official residence of the Portuguese Consul-General to Macau. Sadly it is therefore no longer possible to stop for tea on the verandah. The architecture is still impressive, however.

No sojourn to Macau would be complete without a visit to the early 16th-century **Temple da Deusa A-Ma** (A-Ma Temple), near the entrance to the Inner Harbour. It is the oldest temple in the territory and is dedicated to A-Ma (also known as Tin Hau), the patron goddess of sailors and fishermen to whom Macau owes its name (it is known to the Chinese as A-Ma-Gau). Opposite the temple is the excellent **Maritime Museum** (open Wed–Mon, 10am–5.30pm;

BELOW: the façade of São Paulo.

entrance fee), focusing on both Chinese and Portuguese maritime traditions.
Despite its many sightseeing attractions, most of Macau's visitors come for the gambling rather than the culture. If you fancy a flutter, there are no less than nine **casinos** to choose from, in addition to greyhound and horse racing.

Guangzhou, old and new

At the mouth of the **Zhu Jiang (Pearl River)**, **Guangzhou** ㉘ **(Canton)** was probably founded in 214 BC as an encampment by the armies of the Qin emperor, Qin Shi Huangdi. By the Tang period (618–907), the city was already an international port. In 1514, a Portuguese flotilla reached Guangzhou. After the overthrow of the Ming dynasty by the Manchu in 1644, nationalist ideas survived longer in Guangzhou than in other parts of China. Trade with England increased, particularly the importation of opium which eventually led to two opium wars.

Bird market, Guangzhou.

In the southwest of the city, the island of **Shamian** is a preserved relic of "Old Guangzhou" and its colonial past. It was originally a sandbar on the north bank of the Zhu Jiang (Pearl River) before it was reclaimed and expanded. The small island was divided in 1859 into several foreign concessions, primarily French and British. A canal was dug around Shamian and late in the evening, Chinese were kept off the island by iron gates and narrow bridges. Today, the island is only one kilometre by half a kilometre in size and feels very much like a resort area, in contrast to the bustle of Guangzhou proper.

Half way down Shamian, towards the mainland on Qingping Lu, is **Qingping Shichang**, a market occupying the side alleys to the west of Renmin Nan Lu. A short distance to the north many jade and antique shops can be found. About

BELOW: colonial architecture on Shamian island.

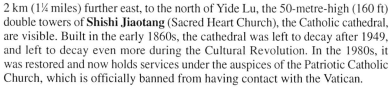

Map on pages 24–5

Duck farms are common in the Pearl River delta.

BELOW: the bicycle is still the main mode of transport. **RIGHT:** monument to Sun Yatsen.

2 km (1¼ miles) further east, to the north of Yide Lu, the 50-metre-high (160 ft) double towers of **Shishi Jiaotang** (Sacred Heart Church), the Catholic cathedral, are visible. Built in the early 1860s, the cathedral was left to decay after 1949, and left to decay even more during the Cultural Revolution. In the 1980s, it was restored and now holds services under the auspices of the Patriotic Catholic Church, which is officially banned from having contact with the Vatican.

Farther east along the river past Haizhu bridge and heading north begins Guangzhou's main shopping street, **Beijing Lu**. Guangzhou's proximity to Hong Kong allows for some classy boutiques and fashionable stores one would not find anywhere else in China.

Between Renmin Zhong Lu and Jiefang Zhong Lu, south of Zhong Shan Lu in Guangta Lu, one can spot the onion dome of **Huaisheng Si**, a mosque dating back to 627 and founded by a trader who was said to be an uncle of the Prophet Mohammed. The 25-metre (80-ft) high minaret, **Guang Ta** (Naked Pagoda), dominates the area, although new high-rises are competing for the skyline. The mosque – the buildings are all of recent construction – is a cultural centre for Guangzhou's 5,000 Muslims.

To the north of Zhongshan Lu, a fairly narrow street leads to **Liurong Si** (Temple of the Six Banyan Trees), and **Hua Ta** (Flower Pagoda), built in 1097 and a symbol of the city.

A few hundred metres northwest is **Guanxiao Si**, a temple preserved during the Cultural Revolution on orders from Zhou Enlai. Local legend has it that the temple is older than the town, dating from around AD 400. The main hall is noted for its ceiling of red-lacquered timbers, and the back courtyard contains some of the oldest iron pagodas in China.

Guangzhou's largest park, **Yuexiu Gongyuan**, due north, is a beautiful example of a landscaped park with three artificial lakes, seven hills, rock sculptures, and lush greenery. It is dominated by **Zhenhailou** (Tower Overlooking the Sea), built in 1380 as a memorial to the seven great sea journeys undertaken by the eunuch Zheng He. Today, the tower houses a museum on the history of Guangzhou. Nearby is the **Sun Yatsen Monument**, built of marble and granite and sitting on a hill above Sun Yatsen Hall. Yuexiu Gongyuan also features some recreational activities, including a golf driving range, bowling alley, and swimming pool.

To the south along Jiefang Bei Lu is the **Nanyue Wangmu** (Museum of the Western Han; open daily, 8am–5pm; fee), the tomb of the Nanyu emperor. In 1983, when bulldozers were clearing the ground to build the China Hotel, they dug up the tomb of the emperor Wen Di, who ruled southern China from 137 to 122 BC. Today, in its place stands the museum that houses skeletons of the emperor and 15 courtiers who were buried alive with him.

Restored after the Cultural Revolution, **Chenjia Ci** (Chen Family Temple; open daily, 8am–5pm) dates from 1894 and lies north of Zhongshan Qi Lu near the intersection with Liwan Lu. The temple features a giant altar of gold-leaf plating and additional wood, brick, and stone friezes along the rooftops. ❑

Taiwan

0 20 km
0 20 miles

N

Taiwan Haixia

Taipei 1
Keelung 4
Shihmen
Liukuaitso
2
Yehliu
Tanshui 3
Yangmingshan
Luchou
2
Kuanyin
Hsinchuang
Hsinwu
Taoyüan 8
Panchiao
Pate
Hsinfeng
Yangmei
Chupei
Lungtan
Kuanhsi
Chutung
Hsinchu
15
Chunan
Toufen
Houlung
Miaoli
Tsaochiao
Tunghsiao
Shihtan
Yüanli
Kungkuan
Tahu
1
Tachia
3
Chingshui
Shalu
Shenkang
Houli
Fengyüan 10
Tatu
Changhua
Lukang
Wujih 14
Taichung
Chihu
Yüanlin 13
Wufeng 21
Tsaotun
Wushe
Fangyüan
Erhlin
Pitou
Nantou
Lushan Hot Springs 11
Tacheng
Tienwei
Shuili
Mailiao
Hsilo
Tzutung
Huwei
Taihsi
Tuku
Touliu
3
Tzŭkuan
Hsinchuang 1
Hsintien
Hsichih
Taipei 1
8
Pate
Sanhsia
Tachi
Wulai 7
Fuhsing
6
9
Fulung
Santiao Chiao
Tahsi
2
Chiaochi
Kueishan
9
on China
3
Kuanhsi
Paleng
Sanhsing
Ilan
Lotung
Tungshan
Suao
Wushih Pi
Chitan
Ssuchi
2573
Hsueh Shan 3884
Nanhuta Shan 3740
Lishan
Tayuling
Hoping
8
Tiensiang
Taroko Gorge 18
Chihan
Jenho
Hsincheng
Chilaichushanpei 3605
Chian
Chilai Pi
Hualien 17
Chichi
Shuilien
Shoufeng
Linjung
Kuangfu
Fengping

Yüchih
Sun Moon Lake
Chuki
Tungshih
Chushan 12
Puli
Tungchünta Shan 3605
Kuanshan
Chishang
Chengkung
Chungan
Changping
Puching
Juisui
Yüli
Goching
Changshan
Fuli
9
20
20

Penghu (Pescadore Islands)
Paisha
Yuweng
Hsiyu
Paisha
Makung 26
Huching
Pachao
Wangan
Tungchi
Chimei
Waisanting
Putai
Peikang
Liuchiao
Potzu
Shuishang
Ichu
Yenshui
Hsüehchia
Chiangchun
Matou
Chiku
Chiai 15
Chungpu
Alishan
Yu Shan National Park 16
Yu Shan 3952
Alishan 2480
Meishan
Talin
Minhsiung
Chiai
Peinanchu Shan 3293
Luyeh
Tungho
Peinan
Taitung 19
Chihpen 20
Ali
22
Taimali

Lu Tao 21
Lu Tao (Green Island)

Tropic of Cancer

Tainan 23
Jente
Yungkang
Nanhua
Chiahsien
Hsinshih
Yüching
Sanmin
Changshan
1
Paiho
3
Coral Lake
Nanhsi
20
21
Hunei
Alien
Chishan 25
Fokuang Shan
Likang
Luchu
Kangshan
Tashu
Pingtung
Kaohsiung 24
Fengshan
Neipu
Wanluan
Chaochou
1
Linyuan
Tungkang
Chiatung
Liuchiu
Fangliao
Fangshan
Fengkang
Shuangliu
Kangtzu
24
Checheng
24
Hengchun
Kenting N.P.
Maopi Tou Pt
Kenting
Oluanpi
Oluan Pi 27
Peitawu Shan 3090
9

Lanyu 22
Lanyu (Orchid Island)

Hsüehshan Shanmo
Chungyang Shanmo
Choshui

PACIFIC
OCEAN

SOUTH CHINA
SEA

TAIWAN

Taiwan's rugged beauty satisfies the Chinese sensitivity
towards aesthetics and the rhythms of nature

Taiwan is an island with a spectacular diversity of terrain and culture, not to mention a superb highway system which not only encircles the island but also slithers through its interior mountains. For a relatively small place, Taiwan reveals itself in an eclectic and resplendent fashion.

Northern Taiwan is the upper terminus of the Central Range that bisects the long and narrow country. The north is of both flat land and foothills. Being so close to the main city, Taipei, the northern sights are sometimes crowded, as residents escape from the urban sprawl. The coastal route along the north shore, while lacking the tropical beaches of the south, skirts an unusually-sculpted sandstone seashore.

Taipei is Taiwan's largest city. Technically, it is considered by the Nationalist government as the provisional capital of the Republic of China, which the Nationalists claim includes the mainland. In any case, it is a city of significant size and prosperity, with all the cultural offerings and urban clutter of any major city. If there's just one stop to be made in Taipei, it would be the National Palace Museum, with its immense collection of artefacts relating to China's ancient past.

Extensive expressways cross the island, and heading south can be as rapid or as leisurely as desired. Landscapes along the eastern coast are rustic and primal; down the west coast they are both agricultural and industrial. The cities along the western coast of – Taichung, Tainan, Kaohsiung – are a mix of ports, industry and history. Tainan is the Kyoto of Taiwan, in a modest way, while Kaohsiung is a distinctly industrial port city. Taichung falls somewhere in between.

Should travellers choose the eastern seaboard, they will find little evidence of urbanisation. Rather, it is a tempestuous shoreline of steep cliffs and crashing Pacific waves. Villages and towns along the coastal road – there are no cities – are pleasantly modest. The most notable sight is Taroko Gorge, a fantastic marble chasm with an equally remarkable road slicing right through the marble.

Between the east and west coasts are the mountains of the Central Range, with numerous hot-spring resorts and honeymoon retreats, such as Sun Moon Lake – romance knows no limits, even if surrounded by bus loads of tourists. There are also rambling bamboo forests here, and one of Asia's tallest mountains, Yu Shan, towering 3,952 metres (12,966 ft) above the Pacific Ocean. ❑

PRECEDING PAGES: Chiang Kaishek Memorial, Taipei; midnight snacks and antics at the Shihlin night market.

Decisive Dates

ISLAND SETTLEMENT

circa 10,000 BC Radioactive carbon-dating of primitive utensils found in caves suggests that there was prehistoric life on the island at this time.

206 BC The most ancient Chinese historical record referring to Taiwan indicates that the island was called the "Land of Yangchow".

AD 239 The earliest attempt to establish a Chinese claim to Taiwan occurs, when the kingdom of Wu sent a 10,000-man expeditionary force.

AD 1000 Ethnic Chinese settlement appears to

have taken place, mainly by Hakkas, a southern Chinese people.

ISLA FORMOSA

15th and 16th centuries Taiwan becomes a haven for marauding pirates and traders. The island is known as "Isla Formosa" or beautiful island, a name bequeathed by admiring Portuguese sailors.

1590 The Portuguese arrive on the north coast, establishing a trading post and port facilities.

1593 The first Japanese attempt to annex Taiwan.

COLONIAL INTERESTS

1622 Dutch forces capture the Pescadores and build a base from which Dutch shops are able to control traffic passing through the Taiwan Strait.

1624 The Dutch reach an agreement with the Chinese government to evacuate from the Pescadores in return for establishing settlements on Taiwan – this marks the beginning of Dutch colonial rule in Taiwan.

1626 Spanish forces seize Keelung and from there expand to control northern Taiwan.

1642 The Dutch capture major Spanish settlements in northern Taiwan, thereby consolidating control over the island.

1652 Chinese revolt against Dutch-imposed poll tax; nearly 6,000 locals are slaughtered.

THE CHENG DYNASTY

1662 Cheng Ch'eng-kung, also known as Koxinga, defeats Dutch forces, bringing an end to Dutch rule and the beginning of the "Cheng Dynasty" in Taiwan.

1683 Koxinga dies. His son and grandson maintain rule over Taiwan until 1684, thus marking the end of the Cheng family rule of Taiwan and the beginning of China's governance of Taiwan under the Manchu dynasty.

COLONIAL INTRUSIONS

1729 The emperor of China forbids immigration to Taiwan, under penalty of death.

1786 Major rebellion against Chinese rule occurs.

1839 China takes up arms to suppress the British opium trade in Canton (Guangzhou).

1858 Treaty ending the first Opium War opens four Taiwanese ports to foreign trade.

1867 25 foreign traders settle in northern Taiwan at Tanshui and Keelung. Trade booms, doubling in volume by 1869, and doubling again by 1870.

JAPANESE OCCUPATION

1874 the Japanese occupy Taiwan and mount a punitive campaign against local aborigines for killing Japanese sailors.

1886 Taiwan is declared the 22nd province of China.

1895 A full-scale war between Japan and China breaks out when the Japanese invade Korea, long a loyal ally. The treaty of Shimonoseki concludes Sino–Japanese War; Taiwan is ceded to Japan.

1918–37 Japan consolidates its regime in Taiwan, exploiting the country's rich natural resources exclusively for their own benefit.

1945 On 25 October, Taiwan becomes part of the Republic of China as a result of Japan's defeat in World War II.

THE REPUBLIC OF CHINA

1948 On 29 December, General Chen Cheng is appointed governor of Taiwan.
1949 The government of the Republic of China flees to Taiwan after being defeated on the mainland. Taipei becomes the provisional capital of the Republic of China.

AMERICAN INVOLVEMENT

1950 Taipei breaks diplomatic relations with the UK after the latter establishes formal ties with Peking (Beijing). The Korean War breaks out and Taiwan is placed under American protection against possible Communist attacks, and also receives substantial economic aid.
1955 The United States and Taiwan ratify the Sino–American Mutual Defense Treaty, and President Eisenhower is authorised to use American forces to defend Taiwan.
1958 On 23 August, the second Offshore Island Crisis begins with forces of the People's Republic of China firing on Quemoy.
1959 On 7 August, Taiwan experiences its worst floods for more than half a century. Later in August, Taiwan receives Nike Hercules missiles from the United States.
1965 The Republic of China and the United States sign an agreement on the status of the US military force in Taiwan. There is a critical test of strength for Taiwan and its leadership as financial aid from the United States is terminated. Nevertheless, industrialisation, modernisation and economic progress accelerate.

CHIANG'S LAST YEARS

1966 The National Assembly elects Chiang Kaishek to a fourth term as president.
1971 The Republic of China loses its membership of the United Nations; the China seat is given to the People's Republic of China.
1974 The island's population reaches 16 million, twice what it was in the early 1950s.
1975 Chiang Kaishek dies.
1976 Chiang Ching-kuo, Chiang Kaishek's son, is elected president.

RELATIONS WITH THE US

1978 The United States announces the recogni-

tion of the People's Republic of China, and ends official diplomatic relations with Taiwan.
1980 The US–Republic of China Defense Treaty is terminated.
1984 President Chiang Ching-kuo is elected to another six-year term.
1988 President Chiang Ching-kuo dies.
1990 The National Assembly officially elects Lee Teng-hui as leader; he is the island's first Taiwan-born president.
1991 Government authorities in China announce that Taiwan has replaced Japan and the United States as the number one investor in the People's Republic.

TENSION RISES

1993 The first official governmental contacts between Taipei and Beijing take place in Singapore.
1996 Beijing indefinitely postpones second set of talks and the uneasy truce falls apart. Taiwan holds its first totally democratic elections for presidency and the Taiwanese vote in their first popularly elected president, 73-year-old Lee Teng-hui.
1998 America's president, Bill Clinton, makes a high-profile visit to China. Pundits once again assess what this means for the future security of Taiwan.
1999 Taiwan's status remains an explosive issue. Officially, Beijing considers the island an out-control-province. Taiwan has never officially declared independence from the mainland. ❏

LEFT: portrait of Taiwan's first Chinese ruler, Koxinga, painted by one of his descendants.
RIGHT: Chiang Kaishek (standing) with his mentor, Dr Sun Yatsen, 1924.

ETHNIC MINORITIES

Despite a largely Chinese population, it's the ethnic minorities in densely-populated Taiwan who captivate visitors with their vibrant culture and traditions

Long before the Chinese ever set foot on Taiwan, the island was inhabited by a colourful array of aboriginal tribes who came to Taiwan from Mongolia, the Malay peninsula, and the South Pacific. Today there are still over 250,000 ethnic aborigines scattered across Taiwan.

With their bold handicrafts, stunning red-on-black ceremonial clothing, and vibrant dance and music, Taiwan's ethnic minorities have woven their own distinctive thread into the fabric of the island's population. More than 375,000 members of minorities, the remnants of nine main groups, live in Taiwan, mostly in the remote valleys and along the rugged slopes of the central mountain range. The nine prevalent groups are the Ami, Atayal, Bunun, Paiwan, Puyuma, Rukai, Saisiyat, Tsao and Yami.

Contrary to traditional Chinese culture, the minority-group society throughout Taiwan remains highly matriarchal. Women often tend the fields and orchards, while men stay home to care for the children and do the housework. However, the increasing exposure of the younger generation of minorities to Chinese and Western ways, through television and schooling, has begun to erode some of these traditions.

The largest ethnic minority group is the Ami, with more than 150,000 members. They populate the scenic mountains and valleys near Hualien, on the east coast. Their annual Ami Harvest Festival, in August, remains one of the island's most colourful and popular events.

The minority group most accessible to Taipei visitors is the Atayal, who live in the lush valleys of Wulai, just an hour's drive away from the capital. Proximity to Taipei has changed their lives and driven them into the tacky tourism business.

A more authentic enclave of minorities are the Paiwan, who inhabit the mountains of eastern Pingtung, in the south of Taiwan. The

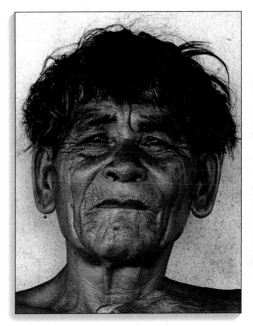

snake-worshipping cult of the "hundred-pacer" still remains strong in Paiwan tradition. The name of the hundred-pacer snake, revered by the Paiwan and several other minority groups, emanates from the belief that victims of its bite drop dead before they can run 100 steps. Venerated as the spiritual elder of the tribe, the hundred-pacer is the embodiment of its ancestors.

The Paiwan are master wood-carvers, making totems, doors, eaves, beams, pipes and other artefacts from the trees of Taiwan's alpine forests. They also weave, sculpt stone, and fashion beadwork using ancient designs and techniques. The faithfulness of this group to its heritage has inspired Chinese anthropologists to research and record their ways.

Another culturally-interesting group, the Rukai, occupies a cluster of hamlets called Wutai, in lofty Pingtung country. The 200 Rukai households engage primarily in agriculture. The buildings of the entire town are constructed from stone slabs that have been

---

LEFT: harvest dance of Lukai people, near Taitung.
RIGHT: Yami elder, Orchid Island.

quarried in the surrounding mountains. The architecture of the dwellings resembles the piled slate homes that dot the Himalayan highlands of western China, northern India and Nepal. The Rukai people love remote, inaccessible cliff-side habitats – the higher the better – and regard 10-hour treks to neighbouring villages as mere strolls.

One fascinating display of Rukai prowess occurs in their "swing contest", one of the most entertaining – if chauvinistic – rituals in Taiwan. Prospective brides mount an enormous swing, with their legs bound to prevent them from flailing. Then burly tribesmen in full ceremonial attire swing the women until they sail like kites to dizzying heights. Afterwards, the girls are carried from their swings and dropped into the arms of their most ardent admirers.

The Puyuma group has traditions similar to those of the Rukai. They live mainly in the foothills of the central mountain range, near Taitung, and occasionally congregate on the city's outskirts for major festivals, which include swing contests.

Another island group of note is the Bunun of Tainan, who still practise a ritual form of night worship that remains essentially unchanged since ancient times – with two exceptions.

BRIDAL POWER

The marriage customs of the Yami group may be of particular interest to contemporary feminists. Unlike the women of the Rukai and Puyama groups, subjected to the chauvinistic "swing contest", the Yami women opt for a more empowering process of mate-selection.

Women significantly outnumber the men of the island and have arranged their numbers into a potent social force. When they become engaged, the male moves into the family home of the female for a one-month trial marriage – or, rather, he becomes a trial husband. During that time, the prospective groom must constantly prove his prowess in hunting and fishing, exhibit his ability to design and build boats, and demonstrate other requisite husbandly skills.

If he fails the tests, he is sent packing in disgrace and another suitor is brought in for the bride's consideration. Even the man who successfully completes the trial period and wins the bride is expected to continually prove his worth to his wife and her family, or else the Yami woman may exercise her most prized right – the unilateral power to divorce a husband at any time on any grounds and seek a new, more worthy mate.

Even the man who successfully completes the trial period and wins the bride is expected to continually prove his worth to his wife and her family.

Severed pig heads have replaced disembodied human heads as sacrificial offerings, and electricity has replaced torches for lighting. Another facet of the ritual is that many of the current participants are ethnic Chinese rather than part of the Bunun minority group. In fact, a large percentage of the group has abandoned its traditional form of worship for Christianity.

The ethnic group that has been least affected by Taiwan's headlong plunge into the 21st century is the Yami, who live on Orchid Island off the southeast coast, and are the only seafaring minority in Taiwan. For half a century during their occupation of Taiwan, the Japanese delib-

women, who turn out bold primitive patterns for capes, shawls, shirts, shoes and sandals. The weaving of red on a black background is a dominant style, although motifs incorporate elements of the three regions from which anthropologists believe the tribes' ancestors may have come.

Minority creativity also finds expression in woodcarving, particularly tribal totems. The totems stress three motifs – faces, snakes and sex. Human heads and sexual organs, rendered as recognisable abstractions, are depicted with bold strokes of the chisel.

In the performing arts, musicians and dancers

erately isolated Orchid Island as a living anthropological museum. Yami fishing boats, each hewn from a single giant tree, are beautiful vessels that glide over the waters of the Pacific.

Creative pursuits

The dazzling costumes of the ceremonial attire remains the most distinctive feature of Taiwan's ethnic groups. They are usually woven by the

FAR LEFT: wooden carving of hunters capturing a wild boar, crafted by Paiwan artists.
LEFT: a potential bride is tied to a rope swing during harvest festivities near Taitung.
ABOVE: portrait of a Lukai couple.

move to the rhythms of nature. They perform their traditional steps with wonderful agility and enthusiasm. Many have gone on to become popular contemporary singers and dancers. The participation of minority groups in local and national politics is also increasing.

There are, of course, many problems for Taiwan's ethnic minorities. The overall educational level is lower, and many minorities face acute social problems. The use of minority-group languages is declining, too, but on such a small land area, especially one that is as developed and as industrialised as Taiwan, it is surprising that these groups have retained any cultural identity at all. ❑

THE TAO OF CHINESE ART

Chinese art fulfils cultural needs, helps human relationships and explores the mysteries of the universe. Like the rotation of the seasons, it stems from nature

The distinctive appearance of a Chinese painting is due to the fact that it was painted by a Chinese artist. The aesthetics of painting are part of Chinese cosmogony (the theory of the origins of the universe). Indeed, the Chinese assign painting and the complementary art of calligraphy an important place in the natural order.

In historical terms, the earliest Chinese characters were pictographic or ideographic. They remain so today, although many characters are derived from the originals on a phonetic basis. The original forms of the characters are difficult to discern, as they have evolved into new shapes over the centuries. But the striking fact about Chinese writing is that, as the script developed, the older forms were not abandoned. Many were preserved and used as they are today. This evolution of Chinese symbols was essentially complete by the 5th century.

Almost without exception, the artist in early China was a calligrapher, and came from a privileged class, otherwise, he would never have had the endless hours needed to acquire skill with the *maubi,* the brush used to write characters. In fact, competence with the calligraphy brush was a necessary facet of education in ancient China.

Four treasures

The *maubi* combined a long, straight handle of wood or bamboo with a round tip that came to a point. It was soft, but firm and springy, and was probably made of rabbit, wolf or deer hair. Softer goat hairs were more often used by the painter than the calligrapher. The artist generally wrote on paper, which may have been invented as early as the second century AD. Lacking paper, he might have chosen silk for his canvas. Paper, however, provided an extremely sensitive surface that readily

LEFT: finishing touches on a character.
RIGHT: temple etching of an unusual form of ancient calligraphy.

revealed the speed of the brush, the manner of its handling, and its charge of ink.

These four treasures – *maubi*, paper, ink and inkstone, the tools of the calligrapher and painter – were the subject of much discussion and critique. The best brush would be made by famous craftsmen, with hairs from the pelt of

an animal captured in the first weeks of March. The best inkstone would grind fine ink quickly and was "cold" enough to keep the fluid wet for long periods. It might come from a famous mountain miles away. The choicest inks were made from the smallest particles of smoke, gathered at the greatest distance from the burning pine wood of *tung* oil, then beaten thousands of times to improve their quality.

The tools of the painter and calligrapher were essentially the same, as was their approach to painting and writing. The difference lay in the painter's use of colour. Although the aesthetic role of colour in Chinese painting never approached the development that occurred in the West, its symbolic role was important. Sze Mai-mai wrote in *The Way of Chinese Painting* that, in its use of colour, painting "was akin to alchemy, for the simple range of colours in Chinese painting symbolised the Five Elements basic to the thought and practice of alchemy, and the methods of preparing colours resembled and perhaps derived from alchemical brewing and distillation".

Calligraphy

There was never a period of Chinese painting or a particular style in which good brushwork was not regarded as critical. Brush control reaches

nature. The concept of *tao* existed even before the formal teachings of the school of Taoism, and is a basic term of Chinese cosmology, expressive of the idea that all things have a common origin.

The Confucianists and Taoists differed more in their preoccupations about society and human relationships than in their concept of *tao*. The Taoists were concerned with humanity's direct, mystical relationship with nature, the Confucianists with an individual's role in society. Both systems, however, reflect humanity's oneness with the harmony of nature, the oneness of *tao*.

its apogee in the subtle art of calligraphy, which the Chinese have always regarded as the highest of the arts. With its abstract aesthetic, it is certainly the purest.

Few examples of ancient calligraphy still exist. Most ancient inscriptions were rubbings taken from cast-metal vessels. The earliest examples of Chinese writing in Taipei's National Palace Museum are Shang-period oracle inscriptions, incised on tortoise shells or the scapulae of oxen.

Painter's tao

The most obvious facet of Chinese painting is its expressions of a life rooted in the *tao* – in

The Chinese universe was an ordered, harmonic whole. People sought to take their place within, and participate in, the natural order. Ritual was important as it involved actual, rather than just symbolic, participation.

The painter's preoccupation with the *tao* occurred at both the ritual level of the Confucianist school and the mystical level of the Taoists. The Chinese painter was often a pillar of society, well-educated, with a responsible position and considerable duties to his family. He was a man of the world. Yet, as an artist, he needed peace and quiet. Chinese literature and poetry abound with references to this conflict between the weight of responsible citizenship and the withdrawal to relative seclusion that marks the life of an artist. Taoism was better suited to the individual effort of painting, as it focused on the relationship between the individual and nature, on the creative act itself, between the painter and his subject, and the magical link between the two: art.

Such concepts apply equally to the painter, as Chang Yenyuan later wrote: "He who deliberates and moves the brush intent upon making a picture, misses to a still greater

NATURAL EXPRESSION

"Writing grew from the need to express ideas, and painting grew from the desire to represent forms. This was the intention and the purpose of nature and of the sages…"

– from a 9th-century treatise on painting by Chang Yenyuan

The strokes, by contrast, are so crucial that they have even been given labels. There are hemp-fibre strokes, big axe-cut strokes, lotus leaf-vein strokes, ravelled-rope strokes and others. It is critical that every line, stroke or dot in a painting be alive and have a validity that plays a part, yet can be separated from the painting as a whole. Each swish of the brush can thus be judged on its own merits, and a painting is perfect in both in its whole and in its constituent parts.

extent the art of painting, while he who cogitates and moves the brush without such intentions, reaches the art of painting. His hands will not get stiff; his heart will not grow cold. Without knowing how, he accomplishes it."

Techniques

Chinese paintings, far more than those of other traditions, are based on line-work. Colour is primarily symbolic and decorative. Tone is more important, but plays a supporting role.

ABOVE: *Autumn Colours on the Chiao and Hua Mountains*, by the Yuan-dynasty master artist Chao Mengfu, 1295.

This is quite unlike the West, where an individual mark contributes to a whole, but can scarcely be subjected to a meaningful appraisal in itself.

What is less obvious, but far more important in the sweep of history, is the debt painting owes to calligraphy. The isolation of the strokes in any painting, with their self-contained beauty and the many special qualities of the calligraphic line, stand as evidence. Capturing the harmony of the parts brought the painter closer to achieving the harmony of the *tao*. Thus calligraphy remains obscure to those who cannot see that a dot may be full of life and that a line may burst with energy. ❏

TRADITIONAL MEDICINE IN TAIWAN

Traditional Chinese medicine is popular in Taiwan and treatments are covered by the country's national health insurance programme.

Historians have traced the beginnings of herbal medicine to the Chinese emperor Shen Nung around 3500 BC. The theoretical foundations of Chinese medical arts, like those of the martial arts, are rooted in the cosmic theories of *yin* and *yang*, the Five Elements (earth, water, metal, wood, fire), and the concept of *chi*, or vital energy. Essentially, Chinese doctors manipulate a patient's internal balance of vital energies by using herbs, acupuncture and other methods to "clear energy stagnation, suppress energy excess, tonify energy deficiency, warm up cold energy, cool down hot energy". By re-establishing the optimum internal balance of vital energies and restoring harmony among the body's vital organs, a doctor can keep his patient healthy. Traditional Chinese medicine takes an approach to disease and therapy that is fundamentally different from that of Western medicine. The Chinese prefer preventive techniques; the West concentrates on cures. The Chinese regard medicine as an integral part of a comprehensive system of health and longevity called *yangsheng*, "to nurture life". The system includes proper diet, regular exercise, regulated sex and deep breathing, as well as medicinal therapies and treatments.

▷ **ESSENTIAL BALANCE**
The concept of balance is key to understanding diagnostic techniques.

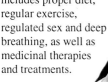

▽ **ACUPUNCTURE**
The flow of positive influences and energy is essential in maintaining good health; acupuncture helps maintain this flow within the body.

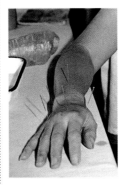

▽ **PRESSURE POINTS**
The Chinese classic *Huang Dineijing* text describes the 365 sensitive points used in acupuncture, in addition to the 12 main conduits in the human body.

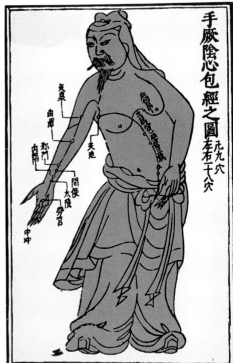

The graceful movements of t'ai chi chuan are instantly recognisable. Apart from the obvious advantages of this gentle form of exercise on the body in terms of flexibility and suppleness, it is thought that any imbalance in the circulation of a person's *chi* is greatly improved with the regular practice of t'ai chi. The discipline is becoming increasingly popular in the West.

In Chinese medicine, illness is a disharmony of the whole body. To be healthy, a balance in the circulation of *chi* in the body must be maintained. If the body is injured, for example, there may be a build-up of *chi* in that part of the body, so causing an imbalance in the energy flow. With the practice of t'ai chi the normal distribution of *chi* is encouraged, and the body will restore itself to its normal state.

The term "t'ai chi" means "supreme pole", while "chuan" translates as "martial art". T'ai chi is essentially an ancient form of self-defence which teaches a flexible and yielding response to confrontation and promotes balance, peace and harmony in daily life.

△ **MEDICINE MAN**
In the past, families paid a physician a monthly fee for preventative care. Today, doctors are mostly employed in times of ill-health.

△ **TEA-TIME**
Teas are prescribed during the acute phase of an illness followed by pills during the chronic phase. Green tea (*above*) is used to reduce fevers.

△ **THE PHARMACY**
Herbal prescriptions come in a variety of forms, including wines, and contain at least a half-dozen ingredients.

▷ **KITCHEN CUPBOARD**
Many pharmaceutical herbs, including cinnamon, ginger, liquorice, rhubarb and nutmeg are used in local cuisine.

TAIPEI AND THE NORTH

Maps:
Area 130
City 148

A sleepy town until 1949, Taipei is now a city of museums, parks and shiny buildings. Beyond, rugged beaches, tranquil mountains, and steaming hot springs lure travellers to Taiwan's northern tip

Taipei, the capital, is the usual focus of a visit to northern Taiwan, but within easy reach of the city's bustle can be found the lush suburb of Peitou, with its therapeutic waters, the fragrant Yangmingshan National Park, and a number of peaceful fishing villages, popular for their seafood restaurants.

TAIPEI

The changes that forever altered the face of **Taipei ❶** during the 1970s were truly dramatic. All the blessings and evils of modernisation gripped the city in a frenzy of growth, which, for better or worse, continues today. Yet this veneer of sophistication cannot mask the fact that Taipei remains one of the most staunchly traditional cities of Asia. For all its modernisations, it has not succumbed to the creeping Westernisation that has woven itself into the social fabric of cities like Hong Kong and Singapore.

Exhaust from the vehicles, combined with smoke from the industrial complexes that ring the city, is another modern malaise. Even more problematic has been the constant flow of newcomers seeking their fortunes in the big city. Despite an earthly philosophy and appreciation of nature, the Chinese have traditionally favoured city life to rural life, especially during healthy economic times. However, for all its newly acquired ills, the underlying currents of traditional Chinese culture continue to make Taipei an attractive destination.

Administrative beginnings

Historically, Taipei's outskirts have attracted more interest than its centre. When Koxinga (Cheng Cheng-ung) drove the Dutch from Taiwan in 1661, he appointed a general named Huang An to command military and naval forces stationed at Tanshui, at the mouth of the Tanshui River and northwest of modern Taipei. New farming methods were introduced along the river banks, and soldiers sent to reclaim land.

Early in the 18th century, reclaimed lands were extended from Hsinchuang to the area of modern Wanhua, now the heart of old Taipei. Wanhua, then known as Mengchia, became a major port in the early 1850s, before port activity shifted to Tataocheng. An emperor of the Qing dynasty was the first to designate the area as an administrative centre, in 1875, when the district of Taipei Fu was established, at the site of modern Chengchung. At the same time, a 5-km (3-mile) protective perimeter was constructed around the city.

The city is divided into northern and southern districts by Chunghsiao Road, site of the Taipei Railway Station. Chungshan North and Chungshan South roads slice the city into eastern and western portions.

PRECEDING PAGES: young martial arts trainees in combat. **LEFT:** an unusually empty side street. **BELOW:** National Day Parade.

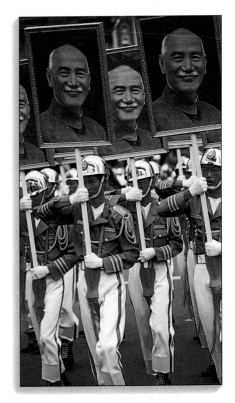

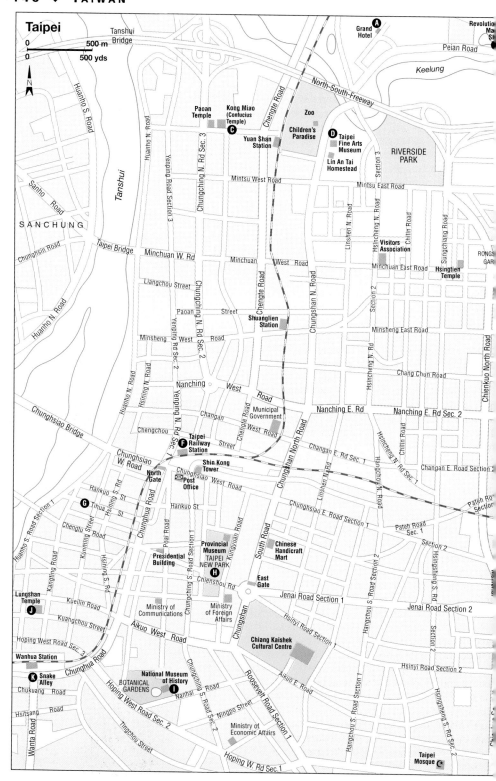

Taipei

0 ———— 500 m
0 ———— 500 yds

N

Tanshui Bridge

A Grand Hotel

Revolutio Ma S

Peian Road

Keelung

North-South-Freeway

Huanho S. Road

Paoan Temple

Kong Miao (Confucius Temple) **C**

Chengte Road

Zoo

Children's Paradise

Yuan Shan Station

D Taipei Fine Arts Museum

Lin An Tai Homestead

RIVERSIDE PARK

Section 3

Mintsu West Road

Mintsu East Road

Huanho N. Road

Chungching N. Rd Sec. 3

Yenping Road Section 3

Sanho Road

SANCHUNG

Tanshui

Chunghsin Road

Taipei Bridge

Minchuan W. Rd

Minchuan

West Road

Linshen N. Road

Hsincheng N. Road

Chilin Road

Visitors Association

Minchuan East Road

Hsingtien Temple

Sungchiang Road

RONGS GAR

Huanho N. Road

Liangchou Street

Chungching N. Rd Sec. 2

Chengte Road

Chungshan N. Road

Section 2

Paoan Street

Yenping N. Rd Sec. 2

Minsheng West Road

Shuanglien Station

Minsheng East Road

Hsinching N. Rd

Chang Chun Road

Minsheng West Rd Sec. 2

Nanching West Road

Chengte Road

Municipal Government

Nanching E. Rd

Nanching E. Rd Sec. 2

Chienkuo North Road

Hsining N. Road

Huanho N. Road

Yenping N. Rd Sec. 1

Changan

West Road

Hsincheng N. Rd

Chilin Road

Chunghsiao Bridge

Chengchou

Changan Street

F Taipei Railway Station

Chunghsiao W. Road

North Gate

Shin Kong Tower

Chunghsiao West Road

F Post Office

Chungshan North Road

Changan E. Rd Sec. 1

Linshen N. Rd

Changan E. Road Section 2

Hsincheng N. Rd Sec. 1

Hangchou N. Road

Hankuo St

Chunghsiao E. Road Section 1

Pateh Ro Section

Huanho S. Road Section 1

Hsining S. Rd

G Tihua St

Chengtu Road

Kunming Street

Hankuo St

Chunghua Road

Poai Road

Chunghsiao E. Road Section 1

Pateh Road Sec. 1

Section 2

Hsingsheng S. Rd

G

Provincial Museum

TAIPEI NEW PARK **H**

Chinese Handicraft Mart

South Road

Kungyuan Road

Presidential Building

Chungching S. Road Section 1

Chienshou Rd

East Gate

Jenai Road Section 1

Jenai Road Section 2

Hangchou S. Road Section 2

Section 2

Lungshan Temple **J**

Kueilin Road

Kangting Road

Kuangchou Street

Hoping West Road Sec. 3

Ministry of Communications

Chungshan

Ministry of Foreign Affairs

Hsinyi Road Section 1

Aikuo West Road

Chiang Kaishek Cultural Centre

Aikuo E. Road

Hsinyi Road Section 2

Hangchou S. Road Section 1

Hsingsheng S. Rd Sec. 2

Wanhua Station

Chunghua Road

K Snake Alley

Chukuang Road

BOTANICAL GARDENS

National Museum of History **I**

Hoping West Road Sec. 2

Chungching S. Road Sec. 2

Nanhai Road

Ningpo Street

Roosevelt Road Section 1

Hsitsang Road

Wanta Road

Tingchou Street

Ministry of Economic Affairs

Hoping W. Rd Sec. 1

Taipei Mosque **C**

Depending on which side of this north–south axis a street lies, it is assigned either East or West. Very long main roads are divided into sections, section 1 being near the city centre, section 5 quite a distance out, so addresses provide a rough indication of where to look on the map.

Map on page 148

One of the city's easiest landmarks for orientation is the **Grand Hotel ⒶA**. Located atop a ridge at the northern end of the city, this 530-room hotel looks somewhat like an ancient palace, built in the classical imperial style of old China. The massive new wing is crowned by the largest classical Chinese roof on earth.

East of the Grand Hotel about half a kilometre is the **Revolutionary Martyrs' Shrine ⒷB** (open daily, 9am–5pm) on Peian Road. The entire complex is built in the palace style of the Ming dynasty. Each structure attempts to reproduce a similar hall or pavilion in Beijing. Dedicated to the fallen heroes of China's wars, the arched portals of the main gate open onto a vast courtyard, past guest pavilions, drums and bell towers. Two gigantic brass-studded doors open onto the main shrine, where the names of the heroes are inscribed beside murals depicting their feats. The late Chiang Kaishek considered this a favourite retreat, frequently spending entire afternoons strolling through the grounds and halls. A changing of the guard occurs every hour.

Guard at the Chiang Kaishek Memorial.

Only a short taxi ride in the opposite direction, to the southwest of the Grand Hotel, is **Kong Miao ⒸC**, the Confucius Temple. It's a tranquil retreat compared to the city's other places of worship, as the throngs of worshippers supplicating their gods with prayer and offerings, the cacophony of gongs and drums, and the gaudy idols are absent. Absent, too, are images of Confucius. The tranquility is apt – Confucius preached the virtues of peace and quiet. The architecture of the temple is subtle yet exquisite, and highlighted by magnificent roofs.

BELOW: the imposing Grand Hotel.

By contrast, the **Paoan Temple**, on Hami Street and next to the Confucian Temple, is a gaudy monument to traditional Chinese folk religion. This 250-year-old Taoist temple sports carved dragons writhing in solid rock on the main support columns, and an interior crowded with the images of many deities. Buddhist elements are also apparent in the architecture, in testimony to the syncretic nature of Chinese religion.

Just south of the Grand Hotel is the **Taipei Fine Arts Museum ⒹD** (open Tues–Sun, 10am–6pm; entrance fee) with 24 galleries of modern art, and the **Lin An Tai Homestead** (open Tues–Sun, 9am–4pm), an original 30-room family home of a wealthy merchant from the Qing-dynasty era, built in the 1820s. Designed for very young lovers of Chinese history and culture – but adults will like it, too – is **Children's Paradise** (open Tues–Sun, 9am–5pm; entrance fee).

Located in the eastern part of the city is an important memorial to Chiang Kaishek's mentor and the founder of the Republic of China, Dr Sun Yatsen – the only common denominator between the rival communist and nationalist regimes, as both revere him as the founder of modern China. On Section 4 of Jenai Road, a long taxi ride away, the main building of the **Sun Yatsen Memorial ⒺE** (open daily, 9am–5pm) has a sweeping, gracefully-curved Chinese roof of glazed yellow tile. A 6-metre (20-ft) bronze statue of Sun Yatsen graces the main lobby.

Downtown walkabout

The best place to begin a downtown walking tour is from the **Taipei Railway Station ⒻⒻ**. This is not just a station, but an impressive and spacious palace, with four floors below street level. Close to the railway station are the bus terminals.

Over the years, this area has been remodelled at the same time as the new underground rail arteries were constructed. Many old buildings were removed giving space to modern skyscrapers. One pride of Taipei is the 245-metre (800-ft) **Shin Kong Tower** (open daily, 11am–10pm), just opposite the railway station and overshadowing the Taipei Hilton. High-speed elevators shoot visitors upwards at 540 metres (1,770 ft) a minute, topping out in 35 seconds at the observatory on the 49th floor (there are 51 in all). A Taipei landmark since 1994, the tower has an unobstructed view on clear days. The inner wall of the observatory is adorned with black-and-white lithographs depicting old Taipei.

East towards the Tanshui River is the narrow **Tihua Street Ⓖ**, perhaps Taipei's most historically important street, running parallel with Yenping Road. In the mid-1800s the first merchant established his business in this area; most of the houses are from the first decade of the 20th century. Back then, goods arrived mainly by boat on the Tanshui River.

West from the railway station and opposite the **main post office** (which has a good philatelic section) stands the ugly **North Gate**, one of the four remaining city gates. Located at the intersection of Chunghsiao and Chunghua roads, just before Chunghsiao crosses the river, the gate was erected in 1984, looking somewhat out of place amidst the tangle of expressway flyovers.

Behind the museum is **Taipei New Park Ⓗ** "newly" opened in 1907 and featuring ponds, pagodas and pavilions. The best time to walk in the grounds o

Blaze of neon lights in a Taipei side street.

BELOW:
Chiang Kaishek Memorial Hall.

Map on page 148

ew Park is at dawn, when thousands of the city's residents stretch, dance, xercise and move through various forms of *ta'i chi, shaolin* and other disciplines. Visitors are welcome to join in with the groups for an invigorating start ɔ a day in Taipei. (Evenings, however, are best spent somewhere else.)

To the east of the New Park are most of the important government ministries nd offices. From the park's southwestern end, it is only a short distance to the overnmental centre of Taiwan. Most prominent is the **Presidential Building**, ronting an enormous plaza that is the site of annual and colourful celebrations uring the Double Tens: 10 October, or National Day. The five-storey complex, finished in 1919, has a central tower 60 metres (200 ft) high.

At the south end of Chungshan Road is the impressive **East Gate**, the biggest f the original five gates in the 19th-century city wall. In 1966, it was renovated ʋith considerable ornate embellishment added to its once very simple façade.

A massive monument to the late president, the **Chiang Kaishek Cultural 'entre** is located at Chungshan South Road, close to the East Gate. Dedicated ɩ 1980, the fifth anniversary of Chiang's death, the enormous 76-metre (250- ɩ) **Memorial Hall** (open daily, 9am–4.30pm) dominates the landscaped rounds. Inside is an imposing 25-ton bronze statue of the late president. From ɩorning until late evening, the adjacent park is full of life – elderly people hatting under a shady tree or feeding the beautiful fat carp in the placid fish onds, mothers with children strolling the walkways, newlyweds posing for he inevitable wedding photos.

The **National Museum of History** ❶ (open Tues–Sun, 10am–6pm), on Nan- ɪai Road, contains 10,000 Chinese art objects dating from 2000 BC to modern ɪmes, including a fine sampling of Chinese currency. This interesting museum s less crowded than its counterpart, the National 'alace Museum. After touring its exhibits, visitors an stroll around the grounds of the **botanical gar- ɪens** next door, containing hundreds of species of rees, shrubs, palms and bamboo. Adjacent to the Museum of History are the **National Science Hall** nd **National Arts Hall** (same hours as National Museum of History).

West of the Chiang Kaishek memorial and near the iver is the oldest and most famous of Taipei's myriad emples, **Lungshan** ❶, or Dragon Mountain, a refer- ɪnce to the large collection of fearsome creatures on ts roof. The temple is on Kuangchou Street, close to he Tanshui River in the heart of old Taipei and outhwest of the Taipei Railway Station. It was built ɩ the early 18th century to honour Taiwan's patron leities, Kuanyin and Matsu.

Market allure

A good way to absorb the city's traditions is to take in he public markets. Most are open from dawn until ɪidnight, selling an amazing variety of fresh vegeta- ɔles, fragrant fruits, meats, fish, poultry, spices and ɔondiments. At night, these vendors retire from the ɩcene, to be replaced by scores of food stalls on ʋheels. These instant cafés serve every conceivable ɩind of Chinese snack food, at reasonable prices. The ɩost exotic night market of all is the two-block-long

The main entrance to the Memorial Hall is a magnificent arch, in traditional Ming style, that towers 30 metres (100ft) high and stretches 75 metres (250 ft) across.

BELOW: Lungshan Temple.

Fish market on Snake Alley.

BELOW: fortune teller, Snake Alley.

lane in the Wanhua district called **Snake Alley**  by tourists, who flock to the street by the bus load. Close to the Lungshan temple, this alley's main thoroughfare is known to everyone else as Huahsi Street.

The Western name stems from the business conducted by some of the vendors whose shops are stacked with cages of hissing snakes. The shopkeepers flip open the cage tops and deftly whip out snakes to sell, and customers watch as the chosen snake is strung live on a wire, stretched taut and unzipped before their eyes with a small knife. Blood and bile from the squirming snake are squeezed into a glass containing potent spirits and herbs. For customers who are keen on seeking an additional "kick", the vendor will even add a few drops of poison venom to the mixture. The carcasses of the gutted snakes are left to hang all night, while the concoction is drunk by men who believe it strengthens the eyes and the lower spine, eliminates fatigue and, inevitably, promotes male sexual vitality. The meat is later taken back to the kitchen to make snake soup.

North of the city

Nestled in the foothills, several kilometres to the northeast of the Grand Hotel and past the Martyrs' Shrine, is the most popular and important attraction in Taipei, if not in all of Taiwan. An imposing complex of beige-brick buildings topped with green and imperial-yellow slate roofs, houses the **National Palace Museum** (open daily, 9am–5pm; entrance fee). The building is impressive and the treasures within are unimaginable. Next to the museum is a small but very attractive *chin-shan-yuan* Chinese garden, that is worth a stroll.

Displayed in the Palace Museum – the exhibitions change from time to time – are some 6,000 works of art representing the zenith of 5,000 years of Chinese creativity. And these are just a fraction of the more than 700,000 paintings, porcelains, bronzes, rubbings, tapestries, books and other *objets d'art* stored in 4,000 crates located in vaults tunnelled into the mountain behind the museum.

Map on page 148

The museum opened in 1965, but the history of its treasures can be traced back more than 1,000 years to the beginning of the Song dynasty (AD 960–1279). The founder of that dynasty established the Hanlin Academy to encourage literature and the arts. The emperor's brother and successor later opened a gallery, where some of the items in the current collection were first housed. The gallery was then established as a government department for the preservation of rare books, old paintings and calligraphy. This imperial gallery was the prototype for Taipei's collection.

The collection expanded considerably during the Qing dynasty (1644–1911), as the Qing emperors were avid art collectors and the majority of items in the present collection are the result of their efforts to seek out and preserve China's most important treasures.

But the real intrigues began in November 1924. The provisional Nationalist government in Beijing gave the last surviving Manchu emperor, Puyi, and his entourage of 2,000 eunuchs and ladies two hours to evacuate the Imperial Palace. Then the government had 30 young Chinese scholars and art experts identify and inventory the overwhelming collection of art treasures that had been hoarded within the palace for more than 500 years.

It took the scholars two years just to sort out and organize the collection. In the meantime, the government formally established the National Beijing Palace Museum and began displaying some of the treasures. By the time the task of identifying all the priceless objects was completed in 1931, however, the Japan-

BELOW: National Palace Museum.

*Exhibit at the
National Palace
Museum.*

ese had attacked Manchuria, and threatened Beijing. To prevent the Japanese from seizing the collection, the government carefully packed everything in 20,000 cases and transported it south to Nanjing.

Thus began a 16-year-long odyssey. The priceless treasures were shuttled back and forth across the war-torn face of China by rail, truck, ox cart, raft and foot, always a few steps ahead of pursuing Japanese and, later, Communist troops. Incredibly, not a single item was lost or damaged. In 1937 the Japanese occupied Beijing and threatened Nanjing. Once again, the precious collection was loaded aboard trucks and transported in three shipments over hills, rivers and streams to China's rugged mountains. After the Japanese surrender in 1945, the Nationalists returned the pieces to Nanjing. But when Communist control of the mainland appeared imminent in 1948, 4,800 cases of the most valuable pieces were culled from the original 20,000 and sent to Taiwan for safekeeping. They were stored in a sugar warehouse in Taichung, and remained there until the Chungshan (Sun Yatsen) Museum Building, in Waishuanghsi, opened in 1965.

NORTHERN TAIWAN

When you've had enough of the sights and sounds of Taipei, take an excursion beyond the city; the northernmost tip, especially, is a microcosm of Taiwan, with its mountains, waterfalls, beaches, paddy fields, villages and temples.

BELOW: jamming, Yangmingshan National Park.

The fastest route of escape from Taipei lies up nearby **Yangmingshan ❷**. About 40 minutes' drive via winding roads north of the city, Yangming is known as the local Beverly Hills. Large numbers of wealthy industrial tycoons, movie stars and entrepreneurs, as well as expatriate business people, live here in luxurious villas clinging to the cliffs in the cool climes above Taipei.

The mountain top is crowned by **Yangmingshan National Park**, a well-maintained park featuring walkways that wind through colourful gardens of trees, bushes, fragrant flowers and grottoes. From the middle of February until the end of March, an annual spring-flower festival is held here, with the entire mountain awash with cherry blossoms and carpeted with flowering azaleas.

A less lofty but an equally entrancing retreat a few minutes from Taipei is the suburb of **Peitou** (pronounced *bay tow*). It nestles snugly in lush green hills north of the city, and can be reached via twisting back roads from Yangming-shan, or from Taipei via a much-less-scenic route that passes through the suburb of Tienmou. (Peitou will soon be a stop at the MRT's Red Line.)

Peitou literally means Northern Sojourn. It has a Japanese feel which has lingered ever since the town was turned into a resort for their officers and magistrates at the end of the 19th century. More recently, Peitou was notoriously used as a getaway for large groups of Japanese men, attracted by the town's therapeutic hot springs and the women who soothed their aching muscles.

Peitou is easy to explore on foot. A street leads directly to **Hell's Valley**, where the open sulphur pits offer a first-hand look at the natural activity responsible for the area's hot springs. Visitors can boil fresh eggs in the medicinal waters that gurgle through the sulphur-stained rocks. These specially-prepared eggs are also on sale at the hawker stands which flank Hell's Valley entrance.

After walking through the centre of town, with its park and Chinese pavilion, you will come to a traffic island. The right-hand fork goes past the New Angel Hotel, near to which Chiyen Road offers access to the climb up **Phoenix Mountain**. This route eventually leads to a double staircase guarded by two huge dogs, symbols of good luck. The stairs lead to the **Chen Memorial Garden**,

Maps:
Area 130
City 148

BELOW: Hell's Valley.

whose chief attraction is its tranquillity. The paved pathway behind the garden is the start of an exhausting mountain ascent. From the summit there are sweeping views of Taipei, Peitou and the surrounding countryside. Trekkers will find well-marked hiking paths leading in four directions from the top of Phoenix Mountain, all of which lead to main roads.

Sandstone erosion at Yehliu.

The western horizon of northern Taiwan is dominated by the 475-metre (1,560-ft) **Goddess of Mercy Mountain**, so-called because its profile resembles that of Kuanyin (Guanyin), the merciful goddess, from a distance. Visitors who make the steep climb to its peak will be rewarded by breathtaking views of the island's northern coastline, and of the Taiwan Strait.

Northern routes

The drive along Taiwan's northern coastline rewards visitors with its scenic natural sights, with little farming towns and fishing villages. The entire route can be covered comfortably in a single day's drive from Taipei. On the way to Tanshui, alongside the Tanshui River, is **Kuantu** with its eye-catching, red, 550-metre (1,700-ft) bridge. Directly on the river and close to a cliff is an extremely large temple complex, **Kuantu Matsu**, one of the most important of its kind in Taiwan. It is worth a stroll around, and there's a viewpoint high above the river accessed via a tunnel through the cliff.

The terminus of the North Coast Highway is a town with a rich historical heritage, **Tanshui** ❸ – together with Kuantu, a popular day-trip from Taipei. The town was the main point of contact in northern Taiwan between the Chinese and foreign traders during its heyday as the island's major port in the 19th century. Today it's very popular for its seafood, sold on numerous stalls and in

BELOW:
the northern coast.

small restaurants: just point to what you want, and they will prepare it for you. The North Coast Highway rounds the northernmost nib of Taiwan. From here on, the East China Sea extends to the horizon. After passing Fukwai Cape, at Taiwan's northernmost point, a natural wonder appears: **Shihmen** (Stone Gate), an impressive natural erosion form, with an 8-metre (25-ft) high opening. Even more evidence of the forces of nature are apparent at **Yehliu Park**, literally Wild Willows. The white, yellow and brownish sandstone promontories here, directly in front of the pounding ocean, have been etched into all manner of artistic shapes by the forces of erosion, creating an other-worldly terrain.

Taiwan's northernmost city and second-largest port is **Keelung ❹**, junction for the North Coast and Northeast Coast highways, and the northern terminus of the North–South Highway. The port has excellent facilities for the loading and unloading of container ships; the container depots are massive. About 80 million tons of freight are handled here annually. Only Kaohsiung has more extensive port facilities. Keelung's main point of interest is an enormous white **statue and temple of Kuanyin**. The 22.5-metre (74-ft) statue is propped up on a 4-metre (14-ft) pedestal that enables the deity to watch over the city.

Fulung ❺, the next stop on the Northeast Coast Highway, belies the notion that Taiwan's best beaches lie in the southern reaches of the island. The white sand beach here hugs the northern shore of a cape that juts into the Pacific Ocean. Enthusiastic walkers will find that the shoreline stretches for kilometres in both directions. A principal attraction in the south of this lovely region is the **Chiaohsi hot springs**. Small restaurants scattered about the town specialise in fresh seafood. Two temples cater to the faithful in Chiaohsi.

Less than 10 minutes' drive into the hills behind the Chiaohsi springs is

Map on page 130

The Kuanyin statue at Keelung.

BELOW: Keelung.

Map on page 130

Wufengchi (Five Peaks Flag Scenic Region). Vendors around the parking lot sell the area's sought-after products of dried mushrooms, preserved plums and other fruits, fresh ginger and medicinal herbs.

Near the Taipei suburb of **Hsintien ❻**, south of the city, is the **Chihnan Temple** (open dawn to sunset), one of the most important landmarks in the north. This Temple of the Immortals has been under constant construction and expansion for 100 years. Perched on a lush green hillside, it exemplifies the concept of a temple as a magic mountain peak. There are supposedly 1,000 steps along the winding approach to the temple, home to 50 Buddhist monks.

South from Hsintien, the mountainous retreat of **Wulai ❼** is the best place in northern Taiwan to witness Atayal traditional culture. Beyond the town, a suspension bridge hangs across a river. From here, a footpath and mini-train take visitors to the Clear Flowing Garden, where a waterfall cascades into a deep gorge. Local ethnic minorities perform traditional music and folk dances in the garden. A cable car carries visitors across the gorge to a place in the mountains appropriately called **Dreamland**, which has additional ethnic performances, a lake for rowing and fishing, plenty of places to eat, and an amusement park for children. Nearby hot springs provide therapeutic bathing.

South of Taipei

BELOW:
Dreamland, Wulai.
RIGHT: Taipei's
hotels climb higher
each year.

Southwest of Taipei are several other places well worth a stop. Only 20 km (12 miles) away is the busy old town of **Sanhsia ❽**, with streets snaking around old brick buildings and the famous Tsushih Temple, originally built in 1770. The temple was in ruins after World War II, but is now reconstructed, with newly-carved stone decorations, making it a fine examples of temple art.

A short hop away is the small town of **Yingko**, a potter's heaven. Some of the factories allow tours, giving visitors a chance to watch how "muddy" clay can be transformed into a beautifully-painted Chinese vase, worthy of a Ming or Qing court. Many shops line the narrow, usually crowded streets, selling everything from simple earthenware to the finest porcelain, from ordinary teapots to delicate figures.

Several other attractions are within hailing distance south of Taipei. Fifty kilometres (30 miles) away to the southwest, down Highway 3 and near the town of Tahsi, is **Tzu Hu** (Lake Mercy), temporary resting place of the late Chiang Kaishek. His body rests above ground in a heavy granite sarcophagus in his former country villa, awaiting the day when political conditions permit returning his body to his birthplace in mainland China, in Zhejiang province.

One of the main attractions to the south of Taipei, beyond Tahsi and near Lungtan, is the **Window on China ❾** (open 8.30am–5pm; entrance fee). On a site covering 10 hectares (25 acres), the most important buildings and temples in Taiwan, as well as many notable buildings in mainland China, have been erected in miniature. Totalling 130 in all, the buildings are on a scale of 1:25, and are populated by some 50,000 miniature model people, some of whom perform parades or dances to music. Vegetation is provided by countless proportionally-sized bonsai trees. ❏

CENTRAL TAIWAN

The beautiful landscapes of Central Taiwan are home to hot-spring resorts, bamboo forests and soaring mountain peaks. On the coast, the old port of Lukang has changed little since the middle ages

Map on page 130

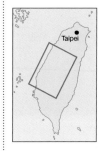

Taipei

C entral Taiwan has the most varied terrain on the island. From the summit of snow-capped Yu Shan, the Jade Mountain, the landscape drops 3,952 metres (12,966 ft) to the harbour at Taichung. The alluvial plain that divides the highlands from the Taiwan Strait is filled with vast green rice fields, and plantations of bananas, pineapples, papayas, sugar cane, tea and other crops.

Taichung

The main urban centre of central Taiwan is **Taichung** ❿ – the name actually means Central Taiwan. The pace and pressure of modern metropolitan Taipei are replaced here by a quieter, slower life; this is what Taipei once looked like, before the big boom of the 1970s. Taiwan's third-largest city with a population of around 100,000, Taichung is located on a plain about 20 km (13 miles) from the coast and 100 km (60 miles) south of Taipei and enjoys the island's best year-round climate, without the seasonal extremes of heat and cold that mark the north and south.

Taichung was founded in 1721 by immigrants from the Chinese mainland, who originally named it Tatun – the Big Mound. The city's current name was adopted by the Japanese after they took possession in 1895. Today, the 20-hectare (50-acre) **Chungshan Park** occupies the hill on which the first settlement was built. The two pavilions rising above the lotus-filled lake are regarded as a local landmark.

Although Taichung is neither as large nor as diverse as Taipei, it has numerous points of interest. The **Martyrs' Shrine**, on Shuangshih Road northeast of Chungshan Park, was erected in 1970. Its design provides a superb example of the harmony and balance inherent in classical Chinese architecture. Many locals claim it is more outstanding than the martyrs' shrines in Hualien or Taipei. Protected by two bronze guardian lions, the shrine commemorates 72 Chinese beheaded in 1911 by the tottering Manchu court, on the eve of the republic's revolution.

Across the island

North and east of Taichung, the **Central Cross-Island Highway** stretches for 200 km (120 miles), from Tungshih through Taroko Gorge to the eastern coast. The Chinese claim no visit to Taiwan is complete without a trip across this road, for it displays – with striking beauty – the full gamut of the island's terrain: lush tropical valleys and snow-capped peaks, alpine forests and rocky ravines, steamy hot springs and roaring rivers, mountain lakes and the shimmering sea. Two hours' drive from Kukuan is **Lishan** – Pear Mountain – on the crest of the Central Range,

LEFT: Central Cross-Island Highway view.
BELOW: the long road to a rice harvest.

close to the Central Cross-Island Highway's halfway point. Highway 7 to Ilan in the northeast begins here. Lishan is the staging point for mountaineering expeditions to **Hsuen Shan**, the second highest peak in Taiwan at 3,884 metres (12,742 ft).

At Tayuling, the highest point on the highway, a road leads southwest through the hills to **Lushan Hot Springs** ⑪, set in a deep valley below the town of Wushe. Lushan village straddles a turbulent stream traversed by a suspension footbridge. Hot-spring inns lie along the river bank. Lushan is famous for its tea, medicinal herbs, petrified-wood canes, wild-blossom honey and dried mushrooms. Potent medicinal deer-horn shavings, tanned deer skins and other products that are either very expensive or unavailable in Taipei are common purchases here.

Southwest of Lushan and Wushe is **Puli**, a village known as the exact geographical centre of Taiwan. On its outskirts is Chenghuang Temple, a monastery founded in 1924, standing in a grove of palms. Nearby, a signposted turning leads 3 km (2 miles) up a pretty valley to Carp Lake, a pleasant picnic spot devoid of people, except for straw-hatted farmers who specialise in growing edible and medicinal fungi on wooden planks and in shaded arbors.

Sun Moon Lake

Taiwan's most enduringly popular honeymoon resort is **Sun Moon Lake** ⑫, 750 metres (2,500 ft) above sea level in the western foothills of the Central Range. Entirely surrounded by mountains and dense tropical foliage, the lake takes the shape of a round sun when viewed from some of the surrounding hills, or of a crescent moon when seen from other heights. The lake was formed

Taiwan has scores of local festivals each year, colourful celebrations held in honour of local city gods and deities.

BELOW: Lushan.

in the early 20th century, when the occupying Japanese built a hydroelectric dam. Prior to that, there had been a major tribal settlement in this area; traces remain on the lake's south shore. Its beauty notwithstanding, Sun Moon Lake's popularity often leaves it crawling with bus-loads of package tourists from Taipei and abroad. However, there are a number of hillside trails and shore-side walks for privacy. The best way to enjoy the scenic beauty of Sun Moon Lake is to rise at daybreak and walk, drive or take a cab along the road that winds around the lake. At dawn, the early birds have the lake to themselves.

A good starting point for an exploration of the lake is the Sun Moon Lake Hotel, perched on a high embankment overlooking the lake. Heading east and south, the road leads first to the majestic **Wenwu** (open dawn–sunset), a temple of martial and literary arts. This Taoist shrine, dedicated to Confucius and the two great warrior deities Kuan Kung and Yueh Fei, is built into the hillside in three ascending levels. The temple complex is interesting for its complicated layout, with various pavilions and side halls connected by ornate passages and stairways.

High on a hill near the southern end of the lake, the **Hsuanchuang Temple** (open dawn–sunset) houses some of China's most precious Buddhist relics. This temple was built for the safekeeping and preservation of the relics, known as *ssu li-tze*. On top of a hill beyond the Hsuanchuang Temple stands the ornate, nine-tiered **Tzuen**, the **Pagoda of Filial Virtue** (open dawn–sunset), which was erected by Chiang Kaishek in memory of his mother. An uphill walk through cool glades of bamboo, fern, maple and pine trees leads to the foot of the pagoda. from where there are spectacular views of the entire lake and the surrounding landscape.

Map on page 130

BELOW: storm over Sun Moon Lake.

Excursions from Taichung

In **Tsaotun** ⓭, about 20 km (12 miles) from Taichung, the Handicraft Exhibition Hall contains an extensive display of local handicrafts and modern manufactured goods. The four-storey, air-conditioned building houses bamboo and rattan furniture, Chinese lanterns, lacquer ware, ceramics, stonecraft, woodcraft, curios, jewellery, and textiles. All items on display are for sale at fixed prices. Another 2 km (1¼ miles) from Tsaotun is **Chunghsing** village, seat of Taiwan's provincial government. Taipei, while regarded by the Taiwanese as the temporary capital of the Republic of China, is not the centre of provincial affairs. (Both the People's Republic and the Republic of China consider Taiwan a province of China; both, of course, have differing versions of exactly how the arrangement should be implemented.)

West beyond Changhua, the ancient harbour of **Lukang** ⓮ lies on the shores of the Taiwan Strait. The narrow residential lanes here have changed little since the Qing dynasty days, and artisans can still be seen making furniture with ancient tools and techniques, in open-fronted shops. The oldest temple in Lukang, and one of the oldest in Taiwan, is **Lungshan Temple** (open dawn–sunset), the Dragon Mountain Temple, dating from the 18th century. It is located on Sanmin Road, just off the main avenue, Chungshan Road. The temple was constructed by early Chinese settlers as an expression of gratitude to Kuanyin, the goddess of mercy, for their safe passage from the mainland. Kuanyin is enshrined in the main hall. The temple structure reflects a classical mainland style of a design that differs markedly from the style that subsequently developed in Taiwan. Note the elaborately-carved wooden ceilings and stone-dragon pillars. Along Chungshan Road from the Dragon Mountain Temple is the impressive **Tienhou Temple** (open dawn–sunset). On the main altar, the image of Matsu, goddess of the sea, is said to have been brought here in 1684 from the original Matsu shrine on Mei Chou Island by Admiral Shih, who captured Taiwan for the Qing emperor. If true, this story substantiates the claim of Lukang's people that this was the first centre of the Matsu cult in Taiwan. There are many other exotic icons here, among them the magnificent Jade Emperor in his own temple in the same compound. Many more temples and shrines are tucked away among Lukang's lanes.

The fragrance of freshly-sawn camphor and wet lacquer drifts through the streets of Lukang. Incense is also produced here, and it is interesting to see the creation of the enormous coils that hang from temple ceilings and burn for days.

BELOW: temple images, Lukang.

Mountain tops

East of Chiayi, the resort area of **Alishan** ⓯ and the peak of **Yu Shan** (Jade Mountain) rise from the mists of the Central Range. Alishan's popularity is due primarily to the famous sunrise view from the summit of nearby **Chu Shan** (Celebration Mountain). It is a spectacular event. As visitors stand shivering 2,490 metres (8,170 ft) above sea level, gazing into the greying mist, the sun glances across it, undulating in vivid hues of gold and silver, red and orange. On holidays and weekends, the summit is overcrowded with thousands of noisy excited visitors – not conducive conditions to witnessing an idyllic sunrise. But on any given day, hundreds of people make the pre-dawn ascent, usually by tour bus. By 7am, most of them will be back at the hotel for breakfast.

Map on page 130

Drifting mountain mists are regarded as possessing extraordinary curative powers, due to their high concentration of *chi*. *Chi* is the life-force or vital energy, the most fundamental of all Chinese physical and spiritual concepts. *Chi* is considered the basic force that animates all life forms. The most potent *chi*, it is believed, rises in the atmosphere and clings as mist to the mountains, like cream rising to the top of milk. From time immemorial, the Chinese have cultivated the custom of *dengagao* – ascending high places. They believe the *chi* found in the mist strengthens their longevity and virtue. One of the most ancient of all Chinese characters – *hsien*, for immortal – combines the symbols for man and mountain. While the practical urban Chinese are unlikely to become mountain-top ascetics, they are nevertheless convinced of the restorative powers of high-altitude mists.

TIP

Prior permission to climb the peak of Yu Shan, now within a national park, is required from the Alpine association of Taipei.

Alishan is the billeting post of mountaineering expeditions to **Yu Shan** ⑯, the Jade Mountain. At 3,952 metres (12,966 ft) in altitude, Yu Shan is the highest mountain in Asia east of the Himalayas, south of Russia's Kamchatka Peninsula and north of Borneo's Mount Kinabalu. Yu Shan is far more visited than the others, however. Indeed, as Taiwan's favourite alpine resort, Yu Shan can lure visitors by the thousands. Even higher than Japan's majestic Mount Fuji, this peak was called New High Mountain during the 50 years of Japanese occupation. Its original name was restored by the Chinese in 1945.

From Alishan there is a road leading 20 km (12 miles) to **Tungpu**, a remote hot spring nestled in the mountains at 2,600 metres (8,500 ft). There is a rustic hotel there for overnight stays; another hostel is high on the mountain slopes, at about 3,000 metres (10,800ft). Four full days should be allotted for this breathtakingly beautiful trip. ❑

BELOW: Yu Shan National Park.

Map on page 130

THE EAST COAST

The raw beauty and wild terrain of rugged eastern Taiwan appeal to the senses, much as the coast does to any traveller who loves remote and unspoiled places.

On the Pacific side of the great Central Range, which bisects Taiwan from north to south, lies the island's rugged eastern coast, unsurpassed for its contours of land, sea and sky. (Parts of this eastern seaboard look much like California's Big Sur coastline.) Insulated by a wall of mountains from the industrial and commercial developments of the western plains, eastern Taiwan remains an enclave of old-fashioned island culture, a refuge where the flavour of human feelings retains its natural taste.

Roller-coaster ride to Hualien

"Breathtaking" is not a cliché when applied to the roller-coaster, 110-km (70-mile) route between **Suao** and Hualien to the south. It is literally a cliff-hanger, with the crashing breakers of the Pacific Ocean eroding the rocks 300–450 metres (1,000–1,500 ft) below. Chiselled into sheer stone cliffs that rise in continual ridges, the road was first built in 1920 along the route of the original footpath that was hewn out of rock in 1875. At first, there was only one lane to cope with the convoys of cars, taxis, buses and trucks. Now, traffic can move freely in both directions, even if the road occasionally gets rather narrow. The journey takes between two and three hours, but travellers are rewarded with magnificent views and a rush of adrenalin.

BELOW:
Suao Harbour.

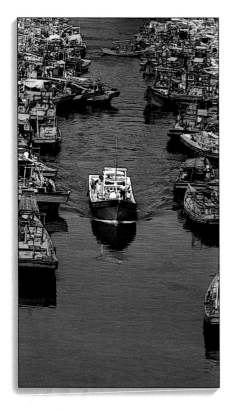

Those who visit **Hualien** ⑰ will find it a pleasant, cheerful town. With 90 percent of the surrounding area dominated by mountains, the city itself – the largest settlement on Taiwan's east coast – fills the narrow strip of flat land separating the mountains from the sea. Hualien's greatest claim to fame is marble, tons of which are contained in the craggy cliffs and crevices of nearby Taroko Gorge.

Hualien is home to Taiwan's largest ethnic minority, the Ami, numbering about 150,000. During the annual Ami harvest celebration, in late August and early September, the town is particularly festive. At other times, authentic performances of traditional tribal dances are staged for visitors in a large marble factory along the road to Taroko Gorge, and in the **Ami Culture Village**, about a 15-minute drive from downtown. But these centres offer more kitsch than class. Those seeking authentic glimpses of Ami life should visit the little coastal town of **Fengpin**, a short drive south of Hualien. The harvest festival's opening ceremonies are especially exciting here.

Taroko Gorge

Nine out of 10 people who visit Hualien tour **Taroko Gorge** ⑱, one of the most spectacular natural wonders of the world. By car, cab or bus, the route from Hualien heads north into the cavernous, marble-rich gorge of Taroko. *Taroko* means beautiful in the Ami dialect, and visitors at once realise that the people who named the site were not exaggerating. A gorge of marble cliffs, through which flows the torrential Liwu River, Taroko winds sinuously for 20 km (12 miles) from the coast to its upper end at Tienhsiang.

The first scenic points along the route are the **Light of Zen Monastery** and the **Shrine of Eternal Spring**. The latter is a memorial to the 450 retired servicemen who lost their lives constructing this road, known as the Rainbow of Treasure Island. It is perched on a cliff overlooking the boulder-strewn river, with a view of a waterfall pouring through a graceful moon bridge.

At **Swallow's Grotto**, the cliffs tower so high on either side of the road that direct sunlight hits the floor of the gorge only around noon. The Fuji Cliff dizzies visitors as they look up its sheer stone face, echoing the roar of the river below. The **Tunnel of Nine Turns** is a remarkable feat of engineering – it cuts a crooked road of tunnels and half-tunnels through solid marble cliffs.

The final stop on the Taroko Gorge tour is **Tienhsiang**. Here, amid a naturally beautiful setting, stands the Tienhsiang Lodge, where overnight lodging and meals are available. A suspension bridge near the lodge leads across the river to an exquisite pagoda perched on a peak. Just a few minutes' drive away, a series of steps at the mouth of a tunnel lead to the dramatic natural setting of the **Wenshan Hot Springs**.

South along the East Coast Highway

Scenery along the East Coast Highway heading south from Hualien grows more gentle and pastoral. On one side, the deep-blue waters of the Pacific either crash frothily against rocky capes or nuzzle the beaches of quiet coves. Inland, the

BELOW: tunnels in Taroko Gorge.

Ami farmers harvesting rice near Taitung.

Central Range forms a massive windscreen, sheltering brilliant green plantations and terraced paddies that cover arable land.

Along the coastal route, a large, seated Buddha image, facing the sea some 15 km (9 miles) south of Hualien, will draw the attention of those not yet suffering temple overload. Another 25 km (16 miles) further on is **Chichi**, the first good swimming beach south of Hualien. The small bay here has clear water for bathing, and sometimes the waves break perfectly for body-surfing. The beach itself is of black sand.

Taitung

Reached from the north by both Highway 9 and Highway 11, the sleepy seaside city of **Taitung** ⓳ is pleasant and airy. At about the same latitude as Kaohsiung on the opposite coast, Taitung is the economic hub for the lower portion of the east coast. The city is not much of a traveller's destination in itself, but it makes a convenient springboard for excursions to nearby places such as the Chihpen hot springs, Lu Tao (Green Island) and Lanyu (Orchid Island), and the East Coast Highway.

The most popular attraction is Carp Hill, with the **Dragon and Phoenix Temple** (open dawn–sunset) providing fine views over the city and the sea. The temple itself is not particularly noteworthy, except for some interesting icons and a small collection of 3,000- to 5,000-year-old archaeological artefacts unearthed in the area. These stone implements include coffin slabs and hand tools, and provide evidence that people lived on Taiwan long before the dawn of written history. On Chunghua Road stands a modest Matsu temple called the **Palace of the Empress of Heaven**, with an ornately enameled and gilded façade.

BELOW: Taitung.

The Chihpen Valley

Tucked against the mountainside at the mouth of a rugged canyon, along the rocky Chihpen River, is **Chihpen ⓴**, one of Taiwan's oldest, quaintest and most remote hot-spring resorts. It was dubbed the Source of Wisdom by the Japanese, who developed it as a resort around the beginning of this century.

The Chihpen Valley, which cuts into the steep mountains behind the spa, is reminiscent of the superb wild gorges hidden deep within the remote mountain ranges of western Sichuan province on the mainland. Here are thick forests and clear streams, steep cliffs and cascading waterfalls, bamboo groves and fruit orchards, robust mountain dwellers and exotic flora and fauna.

The biggest treat in the Chihpen Valley is the **Chinghueh Temple** (Clear Awakening Monastery) (open dawn–sunset), located up a steep hill about a kilometre from the lower hot-spring area, next door to the Royal Chihpen Spa Hotel. A brace of large white-plaster elephants stand at the foot of the steps to the elegant shrine hall. While Taoist temples display the dragon and tiger, the elephant is strictly a Buddhist motif. Inside the hall are two of the most exquisite, tranquil and beautifully-crafted Buddha images in Taiwan. The two statues sit together, one behind the other, gazing in meditative serenity through half-closed eyes, exuding feelings of sublime harmony. The Brass Buddha, 3 meters (10 ft) tall and weighing one metric ton, was made in Thailand and occupies the rear of the shrine. The priceless White Jade Buddha, 2.5 meters (8 ft) tall and weighing 4.5 metric tons, is seated in a lotus flower in the foreground. This solid jade image was a gift from Buddhists in Burma (Myanmar). Along the altar and in front of the White Jade Buddha is a row of smaller but equally lovely icons.

Map on page 130

Chihpen's hot mineral water has therapeutic properties. It is said to alleviate everything from skin irritations to arthritis – all by simply soaking in one of the pools.

BELOW: Chihpen hot springs.

*Traditional
aboriginal canoe,
Lanyu island.*

BELOW:
Green Island.
RIGHT: east coast,
south of Suao.

Visitors should remove their shoes and approach across the carpet for a closer look. To the left of the altar is a small, solid-gold, jewel-encrusted pagoda encased in glass. This houses two of the mysterious relics of the Buddha known as *ssu-li-tzu*, tiny nuggets extracted from the Buddha's ashes after his cremation over 2,500 years ago.

Perhaps no stretch of major road in Taiwan is as untrammelled as Highway 22, which cuts inland and westward from Chihpen to cross the mountains towards Kaohsiung. Travellers will see a lot from the window of a coach, but it is far more convenient and pleasurable to cover this stretch by private car or taxi. There is the train as well, but this spends a lot of its time in tunnels.

Island outposts

For any traveller with a taste for offbeat destinations, there are two islands easily reached from Taitung which offer worlds far removed from the mainstream of Chinese civilisation.

Within sight of Taitung, about 30 km (20 miles) due east, is **Lu Tao ㉑**, or Green Island. Originally known in English as Fire Island – beacons burned there to prevent fishing vessels from wrecking on its coral shoals – it inherited its new name in 1949. The 16-sq. km (6-sq. mile) island has only recently been developed for tourism; it wasn't so long ago that a holiday on Lu Tao meant sitting out a long prison sentence. Today, Lu Tao is accessible by air or sea, with regular flights from Taitung. In addition, three ferries service the island, on infrequent schedules, from Taitung.

The waters and reefs around the island are excellent for swimming, scuba diving and fishing. Glass-bottom boats offer views of coral reefs and colourful fish. Trails lead into the hills for day hikers, and a paved 17-km (11-mile) long road circles the coastline. At the northeast corner of the island is the **Kuanyin Cave**. According to legend, an old fisherman lost his way at sea in a terrible storm, about a century ago. Suddenly, a fireball appeared in the sky and guided him safely back to shore, where he found safe haven in this cave. Within it he saw a stone that resembled Kuanyin, the goddess of mercy. Taking this as a divine sign, he prostrated himself before the stone and gave thanks for his safe return. Ever since then, the cave has been sacred to the Lu Tao's inhabitants.

Lanyu ㉒, or Orchid Island, is an island of 45 sq. km (17 sq. miles) situated 60 km (40 miles) east of Taiwan's southern tip and 80 km (50 miles) southeast of Taitung. Lanyu is home to 4,250 Yami people (*see page 137*), Taiwan's smallest minority group. With their colourful costumes and a strongly-matriarchal society, the Yami are often regarded as representing the northernmost extent of Polynesian ancestry.

The entire island can be driven around in a little over two hours. The coastal rock formations, eroded by weather and seawater, are particularly impressive. Formations include the Lion Rocks, the strange Beauty Stone, and the Battleship Fleet. One thing that is conspicuously missing, given the island's English name, is wild orchids – unfortunately, they have all been dug up and sold. ❏

THE SOUTH

From temple-strewn Tainan to the white sands of Kenting, Taiwan's south has lured many adventurers, including Portuguese sailors, Chinese pirates, and Dutch colonists

Map on page 130

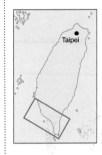

Southern Taiwan is a rich mixture, with something for everyone. From the culture-laden city of Tainan, seat of the 17th-century Ming loyalist, Koxinga (also known as Cheng Cheng-kung – Lord of the Imperial Surname) to the brash and busy port of Kaohsiung, the fishing islands of Penghu, and the Kenting National Park, a haven for exotic flora, it's a challenging and rewarding area to explore.

Tainan

Tainan ㉓ is Koxinga's city. At odds with the new Manchu Qing court, he fled here in 1661, besieged the Dutch fort at Anping, and eventually drove them from the island. The Ming stronghold he established lasted three generations, until his grandson finally capitulated to the Manchu court. His entourage included about 1,000 writers, artists, musicians, craftsmen and master chefs, whose function it was to launch a Chinese cultural renaissance in Taiwan. Modern Tainan remains highly conscious of its rich cultural legacy. For decades a sleepy town of temples and pleasant memories, it is rising in a concerted effort to restore its former glory. Under a forward-thinking administration, Taiwan's fourth-largest city of just under a million people is becoming a tourist mecca. Light industry, agriculture and fishing are all booming, but large industrial plants and their accompanying pollution are kept at arm's length. The goal is to maintain a clean and cultured city, a showcase for visitors. The authorities are especially determined to protect the scenic beauty and delicate ecological balance of Tainan's tropical coastline.

Temples are the hallmark of Tainan. The sobriquet "City of a Hundred Temples" is an understatement: there are 220 major temples and countless minor shrines scattered around the town and surrounding countryside. It is perhaps appropriate to begin at **Koxinga's Shrine** (open daily, 9am–5pm). Set in a garden compound of tropical trees and breezy pavilions, the shrine was built in 1875 by imperial edict from the Manchu Qing court in Beijing. Left in ruins following the Japanese occupation, the shrine was restored after World War II, and once again in 1962.

Three blocks from Koxinga's Shrine is Tainan's **Confucian Temple** (open daily, 9am–5pm), the oldest temple dedicated to the sage in Taiwan. It was built in 1665 by Cheng Ching, Koxinga's son, as a centre for the Chinese cultural renaissance. Restored 16 times since then, it still stands out as Taiwan's foremost shrine to Confucius, reflecting a classical architectural style otherwise seldom seen on the island.

Tainan's residents believe that their behaviour is reported to the emperors of heaven and hell by Cheng

LEFT: Taoist parade at a festival.
BELOW: Koxinga statue, Tainan.

*Relief detail from
Tainan's Confucian
Temple.*

Huang, the city deity. His small, old, and unusual temple – **Cheng Huang Miao** (open dawn–sunset) – is on Chingnien Road, between Chienkuo and Poai roads. The open beam-work on the temple ceiling is noteworthy. Unlike other ceilings, this is varnished rather than painted, its surface etched with fine filigree. Relics and ritual objects hang everywhere, among them two giant abaci. The hardwood beads of each abacus are the size of melons. They are used by the city deity to tally the merits and demerits of each citizen for his annual report to the emperors of heaven and hell.

An indispensable stop on any Tainan temple tour is the **Temple of the Jade Emperor**, commonly known as the **Lord of Heaven Temple** (Tien King) (open dawn–sunset), one of the oldest and most authentic Taoist temples in Taiwan. Located near the corner of Mintsu, a highly-detailed façade of stone, carved in deep relief, graces the entrance to the central hall of this rather gaudy complex. Inside, the Jade Emperor is represented by an austere stone slab engraved with his name. This temple is one of the most ritually-active on the island, attracting a constant stream of worshippers.

Koxinga landed at **Luerhmen** (Deer Ear Gate), a shallow bay north of Tainan. The spot is consecrated by the elaborate **Matsu Temple** (open dawn–sunset). Matsu's shrine, within the main hall, is protected by enough writhing dragons to frighten away an army of devils. Her two fierce guardians, one red and one green, stand fully armed in classical martial-arts postures. Sitting before the large central icon of Matsu are a row of smaller, black camphor wood icons bedecked with finery. The one in the centre is said to be over 1,000 years old, brought to Taiwan from the Chinese mainland by Koxinga.

A few kilometres beyond the Matsu temple is what Tainan calls the largest

BELOW:
downtown Tainan.

temple structure in this part of Asia: the **Temple of the Holy Mother at Deer Ear Gate** (open dawn–sunset). The entire area is carved, etched, painted, cast and gilded in incredible detail. The altar table is a black-lacquered, gold-gilded fantasy of intricately-carved celestial animals, heaped with offerings to Matsu.

In **Anping**, a 20-minute taxi ride from downtown Tainan, are more reminders of Tainan's military past. **Fort Zeelandia** (open daily, 9am–5pm but currently closed for renovations; entrance fee) was built by the Dutch in 1623, then heavily reinforced between 1627 and 1634. Bricks were held in place with a mixture of sugar syrup, glutinous rice and crushed oyster shells. This ingenious mixture must have worked, for much of the original foundation is still intact. Two km (1 mile) to the south of the canal, stands **Yitsai Chincheng**, more often known as the **Eternal Fortress** (open daily, 9am–5pm), an old Chinese fort once used for Tainan's coastal defences. Silt and sand accumulations have left this edifice far from the shoreline it once guarded, as they have with Fort Zeelandia.

Map on page 130

Kaohsiung

Taiwan's economic showcase and a city of superlatives, **Kaohsiung** ❷④ is the island's largest international seaport, the major industrial centre, and the only city on the island besides Taipei with an international airport. The port is the world's third-largest container port after Hong Kong and Singapore, and it also has an extremely large dry-dock for ship repairs and maintenance.

With over a million inhabitants, the city is Taiwan's second largest, and the only one besides Taipei to enjoy the status of a special municipality – equal to a province, and administered by the central government. A city of humble origins, Kaohsiung has experienced meteoric economic growth, but the concentration of heavy industry has caused considerable pollution. Kaohsiung is trying to attract and develop high-technology industries in its central districts, moving smokestack factories out to suburban industrial zones. For the time being, however, the city is often shrouded with smog.

The city centre is dominated by modern tower blocks, including the **Grand 50 Tower**, whose 50 storeys make it one of the tallest buildings in Taiwan. Another overview of the city is atop **Shou Shan** (Longevity Mountain Park), which overlooks Kaohsiung harbour near the fishing wharves. But on most days, the views of the city itself are disappointing.

Temple-addicts can include three complexes on their rounds in Kaohsiung. The **Three Phoenix Palace** (open dawn–sunset), on Hopei Road, is the largest temple in the city, devoted to the demon suppressor, Li Na-cha. Stone lions stand sentry at the foot of the steps, which lead up to an elaborately-carved stone façade. The **Holy Hall of Martial and Literary Arts** (open dawn–sunset), a three-storey Taoist temple dedicated to the deity Kuan Kung and his literary counterpart, Confucius, is on Fu-Yeh Street. Not far away, on Yeh-Huang Street, is the **Shrine of the Three Mountain Kings** (open dawn–sunset). This 300-year-old Buddhist temple is dedicated to three brothers, private tutors to a man who saved the life of the Chinese emperor.

The main wall of the double-tiered shrine at Tainan's Temple of the Holy Mother is divided into six ornate niches, each of which enshrines the icons of major deities of Taiwan.

BELOW: steel works, Kaohsiung.

The stately Restoration Pagoda at Chengching Lake to the north of Kaohsiung.

BELOW: harbour view, Kaohsiung.

Scrapping and shopping

Kaohsiung has the world's largest breakers yard for old ships. Armies of labourers bearing acetylene torches, saws and wrenches break down about 200 steel-hulled, ocean-going ships each year. They harvest an enormous quantity of scrap steel, nautical devices, copper wire and other parts. Those lucky enough to be in Kaohsiung when a luxury liner is being scrapped can sometimes get bargains on lanterns, clocks and other nautical artefacts. The scrap wharf is located at **Little Harbour**, 10 km (6 miles) south of the downtown area.

As Taipei's leading industrial and export city, Kaohsiung is naturally a good place for shopping. Best buys are modern manufactured goods, clothing and other contemporary items, rather than arts and crafts. A good street for window-shopping and absorbing local colour is narrow **Hsinle Street**, which runs parallel to Wufu Road, between Love River and the harbour area.

Kaohsiung is also Taiwan's number-one fishing port, so it offers excellent fresh seafood. A fine culinary experience can be enjoyed on Chichin Island, which can either be reached by ferry from the Kushan terminal, or by car, arriving at the south end via the harbour tunnel. The island is 11 km (7 miles) long but only 200 metres (655 ft) wide. At the northern end, dozens of seafood restaurants stand cheek-by-jowl. Whether kept on ice or alive in tanks waiting for customers to make their choice, the sheer variety of seafood is unbelievable.

After Taipei, Kaohsiung has Taiwan's most active night life. The busy but pleasant **Liuho Night Market**, some blocks south from the railway station, offers plenty of food stalls and many bargains. **Fleet Street**, a one-block section of Chienhsin 3rd Road, between Wufu 4th and Kungyuan, caters to Kaohsiung's transient merchant seamen.

Into the hills

The centre of Buddhist scholarship in Taiwan is **Fokuang Shan** ㉕, at least an hour's drive northeast of Kaohsiung in lush rolling hills. Better known as Light of Buddha Mountain, the complex consists of several shrine halls surrounded by cool colonnades, pavilions and pagodas, bridges and footpaths, libraries and meditation halls, ponds and grottoes, and exquisite Buddhist statuary. Near the entrance, the tallest Buddha image on the island – 32 metres (105 ft) high – is surrounded by 480 life-sized images of disciples.

The major shrine hall is known as the **Precious Hall of Great Heroes**. The size of a large theatre, this hall has no artificial lighting. Sunlight enters through windows running the entire circumference of the hall, along the tops of the walls. Enshrined within are three 20-metre (66-ft) tall Buddha images, seated in meditation and displaying various *mudras* (hand gestures). Unfortunely, the monastery has been closed to visitors since June 1997, although worshippers may still visit. It is not known at present when or if it will be reopened to the general public.

Islands in the straits

As Taiwan's major port city, Kaohsiung is also the gateway to various offshore islands under the jurisdiction of the Taiwan government.

The islands of **Penghu** ㉖, the Pescadores or Isles of the Fishermen, are situated in the straits of Taiwan. The 16th-century Portuguese sailors who first put Taiwan on European maps – as Formosa – also gave these islands their name. This 64-island archipelago, covering only 130 sq. km (50 sq. miles), has a colourful history. Every army that has attacked Taiwan has used the Penghu

Map on page 130

BELOW: Buddhist statues, Fokuang Shan.

Map on page 130

Rickshaws are an excellent way of getting around.

BELOW: Kenting National Park.
RIGHT: the rocky southern coast.

as their springboard. During the Mongul Yuan dynasty, Chinese pirates used these islands as a base from which to sack ships plying coastal waters. Ming authorities finally suppressed the piracy and established a trading post here. Then, in rapid succession, the Dutch, Koxinga, the Manchu Qing, and the Japanese took control of the archipelago, en route to the main island of Taiwan.

Today, Penghu forms Taiwan's only island-county. Half of the archipelago's population of 150,000 live in **Makung**, the county town on the main island of Penghu. Fishing is the primary source of income; the only crops that grow on these flat, windswept islands are peanuts, sweet potatoes, and sorghum, used for making potent Kaoliang liquor. Makung has a number of attractions, including the old town wall and its gates, and several old temples.

East and south of Kaohsiung

Shortly after Fengshan, a large bridge crosses the Kaoping River. In the dry season, only a little running water is visible, but in typhoon season, the whole river bed is filled with raging waters. From the pleasant town of **Pingtung**, worth exploring with its farmer markets and temples, Highway 22 runs directly to **Santimen**, 50 km (32 miles) east of Kaohsiung.

The coastal crescent that occupies Taiwan's southern reaches is known as the **Hengchun Peninsula**. Two arms reach into the sea: Oluanpi (Goose Bell Beak) to the east, and Maopi Tou (Cat's Nose Cape), to the west. The broad bay between the two points has some of the island's best swimming beaches.

The roadside resort valley of **Kenting** ㉗ lies between Kenting Park and Kenting Beach. There are several hotels in the area. Close by is one of the three nuclear power stations owned and operated by the Taiwan Power Company.

In the low hills above the two-pronged peninsula sprawls **Kenting National Park**, a lovely haven for exotic flora and strange formations of coral rock. Offshore, the merging of waters of the Pacific Ocean, Taiwan Strait, South China Sea and Bashi Channel create a tapestry of green and blue swirls. The park was established in 1906 by the Japanese, who combed the earth to find exotic species of plants that could thrive in this climate. The Chinese have continued to expand the collection: currently there are over 1,200 species here, mostly identified in Latin as well as Chinese.

Scenic points include the 100-metre (330-ft) tunnel through contorted rock called the Fairy Cave, and the deep gorge, opened by an earthquake, known as One Line Sky. In the **Valley of Hanging Banyan Roots**, visitors enter a preternatural world where thick banyan roots stretch 20 metres (60 ft) through cliffs of stone to reach the earth, their green canopies whistling in the wind high above. From First Gorge, trekkers can enter the dense groves of the **Tropical Tree Preservation Area**. It takes a little over an hour to walk through a wild jungle of ancient trees, dark ravines, coral-rock formations and shrieking birds.

On the ocean side of town, **Kenting Beach** is a stretch of beautiful, unspoiled white sand that stretches 200 metres (650 ft). The clear azure water is warm and gentle, perfect for swimming from mid-April to the end of October.

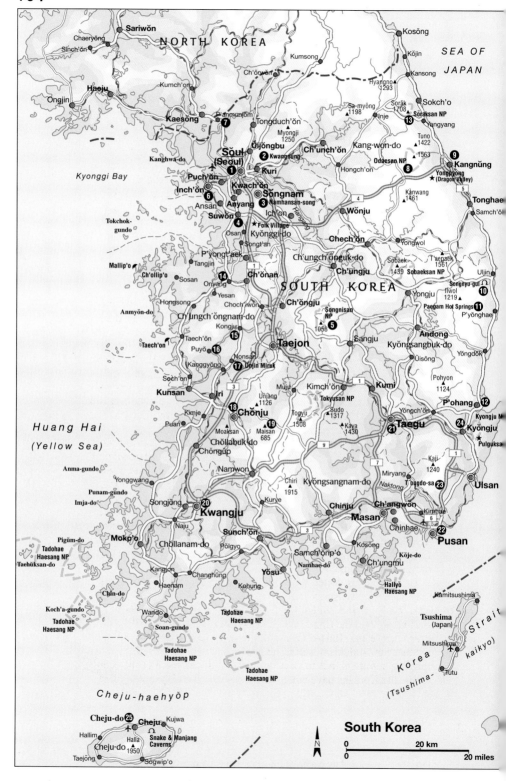

South Korea

0   20 km
0   20 miles

KOREA

*Little-known Korea offers 5,000 years of art and
culture, historic sights and spectacular scenery*

Part of the beauty of Korea is provided by its history. Squeezed as it is between its larger neighbours – Japan, China and Russia – Korea has survived invasions, wars and colonial rule, while remaining fiercely distinct. No small accomplishment.

Until 1945, Japanese colonial overlords had worked aggressively for half a century to eliminate Korean culture, including the Korean language and family names, replacing them with Japanese. Tens of thousands of Koreans were shipped to Japan as slave labour; many of their descendants remain in Japan, more Japanese than Korean now, but without the rights of citizenship. Korea's success as an economic powerhouse following World War II, and the Korean War is as astounding as Japan's own postwar progress.

Yet, like Japan, Korea shares a common cultural heritage with the ancient Chinese kingdom. Indeed, all three nations are closer than they like to admit.

In modern times, the peninsula was first known as the Hermit Kingdom because of its 19th-century policy of retreating from foreign influence. It was not until the 1988 Olympic Games, in Seoul, that Korea burst onto the international scene as a world player. In two short weeks, millions of viewers around the world saw Korea as it is – a modern, vibrant nation, with a long and rich cultural heritage, coming of age as an economic and political power.

Today, part of Korea's attraction is its pulsating modernity. In Seoul, the country's capital for 600 years, skyscrapers reach towards the heavens and traffic jams stall the human race below. Neons light the city at night and workers pile into vehicles early in the morning. Yet in the neighbourhoods of Seoul and throughout the countryside, women still hang out peppers to announce the birth of a baby boy, children bow to their grandparents, fortune-tellers warn of future trouble and offer portents of luck, Buddhist monks wander the streets for alms, and families take to the mountains to worship the natural beauty of their land.

The country is dotted with Buddhist temples and contains some great Buddhist treasures. It also has a rich Confucian legacy from its Yi dynasty period, when it was said that the Koreans were more Confucian than the Chinese. Perhaps they still are, suggest the Chinese themselves. Raised on the strictures of Confucianism and the tolerance of Buddhism, and fashioned by a land of bitter winters and roasting summers, not to mention outside intrusions over the centuries, the Koreans have emerged a proud and strong people. ❑

PRECEDING PAGES: solitary pathfinder; tomb mounds at Kyongju's Tumuli Park.

Decisive Dates

PREHISTORIC PERIOD

circa 30,000 BC Evidence of early settlement is provided by Paleolithic sites discovered in the 1960s.
circa 4270 BC The oldest evidence of a Neolithic society is assigned to this date.

THE OLD CHOSON PERIOD

circa 2333 BC The mythical founder of the nation, Tan'gun, is said to have begun his reign.
1122 BC The establishment of Kija Choson.
circa 800–700 BC The rise of the Chin state.

THE THREE KINGDOMS PERIOD

57 BC The foundation of the state of Saro (later renamed Shilla).
37 BC The state of Koguryo in Manchuria emerges.
13 BC The Paekche tribe arises in central Korea.
AD 382 In Koguryo, Buddhism is officially adopted and a school is established for Confucian studies.
400–500 Shilla is transformed from a tribal league to a kingdom. Another tribal federation, the Kaya league, occupies the southern coast.
598, 612 China, then under the Sui dynasty, launches unsuccessful attacks against Koguryo.
645-660 T'ang forces invade Koguryo.
668 The destruction of Koguryo by the combined forces of Shilla and China occurs.

BUDDHIST TEXTS AND TEMPLES

750 Buddhist texts are printed.
751 Shilla is at the height of its glory, and the Building of Sokkuram and Korea's most famous temple, Pulguk-sa, begins.

KORYO KINGDOM

918 The Kung'ye is overthrown and the Kingdom of Koryo is founded by Wang Kon.
958 A competitive civil examination system is created, filling the highest offices with members of the ruling class most highly schooled in Chinese literature and Confucian Classics.
993, 1010, 1018 Invasions of the Khitans.
1104 Invasion of the Jurchens.
1231 Mongols overrun most of northern Korean and force the government to surrender.
1259 A truce is struck with the Mongols and a decade of comparative peace begins.
1269 Military official Kim Chun falls victim to an internal power struggle and is ousted by another military figure, Im Yon.
1279 The Mongols adopt the dynastic name Yuan and proceed to take over the rest of China.

YI DYNASTY

1392 Yi Song-gye ousts the king and takes the throne, becoming the founder of his own dynasty.
1401 T'aejong, the third king of the dynasty, comes to power after killing his youngest brother, the heir apparent, in 1398.
1592 Invasion by the Japanese in April; in July Yi Sun-sin uses "turtle ships" to foil the invasion by choking off the flow of supplies and troop reinforcements.
1597 Japanese renew the war and invade again.
1627 First Manchu invasion.
1724–76 reign of Yongo: the Yi dynasty recovers some of its earlier vitality.

WESTERNERS ARRIVE

1790s Catholicism is introduced.
1811, 1862 Rebellions occur after decades of social unrest and popular agitation.
1839 A new wave of persecution causes the deaths of 130 Christians.
1860 The Tonghak ("Eastern learning") movement is founded, beginning as a religious society.
1866 Nine French Catholic priests and some 8,000 Korean converts are executed.
1871 Americans occupy Kanghwa island where 350 Koreans and three Americans are killed before the mission is abandoned.

1876 The rise of Japanese influence spurs the Chinese to redouble efforts to preserve their traditional influence, leading to a series of confrontations. **1894** The Tonghak uprising begins followed by the outbreak of the Sino–Japanese War.

RUSSO-JAPANESE WAR

1895 Russia helps weaken the Japanese position. Queen Min, said to be the real power behind the throne, is murdered.
1902 Alliance between Japan and Great Britain begins to turn the situation in Japan's favour.

JAPANESE CONTROL

1905 Japan's control of Korea is recognised, ending the war.
1910 Japanese control the administration of justice and have complete police power, but Korean resistance is unflagging.
1919 Independence Movement of 1 March.
1937 Colonial policy turns toward a complete "Japanisation of Korea".
1939–42 Hundreds of thousands of Korean labourers are conscripted to fill the positions of workers in the Japanese army.

INDEPENDENCE AND THE KOREAN WAR

1945 Despite bitter opposition from the Koreans, the Allied foreign ministers agree to go ahead with an international trusteeship, which is to direct Korean affairs through a provisional government, staffed by Koreans, for at least five years.
1946 Communists begin to dominate politics under the leadership of Russian-chosen, Kim Il-sung.
1948 The Republic of Korea is recognised by the UN and Syngman Rhee is sworn in as the first president. The separate government created in the South is reduced to an advisory group. The Russians supply arms and assistance to create a formidable North Korean army. The stage is set for civil war.
1950: On 25 June, North Korean troops pour across the 38th parallel. US forces are ordered into battle by President Truman.
1951 Truce negotiations begin, dragging on for two years.
1953 An armistice agreement is reached, but not before Korea has been reduced to ruins.

LEFT: an early portrait of the 8th-century Sokkuram Buddha at Kyongju.
RIGHT: Korean Prince Yi Eun was commissioned as "Captain Prince Ri" by conquering the Japanese.

MODERN HISTORY

1960 Yun Po-Son wins the election, marking the beginning of the Second Republic. The Chang government, incapable of maintaining power, falls in 1961.
1961 Military government is formed under Major General Park Chung-hee, who retains control for 18 years until his assassination in 1979.
1980 Major General Chun Doo-Hwan becomes president. After his seven-year term, Chun permits free elections.
1987 Roh Tae-woo becomes the first democratically elected president. Roh's ruling party merges with the forces of opposition Kim Young-sam ("YS").

1988 South Korea hosts the Olympic Games.
1993 YS takes office as the first civilian president in over 30 years and brings a new atmosphere and promise of democratic reform. He changes the name of his ruling party to the New Korea Party (NKP).
1996 Ex-presidents Roh and Cun go on trial for corruption in addition to sedition and treason for their roles in the 1979 coup and 1980 massacre of civilians in Kwangju. Relations between North and South Korea are at a standstill, although the North's deepening food shortage, and the international effort to stop its nuclear programme, present opportunities for renewed relations between North and South. ❑

THE KOREANS

*Despite a superficial overlay of Western dress and manners, Korean people are
underneath a more complex blend of old ways of thinking and modern sensibility*

To understand today's Koreans and their intriguing, paradoxical country – to survive potentially terminal culture shock, and learn to get along smoothly in this fascinating nation – it is necessary to give some consideration to the questions of who the Koreans are, how they became that way, and why they act the way they do.

Three primary qualities have enabled Koreans to survive, and have become their most strongly ingrained attributes: patience, flexibility, and stubbornness. To these qualities might be added a robust, satirical and sometimes uncouth sense of humour.

Korean patience does not mean passivity, nor does flexibility imply a lack of individuality. The third trait, stubbornness – sometimes dignified by being called perseverance – explains and modifies the other two.

It would be easy but misleading to make a neat generalisation here and say that these three basic Korean qualities are derived from the three major outside influences, and to speak of Chinese patience, Japanese adaptability, and American tenacity. But it goes deeper than that: these counterpointed national themes were here before the outside influences, it seems, and were to be developed and orchestrated by subsequent influences and events. Buddhism encouraged the cultivation of patience. Likewise, the Confucian system became in practice a pragmatic philosophy, presupposing adaptability in pursuit of advantage. And Taoism suggests stubbornness in its metaphor of water as the strongest of elements, since it gradually wears away even the hardest stones.

Koreans still find it difficult to speak of the Japanese annexation with any degree of equanimity and they shudder at the suggestion that they resemble their island neighbours. The Japanese did influence Korea in many ways – they introduced social structure, political organisation, education and administration into

an existing vacuum – but the price was so severe that even today Japanese songs and movies are still banned in Korea.

During the occupation, when Christian missionaries from America, Britain, Canada and Australia offered an alternative, many Koreans quickly took up the calling. The Japanese

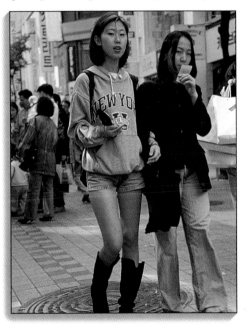

recognised the Christians as leading subversives, but did not directly seek to dismantle the churches until World War II because of their links with foreign powers.

Although there was far wider acceptance of Japanese rule than modern Koreans wish to remember or admit, for the majority the dream of independence never died. Korean anger against foreign powers and frustration over her own weakness underlie the painful memory of both the colonial period and the subsequent division of the peninsula into the northern and southern halves.

In some ways, this sorrow rocks the stability of the southern half of the peninsula – students

---

LEFT: *harboji* (grandfather) with black horse-hair hat.
RIGHT: Seoul mates.

inevitably blame the current government for maintaining the status quo – but it also serves to strengthen the society. Koreans hold onto one another like parents to their children to fend off foreign influence and maintain their traditions. National pride and resilience results, a force far stronger than armies.

Manner over matter

Despite the economic urgency of importing modern science and technology, Koreans still show more concern with manner than matter. As the essayist Lee O-young writes: "In Korea, they say there is no logic... instead there is emo-

Despite the differences, most Occidental visitors receive a favourable impression of Koreans as a warm, friendly, sympathetic and cheerful people, the proverbial salt of the earth – an impression that usually remains, even after the strange experiences some will encounter in the clash of cultural values. The abrasiveness of such a clash is not felt, because the foreigner is considered in the same category as the classless people, or *sangnom*: "unpersons" and outcasts who are not expected to know how to behave in a proper Korean manner, and upon whom it would be pointless to waste anger.

From the vantage point of the foreign *sang-*

tion, intuitional insight and a soulful spirit."

Korean etiquette consists of an elaborate system of formalised gestures designed to produce pleasant feelings and smooth relations. This is done by ensuring maintenance of proper *kibun* (mood or aura) through adroit employment of *nunchi'i* (intuitively assessing another's feelings through observation), and behaving with suitable *mot* (style or taste).

Somewhere along the line, amid the maze of honorifics and the anxiety to determine whether one must talk up, down, or straight-from-the-shoulder to a given individual, any idea of truth, fairness, or brass-tacks agreement becomes distinctly secondary.

nom, a Korean can be seen in his best light – without all the hang-ups he has to deal with among his compatriots – as a courteous, considerate, and tenaciously loyal friend. Korean men tend to be gregarious, fun-loving, hearty, even bibulous, yet remain devoted husbands and fathers, hard workers and solid citizens. They are very likely to be highly cultured – taxi drivers often know Beethoven symphonies, schoolboys gather tasteful wildflower bouquets – with great respect for learning and refinement. They are fiercely nationalistic, not shallowly patriotic, and may exhibit a touching reverence for the natural beauties of their mountainous, storm-tormented land.

But visitors may sometimes glimpse the other side of the coin: an intoxicated Korean often becomes angry or tearful, not euphoric. Korean songs are sad and their poems piercingly nostalgic. This is why they try so hard to be happy, to seize the fleeting moment before it has passed.

Koreans have been called the Irish of the Orient, yet the burden of their history has been even longer and heavier than that of the Irish. This human family may be indissolubly united, but each link in the chain represents a unique

OLD MAIDS?

Stories abound of women suddenly getting married within a few weeks before turning 28, the bewitching age for Korean women.

Passage of life

Marriage used to occur only after the ministrations of a matchmaker who blended astrology with canny psychology and sociology. Nowadays, the dating game is played among the young, with rather stricter rules perhaps than in the West. Traditionally, marriage occurred at quite a young age. A girl's family sent her bedding and trousseau chest to the boy's home, and the boy's family reciprocated with gifts. On the nuptial day, the bride was carried in a palan-

idiosyncratic national entity, with its own customs created or adapted to a set of special circumstances.

In Korea, the hallmark of nationality has for many centuries been symbolised most clearly by family ritual. Indeed, the ancient Chinese used to refer to their Korean neighbours as the ceremonious people of the east – which was an admission that the Koreans had outdone the Sage's own people in adherence to Confucian formalities.

LEFT: traditional Confucian dancers at Sungkyunkwan shrine.
ABOVE: children at Mt Chiri.

quin – a shoulder-borne litter – to the groom's house and the couple – often meeting for the first time – shared a cup of rice wine to pledge their troth. This ritual is now seen only in staged form at folk village shows, for the custom of the *yesik-chang* (wedding hall) pervades town and country.

These marriage factories, often huge buildings with dozens of weddings going on simultaneously in various-sized chambers, provide everything from flowers to Western-style music. Crowds of friend and relatives gather in pew-like seats, with no compulsion to retain order or quiet; children frequently scamper and shout in the aisles. The only remaining trace of the old days is the family-only room at the back, where time-honoured bows are performed and wine shared. The public part of the ceremony is the bridal procession, a short homily by a family member and the indispensable group photographs. Guests arrive bearing gifts of cash in customary white envelopes.

After marriage the birth cycle was expected to begin and keep the family busy with rituals. No further scheduled event was indicated until the 60th birth-

RICE WINE RITUALS

In Korea, rice wine punctuates both weddings and funerals – young couples share a cup of it to seal their vows, and upon death, a vessel of the liquid is ritually poured over the grave.

ritual wailing by servants, shirt-tail relations, or paid mourners goes on, while the family provides a convivial party resembling an Irish wake. On the third day, a procession accompanies the coffin on a bier borne by labourers, fuelled by frequent stops for rice wine, to the grave site, preceded by the wooden tablet (or pennant) lettered in Chinese with the name of the deceased, which will later be enshrined in the house.

Though such old-fashioned funerals may still be encouraged in the countryside, they are obviously impractical in big cities, where the poor have no choice but cremation. Though the funeral completes the life cycle, it does not end the cyclical pattern of Korean family ritual, for twice a year – on the *ch'usok* autumn harvest holiday and in spring on *hansik* (or cold food) day – family members gather at the grave and set up tables covered with fruits and rice cakes that are eaten later.

Taming the world

Although modern-day Koreans continue to practise the ceremonies of the past in order to show respect to their ancestors, they are no longer quite so superstitious. The ceremonies often provide a welcome excuse to reminisce about the forbears they can call to mind, and to enjoy a few hours with their extended family. Many young people are now leaving the parental home after getting married, so the traditional days of gathering together are becoming less frequent.

The streets of Seoul in this day and age look much like the streets of any large international city where people wear business clothes and walk at a clip. Upon first meeting a Korean, there seems to be little mystery to his character and little contrast to the prevalent Western style. It is only after one gets to know the people better that their culture begins to show through in details of behaviour and thought, and they no longer appear unapproachable. Koreans are out to tame the world and they have managed to adapt to the modern age without letting go of their heritage. ❏

day, or *hwan'gap,* one of the most important events in any Korean's life. The 60th birthday is celebrated with all possible pomp and ceremony. The guest of honour sits virtually enthroned on cushions, receiving the kowtows of children and grandchildren. Behind this cushioned throne are low tables piled high with fruit, rice cakes, cookies, candies and other goodies set out among brass candelabra.

After the ceremony comes a feast with drinking, music, and dancing for all, including the birthday celebrant, testing the endurance of the guests to see who will be the last one to give in.

Traditional funeral customs called for the coffined body to be placed in the house, where

LEFT: testing out mobile phone services in Seoul.
RIGHT: honouring Confucius at a special ceremony.

RELIGION

Korea's religious identity is not easily pigeon-holed: Shamanism, Buddhism and Confucianism are all distinctly prevalent elements of Korean society

Most East Asian countries adhere to a spiritual mainstream, but Korea denies a simple religious label. Strong traditions of shamanism, Confucianism, Taoism, Buddhism and various forms of Christianity infuse society, and though many Koreans subscribe exclusively to one religion, they also

allow other spiritual beliefs to play an occasional role in their lives.

Shamanism

If one could peer into the souls of Korean people, one would find fascinating elements of shamanism, the folk worship of a pantheon of household, village, and animate and inanimate forces in nature. Koreans maintain ancient traditions such as the *kut*, or exorcising ceremonies. These practices have not been fully institutionalised into a religion, but shamanism has been kept very much alive – as in the deification of Sanshin, a non-Buddhist mountain god, who has found his way into special shrines

in the courtyards of Buddhist temple complexes. Shamanist elements have also worked their way into Confucian ceremonies dedicated to Sajik ("Gods of Land and Harvest").

The visitor to Korea will notice carved and painted shamanist posts depicting an ancient general "of the heavens" and his female general "under the earth". These posts are placed outside villages to repel evil spirits.

Taoism

Taoism has been practised in Korea for more than 1,300 years, but active examples of its presence are rare these days. Though Taoist texts were often studied in the past, and though some of Korea's Buddhist temples temporarily served as Taoist temples, few remnants of early Taoist art survive today. Taoism was at its height in Korea during the Unified Shilla dynasty (AD 668–918). Practitioners aren't so dedicated today, but Taoism is experiencing something of a renaissance as a number of modern schools draw upon its teachings.

Buddhism

When it comes to the arts and innovative thought, Buddhism stands out as one of the most important of this country's cultural fountainheads. This religion stresses finding a practical and moderate way towards self-actualisation while on earth. The Mahayana school, with its acceptance of local deities as a means of drawing the masses to temples for an eventual study of more orthodox doctrines and practices, proved to the liking of the Koreans.

Buddhism is Korea's largest single religion. One may find Buddhist influences in modern-day Korea subtle but pervasive. In the thought patterns of Koreans, for example, the principle of *karma* allows many to take a passive view of the world. When the negative effects of some past action catch up with them, they may reason that the problem is out of their control. Another element of the Korean Buddhist psyche is the phrase "Creation, Staying, Destruction and Nothing". This basic concept of reincarnation, with an accompanying perspective of a cyclical nature of history, gives Koreans an introspective view of the universe.

Confucianism

Confucianism has become a way of life in Korea. Confucius was never a breaker of traditions but a conservative reactionary who rallied for a return to China's Golden Era, the early days of the Chou dynasty (1112 BC–256 BC). Today, Confucianism thrives more in Korea than in any other nation, and though it has been greatly discredited since the turn of the century by both foreign and domestic intel-

Christianity

First-time visitors to Korea are often surprised at the many church steeples and crosses that punctuate skylines. Yet over 9 million people – by government reckoning almost half of all those who follow a particular religion – are avowed Christians. Korean scholars first came into contact with Christian emissaries in Beijing in the 18th century. Originally the religion was regarded as little more than a curiosity but gradually its influence spread and by the start of the 19th century there were about 4,000 Christians in Korea, many of whom were persecuted by the Confucian establishment. Despite this, mis-

lectual movements, its basic values and premises still effectively dominate the lives of all Koreans.

Ancestor worship continues to be practised much as it has been for more than 1,000 years. In Korea, even an "old fool" is first and foremost an elder. To rebel against the word of an elder is to invite social censure – a conservative and powerful force which is very effective in Korea's small and closed society.

LEFT: young novice monks receive money during the annual festival to mark the Buddha's birthday.
ABOVE: modern Chin-do *mudang* burns an offering to a restless and ancient Shaman spirit.

sionary zeal further strengthened the new religion and by the early 20th century missionaries, both Protestant and Catholic, were playing an important part in the independence movement. Today, Christianity has a disproportionate role in government and opposition power circles.

Other religions

About 500,000 Koreans belong to a wide variety of "minor" religions. The best-known internationally is the Unification Church, a movement started by Moon Sun-myung, a North Korean refugee, in 1954. Moon's church has a wide following overseas, where they are known as the Moonies. ❑

KOREAN ART

Deeply intertwined with Buddhism and flecked with Taoism and shamanism, Korea's pottery, sculpture and painting radiate an energetic, organic feel

For insights into a nation's character, look at its art, particularly its architecture. China's traditional architecture is vertical in feeling, its roofs reflecting a nation out to conquer or control nature. Korean roofs form soft curves which float ever so gently heavenwards, flowing with nature's rhythms. And Korean ceramics appear less perfected, warmer and more approachable, so that the viewer touches the potter's hand in spirit.

Pottery and ceramics

The Korean potter created beautiful elongated curves which soar with controlled energy. These unknown craftsmen decorated their porcelains with a pale, gray-green celadon glaze which sometimes became "kingfisher," a bluish green considered a "secret colour." More than 60 shades can be distinguished by the attuned eye, but the most highly admired are "sky blue after rain," and "sea water washed by rain and wind."

White porcelains were developed for upperclass use. Upon large jars, artisans painted sparsely, creating simple designs with iron-impregnated copper or malachite containing copper oxide or cobalt, "Mohammedan blue." Unlike Ming dynasty blue-and-white ware potters, the Korean craftsman never went to the same excess of treating his pot's surface as though it were an easel for painting. Rather, he limited his decorations to hints of nature – such as a single, blossoming spray, a pair of fish, a dragon, or curving leaves with grapes. The underglaze painting with iron is casual rather than pretentious and so suggests and earthy Korean spirit.

Sculpture

When Buddhism swept out of India and over central and eastern Asia, the artists of each of a dozen countries responded by creating cave sculptures, free-standing images of Buddhas, and temples. They represented the human body thinly disguised as a deity with certain sacred marks, such as long ear lobes, a depression between the eyes and a pronounced "protuberance of wisdom" on top of the head.

Korea's earliest bronze statuettes of Buddha appear relatively flat and linear, also inspired by the calligraphic line; soon its natural genius in metallurgy and its skilled stone chiselers initiated their own directions.

Korea excels in granite sculptural work. The Korean peninsula is dotted with Buddhist figures carved in rocks in the mountains.

Koryo paintings

Almost as remarkable as uncovering the rich treasures of golden crowns from Korea's 5th and 6th century and rediscovering its 12th- and 13th-century pale green celadon wares, has been the unveiling (in the late 1970s) of 93

LEFT: *Kwanseum-posal with Willow Branch,* by the 14th-century Koryo artist Sogubang.
RIGHT: names painted with birds and animals are an old art form.

Koryo-period paintings – Buddhist icons of unsurpassed beauty. It was thought that such art had vanished. Tucked away in various temples and shrines, these rarely-seen paintings reflect Northern Sung works, strongly influenced by Buddhism. The Korean artists refined and enriched the paintings' characteristic lines of gold, and the brilliant scarlet, malachite green and sapphire blue of the painted robes.

An entirely different approach to art is revealed in Yi dynasty folk paintings. Charmingly naive and unpretentious, they reflect the actual life, customs and beliefs of the Korean people. These works are only to be seen in spe-

cialist museums, such as the Emille Museum at Songni-san, as the national museums are administered by a Confucian-type bureaucracy.

Korean folk art – with its blue dragons, white tigers and magical fungi – is based on symbolism which developed and evolved over a long period of time and was understood by all the people. Even today, a basic understanding of this complex system is essential to appreciate this lively art.

Symbols

In the mists of China's remote antiquity, symbolic directions arose as part of a cosmology derived either from Taoism or an even more ancient shamanistic system of concepts. Among the most important were the correlatives of heaven and earth, yang and yin, male and female, along with five directions (north, south, east, west and centre), five colours (black, red, white, blue and yellow), and five material elements (water, fire, metal, wood and earth).

During the peak of Buddhist influence, cosmological symbolism played a minor role in Korean art. The lotus, the official religious flower, and other such Buddhist symbols dominated art. However, following the suppression of Buddhism in 1392, Taoism, Buddhism and shamanism had become homogenised so that they were hardly separable in popular thought. For example, it is very difficult to determine the exact origin of the12 zodiacal images used in Korean art.

The major symbols used and their meanings are as follows:

Four Sacred Animals of Good Luck: Turtle, dragon, unicorn, and phoenix.

Ten Symbols of Longevity: deer, crane, turtle, rocks, clouds, sun, water, bamboo, pine and the fungus of immortality (*pullocho*).

Auspicious Ideograms: *bok* (good fortune), *su* (longevity), *yong* (peace) and *kang* (health).

Fertility Symbols: pomegranate, jumping carp, 100 babies and "Buddha's hand citron".

Special Guardians: tiger (front gate or front door), dragon (gate or roof), *haet'ae* (fire or kitchen), rooster (front door) and dog (storage door).

Three Friends of Winter: pine, plum and bamboo.

Four Noble Gentlemen: orchid, chrysanthemum, bamboo and plum.

Individual Symbolic Associations: peach (longevity), pomegranate (wealth), orchid (scholar, cultural refinement), lotus (Buddhist truth, purity), bat (happiness), butterfly (love, romance), bamboo (durability), peony (noble gentleman, wealth) and plum (wisdom of age, hardiness or independence, beauty, loftiness).

The list could go on and on. A formal list was never compiled in writing; it was simply a part of Korean tradition, familiar to everyone from the itinerant painter to a member of the court's Bureau of Painting. ❏

LEFT: Yi dynasty painting of a *kisaeng* house.
RIGHT: colourful, powerful presence in Pulguk-sa Temple, Kyongju.

CUISINE

Spicy. Fiery. Earthy. Cool. Korean food is diverse and provocative. Its bold and subtle taste, textures and aromas are sure to elicit a response

Most foreigners associate pungent garlic and hot chili pepper with Korean cuisine. It is true that garlic-eating has been heartily appreciated by Koreans since the race's first breath, but it is not widely known – even in Korea – that the chili pepper did not even exist in this country until the 16th century

important annual social events is *kimjang,* or autumn *kimch'i* making. At *kimjang* time, women gather in groups throughout the country to cut, wash, and salt veritable hills of cabbage and white radish. The prepared *kimch'i* is stored in large thick earthenware crocks and then buried in the backyard to keep it from ferment-

when it was introduced by Portuguese traders.

However these two ingredients may have reached Korean plates and palates, they are now used in many dishes – most liberally and notoriously in *kimch'i*. For the newcomer, learning to eat this dish is the first step to becoming a connoisseur of Korean food.

Kimch'i culture

Kimch'i is *the* dish that has made Korean food famous. Next to rice (*pap*), it is the most important component in any Korean meal. It is not known when or how *kimch'i* originated, but like curry in India it's in Korea to stay. So institutionalised is it that one of Korea's most

ing during the winter months. Throughout the dark and cold winter, these red-peppered, garlicked and pickled vegetables are a good source of much-needed vitamin C.

During other seasons, a variety of vegetables such as chives, pumpkin and aubergine are used to make more exotic types of *kimch'i*. The summer heat makes it necessary to prepare a fresh batch almost daily, often in a cool, light brine. Raw seafood, such as fish, crab and oysters are "*kimch'i*-ed" too.

Exotic herbs

Not all Korean food ingredients are quite so bold tasting as the garlic and chili pepper. In actuality, the earliest dishes consisted of under-stated ingredients. To Koreans, almost every plant and animal in the diet has a herbal or medicinal quality and certain dishes are purposely eaten to warm or cool the head and body. Wild aster, royal fern bracken, marsh plant, day lily, aralia shoots and broad bell-flowers are just a few of the many wild and exotic plants included in the typical Korean's diet. Others, such as mugwort, shepherd's purse, and sowthistle, are also sea-sonally picked and eaten.

KIMCH'I POWER

In Korea, a woman's culinary prowess is often determined first and foremost by how good her *kimch'i* tastes.

be found at any proper meal. Especially popu-lar is *twoenjang-guk*, a fermented soybean paste soup with short-necked clams stirred into its broth. Also popular are a light broth made from dried anchovies, and vegetable soups based on dried spinach, sliced radish or dried seaweed (*miyok-guk*). The latter is said to be beneficial to nursing mothers.

A seafood dish of some kind is usually included with various "side dishes" which are called *panch'an*. This may be a dried, salted and charbroiled fish or a hearty and spicy hot

LEFT: enticing food display at a *hwan'gap*, or 60th-birthday feast.
ABOVE: street food in Seoul.

More common table vegetables – such as black sesame leaves, spinach, lettuce and mung and soy beans – are typically grown in the backyard, but others are found only in the wild. All are collectively called *namul* when they are individually parboiled, then lightly seasoned with sesame oil, garlic, soy sauce, and ground and toasted sesame seeds.

Another vital part of the Korean meal is soup (*guk*), which is said to be one of the country's earliest culinary techniques. Soup will always

seafood soup called *mae-un-t'ang*. A delicious *mae-un-t'ang* usually includes firm white fish, vegetables, soybean curd (*tubu*), red pepper powder, and an optional poached egg.

Bulgogi and kalbi

Probably the most popular Korean entré ordered or automatically served to Westerners is *bulgogi* (barbecued beef). Most beef-eaters – whether Texans or Koreans – are unanimous in their appreciation of this dish: strips of red beef marinated and grilled over a charcoal brazier. Another popular meat dish is tender and mar-bled *kalbi* short ribs which are marinated and barbecued in the same way as *bulgogi*.

To Koreans, however, rice – not meat – is considered to be the main dish of the meal. In fact, one of the most common street greetings, *"Pam mogoss-o-yo?"* literally means "Have you eaten rice?"

When Koreans sit down to a traditional meal, they do so on a clean lacquered paper floor. The meal is served to them on a low table. Usually the food arrives in a collection of small metal bowls which are neatly arranged. The utensils used are chopsticks and a flat soup spoon.

Westerners may be surprised to find that Koreans will often eat a bowl of rice and maybe have an extra helping even though tastier side

dishes remain unfinished. Don't let this preference for rice bother you, and don't think that you have to emulate it.

A dish of sliced and chilled fruit is usually served as a dessert. Depending on the season, musk-melon, strawberries, apples, pears and watermelon are among the fresh and sweet selections. At major celebrations, steamed rice cakes *(tok)* are presented as tasty ritual food.

Korean libations

Deep within a cave beneath a hill in northern Seoul, four men sit around a low round table, drinking small bowls of a milky white liquor they pour from a battered aluminium teapot.

Welcome to *kul-jip* (cave-house) one of Seoul's most unusual drinking spots. A bomb shelter during the Korean War three decades ago, today it is operated as a wine-house by several aging ladies. The quality of the potent rice *makkolli* is excellent, so *kul-jip* never lacks customers.

There are only a few other bomb-shelter wine houses in Seoul but there are many other places to drink – probably more per capita than in most other countries. Within a few minutes' walk of *kul-jip* you will find a beer hall selling both draft and bottled beer, a market wine shop which serves several alcoholic beverages, and a roadside drinking cart where passers-by can duck in for a quick snort on their way home from work.

Drinking is an important part of Korean culture. There are few proscriptions against alcohol here and many social reasons for imbibing, so most Korean men – and a growing number of women – drink.

History doesn't reveal when Koreans first discovered fermentation, but drinking was an important part of the culture even in the early dynasties. During the Shilla dynasty, the king and his court relaxed at *P'o-Sok-jong* drinking bower outside Kyongju. Here a spring bubbled up into an abalone-shaped stone channel. The drinkers set their cups afloat in the channel and competed to compose poems before the cups drifted all the way round.

Later Korean dynasties continued drinking. Probably the most popular surroundings were in what is today known as the *kisaeng* party. *Kisaeng* were female entertainers who played musical instruments, sang, danced, composed poetry and practised calligraphy to amuse the male aristocracy at palace parties. They also poured drinks, served the men food, and flirted. According to tradition, high-class *kisaeng* took lovers but they weren't promiscuous. At one point in the Yi dynasty, there were more than 20,000 *kisaeng*.

Today, very few *kisaeng* can play classical instruments, compose poetry or write with a brush. Instead, most *kisaeng* parties include a band with drums and an electric guitar, and the women and their guests dance together around the tables after they have eaten. The majority of the patrons are Korean businessmen – who are more than willing to pay large sums of money to entertain customers – and, increasingly these days, Japanese tourists.

The etiquette of drinking is important: a drinker will often give his cup to another, conveying it politely with both hands, in a gesture of respect and friendship. His companion then receives the cup with both hands and holds it while it is filled to the brim. He may then drink. After emptying the cup, he again uses both hands to return it to the owner. Then, grasping the vessel with both hands, he refills the cup for the owner, to return the favour.

holds ferment at home. It is reputed to be highly nutritious, and farmers found that a few cups during the long working day helped to stave off hunger. *Makkolli* was inexpensive in the cities as well, making it the working man's drink. For many people, until the early 1970s, going drinking usually meant going to a *makkolli-jip*, an establishment that served *makkolli*.

The *makkolli-jip* vary in style and quality, but they are generally comfortable and unpre-

In a group, several drinkers in succession may offer their cups to a single person, leaving an array of brimming vessels before him. A person who has given up his cup cannot drink until the recipient returns it or someone else gives him his. So whoever has received a cup has an obligation to empty it and pass it on without inordinate delay.

The working man's brew

A popular Korean brew is *makkolli*, a milky liquor made from rice that most rural house-

LEFT: local beers and spirits.
ABOVE: a Korean business lunch.

tentious places where nobody can put on airs, and it is easy to feel relaxed.

The two most important factors about any *makkolli-jip* are the quality of the *makkolli*, and the kinds of side dishes, *anju*, that it serves, since all drinking in Korea involves eating. The things that go best with *makkolli* range from fresh oysters, peppery octopus, dried fish, squid or cuttlefish, to soybean curd, soups, bean pancakes, scallion pancakes and omelettes.

The other popular drink is *soju*, a cheap distilled liquor of around 25 per cent alcoholic content, with a taste somewhere between gin and kerosene. Its price and the high alcoholic content make it Korea's cheapest drink. ❑

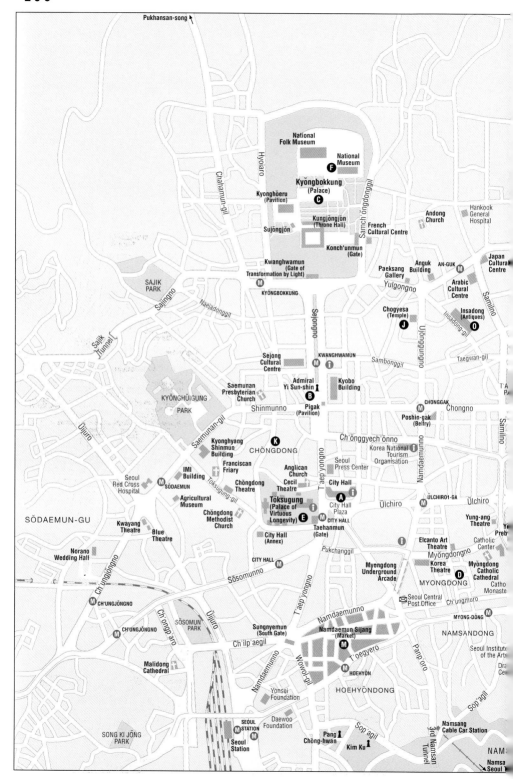

Seoul

0 ——— 200 m
0 ——— 200 yds

N

Songgyun'gwan University ❶

SÕNGBUK-GU

PIWON
(SECRET GARDEN) **H**

HYEHWA Ⓜ

Hansung University

Botanical Garden

National Science Museum

Seoul National University Dental College

MARRONIER PARK

Ch'anggyŏnggungno

Taehangno

...ngdŏkkung
...ce of
...rious Virtue) ❾

Ch'anggyŏnggung (Palace)

Naksŏnje

...gjŏn

Honghwamun (Gate)

...amun

Myŏngjŏngjŏn

Seoul National University Medical College

Ihwajang Museum

Ch'angshin Sijang

...ŏngnyŏngjŏn

Chongmyo (Royal Shrine)

Chŏngjŏn

Yulgongno

Taehangno

Ch'anggyŏnggungno

Yulgongno

Pok-Um Church

Chung-ang Church

Tongdaemun Church

Wangsanno

Olympic Park

CHONGNO-GU

Tasanno

CHONGNO3-GA Ⓜ

Ch'odong Church

CHONGNPO5-GA Ⓜ

CHONGNO3-GA Ⓜ

Kwangjang Sijang (Market)

Chongno

Tongdaemun Sijang (Market) Ⓝ

TONGDAEMUN Ⓜ

Hŭng-injimun (East Gate)

Tongdaemun Chain Store

Tongshin Church

TONGDAEMUN Ⓜ

Hwanghak-dong Flea Market

Seun Arcade

Ch'ŏnggye Elevated Road

Pasang Sijang (Market)

Citizen Hall

Tongdaemun Sijang (Market)

P'yŏnghwa Sijang (Market) Shin P'yŏnghwa Sijang (Market) Tong P'yŏnghwa Sijang (Market) Ch'ŏng P'yŏnghwa Sijang (Market)

...nggyech'ŏnno

Ch'ŏnggyech'ŏnno

Tonghwa Arcade

Taerim Arcade

03-GA Ⓜ ÜLCHIRO3-GA Ⓜ

ÜLCHIRO4-GA Ⓜ

Ülchiro

Tongdaemun Stadium

Seoul Sports Complex →

Ulchiro Underground Arcade

Samp'ung Arcade

Hullyonwon-gil

Chungbu Sijang (Market)

Paegoge-gil

Marunnaegil

TONGDAEMUN STADIUM

Hŭng-imunno

TONGDAEMUN STADIUM Ⓜ

Wangshimnigil

New Korea Wedding Hall

Marünnaegil

CHUNG-GU

Chung-gu Office

T'oegyero

Kwanghuimun (Gate)

Kwanghŭimun Church

Tonhwamunno

Shinsong Arcade

Kyongdong Church

Chinyang Arcade

CH'UNGMURO Ⓜ

Haengbok Wedding Hall

Baptist Church

Cheil Hospital

Hullyonwon-gil

Changch'ungdan-gil

...oegyero

Chung-ang
...versity Hospital

Korea House

Changchungdan Church

Shindang-dong Catholic Church

CH'ŎNGGU Ⓜ

Samjŏngdaesa ✠

DONGGUK UNIVERSITY Ⓜ

Tonghoro

Söngdong Church

Tasanno

Kümsöng Church

Dongguk University

CHANGCH'UNG PARK

Yi Jun ✠

...sa
...gwon-gil

1st Namsan Tunnel

CHANGCH'UNGDAM

Namsangongwon-gil

PARK

2nd Namsan Tunnel

...K

Itaewon **L**

YAKSU Ⓜ

SEOUL AND SURROUNDINGS

Seoul is not just the capital of Korea, but also the magnetic centre of a land surrounded by the Pacific Ocean, Russian Siberia, and Chinese Manchuria

Maps:
Area 184
City 206–7

By government designation **Seoul ❶** is officially a *t'ukpyol-si* or special city. Other provincial capitals are referred to as *chikhal-si*, or self-governing city, which entitles them to administer their affairs separately from the provincial government. Seoul is the central city and has been the capital for more than 5,000 years (the word *seoul* means capital), the eye, as it were, of the Korean vortex.

Centres of the vortex

Topographically, the city's centre is wooded **Nam-san** (South Mountain), a 270-metre (900-ft) elevation that gazes across midtown at conically shaped **Pugak-san** (North Peak Mountain). At the top of Nam-san is the **Seoul Tower**, complete with revolving restaurant and spectacular views. Between these peaks sprawled the old walled city. The 16-km (10-mile) encircling wall made of earth and dressed stone is gone, but a few crumbling stretches on Pugak-san and Nam-san, and other restored patches that were rebuilt for tourist visibility, have survived. The original wall was pierced by nine gates. Five still stand, and the two largest – Sungnyemun (Great South Gate, also known as Namdaemun) and Hung-injimun (Great East Gate, also known as Tongdaemun) – are regal presences in the midst of the modern city's swirl. They are reminders of the capital as it was once laid out.

For most people, the hub of the modern city is **City Hall Plaza ❹**, the fountain square bounded on the north by City Hall, on the south by the Plaza Hotel, on the east by the entrance to Ulchi-ro (one of the main east–west streets), and on the west by **Toksu Palace** (a remnant of the old dynasty that founded the city, see page 211). Running under the plaza are two subway lines. Traffic running in and out of the square from three major arteries swings round the fountain; pedestrians descend underground to cross the square through its underpasses; and, if traffic allows, you can stand in the middle of the north–south street, T'aep'yong-no, and look south to Sungnyemun and north to Kwanghwa-mun (Gate of Transformation by Light), the reconstructed gate in front of the 20th-century capitol building.

Other centrists claim that the Kwanghwa-mun intersection is Seoul's centre. This is the next crossing north of City Hall Plaza and it is dominated by a looming **statue of Yi Sun-shin ❺**, Korea's great 16th-century naval hero. From that intersection, T'aep'yong-no runs south, Sejong-no to the north, Shinmun-no west and Chong-no east – the streets changing name as they cross. Somewhat confusingly, the Kwanghwa-mun intersection is not directly in front of the Kwanghwa-mun gate after which it is

PRECEDING PAGES: cherry blossoms in spring. **LEFT:** overview of downtown Seoul. **BELOW:** glitzy department store.

Stone figure at Kyongbok.

BELOW: Kyonghoeru Pavilion in Kyongbok Palace grounds.

named – that's another long block north of here. People who believe that this intersection is the centre of the city do so because it is the entrance to Chong-no, or Bell Street, the city's original main commercial thoroughfare. When he established Seoul as the capital in 1394, Yi dynasty founder Yi Song-gye, whose royal name was T'aejo, hung a bell there. The bell was rung at dawn and dusk to signal the official opening and closing of the city gates. The bell hanging inside the Poshin-gak belfry at Chong-no intersection today was rebuilt in 1984 and is rung only on special holidays.

The governmental heart of the old walled city was **Kyongbok Palace** (Palace of Shining Happiness) ● (open daily, 9am–6pm in summer, 9am–4.30pm in winter), which was T'aejo's residence and seat of power, and was used by him and his successors until 1592, when it was burned during the war with Japan. If you inquire more closely, you will discover that Kyongbok's throne hall, the **Kunjong-jon** (Hall of Government by Restraint), rebuilt in 1867, was the very centre of Taejo's governmental heart. Here the king sat to receive ministers ranged in orderly ranks before him, made judgements, and issued proclamations. The hall faces south down Sejong-no and once commanded an unobstructed view through Kwanghwa-mun to Sungnyemun.

In 1991, the government launched a 10-year project to restore the palace, rebuilding some places such as the **Kangnyongjon** (Residence of the King) and **Kyotaejon** (Residence of the Queen), destroyed by the Japanese, and removing some pagodas which the Japanese built. Flanking the palace gate are two stone *haet'ae*: mythical animals from Korean lore, which have witnessed Seoul's changes and additions ever since they were carved and placed here in the 15th century to guard the old palace from fire.

Many people think Seoul's real centre today is modern **Myong-dong** , an area of narrow alleys that starts a 10-minute walk southeast from City Hall Plaza directly across from Midopa Department Store. Myong-dong's main thoroughfare is lined on both sides with smart shops selling chic clothes and accessories, and it ends at the top of a low hill before **Myong-dong Cathedral**.

Myong-dong alleyways come alive in the evening when they are crowded with after-work strollers window-shopping – "eye-shopping" in Korean – past the fancy displays of shoes and handbags, tailor-made suits and custom-made shirts, dresses in the latest fashions, handcrafted jewellery, and cosmetics.

Getting around

Seoul is divided into 22 wards – *gu* –with each *gu* again segmented into various precincts – *dong*. A *dong* is an area of considerable size, but the term is often used simply to identify where you live or where you're going. People hoping to share a taxi ride, for example, stand at the side of the street shouting, "*Hannam-dong!*", "*Tonam-dong!*", "*Yaksu-dong!*" and other *dongs* at passing taxis.

Knowing the address of a particular house does not guarantee that you will find it – at least, not quickly. House numbers seldom follow a numerical sequence, instead, thcy are assigned according to when the house was built. Thus, Koreans get a lot of practice in drawing maps. Only downtown, in fact, will you hear the names of certain streets used regularly.

With increasing traffic congestion and the confusion about street names, the subway is the handiest means of transport in Seoul. There are numerous lines which connect to the national railway lines to nearby cities such as Inch'on, Uijongbu and Suwon. Visitors will be happy to hear that signs and maps at subway stations are clearly marked in English, which makes life relatively simple. Line No. 1 is coded red on subway maps and begins at Seoul railway station. The first stop from here is City Hall, which brings you right out onto the city plaza within easy reach of Toksu Palace, the Plaza, President, Westin Chosun and Lotte hotels, the British Embassy and the American Cultural Centre.

Shoppers going to **Tongdaemun (Hung-injimun) Market** or movie-goers heading for the Hollywood, Piccadilly and Danseongsa theatres should get off at stops further down the line.

Virtuous longevity

An essential stop on any tour of Seoul is the central and historical **Toksu Palace** (Palace of Virtuous Longevity) (open Tues–Sun, 9am–6pm in summer, until 4.30pm in winter), whose gate faces City Hall Plaza. Toksu is not the oldest of the surviving palaces – it was built as a villa towards the end of the 15th century – but it is important for its role at the unhappy end of the Yi dynasty. King Kojong, who was forced to abdicate in favour of his son Sunjong in 1907, lived in retirement and died here in 1919 after having seen his country annexed by the Japanese in 1910 and his family's dynasty snuffed out after 500 years.

Among the most conspicuous structures in the palace grounds, regularly open to the public, is a

The Myong-dong district was famous during the Park Chung-hee era for its tiny upstairs and hideaway drinking houses which used to serve cheap liquor up until curfew time.

BELOW: busy Namdaemun-no.

statue of Sejong, the great 15th-century king who commissioned scholars to develop a distinctive Korean system of writing, different from the traditional Chinese characters, and officially promulgated in 1446. There is also a royal audience hall and two startlingly European-style stone buildings, with Ionic and Corinthian columns designed by an Englishman in 1909, which once housed the National Museum of Modern Art, now relocated south of the city. The palace grounds offer a welcome relief from the modern bustle, especially in the autumn when its aisle of gingko trees is aflame with gold.

In the grounds of Kyongbok Palace is the **National Museum** ❻ (open Tues–Sun, 9am–5pm in summer, 9am–4pm in winter), the largest museum in the country, displaying over 100,000 items from ancient times through the Choson Kingdom period. These include Paekche tiles, Silla pottery, gilt Buddhas, Koryo celadons and Yi calligraphy and paintings. The building, once central government offices, holds the largest and finest collection of Korean art in the world. Also within the palace grounds is the **National Folk Museum**, which houses artefacts of everyday life and dioramas showing how they were used.

About 1 km (½ mile) east of Kyongbok lies **Ch'angdok Palace** (Palace of Illustrious Virtue) ❼ (open Tues–Sun, 9.15am–5.15pm), built in 1405 as a detached palace, burned down in 1592, rebuilt in 1611, and used since then as the official residence of various Yi kings, including the last one, Sunjong, until the latter's death in 1926. The best preserved of Seoul's palaces, Ch'angdok has a throne room surrounded by long drafty corridors leading past reception rooms furnished with heavy upholstered European chairs and sofas.

Nakson-je, a small complex of buildings within Ch'angdok's grounds, is still the residence of descendants of the royal family: ensconced there are an

BELOW:
Toksu Palace.
RIGHT:
ceremonial urn.

elderly aunt of Sunjong; the wife of the last crown prince, Sunjong's son (who never ruled), and her son and his wife. In the formal back gardens of Nakson-jae, a series of stepped granite-faced tiers planted with azaleas, it is possible to feel totally isolated from the sounds of modern Seoul.

Behind Ch'angdok lies the extensive acreage of **Piwon** , the Secret Garden (open Tues–Sun, 9.15am–5.15pm in summer, 9am–4pm in winter), so called because it was formerly a private park for the royal family. In wooded and hilly terrain, footpaths meander past ponds and pavilions and over small bridges. The most picturesque of these sites is **Pando-ji** (Peninsula Pond), shaped like the outline of the Korean peninsula. From its shore extending out over the water stands a small, exquisite fan-shaped pavilion from which Injo, the 16th king, could cast a line for a bit of quiet fishing. Piwon and portions of Ch'angdok Palace may be visited by joining one of several daily guided tours at the Piwon entrance. Nakson-je is open to the public twice a year for royal ceremonies.

Confucianisam and Buddhism

Strangely, the teachings of Confucius, who lived in China about 2,500 years ago, became more deeply rooted in Korea than in his native land, especially during the Choson dynasty (1392–1910), when they formed the basis of society. Even today, many aspects of Confucianism live on in Korean society, such as the emphasis placed on education, respect for one's elders and ancestral worship.

Twice a year, in the second and eighth lunar months, many people still gather at the **Songgyun'gwan** shrine located on the grounds of **Songgyun'gwan University**  to the northeast of Piwon. The Sokchon honours the spirit of Kongja (Confucius), the man whose principles formed the basis of government

Map on pages 206–7

The National Museum, in the grounds of Kyongbok Palace.

BELOW: National Folk Museum at Kyongbok Palace.

and code of behaviour in Yi-dynasty Korea. The Confucian Yi court tried hard to extinguish the spirit of the Buddha throughout the country, but it failed miserably. Buddhist temples abound. City temples, though, are hardly places of quiet retreat. **Chogye-sa ❶**, founded in 1910 and the centre of Buddhism in Korea, is in the heart of the downtown area, off Ujonggungno. It hums with activity, and on the occasion of Buddha's birthday – the 8th day of the 4th lunar month – it becomes the hub of Buddhist festivities.

The Buddha's birthday festival, Chogye-sa Temple, Seoul.

The Waeguk Saram

When the first Westerners appeared in significant numbers in Korea, they were not allowed to live within the city walls. In the 1880s, however, King Kojong permitted foreign missionaries, traders and legations to buy land in **Chongdong ❷**, just inside the western wall and behind and to the north of Toksu Palace. Many of the structures they built still stand and are in use: the Chong Dong Methodist Church, which Korea's first modern president Syngman Rhee attended, and the Ewha Girls' High School, founded by Methodist missionaries.

All that remains of the Russian legation are the ruins of a white tower near the present Kyonghyang Shinmun (newspaper) building, but the American ambassador's residence, the British Embassy and an adjoining **Anglican Cathedral** are still in use. The cathedral is a graceful Italianate building, its square belfry visible from City Hall Plaza over the intervening walls. The British Embassy, a red-brick structure dating from the late 1800s, was given a US$6 million facelift and expansion during the early 1990s.

BELOW:
Ch'anggyong-won
in winter.

The American ambassador's residence, behind walls and a heavy gate emblazoned with an American seal, is a one-storey Korean-style house. Its most recent

renovation added a replica of P'osok-jong, a channel in the shape of an outsized abalone shell carved from stone.

In ancient times, a Silla king and his courtiers sat around the contours of the real P'osok-jong (in Kyongju), which was filled with running water. Through the channel floated wine cups. When a bobbing cup hesitated in front of king or courtier, it was his turn either to compose an impromptu poem or down the wine as a fine for lack of instant inspiration. A frequent result was a tipsy king and an equally tipsy court. It is not known if successive American ambassadors have continued this tradition.

Map on pages 206–7

Markets

It'aewon  is an urban area running down from the southern flank of Nam-san and east from the fenced edge of **Yongsan Garrison**, the headquarters of the US Eighth Army. The main thoroughfare bisecting the army base into north–south posts also bisects It'aewon into an uphill Nam-san side and a downhill side, towards the Han River. Foreigners, not all of them Westerners, occupy multi-storey apartment buildings higher up the mountain – which gives them a sweeping view of the **Han River** and mountain ridges south of the city.

Today, It'aewon merchants attract shoppers from civilian ranks as well, and visitors hail from all over the world. By day, bargain-hunters swarm through the hundreds of clothing, eel-skin, brassware, shoe and antique stores, where they stock up on competitive Korean-made goods. However, the life of an urban villager, especially that of a housewife, still revolves around the local market. Though Korean households have refrigerators these days, the housewife (or housemaid) still shops every day for the basic ingredients.

The history of the Tongdaemun Sijang market goes back to the 14th century and the roots of the Yi dynasty. In more recent years, many refugees from North Korea, escaping the communist regime, rebuilt their lives by taking work at the market.

BELOW: candid lanterns at Chogye-sa.

Typical roof detail,
Pong-Won-sa
Temple, Seoul.

BELOW: bicycles are
a good way of beat-
ing the traffic.

Tonam-dong market is typical: it lies along both sides of a roadway, which shoppers share with bicycles, handcarts and an occasional motorcycle delivering goods. The shops are more like open stalls because few of them have fixed doors. The Tonam-dong market also includes a large two-storey building, with open shops selling clothes, household goods, accessories, cosmetics, kitchenware, plastic goods, and textiles in a rainbow of colours and a whirl of patterns. If you multiply this by 50, you have **Namdaemun Sijang** (Great South Gate Market) **Ⓜ**, located east of the gate itself; then multiply the latter by another 50 and you have **Tongdaemun Sijang** (Great East Gate Market) **Ⓝ**, a large area that stretches south of Chong-no 5-ka and 6-ka.

Although there are plenty of underground labyrinthine shopping arcades lying beneath some of the city streets, including the **Sogong Arcade** and the **Hoehyor Arcade**, those looking for items of antiquity should head for **Insa-dong Ⓞ** the time-honoured location for antique dealers, which sits along a narrow street leading south from An'guk-dong Rotary to Pagoda Park. The street is called Mary's Alley by foreigners (although who Mary was has long been forgotten). Some shops offering fine Koryó celadon, Silla pottery and Yi furniture are still flourishing there, but many have fled to other sections of the city, notably to Ch'onggyech'on 8-ka, which is well worth a visit, even by someone who isn' in the market for antiques. It's actually part of P'yonghwa Sijang (Peace Market), itself an extension of Tongdaemun Sijang.

Age-old Korean martial arts such as *t'aekwon-do, hapki-do* and *yu-do* are taught in schools and centres nationally, and around the world. A favourite *t'aekwon-do* viewing spot is the Yuksamdong World T'aekwon-do Headquarters, across the Third Han River Bridge.

BEYOND SEOUL

Even Seoul's most die-hard adherents would admit that the city can get on top of you at times, and when this happens the best thing to do is to board a train or a bus and head for one of the attractions within easy reach of the city.

Maps:
Area 184
City 206–7

To the north

Pukhansan-song (North Han Mountain Fortress), is one of two important ancient fortresses in the Seoul area. This castle is located above the sprawling northeast suburbs of the city along the rocky high ridges of **Pukhan Mountain**.

Kwangnung ❷, the impressive Confucian-style tombs of King Sejo (1456–68) (open Tues–Sun, 9am–6.30pm in summer, 9am–5.30pm in winter), the 7th Yi king, and his wife, are probably the most aesthetically and idyllically located tombs in the Seoul area. These monumental mounds stand about 28 km (17 miles) northeast of Seoul, just past Uijongbu, a town and military camp which sprang to fame courtesy of the American movie and television series M*A*S*H, but which is known as the "City of Ever Righteousness". The tombs are hidden in the middle of a forest of old trees which shade trickling streams and wide greens ideal for a picnic.

At Namdaemun market.

Southward bound

Namhansan-song (South Han Mountain Fortress) ❸, is a popular weekend hiking area about 30 km (18 miles) southeast of Seoul. This grand highland redoubt – with 8 km (5 miles) of stone walls – was originally built around 2,000 years ago during Korea's Paekche dynasty. Most what you see now, however, dates from the 17th and 18th centuries, when the Yi kings used the fortress as

BELOW: suburban Seoul snowscapes.

Pukhansan-song was first built during the early Paekche period and at various times fell into disuse.

Following severe attacks during the 16th century by armies of Ch'ing China, the Yi King Sukjong refurbished its battlements.

BELOW:
Namhansan-song.

a retreat from invading Chinese armies. In 1637, following a six-week siege, Nam-hansansong was the spot where King Injo surrendered himself, some 14,000 of his men, and ultimately Korea, to a huge Manchu invasion force.

Suwon ❹, the capital of Kyonggi Province, is an old fortress-city 50 km (30 miles) south of Seoul in the vicinity of Mt Paltal. The name means "water-source" or "water-field," because this area was traditionally known for its fine artesian wells. These days, Suwon is better known for its recently restored castle walls and support structures, and for its luscious late spring and summer strawberries (called *ttalgi* in Korean) and its *kalbi*, or barbecued short ribs.

King Chongjo wanted to move the Korean capital from Seoul to the Suwon site in the 18th century, but was never able to realise his dream. He did, however, create a beautiful fortified city here in Suwon - complete with parapets and embrasures, floodgates, observation platforms and domes, parade grounds, command bunkers, cannon stands and an archery range. Chongjo's original castle, known as the "Flower Fortress", was heavily damaged over the years, and by bombing during the Korean War. But in 1975 the Korean government undertook a major restoration of this dream city.

One particularly lovely spot near the North Gate, **Changan-mun**, is a strikingly landscaped pond, **Yong-yon**, which sits below an octagonal moon-watching pavilion called **Pang-hwa-suryu-jong**. This meditative spot was created by King Chongjo when he initiated his Suwon master plan in 1794. These days it's a gem of a place, much-favoured by neighbourhood *haraboji* (grandfathers), who sit inside its gabled cupola, smoking long-stemmed pipes, drinking sweet rice wine, and bouncing patriarchal thoughts off nearby castle walls. The whole classical ensemble is officially labelled "The Northern Turret".

The pottery kilns of two of Korea's finest potters are about 70 km (42 miles) southeast of Seoul near Ich'on (also just north of National Highway 4). In **Suk-wang-ni**, **Sindung-myon**, a couple of miles north of Ich'on proper, you can observe Koryo celadons being created by a ceramics master, or marvel at the Yi dynasty whiteware as it's pulled hot from traditional kilns. These craftsmen's fine work can be purchased on the spot or in prominent ceramic art galleries in Seoul. At the other end of the potting spectrum, you will find throughout the great Ich'on area, row upon row of the ubiquitous shiny, brown *kimch'i* pots. These utilitarian wares are hand-thrown and fired in adobe huts.

A morning excursion 45 km (28 miles) south of Seoul to the **Korean Folk Village** (open daily, 9am–5pm in summer, 9am–4pm in winter; entrance fee) near Suwon will give you a full day to tour the 240 homes, shops and other attractions in this authentically rendered Yi-dynasty village. Even in an entire day you may not be able to view all the fascinating exhibits, and the complex manages to avoid the kitsch excesses one might expect from a 'traditional' tourist village.

Some way further southeast, **Songni-san National Park ❺**, a mountain retreat in North Ch'ungch'ong province, is superb at any time of the year, but is most favoured by discriminating Korean weekenders in the autumn when its trees are aflame with colour. Oaks, maples and gingkos try to outdo each other in their autumnal radiance. As one romantic Korean travel writer once said of Songni-san: "The tender green for spring, abundance of forests for summer, yellow leaves for autumn, and snow for winter - all deserve appreciation".

Indeed, since ancient times, Songni has been a popular area: appropriately, the word *songni* means "escape from the vulgar". To achieve this Songni escape, travel from Seoul to **Taejon** by train, then transfer by bus or car through

Map on page 184

The Korean Folk Village isn't just an artificial museum; people live here. It provides a fascinating introduction to Korean culture.

BELOW: shamanist posts at Suwon.

VISITING POPJU-SA

Songni-san's biggest attraction is Popju-sa, uphill from Songni-dong village. This large temple complex is dominated by the massive Miruk Buddha of the Future, appropriately fashioned from modern poured cement. The 27-metre (88-ft) image is often identified by tour guides as "the biggest Buddha in Korea".

The sprawling temple complex was first built at the base of Mt Songni in the 6th century, shortly after Buddhism had been brought to Korea from China. Records note that work began in 553, during the 14th year of the reign of the Silla King Chinhung. The original founder and spiritual master was the high priest Uisang, who had returned home from his studies in India. Uisang contributed several Buddhist scriptural books to Popju-sa's first library.

Remnants of this temple's days of grandeur can be found in every section of the compound. And they are not confined to artefacts connected with spiritual awareness and contemplation. On a far more practical note there is the famous Ch'olhwak, a massive iron rice pot which was cast in 720, during the reign of Silla King Songdong, when some 3,000 priests were living – and eating – here. As you wander around the complex, try to forget the present and imagine yourself transported back to those days.

Okch'on to the Songni area. Alternatively, you can go directly by car or bus from Seoul via Ch'ongju City, which takes about three hours.

Songni-dong village is known for the semi-wild tree mushrooms cultivated in the area and sold at roadside stands. Seoulites try to arrive in Songni village at lunchtime, when they can enjoy as many as six different mushroom dishes served with a dizzying array of side dishes, *kimch'i* and rice.

P'anmunjom was the site of one of the more bizarre exchanges in recent years when a South Korean tycoon (who started the first tours for his compatriots to Mount Kumgangsan in the North) sent a herd of cows across the border as a gift.

Inch'on

Until the 1880s **Inch'on** ❻ was the only place in Korea that foreigners were allowed to visit. Today this erstwhile fishing village has a booming harbour and has become Korea's fourth largest city. In the 20th century, Inch'on became well-known as the place where General Douglas MacArthur, commander of the US Pacific forces, directed an amphibious landing which turned the bitter Korean War around for South Korea and its allies.

Freedom Hill looms over a seaport abustle with international trade. Atop the hill, jaunty in sculpted khakis, stands a statue of General MacArthur, gripping a pair of binoculars. The fastest and easiest way to get to Freedom Hill is to take the Seoul subway train due west through industrial suburbs and rice fields. Once you arrive at Inch'on-dong station, take a cab or hike up to Freedom Hill for a bird's-eye view of the town

Excursion to the DMZ

It's all too easy while travelling round the peaceful, prosperous parts of South Korea to overlook the fact that the entire peninsula was ravaged by war less than half a century ago. Yet North Korea continues to make bellicose noises, which may go beyond mere sabre rattling. In recent years South Korea has had to deal with a number of armed incursions from the north, and despite outward signs of prosperity and normality, it would only take one untoward incident for the calm of this land to be seriously disrupted. The danger is all too real, and to acquaint tourists with this potentially volatile situation, government and UN representatives have sanctioned one of the world's most unusual tourist trips, which takes in the area around P'anmunjom, the site of a small farming village which was obliterated during the Korean War.

P'anmunjom ❼ is the site on Korea's 38th parallel where American and South Korean representatives from a special United Nations Military Armistice Commission hold periodic talks with North Korean and Chinese negotiators in order to supervise the truce signed here on 27 July 1953, which formally divided Korea into North and South political sectors and put an uneasy end to the bloody Korean War.

P'anmunjom sits in a wide valley just northwest of the broad Imjin River and about 56 km (35 miles) due north of Seoul. It also straddles the stretch of land near the western end of Korea's demilitarized zone (DMZ), a demarcation line about 4 km (2½ miles) wide which snakes across the country.

The camp is the only point of official contact between North Korea and the free world. The surrounding area is a heavily mined and barricaded "no-man's land", entered only by well-armed soldiers and a few hundred farmers who carry on working here.

The southern sector of P'anmunjom is policed by the American-led United Nations Command (UNC), not the South Korean army – although the guards include both American and South Korean soldiers. Many meetings have taken place in P'anmunjom between North and South Korean government officials which have led to some low-level trade, but the Cold-War stand-off remains as strong as ever, although a strong faction in South Korea would like to see the two countries reunited.

Visitors used to be allowed to go to P'anmunjom, weather and the political climate permitting, but since a South Korean lieutenant died here in suspicious circumstances in 1998 it has been off-limits. There are hopes this tour might be reinstated in the near future. However, the trip has now been diverted to take in the surrounding area, including one of the tunnels dug beneath the border by the north in an attempt to launch a surprise attack.

Map on page 184

Several formerly endangered species of birds, such as the delicate Manchurian crane, have flourished within the "protected" confines of the DMZ since it was declared off-limits in 1953.

Highway to history

Your tour bus travels due north of Seoul on National Highway 1, following wartime history through plains and valleys. Not so long ago, these peaceful surroundings were the heavily bunkered scenes of massive military advances and retreats during the Korean War and even during a long-ago Mongol invasion. Bridges along the highway have been specially designed so they can be blown up quickly in the event of an invasion, and the military has gone over every inch of ground to decide exactly where mines should be sown and artillery fire brought to bear should the unthinkable finally happen.

BELOW: fishermen at Inch'on.

Map on page 184

The 38th parallel, symbol of the division of Korea.

BELOW: American sentries at the DMZ.
RIGHT: going fishing: Han River shore.

All this seems a little unbelievable, especially as the surrounding landscape is so picturesque. This area is green and lush during the summer months, but when the winter chill sets in, its beauty turns bleak and brittle. The late author James Wade describes this region best in his book West Meets East: "North of Seoul the Korean landscape is austerely beautiful in late winter. A light dusting of snow sets off the dark dots of rice stubble in frozen paddies and the lonely clumps of thatch-roofed farm houses. The steel-gray horizon, rimmed with jagged, ice-streaked mountains, recedes before the jeep as it... approaches the Imjin River, with its symbolically narrow and precarious Freedom Bridge."

Freedom Village

Even from outside the DMZ it's possible to catch a glimpse of an enormous South Korean flag, thumping back and forth when the wind is strong. There is a similar North Korean flag on the other side of the border, and the two countries – mimicking some of the shenanigans which have taken place in the conference room at P'anmunjom – try to outdo each other by building taller and taller flagpoles. The southern flag marks the village of **T'aesong-dong** ("Attaining Success Town"), where a community of ex-refugees were allowed to resettle; you can see the settlement from a specially-built observation platform.

T'aesong-dong, called Freedom Village by the US military, is about a mile from P'anmunjom. Villagers – and soldiers – have to endure propaganda blasted from North Korean loudspeakers, but for their pains they enjoy certain benefits, including exemption from military service and taxation. Otherwise, life generally goes on here in much the same way it does in other parts of the republic, although the villagers must be constantly aware that if hostilities do break out, they are going to be at the very front of the front line.

Across the dividing line in the North Korean half of the demilitarised no-man's-land is the village of Gui-jong-dong, nicknamed Propaganda Village. It has bigger houses than T'aesong-dong – in fact the village is said to be the biggest in the world. The odd thing is that no one appears to inhabit it, although the North's distortive broadcasts constantly enjoin the people of T'aesong-dong to come over and join them.

The highlight of a tour to this area is the Invasion Tunnel, which was discovered in 1978 – the third one the North tried to build in secret. The South Korean military uses sophisticated listening devices along the length of the border to prevent similar incursions in future. The tunnel itself – hacked out of the rock by hand – is quite large and rather eerie, standing as mute testament to the continued state of tension.

Since 1987 Western tourists have been able to make the P'anmunjom trip from the northern side. From Seoul this involves flying to the northern capital, Pyongyang, via Beijing and then a morning's drive, and six-hour train journey to Kaesong, a city near P'anmunjom. As of 1998, South Koreans were allowed to take a cruise to Mount Kumgangsan in the North, although the rest of the country is still barred to them. In 1999 permission was extended to foreigners, for whom tours are also available to other parts of the North.

EAST COAST

Whether you want snow sports or watersports, mountain hikes or quiet contemplation amid temples and shrines, you'll find them all in Korea's East Coast region

Map on page 184

S nowy hills and ski resorts. Highland hot springs overlooking rice terraces and pine forests. The bluest waters and whitest sand beaches in Korea. Caverns dripping with stalactites and stalagmites. All this awaits you on a trip along the East Coast. At the southern end of the coast are P'ohang and Ulsan, recently created industrial cities where steel, automobiles and ships are manufactured at astonishing production rates. To the north – along postcard-perfect pine bluffs, inland lagoons, and cabana-dotted beaches – there are seaside retreats; and in the northeast province of Kangwon-do, lies Sorak-san National Park, a place of breathtaking beauty, where waterfalls and flowers decorate the trails to Mt Sorak.

You can begin your tour of the East Coast at several points up and down the East Sea, but the most central place to use as pivot point is Kangnung, the major city in east **Kangwon Province**, reached by train or bus, although the most interesting way to make the 230-km (140-mile) journey from Seoul is by private car, as it gives you so much more flexibility. Once you get into more mountainous areas, notice the unusual pointed-topped silos of Korean design, bright ears of corn drying along rooftops, and hop plantations which are distinguished by the lacy network of string trellises built to support the bines, from which *maekju* (beer) is made.

LEFT: Kumgang waterfall at Sorak-san National Park.
BELOW: Woljong-sa temple complex.

Land of 10,000 Buddhas

One detour you must make is just beyond the little village of **Chinbu**, about 40 km (25 miles) west of Kangnung. This side-trip carries you along paved and dirt roads to **Odaesan National Park ❽**, an attractive mountain area and the location of two of Korea's best-known temple complexes, **Woljong-sa** and **Sangwon-sa**. The road leading to 1,563-metre (5,128-ft) **Odae-san** is dotted with tiny hermitages, Zen meditation niches, and other impressive remnants of Buddhism which date from the 7th century and Korea's impressive Silla dynasty.

Woljong-sa, which sits on the southern fringe of Odae-san about 8 km (5 miles) off the expressway, is a sprawling temple complex distinguished by a superb nine-storey octagonal pagoda and an unusual kneeling Buddha sculpture. The tiered pagoda, which rises 15 metres (50 ft), is capped with a sculpted lotus blossom and a bronze finial of intricate design; the kneeling Buddha has well-weathered features, and (because of an unusual cap he's wearing) looks very much like a European tin soldier.

Snow, sea and secrets

The Taekwallyong mountain region is where Korea's most modern and well-equipped ski resort is located.

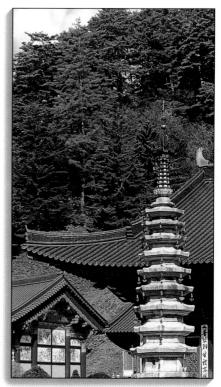

Throughout the **Taekwallyong** area are various ski spots with names such as Talpanje, Chirmae and Third Slope. Most are located in the vicinity of a small town called **Hwoenggye**, but the newest and favourite slopes have been developed in a place called **Yongpyong**, or **Dragon Valley**. The Dragon Valley Ski Resort sprawls over 20 hectares (50 acres) and is equipped with chairlift systems, snow-making machines, a ski school, ski rental facilities, and even lighting facilities for ambitious night skiing.

Kangnung ❾ is a sleepy seaside town rich in traditional architecture and hospitable people, the key trading and terminal point in this part of Korea. The Kangnung area abounds with distractions worth visiting, but among the most prominent is the classical Confucian academy and shrine – **Hyangkyo** and **Taesungjon** (open daily, 9am–6pm) – in the northwest suburbs of Kangnung on the grounds of the Myungnyun middle and high schools. This hilltop structure, which was built in 1313, destroyed by fire in 1403, then rebuilt in 1413, has low, brooding rooflines and tapering colonnades typical of Koryo dynasty structures in other parts of Korea.

A few miles north of Kangnung is the not-to-be-missed resort of **Kyongp'o-dae Lake**, which has long been a popular Korean recreational spa. Waters off Kyongp'o-dae Beach are often busy with zig-zagging speedboats and sailing craft, and on shore you will find numerous tented seafood restaurants.

Other sites along the southeast coast which are well worth a visit include the strangely beautiful **Songnyu Cave** (open daily, 8am–7pm in summer, 8am–5pm in winter) ❿. Just south and then inland from the town of Uljin, this is a proper limestone cavern complete with bizarre stalactites and stalagmites. The easiest way to get there if you don't have a hired car is to catch a local bus from Uljin

TIP

Songnyu Cave has been described as "a spelunker's delight". If you get a thrill out of caving, don't forget to include it on your itinerary.

BELOW: village south of Kangnung.

and travel 8 km (5 miles) south to the Songnyu-gul bus stop. From there the cavern is about a 2-km (1¼-mile) walk west on a dirt path or road across attractive rice paddies and along a curving riverbank.

Approximately 30 km (20 miles) south of Uljin is **P'yonghae**, a quiet farming town where you can book a taxi or chance a bus to Korea's picturesque **Paegam Hot Springs ⓫** on the mountain of the same name. Those who like to get away from it all will embark on a trip to **Juwang Mountain**, a 720-metre- (2,362-ft) peak set in **Mt Juwang National Park** due west of Yongdong and southeast of Andong via Chongsong. It can usually be reached only by country bus.

At the southern end of your East Coast adventure looms **P'ohang ⓬**, a seaport and resort area which since 1968 has been the apple of Korea's industrial eye. This is because P'ohang is the location of the model P'ohang Iron and Steel Company (POSCO), Korea's successful producer of industrial steel and its by-products.

Few foreigners venture out to the island of **Ullung-do**, 270 km (170 miles) northeast of P'ohang. Indeed, because of its location, Ullung-do is one of Korea's best-kept secrets. Some of the best sights and travel experiences in the country are to be had on this island, which is about halfway between Korea and Japan (and is the farthest east one can go and still be in Korea). Embark on the Han II Ho speedboat ferry in P'ohang, and six hours later you'll be strolling into **To-dong** town on Ullung-do's southeast coast.

Sorak-san National Park

Sorak-san, the "Snow Peak Mountain", is now more formally known as the **Sorak-san National Park ⓭**. Not just a lone mountaintop, **Mt Sorak** is in

Map on page 184

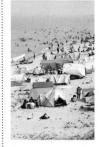

Sun, sea and sand at P'ohang beach.

BELOW: blue-green Ullung-do visions.

Cable car at Sorak-san National Park.

BELOW: Sorak-san is popular with trekkers.

fact a series of peaks in the mid-section of the spectacular **Taebaek Sanmaek**, or "Great White Range", Korea's most prominent geographical feature. This panoramic backbone of South Korea's northeast province of Kangwon-do is a tourist destination that more than lives up to its public relations hype. The Sorak area is a true mountain wonderland – it is easy to see why early Zen Buddhist monks chose this region as a place in which to sit and strive to become one with the universe.

Inje, the "Gateway to Inner Sorak", is a good place to begin such an exploration. En route you'll encounter (at Chang Su Dae) numerous nature trails abloom in the spring and ablaze in the fall, veil-like waterfalls, red-bellied frogs and, at **Osaek Yaksu**, mineral water springs famed for their therapeutic properties. Some travellers like to pause at Chang Su Dae and hike up to the Taesung waterfalls, then upward to **Paekdam-sa** (open daily, 9am–6pm), a lovely Buddhist temple smack in the interior of Inner Sorak. Ex-President Chun and his wife spent a year here from 1989 to 1990 "repenting" for the sins of his 1980–88 dictatorship. Both hikes are spiritually healing after bustling Seoul, but be prepared with warm clothes, good walking gear, food and drink – especially if you plan on camping overnight.

Further east on the Han'gye Pass road, at the very top of the spectacular pass, you can begin yet another trek – this one all the way to the top of Sorak's supreme peak, **Taechon-bong** (also called Sorak-san), the third highest mountain in Korea at 1,708 metres (5,604 ft). You can navigate onwards and enter the **Sorak-dong resort complex** by its back door. However, be advised that the steep zig-zagging through beautiful scenery can be slippery and dangerous during the winter months.

The Osaek Yaksu medicinal springs at the far east end of the Han'gye Pass road are well worth a stop for a recuperative soak. But if you're feeling fit, you may want to rush on down to sea-level to enjoy a grand seafood meal at **Yangyang, Naksan** or **Sokch'o**.

The 15-minute bus ride from the sandy East Coast into Sorak Village is a grand transition from beach cabana chic to mountain resort cool. One moment you're tasting raw fish and clams under your beachside umbrella, and the next, you're in a pine lodge considering hot buttered rum and pinenut soup.

Temples and hermitages

Before you head into the bush, stroll up the main flagstoned and fir-lined path which leads to **Sinhung-sa** (open daily, 9am–6pm), an ancient Zen (Son) temple originally built near its present location in AD 652. The first Sinhung-sa, then called Hyungsong-sa, or the "Temple of Zen Buddhism", was destroyed by a forest fire in 707, rebuilt in 710, burned again in 1645, and rebuilt a third time at its present location in 1648. "If the signboard date at Sinhung-sa is correct," writes Zen and oriental art authority Dr Jon Carter Covell, "then Sinhung-sa is the oldest Zen temple in the world. Nothing in China or in Japan is of this age, not by many centuries."

Just before you reach the actual temple compound, you'll pass (on the right side of the cobbled path) a neatly kept and fenced-in cemetery full of unusual bell-shaped tombstones, erected to honour former illustrious Zen monks who spent much time meditating in this area.

In the temple itself, which sits on a pleasant little bluff with a superb view of the surrounding mountains, you'll pass through lattice doors carved and painted

Map on page 184

Outer Sorak–Sorak-dong resort complex has become one of the finest rural spots in Korea for leisurely hiking and al fresco meals. Nature strolls here can accommodate everyone – from the languid wanderer to the rock-climbing fanatic.

BELOW: the famed Rocking Rock.

Map
on page
184

TIP

There are several ways
to get to the Sorak area
from Seoul. If you've
only got a few days, the
quickest is on a Korean
Air domestic flight to
Sokch'o (50 minutes),
then by bus or taxi to
Sorak-dong (another 20
minutes).

BELOW: temples
abound in the area.
RIGHT: autumn
around Sorak-san.

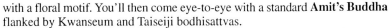

with a floral motif. You'll then come eye-to-eye with a standard **Amit's Buddha** flanked by Kwanseum and Taiseiji bodhisattvas.

Sinhung-sa offers more such fantasy, drawing on combinations of shaman, Taoist and Buddhist imagery. Consider the creatures which are half-tiger, half-leopard, and the writhing dragons, cranes and bats - all brilliantly painted on the ceiling. Or the drawing on the main hall's rear wall which shows a Zen patriarch offering his severed arm to a higher-ranking Zen master.

Next, carry on up this spiritual path to the **Kejo Hermitage**, about 3 km (2 miles) along a singing stream bed. The hermitage, a subsidiary of the mother Sinhung Temple, is partially built into a granite cave at the base of Ulsan-bawi, a spectacular granite formation that dominates this part of the Sorak area. Like much of Sorak, and like the famous **Diamond Mountains** (Kumgangsan) across the DMZ (demilitarised zone) in North Korea, Ulsan-bawi's face is rich with anthropomorphic images. Indeed, about halfway up the Kejo Hermitage, an enterprising fellow with a high-powered telescope charges a small fee for lingering peeks at one particularly erotic formation carved around Ulsan-bawi's mid-section.

The hermitage is identified by a bright red Buddhist swastika carved and painted over an entrance arch (reminding us that swastikas have a longer and more honourably history than that with which we now associate them). A narrow corridor leads to the cave interior where candles on an altar burn before a small but exquisite golden Buddha. When monks are gathered inside this ancient niche, chanting sutras and clacking wooden bells in the flickering candlelight, the effect is Zen Buddhism at its most poignant.

Fronting the Kejo Hermitage and **Ulsan-bawi** is another geological curiosity which has become a major tourist attraction over the years. This is **Hundulbawi**, a massive boulder which rocks alarmingly back and forth in its secure place when given a determined nudge.

A cave and a dragon

The hike to **Pison-dae**, a vertical rock that juts heavenwards at the entrance to an extremely picturesque gorge, is easy enough. In the autumn, fire-red maples and golden gingkos are the seasonal attractions.

From this restful camp at the base of Pison-dae, devoted Buddhist pilgrims head up a smaller path to **Kumgang Cave**, which is located near the top of Pison-dae and requires a serious determination to exercise. After negotiating 649 stairs (count them, it will take your mind off the climb) to reach this pleasing cave-shrine, your heart will be pounding in your ears, but the extraordinary view from up there – and from a promontory at a halfway point – will be your earthly reward. Inside the cave is a small statue of a Buddha surrounded by burning candles, incense and food offerings.

Meanwhile, from back at the Sorak-dong base camp, other hikers will opt to visit the **Flying Dragon** (Piryong) at the top of an awesome gorge beneath the 1,345-metre (4,412-ft) high Hwachae-bong. A suspension bridge across the narrow gorge and stream leads to the Flying Dragon. ❏

WEST COAST

Map on page 184

Hike to the Gold Mountain Temple, visit a museum of folk art and eat what is reputedly the best food in Korea – or simply lie on the beach and lap up the sun

Korea's jagged West Coast, cut by the Yellow Sea, is dotted with myriad peninsula islets floating offshore, and bordered by sandy beaches overlooking quiet pine glens. Along this coast, village fishermen and seasonal beach-goers regulate their activities according to tidal changes, because the differential is so extreme. In certain areas at low tide, the Yellow Sea exposes vast mud flats 5 metres (17 ft) to 7 metres (25 ft) offshore – a distance second in tidal extremes only to the Bay of Fundy in Canada's Nova Scotia.

Travellers en route to the coast may find **Onyang ⓐ**, about 18 km (11 miles) west of Ch'on-an on Highway 21, a refreshing stop along the way. A hot spring and **Hyonch'ungsa Shrine** (open daily, 9am–6pm), which is dedicated to Korea's great 16th-century naval hero, Admiral Yi Sun-shin, have long attracted visitors, but since the **Onyang Folk Museum** (open daily, 8.30am–5.30pm in summer, 9am–5pm in winter) in **Kongok-ni** opened in 1978, tourist traffic to Onyang has increased. Promoted as having the best all-around collection of Korean folk art in the world, the privately-owned Onyang Folk Museum does indeed house over 7,000 traditional Korean folk articles – only a portion of the vast collection Kim Won-dae has accumulated over the past two decades.

Nature lovers will be drawn to popular **Mallip'o Beach** on the western tip of a peninsula which flares into the Yellow Sea like a snarling dragon. Just north of Mallip'o Beach lies **Ch'ollip'o**, a haven for flora and for people fond of flora. In a 81-hectare (200-acre) sanctuary, more than 7,000 varieties of plants, almost exclusively from temperate climes, thrive on the stable climate, the longer springs and autumns in this region.

Veteran Westerners in Korea have long favoured the West Coast's Taech'on Beach, or **Taech'on-dae**, as a resort haven from spring to autumn. The resort is about 14 km (9 miles) from the town of Taech'on, and is reached by bus or train from Seoul.

The beach (Taech'on to the locals) is unofficially divided into two sectors – a northern stretch called KB, or the "Korean Beach", and a southern stretch called the "Foreigners' Beach". This was originally a Christian missionaries' resort. The Korean Beach – where discos and wine houses coexist with fishermen's huts – is a non-stop boogie scene during the peak summer season, but the Foreigners' Beach maintains an air of residential dignity.

Paekche capitals

Further inland from Taech'on, away from frolicking surf and missionary resorts, lie the ancient towns of **Kongju ⓑ** and **Puyo ⓒ**. Kongju was once the capital of the Paekche Kingdom until the administration was moved south to Puyo. Both Kongju and Puyo

LEFT: entrance of Sunamsa (temple), Chollanam-do.
BELOW: Taech'on.

became famous in archaeological circles after a series of Paekche relics were excavated in the central and southeastern provinces. Many remains are displayed in the **Puyo National Museum** (open Tues–Sun, 9am–5pm in summer, 9am–4pm in winter). Prehistoric stoneware vessels, shamanistic instruments, gilt-bronze and stone Buddhist statues, gold and jade ornaments and other treasures attest to the development and excellence of Paekche craftsmen, who were influenced by Central Asian and Chinese artists.

The Paekche legacy extends beyond the museum. Along the serene Kum River at **Paengma-gang** (White Horse River), remnants of the grandeur and the fateful fall of the Paekche kingdom of some 1,300 years ago are preserved. You can have a picnic on the flat rock (Nan-sok, or Warm Rock) on the river bank at **Saja**, just as the Paekche kings once did. On the opposite side of the river is the picturesque **Nakhwa-am** (Rock of the Falling Flowers) bluff with a pavilion on its brow. From these Paekche delights, head southeast along Highway 23 to Kwan-ch'ok Temple outside Nonsan.

Shamanism is still very much alive in modern Korea.

Unjin Miruk and paper making

As you scale the stone steps on the P'anya hillside to **Kwanch'ok-sa** (Temple of the Candlelights), all the superlative descriptions you've heard regarding the **Unjin Miruk** ⑰ – the 1,000-year-old largest standing stone Buddha in Korea – will stir up your anticipation. But when, at the top of a flight of stairs, your get your first glance at the Unjin Miruk through the clear, horizontal window of the temple (if the temple doors are open), all you can see of the Buddha of the Future is the face, with its eyes peering back at visitors through the holy sanctum.

BELOW:
Unjin Miruk statue.

Chonju ⑱, which is 93 km (58 miles) south of Seoul, is the provincial capital of Chollapuk-do. It is the ancestral home of the descendants of Yi Song-gye, founder of the Yi dynasty, and is famous for its paper products (fans, umbrellas and writing paper), *pi pim pap*, and food in general. Paper-making was introduced to Korea by the Chinese about 1,000 years ago, but the Koreans became so adept at this fine craft that both Chinese and Japanese calligraphers came to favour Korean papers over their own.

Technology has encroached on the handmade paper industry, but in Chonju villagers still actively continue the tradition in their homes and in makeshift factories. The sound of new paper pulps swishing in water drifts out of windows, and in many backyards white sheets of fresh paper hang like drying laundry. The entire paper-making process may be observed at Oh Dong-ho's factory at the end of Chonju's main street – just before a small bridge and to the left along a red brick wall.

Horse ears and frozen fairies

The winding road on to **Mai-san** ⑲ (Horse Ears Mountain) is a joy to behold. There are attractive and classical sights at nearly every highway turn. Just five minutes outside of Chonju, for example, you will see on the left a series of hills covered with hundreds of traditional Korean grave mounds. This is an unusually crowded pre-Christian-style cemetery.

Map on page 184

The famous Mai-san "Horse Ears" are not visible until you get quite close to Chinan town. There, they spring up from behind a large knoll above a meandering river bed. Once you reach Mai-san, your expedition has just begun. The hike through narrow **Chong-hwang Pass** between the two horse's ears is a strenuous, heart-thumping ascent of 132 steps. Once there, near **Hwaom Cave**, you can rest and enjoy a panoramic view of Chinan and its environs. Continue into a small valley to the south of the ears, veer to the right (negotiating another 181 steps in segments) and you'll come to one of the most bizarre Buddhist temples in Korea. Built by the hermit monk Yi Kap-yong, this **T'ap-sa** (Pagoda Temple) (open daily, 9am–6pm) site is a collection of stone pagodas, some of them 9 metres (30 ft) high. All were built without mortar and have stood in surrealistic splendour in this narrow valley since the early part of this century.

Kumsan-sa (Gold Mountain Temple) (open daily, 9am–6pm), on the western slope of **Moak-san**, is reputedly the most beautiful temple in **Chollabuk-do**. It is about 34 km (21 miles) southwest of Chonju. The complex was burned during the 1592 Hideyoshi invasion, then finally rebuilt in the early 17th century.

Today, its main hall, **Miruk-jon**, stands three storeys high, making Kumsan-sa the tallest temple in Korea. This space is devoted to housing 10 designated cultural assets from Silla, Paekche, and Koryo periods. Miruk-jon, a worship hall for the god Avalokitesvara, is one of these priceless treasures.

Inside Miruk-jon, a huge golden Maitreya (Buddha of the Future) stands 12 metres (39 ft) tall, holding a red lotus blossom in its left palm. It is flanked by two crowned bodhisattvas, Taemyosang and Pophwarim. Below the statues, behind the wooden grille, a stairway leads down to the Matreya's feet. Devotees and visitors can walk down the steps to kiss the candlelit Maitreya's feet and make an offering. Next to Miruk-jon, above the left slope of the hill, is a stupa made of stone and a six-storey granite pagoda where a monk's body minerals are enshrined after cremation. The pagoda's roofs are flat and subtly curved at the corners in traditional Paekche style.

Kwangju ㉑, the ancient provincial capital of **Chollanam-do**, is a low-key city where at night in the city centre traffic ceases and streets become pedestrian malls, busy with strollers and shoppers. More often than not, these strolling people also eat, and Kwangju competes with Chonju for producing the best food in Korea. The country's premier rice wine is also produced here. **Mudung** (Peerless Mountain) hovers like a guardian over Kwangju. A resort area has been created at its base among acacia trees and beside a stream. There are also two factory buildings, used for tea production during the spring and autumn tea-harvesting seasons.

The **Kwangju Museum** (open Tues–Sun, 9am–5pm in summer, 9am–4pm in winter) was built to house Yuan-dynasty booty rescued from a sunken 600-year-old Chinese ship in the Yellow Sea in 1976. This archaeological find is exhibited on the ground floor gallery. Upstairs on the second floor is a gallery of Cholla treasures, which includes 11th- to 14th-century bronze Buddha bells, Yi dynasty scroll paintings, and fine white porcelain. ❑

Legend notes that before Mai-san was created, two fairies – one male, the other female – lived there. They were enjoying their respite on earth when one day their heavenly creator called for them to make their ascent back home.

BELOW: grave mounds at Mai-san, "Horse Ears Mountain".

THE SOUTH

*The most perfect Buddha, the largest tombs, the most idyllic island –
these are just a few of the claims which keep bringing tourists to
the South. There's even an Irish woollen industry...*

Map
on page
184

A tour of Korea's southern crescent offers a bit of eveything: Taegu, the capital of North Kyong-sang province, is a busy, friendly town; Kyongju has some of the most important tombs and archeological finds; and Cheju-do island has gained the nickname of the Hawaii of the Orient.

A logical starting point for a trip through the south of Korea is **Taegu** ㉑, capital of North Kyong-sang Province. Taegu serves as a clearing house for a variety of produce harvested in this agriculturally rich province and it is an industrial centre as well. It is a very Korean compromise between urban and rural extremes: big enough to offer good hotels, restaurants and contemporary entertainment, yet small enough to retain a relaxed ambiance that is all but lost in Seoul or Pusan. Traditionally-styled clothing is still very much in evidence, especially (for no apparent reason) in the environs of **Talsong**, an earthwork fortress dating back to the prehistoric Sam-Han era. The fort is now a popular park, complete with a small zoo.

Yak-chong Kol-mok, "medicine alley", is the site of one of Taegu's more notable sensory delights. The street is a centre for wholesale purveyors of traditional medicines.

Taegu also has its own brand of nightlife which, if lacking the polish of posher establishments in Seoul, is well-endowed with enthusiasm. Most after-hours partying in Taegu is centralised in several blocks near the "old station" at the centre of town. A spirited confusion of side alley vendors, eclectic shop fronts, nightclub bands, and throngs intent on entertaining themselves.

For tamer daylight diversions, there is **Su-song Reservoir** on the southern outskirts of the city. In winter, the reservoir's ice is crowded with skaters.

Taegu has several other recreational areas: **Tong Chon Resort** and **Mangwuli Park** are located out past the railway station, on the Naktong River where the communist attack that began the Korean War was finally halted. **Ap-san Park** includes a cable car ride up to the summit of **Ap-san** for a panoramic view of the Taegu plain. Near the old railway station are Taegu's small reconstructions of old government buildings. The original structures were built in 1601 as part of an administrative complex which remained in use until 1965.

The **Sobuju-c'ha-jang** (West Depot) will get you to **Yong-yon-sa**, a tiny temple perched high in the mountains with an exquisite set of guardian *deva* paintings, miles of hiking trails, cordial inns, and an invigorating stream for bathing.

The bus to **Unumn-sa** from **Nambu-ju-ch'a-jang** (South Depot) is a challenging, but rewarding, test of stamina. Unmun-sa is a restful sanctuary for a

LEFT: squids drying in the sun.
BELOW: many of Taegu's original city gates still remain.

Kumquats are used for decoration throughout Korea

BELOW:
Pusan fish market.

community of Buddhist nuns. **Chikji-sa**, easily reached from Taegu via Kim-ch'on, is a gem of a temple. Chikji-sa's shrines are populated with a bewildering array of finely-carved statues.

Pusan

Wedged between an imposing range of mountains and the sea, the big port city of **Pusan** ② is a raucous melange of masts, loading cranes and buildings; honking cabs, train whistles, and the throbbing horns of passing ferries; suited businessmen, deck hands, navy cadets and fishmongers mingle in the streets.

For those willing to dare the murky water of Pusan harbour, **Songdo Beach** is just a stone's throw southwest of **City Hall**. Even if you prudently abstain from swimming, it offers an interesting alternative to staying in town, as there are several inns and hotels with a Pusan flavour. Somewhat cleaner waters are available at three sandy beaches to the east of the city. The most popular is **Haeun-dae**, which has good hotels and a bustling resort town. A few small Buddhist temples are scattered around town, and two large important ones are within easy reach by bus or taxi; **Pomo-sa**, the closer of the two and the headquarters of the Dyana sect, is a mountain temple a few miles from Tongnae Hot Springs.

T'ongdo-sa ㉓ is half an hour to the north along the highway to Taegu. With a total of 65 buildings, T'ongdo-sa is Korea's largest temple. Many of the structures are dispersed throughout the surrounding mountainside, so the temple does not appear especially expansive on first encounter.

Ch'ungmu is deservedly the most popular local destination outside Pusan. The dock of this still rustic resort town is small, but always busy with ferries returning from neighbouring islands, small private fishing trawlers, tourist excursion boats, and all manner of hired craft which take water-sportsmen out for an afternoon of fishing or skin diving. On the way to Ch'ungmu, you will pass between the mainland, to the north, and the island of Koje, to the south. **Koje do** is Korea's second-largest island (after Cheju) and one of the most beautiful areas of the country.

Kyongju

Known for its massive burial mounds, **Kyongju** ㉔ was once well known to Asia's ancients as Kumsong the home of powerful and opulent shaman kings. Today, it's an easy-going resort town where rice cultivation and tourism are the most important sources of revenue. Its distinction as a one-time seat of power however, cannot ever be forgotten. This 210-sq. km (80-sq. mile) valley is dotted with tombs from the 1st to the 8th century and later, with tiered pagodas fortress ruins, granite standing and relief sculpture, palace grounds and other remnants of the rich Three Kingdoms Period.

The **Shilla tombs** at Tumuli Park (open daily 8.30am–6.30pm, closes 5pm in winter; entrance fee) lie on the southeast side of Kyongju and house some 20 tombs of varying sizes, which were originally heaped into place as early as the middle of the first century. The largest of the tombs, that of Kin

BELOW: Pusan fish market.

Map on page 184

Mich'u (reigned 262–85), has been identified in ancient chronicles as the **Great Tomb**. However, a secondary tomb, the so-called **Ch'onma-ch'ong**, or Heavenly Horse or Flying Horse tomb (open daily, 9am–7pm in summer, 9am–5pm in winter), is probably the most well-known gravesite in **Tumuli Park** (sometimes called the Tomb Park).

Kyongju National Museum (open Tues–Sun, 9am–5pm in summer, 9am–4pm in winter) houses some of the finest examples of more than 80,000 items unearthed during digs in this area: metal work, paintings, earthenware, calligraphic scrolls, folk art objects, weapons, porcelains, carved jades, and gold, granite and bronze sculptures.

The sprawling temple complex of **Pulguk-sa** (open daily, 7am–6pm), about 16 km (10 miles) due east of Kyongju on the western slopes of Mt T'oham, is one of the oldest surviving Buddhist monasteries in Korea. As one of Korea's most famous temples, its renown is most likely due to the fact that it stands, flawlessly restored, an example of Shilla-era architecture. **Sokkuram** (open daily, sunrise to sunset), northeast of Pulguk-sa, is a grotto temple set among pines and maples, which enshrines a white granite Sakyamuni Buddha image considered by some art historians to be the most perfect of its kind.

TIP

The island of Cheju-do can be easily reached – either by ferry from Pusan, Mukp'o or the island of Wan-do; or by regular Korean Air and Asiana Airlines flights from the major mainland airports.

Cheju-do

Raved about for its people, culture, seafood, climate, beaches, golf courses, horseback riding, challenging hiking trails, sports fishing grounds and volcanic peaks and craters, **Cheju-do** ㉕ has been nicknamed the "Island of the Gods" by the likes of *Newsweek*. The Korean government prefers to call Cheju-do "Korea's Hawaii" and "The Hawaii of the Orient".

On this egg-shaped island, which lies about 150 km (90 miles) south of Pusan in the channel between Korea and Japan, offshore waters are of the same aqua-turquoise colour as those of Hawaii. These colours in turn lap against the same type of black lava shelves, jagged outcrops and steep cliffs which rim the Hawaiian isles.

Cheju-do claims to be home of the world's longest known lava tubes – the **Snake** and **Manjang caverns** located at **Kimnyong**, between Cheju City and Songsanp'o. The Manjang cavern, the longer of the two tubes, is almost 7 km (4 miles) long, and with a diameter that ranges from 3–20 metres (10–66 ft). During the summer, tourists can join local guides on lamplight tours of these caverns filled with bats, spiders, centipedes and unusual lava formations.

Once winter sets in, icy offshore winds knife across Cheju-do and shatter all Polynesian allusions, but this splendid island – which since ancient times has been renowned for its winds, women and stones – is worth any traveller's detour. When the weather gods are cooperating, Cheju-do is one of Asia's great vacation idylls.

The first Westerners to visit and tell the outside world about Cheju-do (and Korea proper) were Dutch sailors who were shipwrecked at **Mosulp'o** on Cheju's south shore in 1653.

It wasn't until 1958 – an incredibly late exploratory

BELOW: the other side of Songsanp'o.

Map on page 184

date by contemporary tourism standards – that the first really significant group of tourists descended on Cheju-do. But the island is now crisscrossed with paved streets and highways, and dotted with hotels and *yogwan* (inns). There are six major hotels, all of which come equipped with casinos.

Among the island attractions one shouldn't miss are Cheju-do's superb beaches. Favourite crescents of sand are located at **Hyopje**, **Kwakji**, **Hamdok** and **Songsan** along Cheju's upper half, and at **Hwasun**, the aforementioned Chungmun and P'yoson in the south sector. Most of these spots feature superb seafood restaurants, gaily-painted tent cafés, and rentable recreational facilities.

Weaving priests and swimming grannies

The **Hallim weavers village** on the northwest shore, where Koreans trained by Colombian Roman Catholic priests and nuns are creating some of the finest Irish woollens outside of Ireland is another site which shouldn't be missed. This village's unusual cottage industry was begun in the early 1960s by Father Patrick J. McGlinchy, who imported 500 sheep and the right kind of grass for grazing. The colourful and industrious priest first arrived on the island in 1954 and has since become something of a legend for his significant contribution to Cheju's development.

The series of waterfalls on both the east and west sides of lovely **Sogwip'o** are a delight. The strong **Chongbang Falls** right in Sogwip'o town is often referred to as the only waterfall in Asia that plunges directly into the sea.

The **Tol-harubang**, or grandfather stones, are intriguing. These carved lava rock statues, 52 in all, are seen on all parts of Cheju-do. However, nobody is quite sure what to make of these phallic fellows with funny smiles. Anthropologists say they are likely to represent legendary guardians who once flanked the entrances to Cheju's largest townships. Other scholars compare them to mysterious statuary found in some parts of the southern Korean peninsula, Tahiti, Okinawa, Fiji and even Easter Island. Suitable places to study these images up close are at the entrance to the **Samsonghyol Museum** (open daily, 8am–6.30pm in summer, 8am–5.30pm in winter) in Cheju City, or in front of Kwandok-jok-jong (a 15th-century pavilion).

Koreans suggest that you also see the curious **Yongdu-am**, or **Dragon's Head Rock**. This rocky formation rests on the sea in Cheju City's western suburbs near the main airport. According to local legends, this dragon descended from Halla-san and, upon reaching the sea, was petrified where he stood.

Probably the most dominant memories you will have of Chehu-do will be the image of the diving women – called *haenyo* – as they have long been a symbol of this island and its purported matriarchal culture. When the sea and weather conditions are favourable, scores of the *haenyo*, who range from teenagers to weathered grandmothers, can be seen bobbing offshore between free dives for seaweed, shellfish and sea urchins, all staples of the local economy. Do remember though to ask for permission before photographing the *haenyo*, since they are often shy, or might at least want to be rewarded. ❑

BELOW: chillies drying outside a traditional Cheju thatched house.
RIGHT: *haenyo* souvenir plate.

濟洲 飯 죽 (海女)
Women divers in Jeju Island, Korea

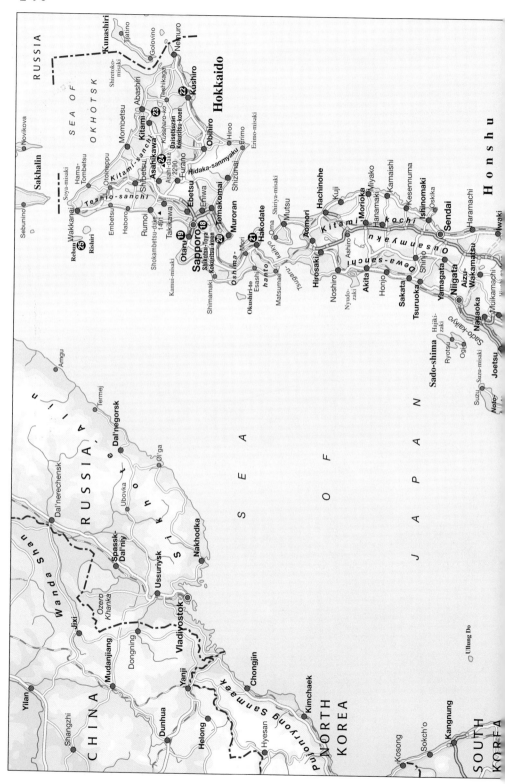

RUSSIA

Kunashiri

Tjatino

SEA OF

OKHOTSK

Novikova

Sakhalin

Sebunino

Golovino

Nehuro

Shiretoko-misaki

Teshikaga

Abashiri

Kushiro

Hokkaido

22

23

Mombetsu

Kitami

Kushsharo-ko
Kokuritsu-koen

Obihiro

24

Hiroo

Soya-misaki

Hama-Tombetsu

Otoineppu

Daisetsuzan
Kokuritsu-koen
2290

Asahi-dake

Erimo-misaki

Wakkanai

Teshio-sanchi

Asahikawa

Hidaka-sanmyaku

Shizunai

Rebun

Rishiri

Embetsu

Haboro

Rumoi

Shibetsu

Kitami-sanchi

Furano

25

Shokambetsu-dake
1491

Takikawa

Enbetsu
Eniwa

Tomakomai

Muroran

Shirya-misaki

Kamui-misaki

Otaru

Sapporo

Shikotsu-Toya
Kokuritsu-koen

Shimamaki

Oshima-hanto

Mori

Hakodate

Oma

Mutsu

Hachinohe

Kuji

Morioka

Miyako

Kamaishi

Kesennuma

Ishinomaki

Oshika

Sendai

Haramachi

Honshu

Okushiri-to

Esashi

Matsumae

Tappi-zaki

Kikko

Aomori

Ashiro

Kitami

Hirosaki

Dewa-sanchi

Noshiro

Nyudo-zaki

Akita

Ou-sanmyaku

Kochi

Shinjo

Yamagata

Aizu-Wakamatsu

Iwaki

Honjo

Sakata

Tsuruoka

Sado-shima

Hajiki-zaki

Ryotsu

Ogo

Niigata

Nagaoka

Joetsu

Suzu

Suzu-misaki

Noto

SEA OF JAPAN

Amgu

Termej

Dal'negorsk

Sikhote Alin

Dal'nerechensk

Ol'ga

RUSSIA

Ubovka

Nakhodka

Spassk-Dal'niy

Ussuriysk

Wanda Shan

Jixi

Ozero
Khanka

Vladivostok

Ullung Do

CHINA

Yilan

Shangzhi

Mudanjiang

Dongning

Yanji

Dunhua

Helong

Hyesan

Chongjin

Kimchaek

NORTH
KOREA

Pulryong Sammaek

Kosong

Sokch'o

Kangnung

SOUTH
KOREA

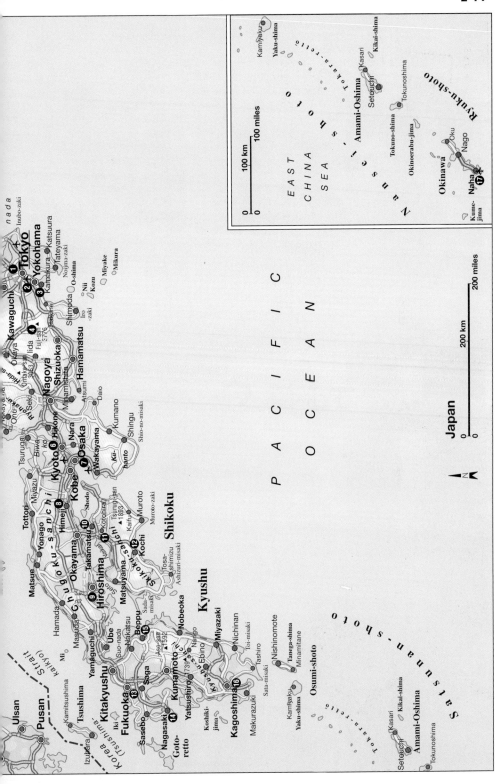

JAPAN

Some see the Japanese turning into Westerners. Others see a
Zen-like serenity. The reality is more complicated

A traveller roaming among the islands of Japan is usually seeking the exotic, or the wondrous, or the unconventional. And indeed, this is what Japan often is, both in the cities and along the back roads. Sometimes what's encountered seems illogical or of dubious purpose, but that is a bias of culture and outlook. The traveller will inevitably compare Japan with the West when confronted with the obvious examples of suits and ties on Japan's *sarariman* – the "salary man" or white-collar worker – and the proliferation of fast-food franchises nearly everywhere. A traveller may then think, "Japan has become like the West".

Big mistake. In its history, Japan has adopted many things, taking what it wants or needs, adapting, and then discarding that which is of no use. Over the centuries, the Japanese have adopted Chinese writing and philosophy, Korean art and ceramics, and most recently, Western technology, clothes and fast-food. Indeed, since it yielded to Perry's Black Ships in 1853, Japan has adopted things foreign with gusto. Yet that which it adopts from the West or elsewhere somehow becomes distinctly Japanese.

Although Japan derives most of its culture from its Asian neighbours and most of its modernity from the West, the Japanese continue to cultivate a unique self-image. They repeatedly refer to Japanese things – including themselves – as "special" or "unique" and thus beyond an outsider's understanding.

There is the nagging legacy of World War II, not to mention the specifically Japanese forgetfulness regarding the subject. Most recently, national self-confidence weakened after a collapsing superheated economy lingered as a decade-long recession. Then there was the 1995 Kobe earthquake that killed over 5,000 people and destroyed a supposedly earthquake-proof infrastructure; and a poison gas attack on Tokyo's subways, right in the heart of the government district.

Nonetheless, the Japanese are rightly proud of their country – recent self-doubts aside – and of the sophistication and depth of its heritage. Much of its progress and advances have been the result of an inward-looking dedication and spirit. The Japanese are perhaps more appreciative of the subtleties of the changing seasons than any other people. Rural people will know if the dragonflies that appear in late spring are three days early, or if the *tsuyu*, the rainy season, is dragging on a bit longer than normal, say by two days. There is a delicate charm and serenity in such observations. It is a quality that says the people know their sense of place. ❑

PRECEDING PAGES: Sakura-jima volcano, Kyushu; leather-clad youths pose for the camera in Harajuku.
LEFT: purification before prayer at a Kyoto temple.

Decisive Dates

THE RISE OF CIVILISED JAPAN

10,000 BC Jomon culture produces Japan's earliest known examples of pottery.
3500–2000 BC Population begins migrating inland from coastal areas.
300 BC Yayoi period begins, with the migration of people from Korea, who introduce rice cultivation.
AD 300 Start of Kofun period as political and social institutions rapidly develop. The imperial line, or Yamato dynasty, begins.
500–600 Buddhism arrives in Japan from Korea.

TIME OF THE WARLORDS

710 A new capital is established in Nara.
794 The capital is relocated to Kyoto. While the court expands, rural areas are neglected.
1180s Estate holders respond to the imperial court's disinterest in the rural areas by developing military power. Conflict among warlords.
1185 Minamoto Yoritomo is victor of the estate-lord struggles and is granted the title of shogun. He establishes his base in Kamakura. The weakened imperial court, however, stays in Kyoto.
1274 Mongols from China unsuccessfully attempt an invasion, landing on Kyushu.
1281 Mongols again attempt an invasion but are turned back by typhoons.

1333 Muromachi period begins as shogun Ashikaga Takauji returns the capital to Kyoto, confronting the imperial court and further eclipsing its influence.
1467 Relations between shogun and provincial military governors break down, leading to the chaotic Age of Warring States. Power of the feudal lords (*daimyo*) increases.
1573 Warlord Oda Nobunaga overruns Kyoto and conquers the provinces, thus beginning the process of unifying the islands.
1582 Nobunaga is assassinated and replaced by Toyotomi Hideyoshi, who continues Nobunaga's unification efforts.
1590 All of Japan is under Hideyoshi's control.
1592 Hideyoshi attempts invasion of Korea.
1597 Hideyoshi again attempts an invasion of Korea, but dies a year later.
1600 Edo Period begins as Tokugawa Ieyasu takes control after defeating opposition warlords in the Battle of Sekigahara.
1603 Tokugawa moves capital to Edo (present-day Tokyo), beginning 250 years of isolation from the world. Edo becomes the largest city in the world.
1853 Perry arrives with US naval ships and forces Japan to accept trade and diplomatic contact. The shogunate weakens as a result.

RETURN OF IMPERIAL RULE

1868 Meiji Restoration returns the emperor to power. The last shogun, Yoshinobu, retires without a fight. The name of the capital is changed from Edo to Tokyo (Eastern Capital).
1872 Samurai class is abolished by imperial decree.
1889 New constitution is promulgated.
1895 Japan wins the Sino–Japanese War.
1904–6 Japan wins Russo–Japanese War, the first time that an Asian nation defeats a European power.
1910 Japan annexes Korea.
1912 Meiji emperor dies. Taisho emperor ascends to the throne.
1918 Japan hit hard by economic chaos, rice riots.
1923 Great Kanto Earthquake hits Tokyo, killing tens of thousands and nearly destroying the city.
1926 Taisho emperor dies. Hirohito ascends the throne to begin the Showa period.
1931 The Japanese occupy Manchuria and install China's last emperor, Pu-yi, as leader of the new Manchuguo. Japan leaves the League of Nations.
1936 A bloody military uprising, one of many during the 1930s, almost succeeds as a coup d'état.
1937 Japan begins a brutal military advance on China. In Nanjing, the army runs riot, killing be-

tween 150,000 and 300,000 civilians in six weeks.
1941 Japan attacks Pacific and Asian targets.
Within a year, Japan occupies most of East Asia
and the western Pacific.
1945 American bombing raids destroy many of
Japan's major cities and industrial centres. In
August, atomic bombs are dropped on Hiroshima
and Nagasaki. A week later, Japan surrenders.
1946 A new constitution is issued under Allied
occupation forces, placing sovereignty with the people rather than the emperor.
1952 San Francisco Peace Treaty settles all war-
related issues and Japan is returned to sovereignty,
except for some Pacific islands, including Okinawa.

1989 Hirohito dies, replaced by his son Akihito,
which begin the Heisei period.

END OF THE DREAM

1990 The "economic bubble" of over-inflated land
values and over-extended banks begins to deflate.
1991 Completely dependent on imported oil, Japan
receives international criticism for not contributing
its share to the Gulf War against Iraq.
1992 Japan's worst post-war recession begins.
1993 A series of publicised scandals, including
institutionalised bribes and collusion, creates a
backlash of voters, who replace Liberal Democratic
Party members with independents.

Japan regains its pre-war industrial output.
1955 Socialist factions merge to form the Japan
Socialist Party; in response, the Liberals and
Democrats join to create the Liberal Democratic
Party (IDP).
1964 Olympic Games held in Tokyo. The bullet train
(*shinkansen*) begins service.
1972 The USA returns Okinawa to Japan.
1980s Japan's economy blossoms into the world's
second most powerful. Banks extend easy loans to
corporations and small companies based on the
inflated land values.

LEFT: Prince Shotoku Taishi with two princely escorts.
ABOVE: blessings for the warriors, 1945.

1995 An earthquake hits the Kobe area, near
Osaka and Kyoto, killing more than 5,000 people and leaving 300,000 homeless. Two months
later, members of a religious cult release nerve
gas in the Tokyo subway system, killing 12 and
destabilising Japanese confidence in the safety of
their society.
1996 The IDP returns to power.
1998 The Winter Olympics are held in Nagano. The
international community prods Japan to resusci-
tate its economy, essential to bring the rest of Asia
out of economic recession. Several banks close
and bankruptcy rates continue to rise. The Chinese
president berates Japan during a state visit for not
sufficiently apologising for World War II.   ❑

THE JAPANESE PEOPLE

One of the most homogeneous societies in the world, Japan is a place of definitive rules of behaviour and some unusual ways of engaging with life

For the Japanese, the group defines a person's individual purpose and function. And the group known as the Japanese – *nihon-jin*, or if especially nationalistic, *nippon-jin* – is the mother of all groups. (That is not exactly an irreverent comment, given that Amaterasu Omikami, or Sun Goddess, is the mythological foremother of the Japanese themselves.)

"Don't understand us too quickly," the Japanese will warn visitors, who are by definition outside of any group of which the Japanese feel themselves a part. Indeed, Japanese people often seem to prefer foreigners not to understand too much about them at all, and there can be a certain pride that outsiders simply don't understand something that is Japanese simply because foreigners are *not* Japanese.

Origins

The Japanese sense of uniqueness extends down to a basic identity of a race and culture distinct from others – if not superior. But the objective evidence strongly points to origins from the mainland.

Theories regarding the racial origins of the Japanese cite both the north and the south – Manchuria and Siberia, and the South China or Indochina regions – as likely possibilities. Students of the subject differ as to which origin to favour. The southern physical type is, of course, the Malay; the northern type is the Mongolian. Today, both north and south Asia are considered equally valid as likely origins of the Japanese. Still, the precise configuration of the migrations and the cultural traits associated with areas of origin are subject to argument. (We could also toss in other legitimate theories about migrations from Polynesia.)

There was substantial human immigration later – in addition to cultural and artistic influences – from the Korean peninsula, a point vehemently denied by Japanese nationalists and racial purists despite the overwhelming archae-

ological and anthropological evidence. Whereas archaeology in many countries is considered the most neutral of disciplines, without political overtones of any kind, in Japan it is rife with factions and rivalries. One group of "experts" has steadfastly refuted and rejected most modern, scientific dating methods, particularly when they are used to authenticate theories proposing a Japan–Korea connection.

Notwithstanding such protests, it may also be possible that the Korean and Japanese languages were mutually understandable, if not identical, some 2,000 years ago and that the people on the Korean peninsula and the Japanese archipelago may have approached a common culture.

Unique or arrogant?

Perhaps the most substantial insulator of the Japanese from the outside is the modern language. In fact, the grammar and syntax are considerably easier to learn than those of most

LEFT: young businessman with a purpose.
RIGHT: concerned girl in trendy Harajuku, Tokyo.

Germanic or Romance languages. The Japanese will retort, however, that it is undoubtedly one of the world's most difficult. The language in fact isn't that difficult, but the context of usage can be very confusing for those not brought up within the culture.

There is much in the Japanese language that buttresses a fundamental notion: that is, the undercurrent in Japanese thinking and traditions that all things Japanese, including the race, are "special", if not unique, in the world. Stay in Japan long enough, listen to conversations and to the media, and it seems that only Japan has earthquakes, typhoons, tasty rice, misery, hot weather, bad memories of war, trees that change colour in autumn, snowfall, and fast trains.

Living on egg shells

In a country where physical crowding and complex interpersonal relationships have shaped the language and social manners over the centuries, even the slightest chance of offending, disappointing, or inconveniencing another person is couched in a shower of soft words, bows, and grave smiles. (Or worse, giggles, a sure signal of acute embarrassment or being uncomfortable.) That foreigners have sometimes

THE AINU

Today with a population of less than 20,000, the Ainu people of Hokkaido were early inhabitants of Hokkaido and also northern Honshu. An enigma is their origins: it was once thought that they were of Caucasian heritage, but blood and skeletal research points most probably to connections with Siberia's Uralic population.

Today there are few speakers of Ainu, which has much in common with other northern Asian languages and also with languages of Southeast Asia and some Pacific cultures. Traditional Ainu culture was one of hunting and gathering. Bears and salmon had an especially sacred place in Ainu traditions.

stereotyped Japanese behaviour as insincere is, to the Japanese, simply ignorant and hurtful.

Notable both for the linguistic hedging and for the insight into Japanese thinking is the difference in the way that Japan remembers World War II. Recent prime ministers have made efforts to address the past, despite the vociferous views of right-wing politicians, nationalists, and university scholars to the contrary.

Yet the linguistic nuances, when properly translated and understood, reveal not the expected apology that at first seems to be offered when translated from Japanese, but rather a promise of "reflection" or "remorse concerning unfortunate events" – which hardly amounts to a sincere apology or an admission of wrong actions or behaviour.

Obligations

If apologies are linguistic puzzles, other expressions of social necessity too are interesting, if not curious. Strangely, the very word for "thank you" – *arigato* – literally means "You put me in a difficult position". *Oki no doku,* which is an expression of sympathy, means "poisonous feeling". And who would think of expressing regret or apology with *sumimasen,* which in strictly literal translation means "This situation or inconvenience will never end"?

easily recognise it without articulating it, the individual must meet and honour that responsibility while putting aside their work or their personal desires.

Family values

Extended families – often cited as the core of Japan's traditional social stability – are nowadays as far flung from the original homestead as education, job opportunities and jet planes can take them. And although nostalgia for the home town and simpler living have become the fashion in recent years, the urban family is increasingly defining the contours of Japanese life.

Then there is that virtually untranslatable word, *giri*. To violate it is simply unthinkable. *Giri* is often translated as a sense of duty and honour, but such a definition ignores the subtle communal and personal responsibilities behind *giri*. In Japan, there are unspoken responsibilities inherent by acceptance and participation within a group, whether in a friendship or with co-workers in an office, or in the sharing of communal village life. When the responsibility beckons, and the member of any group can

In many marriages today the husband still maintains a higher status and exercises greater authority in the family by virtue of being the sole provider. He shows little inclination to help around the house or take care of the children, except when it suits him.

Although comparatively low, rising divorce rates reflect the growing desire of spouses, particularly wives, to put their personal aspirations and concerns over those of the family. Some wives file for divorce when their husbands retire from their jobs, demanding half of their severance pay.

Like her grandmother, the modern Japanese woman feels obligated to show appreciation of

LEFT: morning trot in Fukuoka.
ABOVE: celebrating the emperor's birthday outside the palace.

the family through acquiescence and service. Unlike her grandmother, she is able to regain control over her own life by getting a divorce, particularly once her children have grown up and become independent.

Some couples divorce before they even get started on a proper married life. This is called a Narita Divorce. Many modern Japanese women have spent more time travelling overseas than their new husbands, who may never have been outside of Japan because of the emphasis on working hard and furthering their career. If their first jaunt overseas is on their honeymoon, it becomes ripe with tension and ends in disaster

because the woman is more self-reliant than the man. After returning home to Narita, Tokyo's international airport, they divorce.

Education

Japanese social institutions in general, and schools in particular, are arranged hierarchically in terms of their ability to bestow economic and social status. No institution ranks higher in this regard than Tokyo University.

Entrance to higher education is determined by dreaded examinations, which are administered by the individual universities; for each school applied to for admission, a complete set of entrance exams must be endured. There is no general university admissions exam. The more prestigious a school is, the greater the number of applicants seeking admission and the more difficult the examination.

To help them reach the goal of passing the examinations, parents will budget a considerable amount of their monthly income to send children to *juku,* or private cram schools that are a multibillion-yen business. For the most disciplined of students, every night and weekend is spent at *juku* having their brains crammed with exam-passing information. It is all learned by rote and not by deduction.

Perhaps more importantly, schools reform undisciplined brats into socially predictable and socially responsible people (before starting school for the first time children are often allowed to be especially unruly, the parents knowing their behaviour will be moderated in school). The schools pound down the nail that sticks out. From the earliest days, the educational system focuses on developing such basic Japanese values as harmonious relations with others and establishing group identity through membership in a limited number of social and vocational groups.

Education is respected in Japan, and so are educators. In fact, the honorific for teacher – *sensei,* as in *Nakamurag-sensei* – is the same as for physicians. Unfortunately, the responsibility and professional pressure upon teachers is considerable, especially at the high-school level when students are preparing for their university exams.

The concentration of so much of the nation's educational and cultural resources in Tokyo has its problems. Even the Japanese themselves admit their educational system's shortcomings. The excessive emphasis on entrance examinations is a cause of much national concern and debate. Because of the emphasis on conformity and passing exams, students lack initiative and creative abilities. As a result, Japanese corporations and institutions have to go to North America and Europe for original research and development work. The rigidity of formal education and the alienation of numbers of young people, along with an increased awareness of violence in the schools and bullying of pupils, are also causes of concern. ❏

LEFT: Meiji-era schoolboys.
RIGHT: budding sumo star.

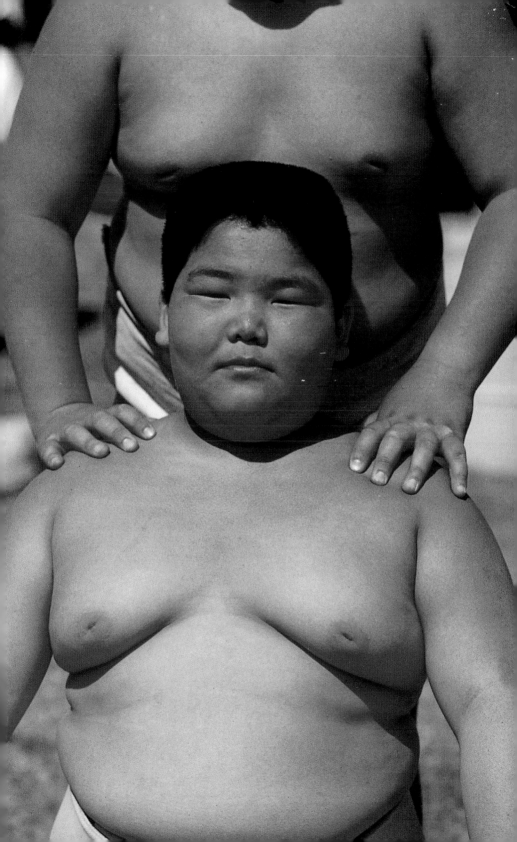

ART AND CRAFTS

With an aesthetic that goes back scores of centuries, Japan's art and crafts
of today retain the depth and layers of history, culture and outlook

The earliest preserved and distinctly Japanese works of art are those of the late Yayoi Period (300 BC–AD 300). These were small, tubular clay figurines called *haniwa*, some of which were set up like fences around imperial mausolea. Whatever their purpose may have been – substitutes for people buried alive in the tombs or magical instruments to ward off evil spirits or bandits – their immediate interest lies in their utter simplicity and charm.

Although many of them are only cylinders, some of the haniwa (and there are hundreds) are figures of men and women, horses, monkeys, and birds. Most are very simple with only a few details of decoration – perhaps a sword or a necklace. They have large hollow spaces for the mouth and eyes, which prevented them from cracking when being fired and which adds not only to their charm, but also to their sense of mystery.

Who are they? What are they saying? Some emotion or song seems to have been eternally suspended here, and while the will to know them may be strong, the recognition of the eternally human, of the eternally here and now, is more compelling.

Aesthetic impulses

The haniwa figures are also important for another reason. We find in them – at the very beginning of the culture – many of the salient characteristics of almost all Japanese art.

Decorative, narrative, human. The decorative extends from modest fence posts to elaborately gilded, painted screens and walls in palaces and castles, to pin-ups in a swordsmith's shop. The narrational can range from rolls and rolls of scrolls illustrating one of the world's biggest (and greatest) novels – *Genji Monogatari*, or *Tale of Genji* – to a single illustration of a young boy playing a flute before a warrior. As for the human, Japanese art embraces everything, from demons to gods to people.

LEFT: from the *Lotus Sutra:* a hermit reciting a sutra.
RIGHT: *Maple Viewers*, Muromachi Period.

Nara and Kamakura sculpture

Before the Nara Period, there are some superb examples of sculpture (such as the Kuze Kannon and the Kudara Kannon, both at Horyu-ji in Nara). To recommend only one, mention must be made of the Miroku at Koryu-ji, in Kyoto. This is a delicately carved wooden statue of the

Buddha of the Future. The young person (gender is blurred in Buddhist art, but one assumes the figure is of a boy) has one leg crossed over the other, his chin rests on a couple of extended fingers, and one detects the slightest hint of the most gracious, lyrical smile imaginable. The Miroku is a hint of the greatness to come.

In the Nara Period (646–794), with Japan's full-scale welcome of things Chinese, the native response to the real is fused with its spiritual aspirations without ever abandoning the former. Work is done in wood, clay, bronze, or by using the curious technique of hollow lacquer.

Sculptures – gods and humans alike – are spiritually powerful because they are so real.

(They were probably based on real models.) And though it cannot now be seen, they were originally coloured. The patinas of age may lend them a spiritual depth, but one should not forget their original splendour. While the Buddha and some of the deities are ruled by convention (the beatific smile, various hand gestures for the former, terrifying gazes for the latter), the portraits of the blind monk Ganjin (Toshodai-ji) and of the Buddha's disciples (Kofuku-ji) are utterly remarkable for their realism.

GENJI'S LOVES

Tale of Genji, the masterpiece of Japanese literature, was written by the daughter of a courtier around 1010. It is about Genji, a Heian-Period courtier, and his pursuit of the art of love.

revive until the Kamakura Period several centuries later. While Nara Period sculpture was both human and ideal, that of the Kamakura was wholly human, personal, and emotional.

For example, the Kamakura Period (1185–1336) produced more portraits of monks and of demons (warriors, really) than of aloof gods. It also produced its Daibutsu, which, though somewhat smaller than that in Nara, is equally affecting. It now sits uncovered in the Kamakura hills, its presence enhanced by time.

It was also during this time that the 16-metre (52 ft) high bronze Daibutsu (Great Buddha) in Nara was created. It is a sorry sight from what it must have originally looked like, housed as it is now in a much smaller hall and worn by age. It was originally gilded with bronze and incised with designs that can now only be barely discerned on some of the lotus petals upon which the figure sits. This is the great tourist attraction at Todai-ji that should not be missed.

The Nara Period ended with the move of capital to Kyoto. With that – the beginning of the Heian Period (794–1185) – Japanese sculpture declined as other arts ascended and did not

Painting

In the Heian Period, life itself became an art, and works of art became its decorative attendant. Kyoto's Byodo-in may have been meant as a model of the next world, but it only showed that life in this one was already exquisite

Japanese painting had long existed, but it had not flowered into great sophistication, particularly in the form of long, rolled, and hand-held scrolls. These paintings, known as *Yamato-e*, might depict the changing seasons, famous beauty spots, or illustrate well-known stories. The best Yamato-e were of the latter type and depicted popular legends, warrior tales, or works of great literature such as the *Ise Mono-*

gatari and *Genji Monogatari*, or the *Tale of Genji*. The popular legends might include a satirical look at pompous officials turned into battling frogs and rabbits, or a man who can't stop farting, or a look into the punishments that await evil-doers in hell. Post-Heian warrior tales drew on the many heroic or sentimental tales collected in the *Heike Monogatari* and other stories (as Western artisans drew on Homer and Virgil).

The Momoyama Period (late 16th century) is Japan's age of Baroque splendour when, as one scholar says, "The simper of the late Ashikaga court went down before the swagger of men like Nobunaga". It is the one of the high points of Japan's decorative genius. The Momoyama Period is filled with gold and silver, with very bright, flat colours (no shading or outlining), and embellished with lush scenes painted on screens and walls of flower-viewing parties, lovely women, and sightseeing spots.

This is not to imply that monochrome was abandoned during Momoyama. Far from it: there was a great deal of superb *sumi-e* (ink picture) screens and paintings done at this time. The overwhelming impression of Momoyama-Period art, however, is of gold.

Floating world

The Edo Period (1603–1868) is the great age of popular art, even though much great decorative art was being made for the aristocracy or the military classes, especially by Koetsu, Sotatsu, and Korin. The latter's gorgeous *Irises* – all violet and gold – is an excellent example of the period art and can be seen at the Nezu Museum of Art in Tokyo.

The merchant class, however, was developing its own pleasures in fiction, drama (*kabuki*), and art, and mass appeal soon became more important than ever.

The art most associated with Edo Tokyo is *ukiyo-e* (lit. pictures of the floating world). Once again, the sublunary, fleshy human existence was a key element. Although woodblock printing had been used to reproduce sutras, for example, the technique first began to be used in a more popular vein in the early 18th century. At first, the prints were either monochromatic

---

LEFT: *ukiyo-e* of Mt Fuji by Hokusai, Edo Period.
RIGHT: the classic image of an 18th-century male *kabuki* performer.

or hand-coloured with an orange-red. In time, two colours were used, then four, and so on.

Although the names of hundreds of ukiyo-e artists are known, it should be remembered that the production of these prints was a cooperative effort between many highly-skilled people. There was the artist who created the design and suggested the print's colours, the carvers of the many blocks, the actual printers, and finally the publishers who financed and distributed them.

Early ukiyo-e, especially those by the first great master, Moronobu, are usually portraits of prostitutes from the Yoshiwara district of old Edo or else illustrations for books. With

polychrome printing in ukiyo-e, a number of "genres" became established. There were, for example, portraits of prostitutes (*bijin ga*), kabuki actors in famous roles, the ever-present scenes of renowned places, and of plant and animal life.

Ukiyo-e, suffice to say, is one of the world's great graphic art forms, but until very recently, the Japanese have never considered it to be "art". Rather, it was a publishing form until foreigners began to show an interest and to start collecting ukiyo-e works. It is only in the past few decades that Japanese collectors have begun to fully appreciate ukiyo-e and to realise its value. ❏

CUISINE

The Japanese islands are home to what is probably the world's most eclectic, detailed, healthy, and aesthetically appealing cuisine

Japan is a country of regional cuisines and, also, of seasonal cuisines. In fact, sampling local dishes is a fundamental purpose of travelling for many Japanese, whether it be a *ekiben* box-lunch bought at the train station or an exquisite dinner at a remote *ryokan*.

Two types of places that particularly deserve attention for their pure Japanese ambience are the *izaka-ya*, or pub, often with a string of red lanterns above its door, and the *taishu-sakaba*, a much larger tavern-like establishment that may also sport red lanterns. These red lanterns (*akachochin*) signify a traditional Japanese place for eating and drinking. Specialties include Japanese-style fried fish, shellfish, broiled dishes, *tofu* (bean curd) dishes, *yakitori* (skewered and broiled meat), fried rice balls, and simple *sashimi*.

Kaiseki ryori

At least one meal in Tokyo should be *kaiseki ryori*, a centuries-old form of Japanese cuisine served at restaurants or in *ryokan* in several elegant courses. Ingredients depend upon the season and region. One might spend a lifetime sampling every regional variation (Be warned that authentic kaiseki ryori is very expensive).

Fastidiously prepared, kaiseki ryori is so aesthetically pleasing that it's virtually an art form. Ideally, the food's visual appeal would be heightened by a proper setting for the meal, whether in the snow-blanketed mountains or on the sea shore. Some of the better restaurants serving kaiseki ryori have succeeded in creating exactly such an atmosphere regardless of outside environment, with brush works, flower arrangements, and views of waterfalls cascading over well-hewn rocks into placid pools. The effect elevates the senses and pleasure of kaiseki ryori.

The ingredients must be as fresh as the dawn. That's a prime requisite of good food in gen-

eral, of course, together with a good recipe and a good cook. Rejoice in the fact that Japan has plenty of all three.

Japanese cuisine focuses on flavour and its subtleties, and on the food's aesthetic presentation. Rather than create distinctive flavours for their dishes, Japanese chefs seek above all

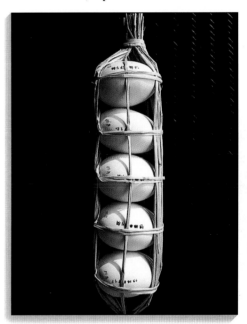

to retain the natural flavours. And rather than alter the appearance of their ingredients, they strive to enhance their visual appeal through artful arrangements.

Noodles

Japanese noodles are of three main types: *soba*, *udon*, and *somen*. Made of buckwheat, soba noodles are thin and brownish, with a hearty consistency. Udon noodles, made of wheat, are usually off-white and thick to very thick. Somen noodles, also made of wheat, are as thin as vermicelli. Udon is usually eaten in hot dishes, while soba and somen may be eaten hot or cold, depending upon season. Additionally,

LEFT this shop owner is in a pretty fine pickle.
RIGHT: traditional packaging of eggs.

eaten cold, is a type called *hiyamugi* (iced noodles), made of the same ingredients as udon but much thinner.

Most common are soba, particularly delicious if not overburdened with non-buckwheat flour extender. It is usually served with *wasabi* (green horseradish), thinly sliced scallions, a dip made of *mirin* (sweet *sake*), and *katsuobushi* (shaved flakes of dried bonito). Soba noodles in this form, when served chilled on a *zaru*, a type of bamboo tray, are called *zaru-soba* and make a delicious summer meal. Soba is not only tasty, but extremely nutritious, the more so in proportion to its *sobako* (wheat

Sushi and sashimi

Taste and visual pleasure converge in *sushi* and *sashimi*, both prepared with uncooked seafood. Japanese simply adore sushi and sashimi, and knowing the Western bias against raw fish or meat will often ask visitors – simply out of sheer curiosity – if they can eat one or the other.

A good sushi shop, or *sushi-ya*, can be both expensive and confounding if one doesn't know what to ask for. Try, instead, a *kaiten sushi-ya,* where small dishes of sushi pass by on a conveyor belt along the counter. It lacks a certain elegance, but in a kaiten sushi-ya the uninitiated can study the sushi offerings at leisure and

flour) content. Another hot weather favourite – just as soba is, but entirely different – is somen, the thin and off-white wheat noodle noted for its delicate flavour and adaptability to many garnishes.

One of Japan's great cold-weather favourites is udon, a somewhat thick to very thick wheat noodle served in a hot, soy-based broth with scallions, other vegetables, and an egg. Udon, a real body-warmer, is appreciated for its excellent texture.

Unlike pasta that's turned around on a fork, Japanese noodles are sucked into the mouth with chopsticks and *slurped* down. Experts say the noodles taste better that way.

sample it for less cost. Then later, armed with new-found expertise, visit a proper sushi-ya.

Good sushi requires that the ingredients should be of good quality, that the rice be properly vinegared and steamed, and that the topping should be absolutely fresh.

Nabemono

If hot-pot dishes are your pleasure, Japan is the place to be in autumn and winter. Every part of Japan, without exception, has its own distinctive *nabe-ryori* (pot dishes). Nabemono are winter dishes, essentially, and include: *ishikari-nabe* (Hokkaido Prefecture), containing salmon, onions, Chinese cabbage, tofu, kon-

nyaku (a jelly made of root starch), and *shungiku* (spring chrysanthemum).

Popular for a quick meal is Tokyo-style *oden-nabe*, a potpourri containing potatoes, tofu, konnyaku, boiled eggs, octopus, carrots, daikon, kelp, and a wide variety of other ingredients. Make a note of oden, which are often presented as pick-and-choose in convenience stores like 7-11. It is one of the better winter body-warmers and a hearty dish.

Bento

Like most developed countries, Japan is increasingly a land of fast-food. The traditional and bento). Some of Japan's most popular forms of food are those sold inside the stations.

Trains often make stops of just long enough duration to permit passengers to get off briefly and buy some of their favourite *meisanbutsu* (local specialties), especially the ubiquitous ekiben, to be eaten aboard the train.

Tsukemono

A Japanese meal always comes with *tsuke-mono*, or distinctive Japanese-style pickles. Historically, pickles probably owe their origins to the practice of pickling foods in anticipation of famines. During the Edo Period, pickles

Japanese box lunch, *bento*, or more respectfully, *obento,* has become a form of fast-food in itself, with both convenience stores and *bento-ya* offering wide selections to take out. A bento box, flat and shallow, is used with small dividers to separate rice, pickles, and whatever else might grace the inside. Just about anything can be used in bento, including Western exports like spaghetti, Vienna sausages and hamburger.

A special type of bento that has become an art in itself, not to mention a pursuit for the connoisseur, is the *ekiben* (from *eki* for train station

LEFT: yakitori, one of Japan's original fast-foods.
ABOVE: counter fare can be fast and economical.

came into their own and the *tsukemono-ya* (pickle shop) emerged as a new type of business. Ingredients used in Japanese pickles include Chinese cabbage, bamboo, turnips, *kyuri* (Japanese cucumbers), hackberry, daikon, ginger root, *nasu* (Japanese eggplant), *udo* (a type of asparagus), *gobo* and many others.

Tsukemono add colour to a meal and offer a wide range of textures, from *crunch* to *squish,* that might be missing from the main dishes. Pickles can serve to clear the palate for new tastes – such as in sushi, in which a bite of pickled ginger root rids the mouth of the aftertaste of an oily fish such as *aji* (mackerel) and prepares it for the delicate taste of *ebi* (prawn).❑

UNDERCURRENTS OF LIFE AND RITUAL

At the core of Japanese life is the ancient, animist belief of Shintoism, which informs daily life in basic ways, enriched by introduced Buddhism

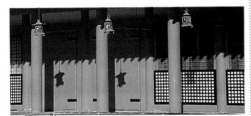

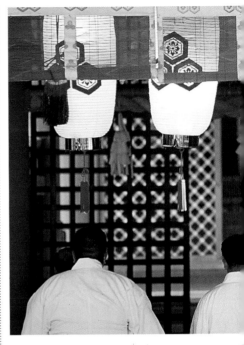

An outsider may perceive a certain fog enveloping the Japanese beliefs in gods and afterlife and in the metaphysical concerns of life. Buddhism and Shintoism coexist, and on occasion appear to meld together. Unlike believers in a monotheistic system, Japanese are more willing to accept a world that has a lot of grey areas with few absolutes, in which compromise and tolerance of thought is essential. It is not uncommon to find Shinto shrines and Buddhist temples sharing the same sacred grounds, each tending to specific needs but complementing one another as a whole.

Shintoism doesn't exist as doctrine, but rather as an integral undercurrent to one's daily life. Shinto is Japan's indigenous religion, but the term Shinto did not appear in any Japanese literature until the 6th century, and in fact the label came into existence only as a way to distinguish it from Buddhism, introduced from mainland Asia. Nor were there visual images of Shinto deities – *kami* – until the imagery of Buddhism established itself in the archipelago. Over the centuries, Taoism and Confucianism also influenced Shinto.

Ancient Shinto was polytheistic, maybe even pantheistic, and people believed kami existed not only in nature, but also in abstract ideas such as creation, growth, and human judgment.

▷ **COEXISTING WITH BUDDHISM**
Buddhist priests, such as these Zen priests at a Kyoto temple, have no qualms in sharing the metaphysical with Shinto priests.

△ **GIFTS TO THE GODS**
Offerings at a small shrine Okinawa. Some of the mos sacred sites are simple and lack grand structures.

△ **GOOD HARVEST WISH**
As in ancient times, praye and imagery of good rice harvests often punctuate festivals in Japan.

A LIFE OF SHINTO BLESSINGS

Traditions of Shinto (and of Buddhism, too) are the traditions of Japan itself. They pepper the daily lives of the Japanese, who perform them as routines of life when the urge or need arises.

The small votives *(ema)* above are hung at shrines to seek good luck in exams or other secular rituals. Infants are brought to the shrine 30 to 100 days after birth to initiate the child as a new believer. On 15 November of every year, Japan is embellished with children in kimono for *shichi-go-san* (seven-five-three). Girls three and seven years old and boys five years old visit the shrine to thank the *kami* for their life so far and to pray for health. In January, 20-year-olds return to the shrine marking their becoming adults. When they are married, it is usually a Shinto ceremony (although a separate Western-style ceremony is increasingly common. Death, however, usually is of Buddhist ritual and family remembrance.

△ **MORNING PRAYERS**
Shinto priests at morning prayers. The sacred image is often kept from view, seen only by the head priest.

▽ **VANISHING POINT**
Torii – dividing the secular world from Shinto shrines – make an unusual tunnel at Fushimi Inari, Kyoto.

◁ **SHRINE IMAGERY**
The rope, white paper, and other symbols announce a sacred site as of Shinto importance.

▷ **SADO**
Tea ceremonies – symbolic of Japanese ways – are mostly Zen Buddhist influenced.

QUICK PRAYER
here are no weekly holy ays. Rather, the Japanese tend a shrine or temple hen the need arises.

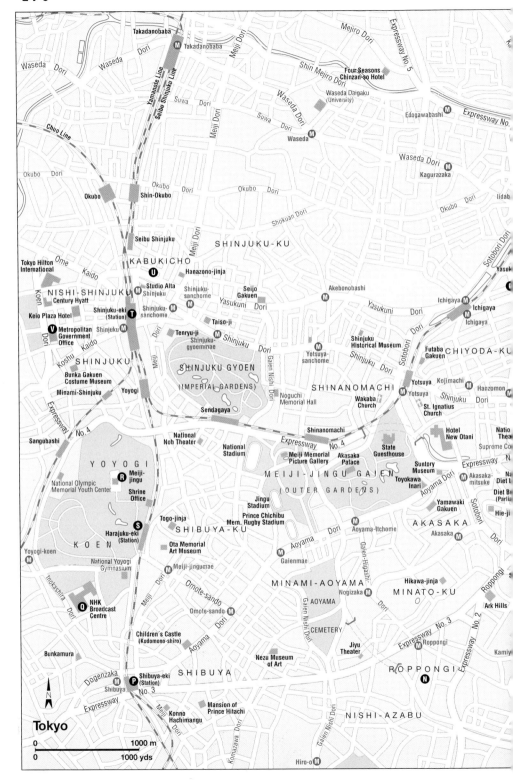

Tokyo

0   1000 m

0   1000 yds

TOKYO

Vying with Mexico City as the world's largest city, the Tokyo metropolitan area, sited on the former capital of the shoguns – and on an earthquake zone – is home to 30 million people

Maps:
Area 246
City 270

Japan has always been a country of villages. If the giant sprawling metropolis of **Tokyo** ❶ can be described as Japan's biggest village – and it is by far at over 620 sq. km (240 sq. miles) and with 10 million people in central Tokyo alone – then one can easily reduce the city itself into a gathering of smaller villages anchored around major railway stations. Indeed, these stations are helpful in understanding the layout of Tokyo, which does not have a central urban core.

Most of Tokyo's smaller "villages" lie on a circular railway line called Yamanote-sen, or Yamanote Line. There are 29 stations on the Yamanote and it takes about an hour to make the complete loop, actually an oval in shape. Look at the layout of the Yamanote-sen, and the placement of the stations along the way, and orientation in Tokyo becomes much easier. The important stations on the line – and the ones with which to become most familiar – are Tokyo, Ueno, Shinjuku, and Shibuya. In the centre of the oval defined by the Yamanote-sen, a bit off-centre to the east, are the grounds of what once was the Edo Castle. The Imperial Palace has replaced it, but the symmetry of the old castle defences – moats and gates – are still evident today.

Most of Tokyo is accessible by one station or another, by one train or subway line, or by many. Use them. They're fast, cheap and utilitarian. Just stay off the trains during rush-hour for obvious reasons. Or you could walk, for only then do the many villages feel connected, giving a true sense of Tokyo itself.

Imperial Palace

In the centre of Tokyo stands **Kokyo**, the **Imperial Palace** Ⓐ, a functional palace where the emperor and his family reside. Much of the grounds – as well as the palace itself – secluded behind massive stone walls, trees and Edo-Period moats, are closed to the public.

Most of the 110-hectare (270-acre) palace complex is forested or given over to private gardens and small ponds. The Showa emperor (Hirohito), who reigned from 1926 until 1989, was a skilled biologist and much of the inner garden area is a nature preserve. The Imperial Palace building itself is an expansive, low concrete construction, veiled with a green roof. It was completed in 1970 to replace the wooden residence destroyed in a 1945 Allied air raid.

Kokyo Gaien, the palace's outer garden to the southeast, is a spacious area of green lawns and impeccably sculpted pine trees, planted in 1889 directly east is Tokyo Station). Kokyo Gaien is where most tourists come to take their obligatory photograph, for here a large, gravel-covered area leads to the famous postcard scene of **Niju-bashi** Ⓑ, a dis-

PRECEDING PAGES: Mt Fuji seen from Shinjuku on a clear day. **LEFT:** Harajuku's Takeshita-dori. **BELOW:** back alley in Shinjuku.

Yasukuni-jinja's torii *is made of steel.*

BELOW: Niju-bashi and Fushimi-yagura.

tinctive bridge across an inner moat and one of the most widely recognised landmarks in Japan. Tourists come here by the bus-load for a group portrait in front of the bridge (*bashi*) and moat. Behind is the **Fushimi-yagura**, a lookout turret of the original Edo castle.

Visitors are permitted to enter the **Kokyo Higashi Gyoen**, the East Imperial Garden of the palace. It is open most days and can be entered through Ote-mon, Hirakawa-mon and Kitahanebashi-mon, three of the eight gates (*mon*) into the palace grounds. Inside are the remains of the defences of Edo-jo, the shogunate's castle (*jo*), and the foundations of the castle's *donjon*, the primary lookout tower of the shogun's residence.

At the northern end of the old castle grounds in **Kitanomaru-koen** is the **Kokuritsu Kindai Bijutsukan** (National Museum of Modern Art) (open Tues–Sun, 10am–5pm; entrance fee). In well-presented galleries the modern building displays excellent examples of Japan's contemporary artists, many of whom studied in Europe.

West from Kitanomaru-koen, Yasukuni-dori leads to **Yasukuni-jinja** ⓒ. What is said to be Japan's largest *torii* – eight storeys in height, made of high-tension steel plates and weighing 100 tons – boldly announces the shrine. Its entrance nipping the northern tip of the Imperial Palace grounds, this Shinto shrine is Japan's most controversial. Proponents say it honours those who died for Japan and the emperor; opponents say it glorifies Japanese aggression and honours convicted war criminals. Pinched between the two extremes are politi-cians, who must decide for themselves whether or not they should attend annual ceremonies at the shrine. When a prime minister visits, governments through-out Asia respond with highly vocal disapproval.

Tokyo Station, Ginza, and Nihombashi

While not Japan's busiest station – **Tokyo-eki** (Tokyo Station) is nonetheless sizable with 19 platforms side by side, including the terminus for the *shinkansen* (literally, new trunk line), or bullet train. Deep beneath the station are additional platforms for more subway and JR lines.

The Marunouchi side of the station is fronted by the original Tokyo Station, built in 1914 of red brick in an Old World European style. Air raids in 1945 damaged the station, taking off the top floors; renovations, finished in 1947, left it somewhat lower than before.

Immediately south of Tokyo Station is the **Tokyo International Forum**, an echoing complex of concert and exhibition halls. There is a **Tourist Information Centre** (open Mon–Fri, 9am–5pm, Sat, 9am–noon; tel: 03 3201 3331) in the basement here. If you are expecting to travel in Japan, you should visit this centre to get extensive information about the country (the staff speak English). South again are elevated railway tracks extending from **Yurakucho-eki** (Yurakucho Station) , constructed in 1910; the shinkansen and Yamanote-sen trains snake along the overhead tracks.

Of all places in Japan, the name of **Ginza** is perhaps better known outside the country than any except Tokyo and Kyoto. During the super-heated bubble economy of the late 1980s, land in Ginza was literally priceless, the most expensive real estate anywhere, and priced in square centimetres. Likewise, an evening's entertainment in the exclusive and unmarked clubs of its back alleys seemed almost priceless – and still is.

The Mitsukoshi store anchors **Ginza 4-chome**, where Chuo-dori intersects Harumi-dori, the second main avenue (*dori*). (Most Tokyo districts are subdi-

> **Map on pages 270–1**

> **TIP**
>
> Take care when considering a place to eat or drink in Ginza: prices can be astronomical. On the other hand, beneath the elevated train tracks of nearby Yurakucho are many cheap stands and shops offering *yakitori* and cold beer.
>
> **BELOW:** famous Ginza 4-chome in the rain.

Woodblock print of Nihom-bashi during the Edo Period.

BELOW: homeward bound: fighting the boredom on the subway.

vided into *chome*; Ginza has eight.) Chuo-dori, sometimes called Ginza-dori, is one of two main arteries through Ginza and extends northwards to the east of Tokyo Station and into Nihombashi. A few blocks past the overpass separating Ginza from Nihombashi and Yaesu is a monument to the original site of Ginza. Further on, numerous fashionable boutiques and galleries line the wide boulevard, and immense department stores – including Matsuya (Ginza's largest) and Mitsukoshi (founded in 1673, with the current Ginza store dating from 1930) – cascade onto the sidewalks. A popular meeting place is the **Sony Building** – note the waiting and expectant faces outside; inside are the latest in consumer electronics and a Toyota showroom.

Along Hibiya-dori is the towering **Imperial Hotel** (Teikoku Hoteru) ❻ Always a place of impeccable standards, by which other hotels are measured, the first Imperial Hotel opened in 1890. Its modest structure was later replaced by a wonderful Frank Lloyd Wright design; the day after it opened to the public in 1923, the Great Kanto Earthquake hit Tokyo, and the hotel was one of the few structures to escape destruction. The Wright building was replaced by this modern structure in 1970. It is a great shame the Wright building wasn't kept in Tokyo, but it is now in Nagoya, reassembled in its original form.

Returning north to the Yaesu side of Tokyo Station, Chuo-dori crosses Nihombashi-gawa over **Nihom-bashi** (Nihon Bridge) ❼ (the Nihom/Nihon variation is a phonetic one of pronunciation, not meaning). The concrete-lined river and expressway diminish the significance of the original 1603 arched wooden bridge that was the centre of Edo Period Tokyo and the zero point for the five main roads leading out of Edo to the rest of Japan. The present stone bridge, dating from 1911, retains little, if any, of its Edo Period ambience.

On the eastern periphery of Nihombashi, towards the Sumida-gawa, the **Tokyo City Air Terminal** (TCAT) is a downtown check-in facility for flights departing from the international airport at Narita.

Map on pages 270–1

Kanda and Akihabara

If there is a book, however old and in whatever language, that seems unattainable, it can be found in **Kanda**, especially around the Jimbocho station. There have been bookshops here in Kanda since the 1880s, nearly as long as the nearby universities have stood.

The neighbourhood of **Akihabara** epitomises the old Edo tradition of merchants or craftsmen of a particular commodity congregating together. Akihabara's reputation for electrical goods originated shortly after World War II, when a black market for scarce electrical and radio components evolved near the station. Now Akihabara accounts for around 10 percent of Japan's domestic electrical and electronic sales.

East of Akihabara and on the other side of the Sumida-gawa, the area known as **Ryogoku** is the site of Tokyo's sumo arena, **Kokugikan**. A lot of very large men live in Ryogoku – it is the site of many of the sumo *beya*, or stables, as the training centres and dormitories for the *rikishi* (wrestlers) are called. Behind the Kokugikan is the **Fukagawa Edo Tokyo Museum** ❻ (open Tues–Sun, 10am–6pm; entrance fee), a spectacular hall that encompasses a massive reconstruction of part of Shitamachi Edo (the area of town where the commoners lived) from the 19th century. This is one of the finest museums in Japan, well-planned and meticulously thought out, with intricately constructed models of villages and a life-sized reconstruction of Nihom-bashi, the Edo-Period bridge.

Banners outside the Kokugikan with the names of tournament sumo wrestlers.

BELOW: Fukagawa Edo Tokyo Museum.

Ueno

North of Tokyo Station and Akihabara, exactly eight minutes on the Yamanote train, is **Ueno-eki** (Ueno Station) ❶. It's a subjective and subtle impression, but the area around the station seems somehow more down to earth, if not grittier than other parts of urban Tokyo. West of the station, **Ueno-koen** (Ueno Park) is Tokyo's most park-like park: sprawling grounds with trees, flocks of scrounging pigeons, monuments and statues, homeless Japanese people, a zoo (less than inspiring), a big pond with lilies and waterfowl, and national museums.

The **Tosho-gu** ❷, a shrine adjacent to a five-storey pagoda, was established in 1627 (the present buildings date from a 1651 renovation) by a warlord on his own estate to honour the first Tokugawa shogunate, Tokugawa Ieyasu. Although not as embellished as it was in the Edo Period, the main shrine building is still a magnificently ornate building. The outer hall features murals painted by the famous Edo artist Kano Tanyu.

Shinobazu-no-ike (Shinobazu Pond) was once an inlet and is now a pond (*ike*) dense with lily plants. A small peninsula juts into the pond with a Buddhist temple to Benten – a goddess of good fortune and the only female among the Seven Deities of Good Luck – perched on the end. A promenade follows the pond's square 2-km (1¼-mile) circumference. The **Shitamachi Fuzoku Shiryokan** ❸ (Shitamachi Museum) (open Tues–Sun, 9.30am–4.30pm; entrance fee), near the pond at the park's south entrance, is a hands-on exhibit of Edo commoners' daily life in Shitamachi, as this part of Edo Tokyo was once known. Children love it.

The **Kokuritsu Seiyo Bijutsukan** (National Museum of Western Art) (open Tues–Sun, 9.30am–5pm; admission fee) is anchored by a collection of nearly

BELOW: Tokyo National Museum.

housand pieces, and the **Tokyo Kokuritsu Hakubutsukan ❶** (Tokyo National Museum (open Tues–Sun, 9am–4.30pm; entrance fee) offers a superbly displayed collection of Asian art and archaeology. Arching over the outside entrance to the museum grounds is an immense samurai-estate gate.

Map on pages 270–1

Asakusa

From the mid-1800s until World War II, **Asakusa** was the centre of all fine things in Tokyo, a cultural nucleus of theatre and literature, cuisine and the sensual delights. Imagine today's Shibuya, Ginza, Roppongi, and Shinjuku tossed together, countrified, and without the benefit of neon, fast-food, and loudspeakers.

Anchoring Asakusa was **Senso-ji**, or **Asakusa Kannon ⓜ**, perhaps the oldest Buddhist temple in the region and a draw for people from around Japan who brought with them spending money to make Asakusa prosper. The south entrance to the temple, on Asakusa-dori, is a large gate, Kaminari-mon, dating from 1960 (the original burned down a century earlier). Here begins Nakamise-dori, where two rows of red buildings funnel temple-goers northwards through a souvenir arcade before spilling out onto the temple grounds.

In the other direction, east of Senso-ji, is the **Sumida-gawa** (Sumida River), which empties into Tokyo Bay. The exit for the Ginza Line, Tokyo's first subway line which opened in 1927, surfaces near the Azuma-bashi (Azuma Bridge). Just north of the bridge is **Sumida-koen**, a park intended to open up the river that passes through the old core of Tokyo.

Schoolgirls posing at Senso-ji's south gate, Kaminari-mon.

BELOW: Tokyo Tower from across Tokyo Bay.

Roppongi and Minato

In the lower centre of the oval defined by the Yamanote-sen and just to the southwest of the Imperial Palace is an area favoured by Tokyo's expatriate community: **Minato-ku**, a Tokyo ward (*ku*) made up of Aoyama, Akasaka, Roppongi, Azabu and Hiroo. The area is peppered with embassies and high-priced expatriate and company-subsidised housing – US$10,000 a month is not unusual – and liberally spiced with nightclubs and restaurants.

Up on a hill, **Roppongi ⓝ** is the heart of the area's social life, nightlife and courting life. It crawls with both foreigners and Japanese on the prowl for the opposite sex. Its main avenues are bright and loud, the back alleys lined with drinking establishments laced by themes meant to nurture nostalgia or homesickness in strangers in a strange land. But don't confuse the activity here with the blatant sex trade of Shinjuku's Kabukicho. In Roppongi, it's only upscale food and drinks garnished by probing smiles.

Check the horizon to the south, towards the area known as Shiba: the red-and-white **Tokyo Tower ⓞ** (open daily, 9am–8pm; entrance fee) juts skyward, looking industrial and out of place. Completed in 1958, its primary purpose was to broadcast television signals. Subsequent lyrical allusions to the Eiffel Tower or urban elegance were examples of creative writing. At 333 metres (1,093 ft), it's an ugly projection marring the skyline – but the views from the observation deck, 250 metres (820 ft) up, are excellent.

Shibuya and Harajuku

Although many resident foreigners might nominate Roppongi to the east, **Shibuya** is one of the trendiest commercial neighbourhoods in Tokyo. Roppongi caters to foreigners and has done so with style for decades. Shibuya, on the other hand, caters to Japanese youth with money to spend and style to flaunt. The area was a rural but bustling stop along one of the great highways built during the Tokugawa years and leading from Edo Tokyo. Later, mulberry (for an abortive attempt at silk production) and tea fields surrounded Shibuya's first train station, which opened in 1885. Nearby, along the Shibuya-gawa, were mills powered by water wheels.

Bullet train

The most popular exit of **Shibuya-eki** (Shibuya Station) ➋, opening to the northwest, is named after a hound dog. And outside that entrance one will find a statue erected in 1964 of said dog, an Akita named Hachiko. For a rendezvous in Shibuya, Hachiko's statue is the preferred spot.

Beyond the Hachiko entrance is an immense intersection. Looking straight ahead, note the tall cylindrical building: the Shibuya 109 building is a good reference for orientation. The crowded road to its right leads up a gentle hill to Tokyu department store, and adjacent to it, the **Bunkamura**, a performance hall built during the roaring 1980s. Something's always going on inside – art, music, cinema, theatre – and the interior spaces are refreshing on a hot day.

At the top of the hill to the left is the huge NHK **Broadcast Centre** ➌, a 23-storey building with two dozen TV studios and an equal number of radio studios. NHK is the government-run, viewer-subsidised television and radio broadcasting centre. More than 1,500 shows are produced here each week.

Nearby **Yoyogi-koen** served as the Olympic Village during the 1964 summer

Map on pages 270–1

games. Previously, the area was a barracks for the American army, known as Washington Heights. Everything was eventually torn down, but rather than erecting something new, the site was turned into the park. It now includes a wild bird park and playground. Yoyogi gained notoriety for some of the worst free music in the city when wannabe rock groups gave weekend concerts on a closed-off street, until the government put a stop to such spontaneity.

Yoyogi-koen is an extension of one of Japan's most famous Shinto shrines, **Meiji-jingu** ®. The shrine deifies Emperor Meiji and Empress Shoken. (Their remains, however, are in Kyoto.) The emperor, of course, was restored to rule in the 1868 Meiji Restoration when the Tokugawa shogunate collapsed. The emperor died in 1912 and the empress two years later. The original shrine, built in 1920, was destroyed during World War II; the current buildings were reconstructed in 1958. The shrine itself is constructed of Japanese cypress. The grounds cover 70 hectares (175 acres) and were a favourite retreat of the emperor. The park is populated by nearly every species of tree growing in Japan, all of them donations to the shrine.

The entrance to Meiji-jingu is near **Harajuku-eki** (Harajuku Station) ⑤, architecturally interesting for a Japanese railway station. Leading from it are a number of currently hip avenues, lined with shops, which get extremely crowded at weekends. (Harajuku itself was once a post station on the road from Kamakura in the rather less-hip 11th century.)

Less crowded is the wide and upscale **Omote-sando**, a boulevard running from the southern end of Harajuku Station. Omote-sando has a European feel about it, from the expansiveness of the boulevard (at least they are expansive for Japan) to the zelkovea trees that line it. Even the architecture of some of the

Tokyo was the world's largest city with over 1 million people in the 17th century. Following World War II, the population was around 3 million. By 1970 it had reached 9 million.

BELOW: seeking a cozy evening in Roppongi.

Map
on pages
270–1

*During the morning
rush hour, peaking
around 8am, a 10-
car train with 3,000
severely compressed
people stops at
platforms for the
Chuo and Yamanote
lines every 90
seconds, and white-
gloved "wranglers"
squeeze in the last
passengers.*

BELOW: shopping
in Harajuku.
RIGHT: towers in
west Shinjuku.

older buildings lends it a cosmopolitan air. In the summer, outdoor cafés with suave-sounding French names offer expensive coffees and draw a decidedly expensive crowd. They're a good place to sit and watch the people go by.

Shinjuku

After building Edo castle and settling down, Tokugawa Ieyasu had the **Shinjuku** area surveyed at the urging of some entrepreneurs. He then established a guard post along the Koshu Kaido, a road that led west into the mountains. Shinjuku (literally, new lodging) quickly became one of the largest towns in Edo, filled with shopkeepers, wholesale distributors, inns, and tea houses. Shinjuku was also known for the male sensual delights, with 50 euphemistically named inns catered by "serving girls". Unlike those in Asakusa, the women of Shinjuku had no licences to practise and were considered downscale.

In its early days when the railway line through Shinjuku was a mere 21 km (13 miles) long, only about 50 people a day used the wooden station, surrounded by a forest of trees. Nowadays, it's said by the Japanese that **Shinjuku-eki** (Shinjuku Station) ❶ is the world's busiest. Maybe, maybe not, but it is a furiously congested place – used by approximately 3 million people daily – and can test a traveller's patience. As with most large urban stations in Japan, there are multitudinous shops and restaurants filling every unused space in the multilevel labyrinth above and below ground. There are also four huge department stores within Shinjuku Station itself; two have their own private railway lines.

If the four department stores within the station are somehow lacking, tumble out the station's east entrance onto Shinjuku-dori, where there are more department stores, thousands of ordinary shops, and tens of thousands of people. This entrance is a popular meeting and rendezvous spot, and a small open plaza tempts the idle to linger, especially when there is something to watch on the immense outside television screen at Studio Alta. This side of the station is also a superb area for rambling which one can do for hours with little purpose. Many of those with a purpose enter **Kabukicho** ❷, north of Yasukuni-dori. After World War II, residents of this area tried to establish a sophisticated entertainment area of cinemas and dance halls, and perhaps most importantly, a *kabuki* theatre. Hence the name Kabukicho (*cho* means "ward" or "district"). But the naming of the neighbourhood was somewhat premature: the *kabuki* theatre was never built.

For more stately pursuits, follow Yasukuni-dori under the tracks to the west side of Shinjuku. The twin towers of the **Tokyo Metropolitan Government Office** ❸ were conceived and started at the beginning of the so-called bubble economy in the 1980s. They were intended to make the statement that Tokyo was now one of the world's greatest and most powerful cities. Around 13,000 city employees file in each day. The main building has two upper towers: finished in 1991, they are both 243 metres (797 ft high. Near the top, on the 45th floors, expansive observation decks with cafeterias offer Tokyo's finest views (open Tues–Fri, 9.30am–5.30pm, Sat–Sun and holidays, 9.30am–7.30pm; free).

THE KANTO REGION

Trains make travel outside Tokyo easy. To the south are Yokohama,
Kamakura and Fuji-san, while northward is the outstanding
Tosho-gu and majestic scenery of Nikko

Map
on pages
246-7

When US Commodore Matthew Perry and his armada arrived in 1853,
Yokohama ❷ was just a poor fishing village next to a smelly swamp.
Today, with a superb natural harbour and a population of more than
3 million, it is a city second in size only to Tokyo, and many consider it a far
more pleasant place to live and to visit.

Under the terms of a treaty negotiated in 1858 by the first US envoy to Japan,
the port of Kanagawa, located on the Tokaido (the East Sea Road between Edo
Tokyo and Kyoto), was to be opened to foreign settlement. But given its proximity to the important Tokaido, the *shogunate* reconsidered and built an artificial island on the mud flats of Yokohama instead for the foreigners.

That attempt to segregate the "red-haired barbarians" proved fortuitous for
all concerned, since Yokohama's natural harbour helped international trade to
flourish. Eventually, foreign garrisons were brought in and the merchants were
able to concentrate on their dealing in a more sedate environment. Honcho-dori
became the centre of commercial activities, and the wide street is still brack-
eted with banks and office buildings.

A walking tour of the centre

Happily, many of the areas of the city worthy of
exploration are concentrated in a relatively small area
and can be covered for the most part on foot. Another
aspect that makes Yokohama – only a 30-minute train
ride from Tokyo – alluring is that its broad, relatively
uncrowded streets (except at weekends) and laid back
atmosphere provide a perfect antidote to Tokyo's
claustrophobia and frantic pace.

Start a walking tour of central Yokohama at
Sakuragicho-eki (Sakuragicho Station), which is
the terminus for the Toyoko Line originating at
Tokyo's Shibuya Station. Sakuragicho was also the
last stop on Japan's first railroad, which began service to Shimbashi in Tokyo in 1872.

Central Yokohama is now dominated by the massive **Minato Mirai 21** shopping and leisure complex,
between Sakuragicho Station and the ocean. The complex is dominated by the 73-storey **Landmark
Tower**, Japan's tallest building at 296 metres (970 ft)
with one of the highest observatory decks in Japan on
the 69th floor (open daily, 10am–9pm; entrance fee).
Other buildings of note are the Yokohama Grand
Inter-Continental Hotel, strikingly designed to
resemble a sail, and the **Maritime Museum** (open
Tues–Sun, 10am–5pm; entrance fee). The *Nippon
Maru*, a traditional sailing ship, is anchored nearby.
The **Yokohama Museum of Art** (open Fri–Wed,
10am–5pm; entrance fee) has an excellent collection

LEFT: Daibutsu, the
Great Buddha of
Kamakura.
BELOW: Yokohama's
modern port.

Steamship berthed at Yokohama, 1930s.

of 19th- and 20th-century paintings and modernist sculptures. Also part of Minato Mirai 21 is the world's (allegedly) largest Ferris wheel.

On the southeast side of the Oka-gawa, a stream that bisects Yokohama, leading from Sakuragicho Station is an area of old government buildings and banks. Further on is a tree-lined street with red-brick sidewalks: Bashamichi-dori (Street of Horse Carriages). Here, the **Kanagawa Prefectural Museum** is housed in a 1904 building which was formerly the head office of a bank. As one of the best surviving examples of the city's old commercial architecture, it has been designated an Important Cultural Property by the government.

The **Yokohama Archives of History**, on the site of the former British consulate, houses a museum with various exhibits on Yokohama's fascinating history. Across the boulevard is the **Silk Centre**, with a delightful museum on the subject: Yokohama once owed its prosperity primarily to silk, in the production of which the local Indian community was intimately involved.

Yamashita-koen (Yamashita Park) though rather undistinguished itself, offers attractions such as the "Girl with the Red Shoes" (a statue dedicated to international friendship among children), live music, a beer garden and boat tours of the harbour.

No visit to Yokohama would be complete without a visit to **Chukagai**, the Chinatown district, the largest one in Japan, and nearly as old as the port. The shops here sell a fascinating variety of foods and there is a wide choice of restaurants. The area contained within its five old gates accounts for some 90 per cent of former foreign settlement. Chinatown also takes pride in the historical role it played in providing staunch support to Sun Yat-sen when he was here in exile trying to rally support for revolution on the Chinese mainland.

BELOW: Victorian house in Yamate Heights, and the city's Chinatown.

Back in the old days, the waterfront Bund often stood in contrast to the **Bluff**, or **Yamate Heights**, where the leading foreign merchants lived in palatial homes. Nanmon-dori in Chinatown was the central street that ran through the international settlement and connected the two. There is a foreign cemetery (*gaijin bochi*) where around 4,200 foreigners from 40 countries are buried. The adjacent Yamate Museum, with quaint displays on the life of early foreign residents, sits near the spot where one of Japan's earliest breweries was located.

Map on pages 246–7

Kamakura

Cradled in a spectacular natural amphitheatre, **Kamakura ❸** is surrounded on three sides by wooded mountains and on the fourth by the blue Pacific. For roughly 150 years – from 1192, when Minamoto Yoritomo made it the headquarters of the first *shogunate*, until 1333, when imperial forces breached the seven passes believed to be impregnable, and annihilated the defenders – Kamakura was the *de facto* political and cultural capital of Japan. During those years, the military administrators based here built impressive temples and commissioned notable works of art, a great deal of it Zen-influenced. Surprisingly, despite the endemic violence of Japan's middle ages, most of it has survived and can be viewed today.

Visitors customarily begin their sightseeing from **Kamakura-eki** (Kamakura Station). In addition to the main railway line, there is a private electric-trolley line, the delightful **Enoden** (Enoshima Dentetsu). This began operations in 1902, and plies a meandering route with some wonderful views between Kamakura and Fujisawa, with 13 stops in between. For about half its 10 km (6 miles) length, the cars run beside the ocean. When the trains are not crowded,

TIP

Yokohama and Kamakura are easily accessible from Tokyo Station on the same train, the Yokosuka Line. Yokohama is exactly 30 minutes from Tokyo, Kamakura just 1 hour.

BELOW: Yokohama harbour from Yamashita Park.

Three generations often share a family home.

BELOW: view of Kamakura Bay over the temple rooftops.

the conductors allow surfers to bring their boards aboard. Unfortunately, the delightful old cars have been replaced with modern ones. If time permits, take a trip on the Enoden for its entire length.

Hop off the Enoden at Hase, the station closest to the **Daibutsu** (Great Buddha), from where a road leads to the statue. In the hills to the left and along the way is **Goryo-jinja** (next to the Enoden tracks), which holds an unusual festival every 18 September, featuring humorous characters sporting macabre masks; **Hase-dera**, a temple with a 9-metre (30-ft), 11-headed Hase Kannon statue, along with thousands of small *jiso* statues decked out in colourful bibs and bonnets and dedicated to lost babies (mostly due to abortion); and **Kosoku-ji**, a temple known for a collection associated with the priest Nichiren.

On a knoll to the right of the approach to the Buddha is the 1,200-year-old **Amanawa Myojin**. Dedicated to the Sun Goddess, Amaterasu Omikami, the shrine offers majestic views.

Even first-time visitors to Japan have probably seen photos of Daibutsu, the Great Buddha. But if not, there's little chance of missing the colossus. At 11 metres (40 ft) in height – minus the pedestal – and weighing 93 tons, this representation of the compassionate Amida is unlikely to get lost in the crowds posing for pictures below. The features of the statue were purposely designed out of proportion when it was cast in 1252 so that the proper proportions come together when one is standing 4 to 5 metres (15 ft) in front of it. For a fee, you can crawl around inside the statue.

Astonishingly, the Great Buddha has survived the onslaughts of earthquakes, typhoons, and *tsunami* (tidal waves), like the one in 1495 which ripped away the wooden building that once enclosed it.

On the east side of Kamakura Station is **Wakamiya-oji**, a broad boulevard that begins at the beach and heads inland under three massive *torii* archways to the Tsurugaoka Hachiman-gu. Parallel to Wakamiya-oji is **Kamachi-dori**, Kamakura's modest answer to the Ginza which, like its Tokyo role model, has little elbow room at weekends. The area abounds with all kinds of trendy shops and eating places, and many of the Japanese-style restaurants here and elsewhere in the city have incorporated Zen principles of cooking.

Along Kamachi-dori and especially in some of the side alleys, craft shops encourage serious browsing. Kamakura is most famous for *Kamakura-bori* (lacquer ware), which originated in the area in the 13th century to produce utensils used in religious ceremonies. Unlike the traditional Chinese lacquer ware from which it drew its inspiration, Kamakura-bori is begun by carving the design first and then applying the lacquer. Like fine wine, Kamakura-bori improves with age, taking on richer and more subtle hues and lustre. You can learn more about this ancient art at the **Kamakura-bori Kaikan**, to be found on the right as you start up Wakamiya-oji from the railway station towards Tsurugaoka Hachiman-gu.

The area due east of Kamakura Station, on the other side of Wakamiya-oji, is largely the province of temples of the Nichiren sect. Although most foreigners have heard of Zen, few know much about Nichiren (1222–82) and his teachings, despite the fact that the iconoclastic priest founded the only true Japanese Buddhist sect. Nichiren was an imposing personality who only narrowly escaped execution, was exiled twice, and set upon by mobs on more than one occasion. He continues to generate feelings of respect and disdain centuries after his death. Nichiren's importance in political (as opposed to religious) history lies in his prediction of the Mongol invasion as divine punishment for the failure of the authorities to accept his arguments. The irascible Nichiren seems to have been quite put out that the Mongols did not actually conquer the country.

The temples of **Myohon-ji, Hongaku-ji, Chosho-ji, Myoho-ji**, and **Ankokuron-ji** are all Nichiren temples and are worth a visit. The Myohon-ji, for example, although only 10 minutes from the station, seems a world apart.

At the top end of Wakamiya-oji, the approach into **Tsurugaoka Hachiman-gu** crosses a steep, red, half-moon bridge that separates the Gempei Ponds. The name Gempei refers to the Minamoto (Genji) and Taira (Heike) clans, which fought to the end in the samurai power struggle known as the Gempei War. The three islands on the right – the Genji side – signify the Chinese character for birth, symbolising the victory of Yoritomo and his followers, while the four in the Heike pond stand for the death of the rival Taira. Yoritomo's indomitable wife, Masako apparently built the pond to celebrate her husband's victory over the ill-fated heirs of Taira.

Behind the Heike Pond is the Kanagawa Prefectural Museum of Modern Art, and a little past the Genji Pond is the modern and earthquake-proof **Kokuhokan** (National Treasure Hall) (open Tues–Sun, 9am–4pm; entrance fee). Each month the

Map on pages 246–7

Zen and Nichiren forms of Buddhism reflect the removal of boundaries between Buddhism and Shinto, with Shinto the realm of daily life and Buddhism of the afterlife.

BELOW: Daibutsu.

Minamoto Yoritomo.

Kokuhokan changes the limited displays of the 2,000 treasures from the temples of Kamakura that are in its possession. This can be rather confusing, but whatever is being shown at any given moment should be stimulating for those interested in Buddhist art. (Incidentally, the Kokuhokan building is a copy of the Shoso-in repository in Nara.)

Continuing up towards the main shrine, you will cross a 25-metre (80-ft) dirt track, along which, on the 16 September every year, mounted archers gallop and fire their arrows at targets in the ancient samurai ritual of *yabusame*. Next you come to an open area below the steps to the *hongu*, or shrine hall. Here stands the red stage upon which Shizuka, Yoritomo's pregnant paramour, is said to have danced defiantly, using the occasion to sing the praises of her lover. Just past the stage on the left of the steps is a huge gingko tree measuring 8 metres (26 ft) in diameter and reputed to be 1,000 years old. It was near here, in 1219, that Yoritomo's second son, Sanetomo, at 26 years old already an accomplished poet, was assassinated by his own nephew. Thus came to an end Yoritomo's line; thereafter, the *shogunate* was controlled by Masako's family, the Hojo, through a regency.

Tsurugaoka Hachiman-gu's prominence on the top of Stork Mountain and the shrine's dedication to Hachiman, the god of war and tutelary deity of the Minamoto, made it the central point of reference for the numerous offices of the military government situated below. Actually, the shrine was founded way back in 1063 by one of Yoritomo's ancestors. Yoritomo's unpretentious tomb is to be found to the right of the shrine near a hill. It is an austere grave befitting a samurai, unlike the monstrous mausoleums for the Tokugawa shoguns at Nikko, which look as if they were built for *mafioso* dons.

BELOW: main temple building at Hachiman-gu.

Two isolated temples of great interest and few crowds are the **Kakuon-ji**, back in the hills behind Yoritomo's tomb, and the **Zuisen-ji**, considerably to the east. The former was founded in 1296. Its Buddha hall, dating to 1354, houses a beautiful Yakushi Nyorai flanked by guardians representing the sun and moon, as well as a shrine to the Black Jizo, whose indelible colour results from its constantly being scorched by the flames of hell in its efforts to save souls. Access to this temple is strictly controlled. Zuisen-ji has a Zen rock-and-water garden designed by its founder, the monk Muso Kokushi.

Another spot to visit that is not so far off the beaten track, but which is nevertheless largely missed by the tourist groups, is so-called **Harakiri Cave**, a 20-minute walk to the northeast of Kamakura Station past the shallow, meandering Nameri-gawa. In 1333, in what was then a temple called Tosho-ji, the last Kamakura regent, who had been scorned for his patronage of dogfights, died by his own hand while surrounded by more than 800 of his cornered followers.

North of Tsurugaoka Hachiman-gu is **Kencho-ji**, established in 1253 and perhaps Kamakura's most significant Zen temple. Before fires in the 1300s and 1400s razed the building, Kencho-ji had 49 sub-temples. To the right of the main gate, San-mon, is the temple's bell (*bonsho*), cast in 1255 and inscribed by the temple's first abbot, a priest from China. The large juniper trees beyond the main gate are said to have been planted by the Chinese priest. The *Butsu-den* (Buddha Hall) has a floor of stone rather than the more traditional *tatami*.

To the north is the station at **Kita Kamakura** (North Kamakura), the first stop beyond Kamakura towards Tokyo. West of the station is **Engaku-ji**, which dates from the late 13th century and was intended for the souls of those killed during the unsuccessful Mongol invasion the previous year. After the main

Map on pages 246–7

TIP

The hills above Kamakura are laced with hiking trails good for an hour or a day of rambling. To find them, just follow the Japanese walkers seemingly dressed for a hike in the Swiss Alps.

BELOW: *jizo* images at a temple.

Fuji and Hakone

The region around **Fuji-san ❹** (or Mt Fuji, but never Mt Fuji-san) has been the inspiration for the works of many of Japan's most celebrated writers, poets and artists. It would be hard to find a mountain more highly praised for its beauty than Fuji-san or a lake more often photographed than Hakone's **Ashi-ko**. Most of the region is designated a "national park", but due to Japan's rather weak laws protecting and restricting commercial exploitation of such assets, a national park is often more of an amusement park in a natural setting.

Sweeping up from the Pacific to form a nearly perfect symmetrical cone 3,776 metres (12,388 ft) above sea level, the elegantly shaped Fuji-san watches over Japan. Fuji's last eruption in 1707 covered Edo Period Tokyo, some 100 km (60 miles) away, with ash. Like many natural monuments held to be sacred and imbued with a living spirit, Fuji-san was off-limits to women for many centuries. It was not until 1867, when an Englishwoman boldly scaled the mountain, that there is any record of a woman climbing the peak. Today, about half of the 400,000 annual hikers are women.

Although climbers are known to set out to challenge the mountain throughout the year, the "official" climbing season for Fuji-san begins on 1 July and ends on 31 August. The mountain huts and services found along the trails to Fuji's peak are only open then. Expect thick crowds and a distinctly commercial atmosphere, not only around the facilities but along the entire trail to the top.

Those who wish to see the rising sun from Fuji's peak should start in the afternoon, stay overnight (forget sleeping – it's noisy) at one of the cabins near the top, and make the remaining climb while the sky is still dark. The other option is to climb through the night. The trails are well travelled and are hard to miss, especially as there'll be a continual line of people on them.

Fuji Go-ko (Fuji Five Lakes) skirts the northern base of Fuji-san. It's a year-round resort, offering more than most visitors seeking Japan's sacred mountain would probably expect or want. From east to west, the lakes are Yamanaka, Kawaguchi, Sai, Shoji, and Motosu (-ko added to the end of these names signifies "lake").

Yamanaka-ko, which is the largest in the group, and the picturesque Kawaguchi-ko are the most frequented of the five, but some of the best spots are hidden near the smaller and more secluded Motosu-ko, Shoji-ko and Sai-ko. Some recommended visits include the Narusawa Ice Cave and Fugaku Wind Cave, both formed by the volcanic activities of one of Fuji's early eruptions.

Hakone is set against the backdrop of Fuji-san and has long been a popular place for rest and recreation. Hakone's 16 hot springs are nestled in a shallow ravine where the Hayakawa and Sukumo rivers flow together. The inns here have natural mineral baths. If on a daytrip, the Tenzan public bath provides a hot-spring treat for just a few hundred yen. Miyanoshita is the oldest and the most thriving of the spa towns. ❑

LEFT: beautiful autumn colours beneath towering Mt Fuji.

gate and on the right are steps to a 2.5-metre (8-ft) high bell, cast in 1301, the largest temple bell in Kamakura. The bell's sound, it is said, guides the souls that have been spared by the king of hell back to earth and the living. Engaku-ji's Butsu-den dates from 1964 and has been rebuilt numerous times over the centuries after fires and earthquakes.

Map on pages 246–7

Nikko

The small city of **Nikko** ❺ itself is of little interest, serving merely as a commercial anchor to the splendours that decorate the nearby hillsides and plateau across the river to the west from the main railway stations. Nikko's *pièce de résistance* is a temple called **Tosho-gu** which comprises 42 structures, 29 of them embellished with some sort of carving, making 5,147 carvings in all.

How this region – once a several-day trek from the shogunate's capital in Edo (present-day Tokyo) – was chosen as the site of Tokugawa Ieyasu's mausoleum is a story in itself. True, Nikko forms a sort of crown at the northern perimeter of the great Kanto Plain, of which Edo was the centre, but Ieyasu was from Kansai, not Kanto, and he had established his capital in Kanto primarily to distance himself from the imperial forces in Kansai's Kyoto, forces he had vanquished in order to seize power in the first place.

Building at Tosho-gu.

Through the gates

Ironically, however, given the Tokugawa aversion to things from outside Japan, many of the 5,000-odd carvings at **Tosho-gu** depict foreign objects. Most ironic of all – and most hypocritical, considering its importance in the annals of Japanese art – is the famous **Yomei-mon**, the gate beyond which only the highest-ranking samurai could pass into the inner sanctum of the shrine, and then only after laying aside their swords. This gate is a masterpiece. Technically, it is a 12-column, two-storey structure with hip-gable ends on right and left, and with cusped gables on four sides. This description, while accurate, is somewhat misleading, however. Even though its *keyaki*-wood columns are painted white to make it appear larger, the gate is quite small.

BELOW: old print of Tosho-gu's pagoda.

A large, white dragon (one of 92 in and around the shrine) is the main feature of the central beam in front of the second storey of this fanciful structure, and two drawings of dragons appear on the ceiling of the porticos. The drawing nearer the entrance is known as *nobori-ryu* or ascending dragon, while the other is *kudari-ryu* or descending dragon.

Lying beyond this gate is yet another one: **Kara-mon** (Chinese Gate), also a National Treasure. It is even smaller than the Yomei-mon (about 3 by 2 metres/9 by 6 ft overall) and is also laden with carvings – dragons (ascending and descending, and lounging around), apricots, bamboo, tree peonies, and more.

Shogunate tomb

While here, climb the 200-odd stone steps to the top of the hill and the Tokugawa tomb, called **Hoto**, wherein it is said are the remains of Tokugawa Ieyasu.

Map
on pages
246–7

Some spectacular views of rooftops and the surrounding terrain can be had from here. On the way past Tosho-gu, through the Yomei-mon to the main entrance and beyond, be sure to stop at the **Yakushido**, one of the few places in these sacred Shinto surroundings with a Buddhist atmosphere. You will find it off to the right. The attraction of this building is the huge *naku-ryu*, or crying dragon, drawn on the ceiling.

Beyond the 40-metre (130-ft) five-storey pagoda, its first storey decorated with the 12 signs of the Chinese zodiac, and just before reaching the 9-metre (30-ft) **Omote-mon** (Front Gate), with its large images of the two deva kings, you will find what may be the most famous carvings of all – not just in Nikko, but in the world. Just under the eaves of the royal stables building (which happens to be the only unlacquered structure in the shrine precincts) are the **Three Monkeys** – Hear no evil, speak no evil, see no evil – copies of which can be found in gift shops and on mantelpieces all over the globe. They are surprisingly small pieces, despite their fame, but so too are all 5,000 and more carvings to be seen at Tosho-gu.

In the forests and into the hills

The lush forests of Nikko are filled with ancient trees. The majority are *suji*, or Japanese cedar, planted under the direction of a man named Matsudaira Masatsuna (1576–1648). Matsudaira, so the story goes, was the *daimyo* (a territorial noble in the feudal era) of Kawagoe, and one of the two people honoured by edict of the *shogun* to supervise the construction of Tosho-gu. The extent of the man's personal wealth is not recorded, nor how much of it was spent in planting the trees. However, it appears that he wasn't very well off to begin with. When his turn to present a grand offering to the shrine came – which all the *daimyo* were obliged to do – Matsudaira was broke, and desperately needed to find something he could give as an offering. Around 1631, several years before the shrine itself was finished, he began to transplant cedar seedlings – plentiful in the surrounding mountains (which he owned) – into strategic positions around the shrine grounds and along the seemingly endless roads. It took him 20 years and an estimated 25,000 seedlings. Today, these trees are what in part define Nikko and its surroundings for travellers. The beneficence continues. The trees and the banks along the avenues are protected as Natural Treasures and Places of Historical Importance under Japanese law.

Thanks to the numbers of visitors who flock to Nikko and the region's fine scenery, the area abounds with other diversions. Unfortunately, getting around without a vehicle is a problem. If money permits, rent a car, but this is not a cheap option. If time permits, take a taxi (not a bus) up the well-known I-Ro-Ha switchback road to **Chuzenji-ko**, a large and picturesque lake due west of Nikko. Its heavily wooded shores are lined with hotels, inns, camping grounds, and other tourist facilities. If you choose not to stay overnight at the lake, try one of the several *onsen* on the picturesque Kinu-gawa, somewhat closer to Nikko itself. ❏

BELOW: one of Nikko's bridges. **RIGHT:** natural splendour in Nikko.

KYOTO AND OSAKA

Less than three hours by train from Tokyo, Kyoto has exquisite Buddhist architecture and an Imperial Palace, while in Osaka you will find rose gardens amid the bustle of a money-oriented city

Maps:
Area 246
City 298

This bustling region of Central Honshu is a place of infinite variety. Kyoto is home to no fewer than 17 United Nations World Heritage Sites of religious and architectural significance, while the energy of brash gritty Osaka, renowned as an entrepreneurial centre since the 4th century, make it a stimulating place to visit.

KYOTO

Tokyo might have the national government and Osaka the entrepreneurial savvy, but **Kyoto ❻** defines traditional Japan and possesses an ingrained aristocratic bloodline, and a history unrivalled by any other Japanese city. As the country's artistic and cultural depository, Kyoto ranks with Athens, Cairo, and Beijing as a living museum. But don't expect a quiet, idyllic place: Kyoto is Japan's fifth-largest city, with a population of 1½ million; Kyoto is a huge metropolis, crowded and noisy and, like most other Japanese cities, lacking aesthetic appeal in its modern contours.

Rapid post-war modernisation saw tens of thousands of old traditional houses lining Kyoto's narrow back streets razed to the ground in favour of modern, convenient living spaces. These old houses – splendid *kyo-machiya* – were of simplistic wooden façades and dancing rectilinear patterns; sliding paper doors; window slats in clay walls; lattices, trellises, benches, and hanging blinds of reeds and bamboo; and the *inuyarai*, or curved bamboo fences, that protruded out from the houses to protect against street traffic and passing dogs.

The city sits in a gradually sloping basin enclosed by a horseshoe of mountains on three sides, and open southwards to the Nara plains, between the rivers Katsura-gawa to the west, Kamo-gawa to the east, and the towering Kitayama mountains that stretch north to the Japan Sea.

Beginnings

For nearly 1,100 years, from AD 794 until 1868, Kyoto was home to the emperor, thus capital of the nation. Japan's first permanent capital was established in Nara in 710, but by 784, the intrigues of power-hungry Buddhist priests forced Emperor Kammu to move the capital to Nagaoka, a nearby suburb of present-day Kyoto. It wasn't until 988 that the use of *kyoto* (capital) began to appear in official records. A century later, Kyoto was the city's proper name.

Heian-kyo was built to a scale model of the Chinese Tang dynasty's (618–906) capital of Chang'an (now Xi'an), in China. Heian-kyo extended in a regular grid pattern still in evidence today for 5.2 km (3¼ miles) from north to south and 4.4 km (2¾ miles)

LEFT: Kiyomizu-dera, the most popular temple complex in Kyoto.
BELOW: costumes from the *jidai matsuri* historical festival.

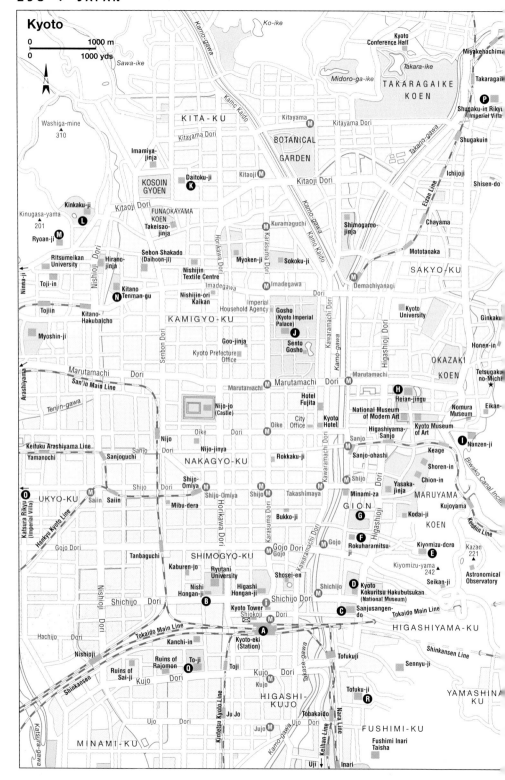

Kyoto

0 ————— 1000 m
0 ————— 1000 yds

Ko-ike

Kyoto Conference Hall

Miyakehachima

Sawa-ike

Takara-ike

Midoro-ga-ike

TAKARAGAIKE KOEN

Takaragaike

Washiga-mine
310

KITA-KU

Kitayama

Kitayama Dori

Shugaku-in Rikyu (Imperial Villa)

Kamo Kaido

Kitayama Dori

BOTANICAL GARDEN

Shugakuin

Imamiya-jinja

Daitoku-ji

Kitaoji

Kitaoji Dori

Ichijoji

Shisen-do

KOSOIN GYOEN

Eizan Line

Kinkaku-ji

Kitaoji Dori

FUNAOKAYAMA KOEN

Kuramaguchi

Shimogamo-jinja

Chayama

Kinugasa-yama
201

Takeisao-jinja

Ryoan-ji

Mototanaka

Ritsumeikan University

Hirano-jinja

Sebon Shakado (Daihoon-ji)

Myoken-ji

Sokoku-ji

SAKYO-KU

Ninna-ji

Nishioji Dori

Nishijin Textile Centre

Imadegawa

Imadegawa

Demachiyanagi

Toji-in

Kitano Tenman-gu

Nishijin-ori Kaikan

Dori

Tojiin

Kitano-Hakubaicho

Imperial Household Agency

KAMIGYO-KU

Gosho (Kyoto Imperial Palace)

Kyoto University

Ginkaku

Myoshin-ji

Goo-jinja

Sento Gosho

OKAZAKI KOEN

Honen-in

Arashiyama

Kyoto Prefecture Office

Marutamachi Dori

Tetsugaku-no-Michi

Marutamachi

Dori

San'in Main Line

Marutamachi

Marutamachi Dori

Heian-jingu

Tenjin-gawa

Nijo-jo (Castle)

Hotel Fujita

National Museum of Modern Art

Nomura Museum

Eikan-

Oike

City Office

Kyoto Hotel

Higashiyama-Sanjo

Kyoto Museum of Art

Keifuku Arashiyama Line

Oike

Dori

Sanjo

Nanzen-ji

Yamanochi

Sanjoguchi

Nijo
Dori

Nijo-jinya

Sanjo-ohashi

Keage

Keishin Line

NAKAGYO-KU

Rokkaku-ji

Shijo

Shoren-in

UKYO-KU

Saiin

Saiin

Shijo-Omiya

Shijo
Dori

Shijo-Omiya

Shijo

Takashimaya

Minami-za

Yasaka-jinja

Chion-in

MARUYAMA KOEN

Katsura Rikyu (Imperial Villa)

Hankyu Kyoto Line

Mibu-dera

GION

Kodai-ji

Kujoyama

Gojo Dori

Tanbaguchi

SHIMOGYO-KU

Bukko-ji

Gojo Dori

Gojo

Rokuharamitsu-ji

Kiyomizu-dera

Kazan
221

Kaburen-jo

Ryutani University

Shosei-en

Kiyomizu-yama
242

Astronomical Observatory

Nishi Hongan-ji

Higashi Hongan-ji

Shichijo

Kyoto Kokuritsu Hakubutsukan (National Museum)

Seikan-ji

Shichijo Dori

Shichijo Dori

Sanjusangen-do

Shijo
Dori

Kyoto Tower Shiokoji

Dori

HIGASHIYAMA-KU

Hachijo
Dori

Tokaido Main Line

Kanchi-in

Kyoto-eki (Station)

Tofukuji

Shinkansen Line

Nishioji

Ruins of Rajomon

To-ji

Toji

Sennyu-ji

Ruins of Sai-ji

Kujo

Dori

Kujo
Dori

Tofuku-ji

YAMASHINA KU

Shinkansen

HIGASHI-KUJO

Katsura-gawa

Ju Jo

Tobakaido

Ujo
Dori

Jujo

Ujo
Dori

Nara Line

FUSHIMI-KU

MINAMI-KU

Fushimi Inari Taisha

Uji

Inari

east to west. Walls with 18 gates and a double moat surrounded the city. And because of earlier and persistent trouble with priests in Nara, Buddhist temples were forbidden inside the capital, explaining in part why many of Kyoto's most venerated temples are isolated in the hills surrounding the city.

Frequently levelled by earthquakes, floods, fires and wars over the centuries, the buildings of Kyoto have been moved, rebuilt and enlarged, and now represent a mosaic of historical periods. As a result, a scant few structures in Kyoto predate 1600, though many temples and shrines faithfully reproduce the earlier styles. It is commonly understood that a decision by the Americans not to bomb Kyoto during World War II – its historical heritage was considered too valuable – assured that these ancient structures stand today.

Map on page 298

Around Kyoto Station

Most people first encounter Kyoto from inside the gargantuan **Kyoto-eki** (Kyoto Station) **Ⓐ**, less than three hours from Tokyo by *shinkansen*. Directly north of Kyoto Station are two notable temples, Nishi (West) Hongan-ji and Higashi (East) Hongan-ji. As with many of Kyoto's historical treasures, Japan's great unifier, Toyotomi Hideyoshi (1536–98), was responsible for establishing **Nishi Hongan-ji Ⓑ**. In 1591, Toyotomi brought the Jodo-shinshu Buddhist sect to the temple's current location. Its Chinese influences are many, and many historians consider it to be the best remaining example of Buddhist architecture.

To the east, **Higashi Hongan-ji** was established in 1603 when the first Tokugawa *shogun*, wary of the Jodo-shinshu monks' power at nearby Nishi Hongan-ji, attempted to thwart their influence by establishing an offshoot of the sect. Only the main hall and founder's hall are open to the public.

BELOW: Kyoto's mix of architecture.

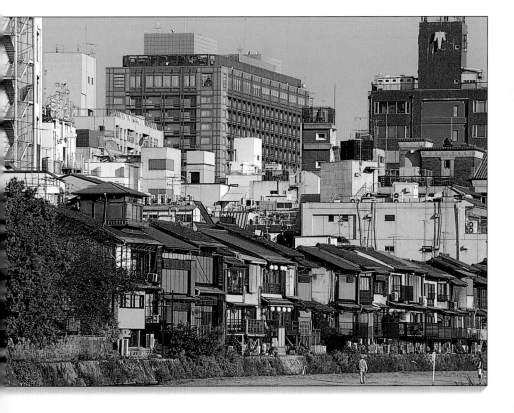

Eastern Kyoto

Just east of Kyoto Station and across the Kamo-gawa, **Sanjusangen-do** (Sanjusangen Hall) **C**, also called Rengeo-in, was last rebuilt in 1266. The temple houses 33 (*sanju-san*) alcoves nestled between 33 pillars under a 60-metre (200-ft) long roof. Inside is a 1,000-handed Kannon, the *bodhisattva* of mercy and compassion, and her 1,000 disciples.

On the opposite side of Shichijo-dori to the north is the **Kyoto Kokuritsu Hakubutsukan** (Kyoto National Museum) **D** (open Tues–Sun, 9am–4.30pm; entrance fee), founded in 1897 and exhibiting historical artefacts and arts and crafts. Several other temples lie east of the museum. Up the Kiyomizu-zaka, a slope on the east side of Higashioji-dori, is **Kiyomizu-dera E**. The temple's main hall (*hondo*) sits perched out over the mountain side on massive wooden pilings. The veranda, or *butai* (dancing stage), juts out over the valley floor overlooking the city below.

Back across Higashioji-dori sits **Rokuharamitsu-ji F**, one of Kyoto's gems. At the rear of the main hall, built in 1363, is a museum with two fine Kamakura-Period (1185–1333) sculptures: Taira-no Kiyomori, of the Heike clan, and Kuya, founder of the temple. The eyes of Kiyomori, presaging the tragic destruction of his clan, sum up the anguish often seen in Kamakura Period art. Kuya, who popularised the chanting of the lotus sutra, is shown reciting magic syllables, each of which becomes Amida, the saviour.

North are the brilliant orange buildings of **Yasaka-jinja**, affectionately called Gion-san after the adjoining Gion pleasure quarter. One of the tallest granite *tori* in Japan, at 9 metres (30 ft) in height, marks the portal to the shrine. From the shrine's back gate, one enters adjoining Maruyama-koen. The park is known for its beautiful garden and magnificent cherry blossom in early April. Two interesting temples sit just beyond **Chion-in** and **Shoren-in**.

East of the Kamo-gawa in central Kyoto, **Gion G** is Kyoto's famous pleasure quarter or *geisha* district today an uncanny blend of traditional and grotesque modern architecture. The tea houses in the quarter are in the style of Kyoto's old *machiya* town houses, but with added delicate touches such as the orangey-pink plastered walls (*ichirikijaya*). The best place to see the houses is along the alleyways that splinter off Hamani-koji, south of Shijo-dori. Just north of here is Gion Shimbashi, another well-preserved neighbourhood of old wooden buildings. At the intersection of Shijo-dori and the Kamo-gawa, **Minami-za**, built in the early 1600s, is the oldest theatre in Japan and is still used for *kabuki* performances.

Cross over Sanjo-dori and continue north to **Okazaki-koen**. This park holds museums, halls, library and zoo. An arching 24-metre (80-ft) *tori* leads from Okazaki-koen to the vermilion-coloured gate of **Heian-jingu H**, more of an architectural study than a Shinto centre. The shrine, dedicated to Kyoto's first and last emperors, is a replica of the original Imperial Palace built in 794 and last destroyed by fire in 1227.

From Heian-jingu, walk east a bit to **Nanzen-ji I** which was originally the residence of 26-year-old

BELOW: purification at Heian-jingu.

Emperor Kameyama (1249–1305) after his abdication in 1274. Nanzen-ji sits nestled in a pine grove at the foot of Daimonji-yama and is part of the Rinzai school of Zen Buddhism, Zen's largest and best-known school. It's also one of Kyoto's most important Zen temples. The complex consists of the main temple and 12 sub-temples, of which only four are regularly open to the public. Nanzen-ji provides an example of the Zen belief in the relationship between all things. The pine grove influences the architecture, art influences the garden, and taken together they all influence the observer. The temple reflects the Chinese style (kara-yo) that arrived in Japan along with Zen.

From Nanzen-ji, follow **Tetsugaku no Michi**, or the Philosopher's Walk, north past the Nomura Museum, Eikan-do temple, and the intriguing hillside temple of Honen-in. The walk, which was the strolling path of Japanese philosopher Nishida Kitaro (1870–1945), snakes about 2 km (1 mile) along the bank of a narrow canal to Ginkaku-ji. The quiet path – save for the crowds of tourists at times – is noted for its spring cherry blossom and fall foliage. Along the way are interesting houses, shops, tea rooms, and small restaurants – try a bowl of Kyoto's famous tofu and vegetable stew (kyo-yudofu).

Philosopher's Walk, ends at the **Silver Pavilion**, or **Ginkaku-ji**. The Ashikaga-era *shogun* who erected it in 1489 died before its completion and despite its name it is not silver at all, but has an exquisite pavilion and Zen garden.

Central Kyoto

Due west on the other side of the Kamo-gawa, the **Gosho** (Kyoto Imperial Palace) ❶ remains the emperor's residence in Kyoto and thus under the control of the Imperial Household Agency, which dictates every nuance and moment of

Temple signs are generally explicit.

BELOW: Ginkaku-ji, the Silver Pavilion, exudes a sober atmosphere.

Young boy in ancient costume during the jidai matsuri.

BELOW: Kinkaku-ji.

the imperial family's life. Originally built as a second palace for the emperor the Kyoto Imperial Palace was used as a primary residence from 1331 until 1868, when Tokyo became the new residence with the fall of the *shogunate* and with the Meiji restoration of the imperial system.

From the palace, a few blocks west is **Nishijin**, the weavers' quarter. The **Nishijin Textile Centre** has excellent displays of working looms and woven goods. Here, you could try on a kimono and try to picture yourself in one back home. South is **Nijo-jo**, a castle begun in 1569 by the warlord Oda Nobunaga and finished by Tokugawa Ieyasu, ally to Oda Nobunaga, to demonstrate his military dominance over the city. In 1867, it served as the seat of government from where Emperor Meiji abolished the *shogunate*. Rectangular in dimensions, the castle's magnificent stone walls and gorgeous gold-leafed audience halls reflect the power of the Edo Period *shoguns*. The linking corridors of the castle's Ninomaru Palace feature "nightingale" (creaking) floors to warn of intruders.

Just south of the castle is **Nijo-jinya**, originally the home of a wealthy merchant and later used as an inn by visiting *daimyo*. The old manor house is full of trap doors, secret passageways, and hidden rooms – the stuff from which *samurai* and *ninja* dramas are made.

To the northwest and west

To the north and west of the city centre, skirting the foothills, are three renowned Zen temples that should not be missed. Established as a small monastery in 1315, the present buildings of **Daitoku-ji** Ⓚ were built after 1468 when one of the several fires in its history burned down the temple. It is the holy of holies

where Zen married art. Some eight of Daitoku-ji's 22 subsidiary temples are open to the public. The three best-known are Daisen, Zuiho and Koto. In Daisen-n is Kyoto's second most famous – and maybe the best – Zen garden. Unlike the abstractions of other gardens, the Daisen garden more closely resembles the ink-wash paintings of Zen art. Look for the mountains, rivers and islands in the water, which appears to flow under the veranda.

Walk west along Kitaoji-dori past Funaokayama-koen to the best-known temple in Kyoto, if not all Japan: **Kinkaku-ji ❶**, the Golden Pavilion. It's a replica built in 1955 of a 15th-century structure and received its last covering of gold-leaf in 1987. Each of the pavilion's three storeys reflects a different architectural style. The first floor is of the palace style, the second floor of the *samurai-house* style, while the third floor reveals the Zen-temple style. The large pond in front of the pavilion and surrounding grounds make it a perfect setting.

The original temple was burned down in 1950 by a man who entered the Buddhist priesthood after being seduced by the pavilion's beauty. Thinking that his sense of aesthetics might approach perfection if he burned down the very object that had enchanted him in the first place, he did exactly that. The author and right-wing nationalist Mishima Yukio fictionalised the burning episode in his 1956 book, *Kinkakuji*.

Further west, visit **Ryoan-ji ⓜ**, or Temple of the Peaceful Dragon, early in the day before the peace is shattered by the bus-loads of tourists and students. Here is the most famous Zen rock garden (*karesansui*, or dry landscape) in the world and one of Kyoto's main tourist attractions. The 16th-century garden is an abstract of an ink-wash painting executed in rock and stone.

Tenth-century **Kitano Tenman-gu ⓝ** is one of Kyoto's most earthy shrines and hosts a popular antique market on the 25th of each month. Its restrained wooden architecture enshrines Sugawara Michizane, a 9th-century scholar and states-man. Small wood votives, or *ema* – with a picture of a horse on one side and a wish or prayer (most for success in school exams) written on the other side – hang in the courtyard. The first calligraphy day of the year is also celebrated, when school children offer their writings to the shrine. The present structure was built in 1607. Tenman-gu is known for its splendid plum trees that bloom in the snows of February, and for the geisha that serve tea under the flowering trees.

Out in the western hills, **Arashiyama** was once the playground of Heian aristocrats. Today it is punctu-ated by temples. Cross over the Hozu-gawa on pic-turesque Togetsu Bridge to the shop-lined promenade along the river. Just beyond sits **Jikishian**, a refuge temple for women escaping violent or distressing rela-tionships; women have written their accounts in some 2,000 books of reminiscences.

One of Japan's most famous strolling gardens lies inside **Katsura Rikyu** (Katsura Imperial Villa) ⓞ, due west of Kyoto Station on the west side of Kat-sura-gawa. Its garden features a number of splendid tea houses overlooking a large central pond. Katsura, with its severe refinement, has exercised more influ-ence on contemporary architecture than perhaps any other building in Japan.

Map on page 298

Original structure of Kinkaku-ji in the early 1900s. It was destroyed by arson in 1950.

BELOW: Buddha of Paradise at Byodo-in.

Shoes are never worn in the house or school but are kept near the entrance.

BELOW: *sayanora* to guests at a *ryokan*, or traditional inn.

To the northeast

In the northern foothills, the **Shugaku-in Rikyu** (Shugaku-in Imperial Villa) Ⓖ was built in 1659 as an emperor's retreat. The imperial villa at Shugaku-in seems like pure fantasy compared to the Katsura Imperial Villa. It consists o three large, separate gardens and villas. In Rakushiken (Middle Villa) stands cedar door with carp painted on both sides. It's said that the carp would escape each night to swim in the villa's pond. Not until golden nets were painted over them, in the 18th century, did they stay put. (Permission is required from th Imperial Household Agency before you may visit.)

South of Kyoto Station

Just south of Kyoto Station, **To-ji** Ⓠ has one of the nation's enduring postcar images: the five-storey **Goju-no-to pagoda**. Rebuilt in 1644, it stands 55 metre (180 ft) high, making it Japan's tallest pagoda. The temple itself was estab lished in 796 and today draws large crowds to its flea markets. Built next to th old city's south gate, To-ji became Japan's main Buddhist temple. Its main ha (*kondo*) reflects Buddhist traditions from India, China, and Japan.

To the east, up against the hills, **Tofuku-ji** Ⓡ is rightly known as one of th best places to see colourful autumn foliage. It contains Japan's oldest and per haps most important Zen-style gate, dating from the 15th century. Yet its 2 subsidiary temples are rarely visited and the grounds are usually quiet, makin it a peaceful place for contemplation. Walk through the abbot's quarters (*hojc* to the platform over the ravine looking down on Tsuten Bridge – it's one of th most delightful views in Kyoto. If you are here during the last week of Noven ber, don't miss the festival of old brushes and pens, when writers and painte

bring their used pens and brushes to be cast into a sacred fire. A few blocks south of Tofuku-ji is where tunnel-like paths of hundreds of bright-red *torii* tempt walkers. Actually, there are more than 10,000 *torii* covering the paths of **Fushimi Inari Taisha** – the fox shrine founded in the 9th century in honour of the fox that farmers believe is the messenger of the harvest god. Unless you're exhausted from sightseeing, walk the full 4-km (2½-mile) course.

Maps:
Area 246
City 298

OSAKA

Some Japanese look askance at **Osaka ➐**, as if it belonged to another, somewhat unrelated part of the hemisphere. Its humour is different, a bit more rollicking than Tokyo's. Osaka is known for the character of its people: straightforward, business-savvy jay-walkers who know how to eat well.

Osaka's business connection is documented as far back as the 4th century, when Emperor Nintoku made Naniwa (Osaka) his capital. His business acumen was considerable for a politician; for example, he decided to rebate all taxes to local businesses for three years after he was informed of an impending recession. His ploy worked rather well and the Osaka business ethic was conceived, as was its special language of the merchants, *akinai kotoba*.

The city's stellar port and river connections to the capital in Kyoto played a central role in its economic and cultural development. Merchants from around the country – and from China and Korea – flooded the city. Osaka grew in strength and economic power, culminating with the *shogunate* of Toyotomi Hideyoshi (1536–98), who chose the city as his seat of government, built himself a fine castle, and then turned Osaka into Japan's foremost commercial and industrial centre. For the next 270 years, Osaka was known as the "kitchen of

TIP

Domestic flights to Osaka arrive at the older airport near downtown, while international flights use the newer Kansai International Airport, in Osaka Bay.

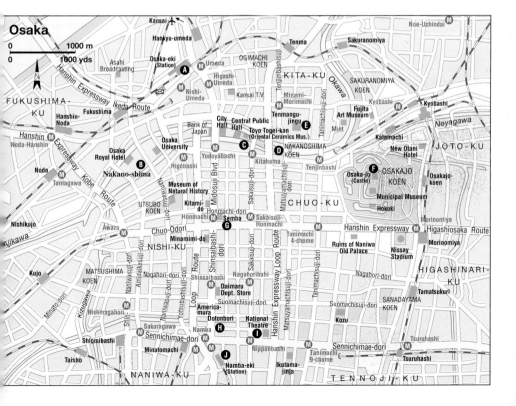

Japan" with raw materials pouring in and high-quality finished products flowing out. Kyoto and fledgling Edo (present-day Tokyo) were the consumers, Osaka the willing provider.

Contemporary Osaka

Lanterns at Yasaka shrine, Kyoto.

Since most trains (except the *shinkansen*, or bullet train) arrive at the **Osaka-eki** (Osaka Station) **A** complex in Umeda, it is from here that a tour of the city might start. At Osaka Station, three train lines (JR, Hankyu and Hanshin lines) meet with Osaka's three main north–south subway lines. Like most railway stations in Japan, Osaka Station offers an underground shopping mall, perhaps one of the largest underground malls in the world.

Back up on the street from the station complex is **Midosuji**, Osaka's main north–south boulevard. South of Umeda is **Nakano-shima** (Nakano Island) **B**, one of the most valuable pieces of real estate in the city. This narrow island between the canals of Dojima-gawa and Tosabori-gawa is the centre of city government and home to many major Osaka companies. A footpath runs most of the way around Nakano-shima; sightseeing boats to tour the canals can be picked up nearby.

From Midosuji, follow the path on Nakano-shima east along the river, passing in front of Osaka city hall, library, and the quaint, red-brick public hall. Across from the public hall is the superb **Toyo Togei-kan** (Museum of Oriental Ceramics) **C** (open Tues–Sun, 9.30am–5pm; entrance fee), housing the famous Ataka collection of Chinese and Korean porcelain. East of the museum is **Nakanoshima-koen** (Nakanoshima Park) **D**, with a rose garden and willow-draped paths.

BELOW: canal along Dotonbori.

Map on page 305

The hard-to-miss Osaka Castle rising to the east is reached by following the footpath to the eastern end of Nakano-shima, then up the spiral ramp onto Tenjin-bashi. Walk north across the bridge, then right at the police box. A short jaunt ends at the entrance of **Sakuranomiya-koen** (Cherry Garden). A few blocks north of this point sits funky **Tenmangu-jingu** ⓔ, dedicated to the god of learning. Sakuranomiya-koen has extensive trails lined with cherry trees. **Osaka-jo** (Osaka Castle) ⓕ is the most visited site in the city. The main *donjon*, towering above the expansive gardens and stone walls, is a 1931 concrete replica of the original that was built by Toyotomi Hideyoshi in 1585. With the conscripted help of all the feudal lords of the nation and the labour of tens of thousands, the massive structure was completed in just three years. Much of the original grounds, moats and walls still stand.

South on Midosuji is the district of Honmachi, where Midosuji and Honmachi boulevards cross. Just north of the crossing is **Semba** ⓖ, the apparel wholesale area of Osaka. Most large wholesalers have outgrown their Semba origins, but some 800 small wholesalers still operate in the Semba Centre Building, a two-storey structure entirely under a 930-metre (3,000-ft) long expanse of elevated highway.

Follow Midosuji south until the next major crossing, Nagahori. The first landmark to look for is the **Sony Tower**, at the mouth of Osaka's premier covered shopping street, Shinsaibashi-suji, which extends south towards Namba Station. Here are ancient little shops sitting in apparent ignorance of the outrageously fancy boutique plazas towering on either side.

South on Shinsaibashi is one of the most fascinating stretches in Osaka, the **Dotonbori** ⓗ amusement quarter. At the Dotonbori Canal, Shinsaibashi ends and Ebisusuji begins. Here, Shin Takamatsu's *son et lumière* **Kirin Plaza Building**, architecturally akin to something out of the dystopian sci-fi movie *Blade Runner*, stands on the north bank of the canal.

There is more to Dotonbori than just the passing crowds, however. For hundreds of years, this was the theatrical heart of Japan with six *kabuki* theatres, five *bunraku* playhouses, and a myriad of other halls where the great storytellers and comics of Osaka performed. Today, most of the old theatres have been replaced by cinemas, among which the elegant old **Shochiku-za** is an architectural link with the golden age of black-and-white films. The venerable **Naka-za**, with its *kabuki* and *geisha* dances, and the vaudevillian **Kado-za** are still active, but they are the last of the legitimate theatres left in Dotonbori. Several years ago, the Bunraku Puppet Theatre moved from its old Asahi-za home to the **National Theatre** ⓘ, a few blocks to the east. Performances are only held at certain times of the year.

Namba-eki (Namba Station) ⓙ offers little that is remarkable, save the vast underground shopping arcade of Namba City and Rainbow Town. Three main subway lines connect at Namba Station, which is also the terminus for both the Kintetsu and Nankai railways serving Nara, Wakayama and points south. Namba is also a good connecting point from downtown Osaka to **Kansai International Airport**. ❏

Late at night Japan's urban areas are often punctuated by the shriek of racing motorcycles with no mufflers, driven by bosozuku ("speed tribes"), who are renegade youth intent on disrupting the norms of society.

BELOW: bar reading material.

Map on pages 246–7

THE SOUTH

The south is a scattered region of great diversity, where medieval castles, ceramics centres and kabuki theatre provide a contrast to the hot springs at Beppu and the wild cat of Iriomote

The South is a bit of a misnomer, as the Japanese refer to this area as western Japan, but this part of the archipelago does extend southwards. Chugoku, Shikoku and Kyushu are exceedingly different yet have one element in common: Seto Naikai, or the Inland Sea. All three regions also face the open ocean, and therefore each has its own climate and local qualities. And Okinawa, a name familiar for its wartime connotations, would prefer to be known for its lofty hills, pristine coral reefs and rare flora and fauna.

Chugoku

At the upper end of Chugoku, the industrial city of **Himeji** ❽ is dominated by the marvellous snow-white castle that seems to hover above the town. Variously called the White Egret or Heron castle, **Himeji-jo** (open daily, 9am–6pm; entrance fee) is a 15-minute stroll from the *shinkansen* station along a road lined with modern sculptures. Resting resplendent on the banks of the Senbagawa, the castle of Himeji is the largest and most elegant of the dozen existing medieval castles in Japan. Its construction was a Herculean task requiring 400 tons of wood, 75,000 tiles weighing a total of 3,000 tons, and a huge number of very large stones, some procured from ancient nearby tombs.

Hiroshima

One moment – 8.15am, 6 August 1945 – irrevocably changed world history. An atomic flash signalled the instant destruction of **Hiroshima** ❾, the eventual loss of over 200,000 lives, and forever linked the city's name with nuclear holocaust. The immediate and lasting impact on Hiroshima gives concrete reality to the horrors of atomic and nuclear war. There seem to be reminders of Hiroshima's atomic bombing around virtually every corner. Amazingly, Hiroshima's people quickly rebuilt a vibrant city from the ashes, making it larger and more prosperous than the old one and leaving a few carefully chosen scars to memorialise its abiding atomic legacy.

The **Heiwa Kinen-koen** (Peace Memorial Park), is adjacent to the **Genbaku Domu** (Atomic Dome), which marks ground zero of Hiroshima's atomic explosion. At its maximum intensity, the temperature approached that on the sun's surface and almost everything within sight was vapourised instantly. The famous building with the carefully maintained skeletal dome once housed the Industrial Promotion Hall and was one of the few surviving vertical structures.

Tange Kenzo designed the heart of the park complex, which comprises the **Peace Memorial Museum** (open daily, 9am–5.30pm; entrance fee), the Peace Memorial Hall, the Cenotaph, and the Peace

LEFT: tending to the cherry trees.
BELOW: Himeji-jo.

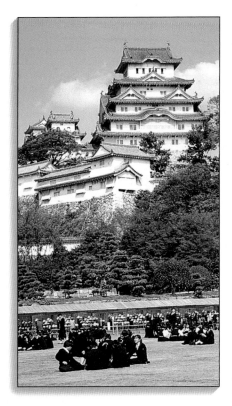

The mushroom cloud over Hiroshima about an hour after the atomic blast.

Flame. The museum contains graphic portrayals of the bombing, but although it is filled with powerful images of terrible suffering, it certainly is not the hall of horrors one might expect.

Shikoku

Shikoku is the least-developed and rarely visited of Japan's four main islands, and its attractions (and drawbacks) are attendant on its relative isolation. The island can provide a more "Japanese" experience than either Honshu or Kyushu. Its people are less familiar with foreigners and its ambiance has been less influenced by the homogenising aspects of modern culture. It is also more diffused. Places likely to be of interest to travellers are relatively far apart and more difficult to get to than on more widely travelled pathways.

The capital of Kagawa prefecture, **Takamatsu** ❿ is the main railway terminal and ferry port in eastern Shikoku. **Ritsurin-koen** (Ritsurin Park) contains one of the finest traditional gardens in Japan with 54 hectares (133 acres) of ponds, hills, pine forests, and a botanical garden.

About 20 minutes and a few kilometres east by train from the centre of Takamatsu is **Yashima**. It was one of the countless battlefields of the Gempei War (1180–85) between the Minamoto and Taira clans. The architectural embodiments of Shikoku's past – an open-air *kabuki* theatre, a vine suspension bridge, thatch-roofed farmhouses, and a variety of other traditional buildings – have been collected and preserved in **Shikoku-mura** (Shikoku Village).

Southwest of Takamatsu, **Kotohira** ⓫ is home to one of the most famous and popular shrines in Japan, **Kotohira-gu** (also called Konpira-san). It is dedicated to Okuninushi no Mikoto, the guardian of seafarers. The **Kanamaru-za**,

BELOW: harvesting cultivated pearls.

restored to its original early 19th-century condition, is the oldest existing *kabuki* theatre in Japan. Its stage, resonating with the fading echoes of thousands of performances, is exciting to visit even when empty. In the third week of April, the nation's best *kabuki* actors bring it alive.

The capital of Kochi prefecture is **Kochi ⑫** itself, best known for the role its leading families played in forging the alliance between the Satsuma and Choshu clans and the ensuing imperial Meiji Restoration of 1868. On the far eastern side of Kochi from Ashizuri-misaki, **Muroto-zaki** points out southwards into the Pacific Ocean. The cape is warm year-round and at its tip the towering waves of the Pacific have eroded the rocks and reefs into strange shapes. The area is also noted for its connection with the venerable Kobo Daishi, founder of the Shingon sect of Buddhism.

Kyushu

Fukuoka ⑬ is reportedly where both tea and Buddhism were introduced to Japan, and Korean captives brought back here were responsible for starting up a sizeable pottery industry. Today, with a population of 1.2 million, Fukuoka competes with Kitakyushu as the largest city on Kyushu. The city remains an important hub in regional trade and commerce while managing to retain a lot of charm at ground level.

In its role as the cross-roads between Japan and China, Fukuoka was the place where Zen Buddhism first touched the archipelago. **Shofuku-ji,** founded in 1195 by Eisai after years of study in China, is the oldest Zen temple in Japan. The **Sumiyoshi-jinja**, the oldest extant Shinto shrine on Kyushu, was built in 1623. Other points of interest in Fukuoka include **Fukuoka-shi Bijutsukan,** a

Map on pages 246–7

Much of the pottery and ceramics found in western Honshu and Kyushu is defined by elegance and rustic simplicity.

BELOW: Kyushu farms are small and family-owned.

museum housing a collection of Japanese art, and **Ohori-koen** (Ohori Park), a pleasant park harbouring the remains of **Fukuoka-jo** (Fukuoka Castle) and reconstructions of its turret and gates. **Karatsu**, **Imari**, and **Arita**, west of Fukuoka, are pottery towns whose fame dates from the 16th century, and are of significant interest to Japanese-ceramics enthusiasts.

Like Hiroshima, **Nagasaki** ⓮ is a name automatically associated with the atomic bomb that brought World War II to an end. Now home to more than half a million people, Nagasaki clings to steep hills wrapped around a very active deep-water harbour, competing with Kobe for the designation of Japan's San Francisco. Like San Francisco, it has a lively Chinatown and a continuing spirit of receptiveness to novel ideas.

A simple stone obelisk stands at the epicentre ("hypocentre" in Japan) of the atomic blast that devastated much of Nagasaki on the morning of 9 August 1945. The **Atomic Bomb Museum** (open daily, 9am–6pm; entrance fee) at the International Culture Hall contains photos, relics, and poignant details of the blast and its 150,000 victims.

If you are seeking to go to hell and back, head for **Beppu** ⓯ on the northeastern coast of Kyushu. The resort town is famous – and thus highly commercialised – for its *jigoku*, variously coloured ponds of water and mud that steam and boil, as well as its hot springs. Although a popular destination for Japanese tourists, Beppu is gaudy and rather tacky.

The prefecture in the far south of Kyushu consists of two peninsulas, Satsuma and Osumi, which encircle **Kagoshima** ⓰, the southernmost metropolis in Kyushu, famous for being Japan's most unintentionally polluted city. The pollution comes from **Sakura-jima** (Cherry Island), the active volcano east across

TIP

Like nearby Fukuoka, Nagasaki is thought by many foreigners to be one of Japan's most pleasant large cities.

BELOW: an old man and his rising sun.

the bay, rising 1,120 metres (3,670 ft) directly above the water. The mountain has erupted more than 5,000 times since 1955, sending clouds of ash and sometimes large boulders raining down on Kagoshima.

Map on pages 246-7

Okinawa

Extending for 1,200 km (600 miles) southwest from Kyushu, the 70-plus islands of the Ryukyus, or **Nansei-shoto**, stretch across the ocean to within 200 km (125 miles) of Taiwan. For centuries, the Okinawans minded their own business and accommodated themselves to outsiders. But during the age of imperialism in the late 19th century, their independence fell prey to the ambitions of powerful neighbours.

The centre of Okinawa's tourism is the city of **Naha** ⓱, and Naha's centre of tourist activity is **Kokusai-dori** (International Road), which is a jangle of typical Japanese urban architecture – cluttered and without aesthetic appeal – together with crowds of walkers and swarms of vehicles. Indeed, Kokusai-dori is nearly indistinguishable from any other urban centre in Japan, yet only a short distance away are typically Okinawan neighbourhoods. **Naminou-gu**, a small Confucian shrine, and the **Gokoku-ji**, a temple that was once considered a national religious centre, sit along the waterfront not far from the central post office and just north of an old pleasure quarter that retains its fair share of bars, cabarets, and steak houses. Okinawan crafts are a delight. Active since 1617, the **Tsuboya** pottery-making district, off Himeyuri-dori and southeast of Kokusai-dori, is not to be missed.

The first castle on **Shuri**, due west of the downtown centre on a lofty hill overlooking Naha and the vast oceans beyond, was established in 1237. Under the

American influence over Okinawa.

LEFT: lush scenery on the island of Yaku-shima.
BELOW: taking the sands at Ibusuki.

Map
on pages
246–7

Shisa *images are*
placed atop buildings
for protection from
evil demons.

BELOW: Okinawan
beach resort.
RIGHT:
Nakijin Castle.

second Sho dynasty, established in 1469 by King Sho En, Shuri became a mighty palace and temple complex. It remained the political and cultural centre of the Ryukyus until 1879, when the last Okinawan king, Sho Tai, was forced to abdicate by the Meiji government in Tokyo.

During the 82-day battle in 1945, when the Japanese army chose Okinawa as the definitive last stand against the Allies before an anticipated invasion of the main Japanese islands, **Shuri-jo** (Shuri Castle) was the headquarters of the Japanese forces. It was destroyed during the fighting, but much of the castle's stonework has been rebuilt in the past decade. Two poignant spots in the far south are the tunnel labyrinths at **Romogusuku**, near the Naha Airport, which was the last headquarters of the Imperial Navy, and in which more than 4,000 Japanese men committed suicide; and the **Himeyuri no To** (Lily of the Valley Tower), a deep pit where a group of high school girls and their teachers also killed themselves, rather than endure the possibility of capture by the Americans.

The central portions of Okinawa are largely occupied by controversial US military bases, the most important of which is the air base at **Kadena**, about a quarter of the way up this skinny island. Jutting out from the west coast about two-thirds of the way to the northern tip of Okinawa is **Motobu-hanto** (Motobu Peninsula). The restored ruins of **Nakijin-jo** (Nakijin Castle), on the peninsula's northern tip, are a fine place to watch a sunset.

The outer islands

The best bet for experiencing the Ryukyuan way of life is to visit the outer islands, or *saki-shima*, reached by ferry or air from Naha. **Kerama**, only 35 km (20 miles) west of Naha, is an excellent scuba-diving site although there are sea snakes among its gorgeous coral reefs. **Kume-jima**, three hours by ferry from Naha's main harbour, has preserved several fine traditional homes in Nakazato and elsewhere. Further afield is the Miyako group of eight islands. **Miyako-jima**, the main island, is an hour by air or 10 hours by boat from Naha. Nearby **Irabu Island,** reached by boat from Hiraya, offers attractive scenery and fine diving.

The island group of **Yaeyama-shoto**, best reached by air (the ferry only puts in about once a week), was long relatively isolated from the rest of the Ryukyus. It will appeal to those interested in folklore or the outdoor life. The main island of **Ishigaki-jima** was for years embroiled in controversy over an offshore airport scheduled to be built near Shiraho, one of the largest and rarest coral reefs in this part of the Pacific.

A short ferry or hovercraft ride from Ishigaki takes you to **Taketomi**, a beautiful, peaceful island famed throughout Japan for the star-shaped sand at Kondoi. A ferry also goes to the large island of **Iriomote**, a touch of New Guinea in Japan. Except for the towns of Ohara in the southeast and Funaura in the north, the island is mostly tropical rain forest. Thankfully, development on the island has been limited to just one resort, although others have been proposed. Iriomote is noted for its rare flora and fauna, especially the Iriomote cat, a wild feline that is found nowhere else, and a large moth over 30 cm (1 ft) in diameter.

HOKKAIDO

The northern island of Hokkaido holds a special place in the Japanese imagination, conjuring up images of wild lands, misty mountains and relaxed friendly people

Map
on pages
246–7

Hokkaido has been part of the Japanese nation only since it was settled in the 19th century as an example of Meiji Restoration development. Japan's northern island is where the temples and castles of the southern islands give way to mountains, forests and farms. One will find the residents here more direct and friendlier than their southern counterparts, and due to the Meiji-era Westernisation, quite sophisticated. Hokkaido is also home to Japan's last indigenous people, the Ainu (*see page 254*), who are of Caucasian ancestry and have no genetic connection to today's Japanese.

The island feels remote, but this is mostly psychological. The Tokyo–Sapporo air corridor is one of the busiest in the world, and Hokkaido has the usual overdeveloped and tacky tourist traps common throughout Japan. But Hokkaido also contains some of Japan's most undeveloped areas, and can be a place of high adventure in the rustic north.

Sapporo

In southwest Hokkaido, **Sapporo** ⓲ is the island's capital and its largest city with 1.7 million people. It is an immensely livable city, especially by Japanese standards. The downtown area is anchored by one of Japan's liveliest, most charming boulevards, **Odori-koen** (Odori Park), broader and more spacious than most, running east to west through the neighbourhood. In the first week of February, this broad avenue is the venue for Sapporo's world-famous **Snow Festival**. Snow statues and ice sculptures – often large and complex – are made by corporate, professional and amateur teams. In summer, beer gardens spring up on the grassy areas and people linger outdoors long into the night.

To the south of Sapporo station is **Tokei-dai** (Clock Tower). Two blocks south of Odori-koen is **Tanuki-koji**, a vibrant strip of restaurants and shops. Finally, south of Odori-koen is **Susukino**, Sapporo's nightlife and strip-joint district of "soaplands" (full-body massages lubricated by soap).

West of Sapporo is **Otaru** ⓳, once a fishing and trading centre and where many of the buildings are an eclectic blend of Western and 19th-century Japanese influences.

Otaru is gateway to the **Shakotan-hanto**, a peninsular microcosm of Hokkaido with its rugged coastlines, abundant campsites, ski areas, boating and fishing in the Sea of Japan, and glorious sunsets from the capes (*misaki*) of Shakotan and Kamui. This area's proximity to Sapporo makes sightseeing hectic at times, especially on holidays and at weekends. But along the side roads and in quiet villages there is always an inn with a room, if not a view.

LEFT: sunrise over Kussharo-ko.
BELOW: snowy Sapporo.

Buddhist tomb on the island of Rishiri.

BELOW: farm with an American look.

To the south of Sapporo

The **Shikotsu-Toya Kokuritsu-koen** (Shikotsu-Toya National Park) ㉑ is Hokkaido's most accessible national park and thus highly commercialised and often crowded. Within easy reach of Sapporo is **Shikotsu-ko**, an extremely large caldera lake.

Toya-ko, south of Shikotsu, is another caldera lake with a large island smack in the centre. Tour boats visit its islands, where the view of **Yotei-zan**, at 1,893 metres (6,200 ft), to the north is best. The resort areas around Toya-ko are boisterous in summer, with fireworks during the August festival season, and there are hot-spring baths (*onsen*) with views of the lake.

The best route from Toya-ko east to the tourist hot spring of **Noboribetsu** is by bus through the gorgeous Orofure Pass. Noboribetsu's most notable sight and activity is at the Dai-Ichi Takimoto-kan Hotel, where 40 indoor, sex-segregated hot-spring baths, once built of wood but now of marble, can accommodate 1,000 bathers simultaneously.

Hakodate

Hakodate ㉒ is Hokkaido's historic city, where Japanese settlers arrived from the south as early as the 13th century, and Russians followed in the mid-1700s. At the base of Hakodate-yama is **Motomachi**, which has been a foreign enclave since the 1850s. The tower nearby offers good views of the fort and over the city. If you can get up early, try not to miss the fish market at dawn, when the squid fleet and the crab trappers return to port. West of the city is a Trappist convent, established in 1898 and today famous for its biscuits and sweets. South is Matsumae, Hokkaido's only castle town.

Kushiro and Akan National Park

To the east of Sapporo along the southern coast is the port city of **Kushiro** ㉒, where ultramodern architecture contrasts with one of Japan's most congenial dockside scenes. Among the Japanese, Kushiro is noted mostly for the migrating cranes that put on elaborate and well-attended mating displays in the fields outside the city.

Akan-ko is also nationally famous for *marimo* – odd green algae balls also known as God's Fairies which may or may not delight you. Two volcanic peaks, Oakan-dake and Meakan-dake, tempt keen climbers; Meakan is the preferred jaunt, partly because an *onsen* (hot spring bath) awaits the weary climber. North of Akan Kohan, Bokke features bubbling hot mud.

Less touristy is **Kussharo-ko** ㉓, at 80 sq. km (30 sq. miles) the largest inland lake in Hokkaido and allegedly home to "Kusshi", Japan's own version of the Loch Ness Monster. Three congenial *onsen* surround Kussharo: Kawayu, Wakoto and Sunayu, where hot sands provide a welcome novelty. **Io-san**, or Mount Sulphur, steams and reeks impressively and is worth a visit despite the commercialisation. **Bihoro**, a pass above Kussharo's west shore, has breathtaking vistas.

Daisetsuzan National Park

Wilder and colder than Akan and Shikotsu-Toya, **Daisetsuzan Kokuritsu-koen** (Daisetsuzan National Park) is the largest national park in Japan, comprising 230,900 hectares (570,500 acres). Anchored directly in the centre of Hokkaido and to the west of Akan, the climate is nearly always cool, even in summer. This is a landscape of volcanic peaks and steep highlands, magnificent gorges, carpets of alpine wild flowers, and assured sightings of the park's rich wildlife, including deer, foxes, bears and exotic birds. In the park there are several good youth hostels and a series of campsites. Hokkaido's highest peak, **Asahi-dake** ㉔ (2,290 metres/7,500 ft) towers over the park.

Rishiri and Rebun

The volcanic islands of **Rishiri** and **Rebun** ㉕, part of the **Rishiri-Rebun-Sarobetsu Kokuritsu-koen** (Rishiri-Rebun-Sarobetsu National Park), are just west of Wakkanai, from where the ferry to the islands departs. Before boarding the ferry, visit the alpine wildflower reserve at **Sarobetsu**, a rainbow of colour as far as the eye can see, especially in July. (This is one of Hokkaido's wonders really worth investigating.) Rishiri and Rebun themselves offer delights for the biker, hiker, camper, and fisherman. It's possible to lodge at a *minshuku* (family-style inn) on either island and get up early in the morning with your host to go fishing in the Sea of Japan.

Hiking is excellent. Rishiri offers the best hiking with a climb up Rishiri-san, poking upwards to 1,720 metres (5,620 ft) above sea level, like Neptune's elbow. On Rebun, which is comparatively flat, hike from Sukotan-misaki to Momiwa, or bike from Kabuka to Funadomori to make the most of the rewarding coastline scenery. ❑

Map on pages 246–7

Eggs cooked on a steam vent on Io-san for sale to tourists.

BELOW: Onuma National Park. **FOLLOWING PAGE:** first snow in northern Hokkaido.

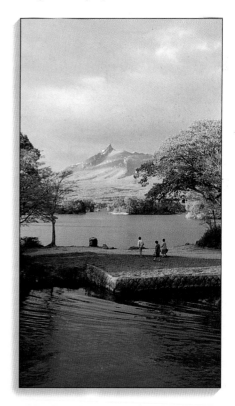

INSIGHT GUIDES
Travel Tips

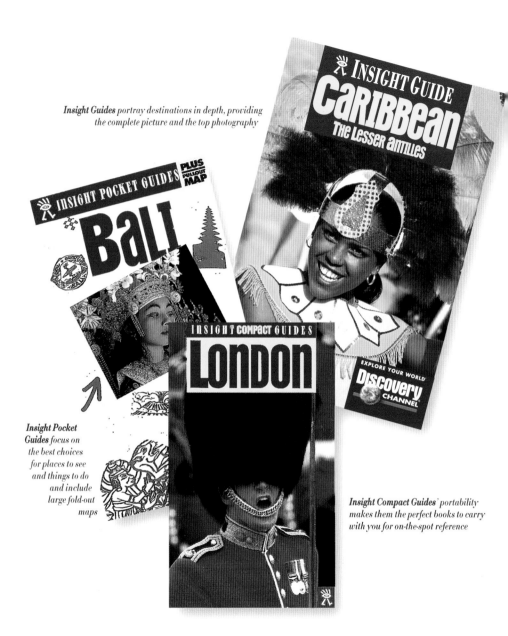

Insight Guides *portray destinations in depth, providing the complete picture and the top photography*

Insight Pocket Guides *focus on the best choices for places to see and things to do and include large fold-out maps*

Insight Compact Guides' *portability makes them the perfect books to carry with you for on-the-spot reference*

Three types of guide for all types of travel

INSIGHT GUIDES Different people need different kinds of information. Some want *background information* to help them prepare for the trip. Others seek *personal recommendations* from someone who knows the destination well. And others look for *compactly presented data* for on-the-spot reference. With three carefully designed series, Insight Guides offer readers the perfect choice. Insight Guides will turn your visit into an experience.

The world's largest collection of visual travel guides

CONTENTS

CHINA

Getting Acquainted

The Place

China is the third largest country in the world. The land comprises 35 percent mountains, 27 percent high plateau, 17 percent basin or desert, 8 percent hilly areas, and 13 percent plains. Only about 11 percent of the land area is agriculturally useful. The highest population densities are along the coast.

Local Time

Despite its immense size, there is only one time zone throughout China: GMT +8 hours.

Climate

China covers 35 degrees of latitude, resulting in a great variation of regional climates. In many areas, the summer is hot and rainy, with a high level of humidity, while the winter is dry. In northern China, more than 80 percent of rainfall occurs in the summer months, but only 40 percent of the annual rainfall occurs in southern China during the same period.

There are frequent typhoons in southeast China during the rainy season, between July and September. North of the Chang Jiang (Yangzi), the winter can be extremely cold with piercing winds.

The northeast and the desert regions of Xinjiang and Inner Mongolia have hot, dry summers and long, cold winters. In central China, the summers are hot and humid, with a lot of rainfall in the late summer. In the low lying re-gions of the Yangzi, winter is milder than in the central Chinese loess mountain regions or in Sichuan. In the regions around Beijing, Xi'an and Zhengzhou, there are occasional sand storms in winter and spring.

On the Tibet-Qinghai Plateau (average altitude: 4,000m/13,100ft), summer is short and moderately warm, while winters can get very cold; there is little rainfall throughout the year, and great differences in day and night temperatures. A mild climate with warm summers and cool winters generally prevails on the Yunnan-Guizhou High Plateau, with little rainfall, and very rare frosts.

Southern China has a sub-tropical climate. Rainfall is distributed throughout the year; summers are humid and hot, and the winters are short and cooler.

Generally, the best times for travelling are spring (May) and autumn (September/October).

The People

The People's Republic of China is the world's most populous nation, with around 1.2 billion people, about 20 percent of them in urban areas. A little over 90 percent of the population are Han Chinese; the remainder includes 55 minorities who differ fundamentally in their customs, traditions, languages and culture. The minorities have been exempted from China's strict population controls.

Culture & Customs

Chinese etiquette is polite and formal, following strict rules, which can seem impolite by Western standards in some situations. If you encounter diffiiculties, stay calm and indicate your problem or enquiry politely and firmly. Politeness is unknown on public transport, as the overcrowded conditions always encourage a struggle. No priority is given to pedestrians on the roads, so be careful when crossing.

For the Chinese, it is bad to lose face, especially in front of a foreigner, so don't put anyone in a position where they might do so. Any criticism should be done discreetly and tactfully.

It is not customary to greet people with a handshake, and embracing or kissing when greeting or saying goodbye is highly unusual. The Chinese do not show their emotions and feelings in public, so follow their example. Be cautious if you get involved in political discussions.

It is very important for the Chinese to make and maintain good connections, and it is equally important for foreigners on business. Expect lots of invitations and gifts. *Qingke*, the wining and dining of guests, is an old Chinese tradition still used today to thank friends for a favour or make new business contacts. If invited by a Chinese, you are obliged to return the invitation.

It is considered quite normal in China to eat noisily and belch during a meal. This doesn't mean that a foreign guest must do likewise. An increasing number of Chinese, particularly in the big cities, don't find it very pleasant either. In many simple restaurants, bones and other remnants are thrown on the table or the floor. Spitting is also quite common, despite official campaigns to restrain the habit.

Names: The family name comes first, the given name second. Mao Zedong's family name, for example, was Mao and the given name Zedong. Only among family and very good friends are given names used. Address people by their family name, with an honorific following it: *xiansheng* for men, *furen* for women. The same goes for the form of address referring to a person's position. For instance, Manager Li in Chinese is Li *jingli*, and Professor Wang is Wang *jiaoshou*.

Government & Economy

The People's Republic of China is a socialist state. It was founded on 1 October 1949. The country is divided into 23 provinces (including

Taiwan), five autonomous regions (Inner Mongolia, Xinjiang, Tibet, Ningxia and Guangxi), and five locally-governed cities (Beijing, Tianjin, Shanghai, Hong Kong and Chongqing, which recently split from the rest of Sichuan and became a separate city state. All provinces and autonomous regions are strictly subordinate to central government.

The **autonomous regions** are mostly populated by members of ethnic minorities who have the right to determine their own affairs – within the framework of a central state policy; they retain their own customs, traditions and language.

The **National People's Congress** is the highest governing body. Only the people's congresses at the lowest local level are directly elected, although the party retains the right to propose candidates. The People's Liberation Army, overseas Chinese and the national minorities send representatives to congress.

The **Communist Party**, founded in 1921, has the leading role in state and society. Since the Cultural Revolution the party has been held in low esteem because of bureaucracy and misuse of power and privileges. Mao Zedong led the party from 1935–76; after his death, Hua Guofeng became leader. By 1978, Deng Xiaoping had consolidated his position, and even after officially retiring in the early 1990s he has held on as *de facto* leader. There is no mechanism for an orderly succession.

The **Four Modernisations**, which are official party policy, refer to agriculture, industry, science and technology, and defence. the Modernisations are an attempt to transform China from a backward agricultural country into an industrial nation, in which socialist planning will be combined with a market economy.

Note
Hong Kong is treated separately in this section of the guide. Although now re-integrated with China, regulations and facilities are very different from those in the rest of the country.

Planning the Trip

What To Bring

It is advisable to take your usual toilet articles and medicines. Hotel shops will have a good choice of Western goods, and more and more local shops in the large cities are stocking Western items, but elsewhere, things such as tampons are still difficult to find.

Photographic film and batteries are available, but may be cheaper and fresher if bought at home. If you buy the versions made for sale in China they are cheaper. Kodak, Fuyi and Konica cost more. Slide film is hard to get. It is worth taking a small flashlight, especially if you're going to stay in modest hostels. Chinese-made batteries tend not to last long. Take an international electrical adaptor, with 3- and 2-pin plugs, and/or battery-operated equipment.

What to Wear

In the summer months, take light cotton clothes that are easily washed and not too delicate. Something warm is also useful, even in the hottest season, as the air conditioning in hotels is often vigorous. Footwear should be comfortable and strong.

Most Chinese wear ordinary clothes to evening performances at the Beijing opera, the theatre or cir-

Electricity

Electricity in China is 220 volts, 50 cycles AC. Don't foget to take an international adaptor, to accommodate different style plugs.

cus. It is best to follow this custom, especially in rural areas, where the floor is often of compressed mud, and high-heeled shoes would be foolish. In contrast, people dress up more for urban discos and clubs.

Rain gear is useful, especially during the summer months – China's rainy season is from May to August.

Entry Regulations

Visas & Passports
All foreigners need an entry visa. If you are part of a group, the tour operator will often obtain it; group visas will usually be issued for groups of at least 10, and the accompanying guide will keep the visas. Individual travellers can apply at any Chinese embassy, and the procedure is usually straightforward, taking about a week. Duration depends on current regulations, and on your own country's regulations for visiting Chinese citizens. Typical is a 30-day single-entry visa. Your passport must be valid for six months after the expiration of the entry visa.

Traditionally, it has been quicker and easier to obtain or renew visas in Hong Kong, including long-term, multiple-entry visas, than anywhere else, and this has not changed much since the handover. If your visa expires while in China, it can be extended by the local Public Security Bureau – the ubiquitous police (*Gongan Ju*).

There was a time when many areas were off-limits to foreigners, or else special travel permits, exceedingly difficult to obtain, were required. Nowadays, most of the country is open to foreigners, except some delicate border areas.

Customs
On arrival, each traveller must complete a form declaring foreign currency and valuables such as cameras, antiques and jewellery. The declaration must be handed in on departure; if required, the listed objects must be shown to verify that they haven't been sold within China. Tourists can import two bottles of alcohol and 600 cigarettes, as well

as foreign currency and valuables for personal use without restrictions. The import of weapons, ammunition, drugs and pornographic literature (broadly interpreted, this would probably include bibles and pictures of the Dalai Lama) is prohibited. On departure, antiques such as porcelain, paintings, calligraphy, carvings and old books must carry the red lacquer seal of an official antique shop; otherwise they can be confiscated by customs officials without compensation.

Health

Travellers to East Asia may be exposed to potential illnesses or diseases from a number of sources. The most frequently reported is traveller's diarrhoea. The best prevention is maximum hygiene while travelling, especially in restaurants and roadside snack bars. Never eat raw, uncooked or partially-cooked food, including salads other than in the top hotels. Animal or human excrement is still frequently used as fertiliser, so bacteria on uncooked vegetables can easily be ingested. If travelling outside a tour group acquire chopsticks and a tin bowl with lid for train journeys and meals in small roadside restaurants. Drink only boiled or bottled water, even though the tap water is drinkable in some places, and reduce exposure to insects as much as possible.

The adjustment to a different climate and food frequently leads to colds or digestive problems that, although rarely serious, can spoil one's enjoyment.

Tibet, the northwest, and tropical Yunnan make particularly high demands on the body. Heart disease and high blood pressure can lead to serious problems in Tibet. Along the Silk Road, expect high temperatures and dry conditions.

If planning to visit areas outside of Beijing, Shanghai, Guangzhou and Hong Kong, consider carrying emergency evacuation insurance. If injured in the deserts of western China, for example, medical and transportation costs could leave you indebted for a long time. Two of the largest emergency evacuation companies are SOS Assistance and Asia Emergency Assistance. They have offices in many major cities throughout the world, or contact them in Hong Kong or Beijing:

International SOS Assistance
Hong Kong:
507 Kai Tak Commercial Bldg,
317 Des Voeux Road,
Central, Hong Kong
Tel: 2541 6483; fax: 2544 1677.
Beijing:
Kunlun Hotel, Xinyuan Nan Lu,
Beijing.
Tel: 6591-6094/6500-3388 ext. 433
Asia Emergency Assistance (AEA)
Hong Kong:
Allied Resources Bldg 9F, 32-38 Ice House Street, Central, Hong Kong,
Tel: 2810 8898; fax: 2845 0395.
Beijing:
Clinic, tel: 6462-9112;
24-hours: tel: 6462-9100;
Admin: tel: 6462-9199/9111.
The International Medical Centre
at the Beijing Lufthansa Centre also has a short-term medical plan for people travelling to Beijing for a month. It also offers evacuation insurance for individual travellers.

Insect-Transmitted Illnesses

Malaria: Transmitted to humans by mosquitoes which are most active around dawn and dusk. *Symptoms*: Fever and flulike symptoms, chills, achiness, and tiredness. Up to one year after returning home, travellers should consult a physician for flulike illness. *Risk*: Little or no risk in urban areas and popular tourist destinations; there is no risk in provinces bordering Mongolia or in Heilongjiang, Ningxia, Qinghai, or Hong Kong. Risk exists in rural areas not visited by most travellers. In such areas, transmission is highest from May to December; in the south, transmission occurs yearround. Whether taking preventative drugs or not, travellers in risk areas should reduce exposure to mosquitoes.

Taking drugs to prevent malaria is recommended only for travellers to rural areas who will have outdoor exposure during evening hours. Knowing what medication to take is not as easy as it used to be. There is increasing evidence that mosquitoes in many parts of the world, including parts of northern Thailand and Durma, are developing resistance to traditional preventative drugs such as choloroquine and Mefloquine (Lariam).

Moreover, some people have extreme reactions to many of the more recent drugs. Consult medical authorities or a physician knowledgeable in travel medicine.

Dengue fever: Primarily an urban viral infection (in or around human habitations) transmitted by mosquitoes, which are most active around dawn and dusk. *Symptoms*: sudden onset of high fever, severe headaches, joint and muscle pain, and a rash, which shows up 3 to 4 days after the fever begins. *Risk*: Occurs in parts of southern China and Taiwan. The risk is minimal for most travellers. Those who have lived several years in highrisk areas are more susceptible than short-term visitors. There is no vaccine or specific treatment available.

Japanese encephalitis: A mosquitoborne viral disease prevalent in rural areas, often in ricegrowing areas. *Symptoms*: none, or headache, fever, and other flulike symptoms. Serious complications can lead to a swelling of the brain (encephalitis). *Risk*: Occurs in rural China and Korea, and occasionally in Hong Kong and Taiwan. The mosquito is most active in the late afternoon and early evening. Low or minimal risk for most travellers. Transmission is usually during the rainy season. There is no specific drug for treatment, but there is a preventative vaccine, which should be considered for people who plan longterm – 4 weeks or more – visits to rural areas.

Contamination

Food and water-borne diseases are the primary cause of travellers' illness. The main one is diarrhoea, which is caused primarily by viruses or bacteria, usually through contaminated food or water. The

More colour for the world.

HDCplus. New perspectives in colour photography.

http://www.agfaphoto.com

AGFA

Probably the <u>most</u> <u>important</u> TRAVEL TIP you will ever receive

Before you travel abroad, make sure that you and your family are protected from diseases that can cause serious health problems.

For instance, you can pick up *hepatitis A* which infects 10 million people worldwide every year (it's not just a disease of poorer countries) simply through consuming contaminated food or water!

What's more, in many countries if you have an accident needing medical treatment, or even dental treatment, you could also be at risk of infection from *hepatitis B* which is 100 times more infectious than AIDS, and can lead to liver cancer.

The good news is, you can be protected by vaccination against these and other serious diseases, such as *typhoid*, *meningitis* and *yellow fever*.

Travel safely! Check with your doctor at least 8 weeks before you go, to discover whether or not you need protection.

Consult your doctor before you go... not when you return!

SB
SmithKline Beecham
V A C C I N E S

Produced as a service to public health

more serious illnesses are:

Hepatitis A: A viral infection of the liver transmitted by fecal-contaminated food or drink, or person-to-person contact. *Symptoms:* Fatigue, fever, no appetite, nausea, dark urine and/or jaundice, vomiting, aches. There is no specific treatment, but an effective vaccine is available, especially for those who plan to travel repeatedly or reside in risk areas. Immune globulin is recommended for short-term protection only.

Hepatitis B: All countries in Asia, including China, report high levels of infection. Hepatitis B is a viral infection of the liver transmitted through the exchange of blood or blood-derived fluids, or through sexual activity with an infected person. Unscreened blood and unsterilised needles, or contact with potentially-infected people with open skin lesions, are sources of infection. An effective vaccine is available, which should be started six months prior to travel.

Public Holidays

In contrast to the traditional festivals, such as the Spring Festival (Lunar New Year), which follow the lunar calendar and vary in timing from year to year, important official holidays follow the Gregorian calendar. Most shops are open on holidays, but don't plan to travel unless reservations have been made well in advance. Especially make no travel plans during the Spring Festival, when everyone is travelling home.

- **1 January** New Year's Day
- **February** Variable. Lunar New Year (Spring Festival)
- **8 March** International Women's Day
- **1 May** International Labour Day
- **4 May** Youth Day
- **1 June** Children's Day
- **1 July** Founding of Communist Party
- **1 August** Founding of People's Liberation Army
- **1 October** National Day

Typhoid fever: A bacterial infection transmitted by contaminated food and water, or directly between people. Travellers to East Asia are susceptible to typhoid, particularly in smaller towns or rural areas. *Symptoms:* Fever, headaches, tiredness, no appetite, and constipation (rather than diarrhoea). Be cautious: drinking bottled or boiled water and eating only well-cooked food lowers the risk. Typhoid is treated with antibiotics. Vaccination is recommended for travellers off the tourist routes, especially if staying for six weeks or more. Available vaccines protect 70–90 percent of users.

Cholera: Although some cases have occasionally been reported in China, the risk is virtually non-existent. An acute intestinal infection caused by bacteria, most often through contaminated water or food. *Symptoms:* Abrupt onset of watery diarrhoea, dehydration, vomiting, and muscle cramps. Medical care must be sought quickly. The available vaccine is only 50 percent effective, and is not recommended for the majority of travellers.

Schistosomiasis (bilharzia): An infection from a flatworm larvae that penetrates the skin, including un-broken skin. *Risk:* Schistosomiasis is found in some areas of China, including rivers and lakes of southeastern and eastern China, especially along the Chang Jiang (Yangzi River) and tributaries. The risk comes from bathing, wading, or swimming in contaminated freshwater. There is no easy way to identify infested water. If exposed, immediate and vigorous drying with a towel, or the application of rubbing alcohol to the exposed areas, can reduce risk. Water treated with chlorine or iodine is virtually safe, as is saltwater.

Money Matters

The Chinese currency is called *renminbi* (people's currency), often abbreviated RMB, but people generally use *kuai* when speaking. The basic unit is the *yuan*. Ten *jiao* make one yuan, and ten *fen* make

one *jiao*. Thus, 100 fen make one yuan. Notes are currently issued for 2, 5, 10, 50 and 100 yuan. Coins include 1 yuan, 5 jiao, and 1, 2 and 5 fen.

Since the RMB is not completely convertible on the world markets, a black market exists, but it is highly illegal and the exchange rates are laughable and not worth the risk of being short-changed, receiving counterfeit bills or being arrested.

Most of the world's primary currencies are accepted in banks and hotels. Eurocheques, however, are not accepted anywhere, including branches of European banks.

ATM machines are appearing in all major cities but usually only the Bank of China's ATMs are connected to a global network. Look out for CIRRUS or PLUS. Most banks have agreements with these networks. Citibank is also showing a presence in Beijing, Shanghai and Guangzhou and their ATMs usually accommodate lots of different cards. There is a useful Citibank at the Bright China building on Jianguomennei Dajie in Beijing, close to the main railway station.

Increasingly, places frequented by foreigners take the usual **credit cards** such as American Express, Visa, Diners Club, and MasterCard. They are of little use outside of the major cities, however. Most transport costs – domestic air and train tickets – must be paid for in cash.

Cash advances may be obtained from major branches of the **Bank of China**, including, in Beijing, the head office at 410 Fuchingmennei Dajie, tel: 6601 6688, or the branch at 19, Dong An Men St, tel: 6519 9115/4.

Getting There

BY AIR

Beijing

The international airport connects Beijing to all parts of China and to the world's major cities. Beijing's airport is 27km (17 miles), a 25-minute drive from the centre.

Taxis are on the left as you leave the terminal. Air China has a coach service to its offices at Xidan, west of Tiananmen Square and Dongsi, in the northeast of the city. This is recommended only if you have light baggage. Most major hotels offer limousine or bus transfers. Passengers on international arrivals must fill out arrival cards, customs and health declarations. Travellers with tuberculosis and AIDS carriers are barred from entry.

If leaving on a domestic flight from Beijing, check in at least 30 minutes before the flight or you will lose your seat – 29 minutes before the flight is not good enough. International flight check-in should be done at least one hour before the flight. Foreigners leaving China by air are required to pay a 100 yuan airport tax. Domestic flight tax is 50 yuan (at 1999 rates).

Other cities

Shanghai is set to become a major international gateway to China with the opening of the new airport at Pudong in late 1999. The major airports in south China are at Guangzhou and Shenzhen, as well as Hong Kong. Guangzhou's Baiyun Airport is 10km (6 miles) north of the city. Shenzhen's Fuyong Airport is about 25km (15 miles) from Shekou, at the western end of Shenzhen, and 55km (34 miles) from the centre of Shenzhen.

Bear in mind that buying a return ticket on a domestic route is difficult, except to cities like Beijing and Shanghai. All pricing discounts have been dropped. Overseas visitors now pay the same fare as Chinese citizens and no discounts are offered for advance bookings.

BY RAIL

Beijing

Beijing has five railway stations with lines running to most major cities throughout China. The new West Railway Station, the largest station in Asia, opened in 1996, providing badly need relief for the overloaded Beijing Railway Station.

If arriving from Europe via the **Trans-Manchurian** or **Trans-**

Mongolian railways (often called the Trans-Siberian, which in fact goes to Siberia's Pacific Coast, not China), all the same health and customs procedures apply as if arriving via an international flight.

There is a choice of two routes. The Chinese train – which is better equipped and maintained – takes 5 days via Ulan Bator through Mongolia, entering China via Erlian. The Russian train, which goes through Manchuria, takes a day longer, and enters China at Manzhouli. Both leave once a week from Moscow.

Luggage

Take sturdy, strong luggage, which should be lockable; sometimes it won't be transported unless it is locked.

Depending upon the type of train, there are two or three classes. Food is not included in the ticket price. Initially, the food seems fairly reasonable, but becomes increasingly monotonous as the journey continues.

If you want to interrupt the train journey in Russia for longer than 24 hours, you need a tourist visa and will have to show a hotel booking.

For train tickets from Beijing to other parts of China, go to the foreigners' booking office. One word of caution: train tickets must be bought at the point of departure; return tickets can't be purchased.

Guangzhou

There are trains to most large cities in China. Four daily trains link Guangzhou and the Hunghom station on the Kowloon side of Hong Kong (departure times 8.50am, 12.05pm, 1.23pm and 4.08pm), with two extra trains added during special festivals, the Guangzhou Fair and other peak periods. Travelling time is 2 hours. There is also a direct train between Foshan and Hong Kong (3 hours).

In Guangzhou, most hotels and the CTS office can help get train tickets. In Hong Kong, tickets can be purchased through travel agents, hotels, CTS offices or at the lobby of

the Hunghom railway station (tel: 2627 4400). A much cheaper alternative, or if tickets to Guangzhou are sold out, is to take the Kowloon–Guangzhou Railway (KCR) to the border terminus of Lo Wu (a 40-minute journey, with three departures an hour from 5.30am–10.19pm). The Shenzhen station is right across the border. There are approximately two departures every hour on the express trains between Shenzhen and Guangzhou. Travelling time is 1 hour 10 mins. Trains arrive in Guangzhou either at the central station or at Guangzhou East Railway Station (Guangzhou Dong), in Tianhe, a 30-minute taxi ride from the city centre. All trains between Kowloon and Guangzhou are air-conditioned, but not all between Shenzhen and Guangzhou. Look for the express trains which cost about 60 percent more than the slow trains. Four departures per day are on the new high speed train imported from Spain. Speeds of up to 200km/125miles an hour are claimed and travelling time is 55mins. Ask for the air-conditioned class when buying a ticket, a small price to pay when temperatures soar in the heat of summer.

BY SEA

From Hong Kong

There used to be an overnight steamer between Hong Kong and Guangzhou, which took 8 hours (but at present service is suspended with no news of any resumption). There is also a daytime catamaran service, which takes just over 3 hours. Ferry journeys from Hong Kong to Shantou take 14 hours; to Xiamen, 20 hours; and to Shanghai, 60 hours. All ferries have restaurants on board and the catamarans have a small canteen serving hot cup noodles and drinks.

From Korea

Ferry service is available from Inchon, South Korea, to Weihai (18 hours, departing twice weekly), Qingdao (24 hours, departing weekly) and Tianjin (30 hours, operating every five days).

From Japan
There is a weekly de-luxe cruise ship between Shanghai and Japan, alternating every week between Yokohama and Shanghai. There is also a weekly boat between Kobe and Tianjin/Tanggu. Trips take two days.

OVERLAND ROUTES

Several of China's international borders are open for crossing. Other parts, like the frontier with Bhutan, are restricted areas. A border crossing with Burma opened in 1996, but the Burmese authorities go out of their way to discourage foreigners from using it.

Nepal
Crossing via Nepal by bus or taxi has been possible since 1985, with sporadic periods of closed borders. Procure a Chinese visa anywhere else but Nepal, unless part of a tour. It's possible to travel by road between Kathmandu and Lhasa, but it requires considerable time, not only for travel, but for bureaucracy, including mandatory tours of Lhasa upon arrival. Independent travellers should note that transport on the Nepal side is good, but scarce on the Tibetan side. Plan on a vehicle hire/share to Lhasa.

Pakistan
Since 1986, it has been possible to travel the Karakorum Highway between Kashi (Kashgar), in northwest China, and Islamabad. Pakistan requires a visa for most nationalities. Visas are not available at the border for either China or Pakistan.

On both the Pakistani and Chinese sides of the border the roads may be blocked by landslides, and you may have to walk a fair distance, carrying your luggage. Accommodation en route is quite modest.

Kazakhstan
There is a daily bus service and a twice-weekly train service between Urumqi and Almaty, in Kazakhstan.

Vietnam
In 1995, train services began between Hanoi and Beijing via the Friendship Gate crossing. Unfortunately they have been plagued by red-tape at the border. Travelling from Vietnam to China requires a special visa. One may also cross the border by foot at Hekou (China) and Lao Cai (Vietnam), and at Friendship Gate (Dong Dang, Vietnam/Pingxiang, China).

PSB Offices

Beijing: 2 Andingmen Dongdajie, tel: 8522-5050/8401-5300, Mon–Fri 8.30am–5pm, Sat 8.30am–11.30am.
Shanghai: 210 Hankou Lu, tel: 6321-5380.
Guangzhou: 863 Jiefang Beilu, tel: 8333-1326.

Visitor Hot Lines:
Beijing: tel: 6513-0828.
Shanghai: tel: 6252-000.
Shanghai Visitor Association: tel: 6275-5880.
Guangzhou: tel: 8667 7422.

If you've lost something, notify the hotel, tour group leader or transportation authorities, and the police, who will usually make a serious effort to recover items.

Tour Operators

There are countless travel agencies within and outside China that handle domestic travel arrangements. Prominent among them is **China International Travel Services (CITS)**, until recently the sole agency handling overseas tourists. It now has branches throughout China, which operate independently. **China Travel Services (CTS)** is a similar organisation, originally responsible for domestic tourists and overseas Chinese, but now also catering to foreigners. While the efficiency of both organisations can be lacking, some say CTS is slightly better than CITS.

Agencies may also have business interests extending beyond simply arranging tours and bookings; they may own or partly own hotels. An agency that arranges a tour may do so by contacting agencies in places you will visit, and asking them to deal with local bookings. This means that if you go direct to an agency in the area you are visiting, savings are possible.

Sometimes, agencies such as CITS may hold tickets for rail journeys, operas, acrobatic performances and concerts even when such tickets are sold out at the stations or venues. Prices will be high, however.

There are also small-scale unlicensed tour operators. Reportedly, some of these use unroadworthy vehicles, take their customers to shops and restaurants that give the guides 'backhanders' (although this could also happen with licensed operators), and demand mark-ups of 100 percent or more for tickets to tourist sites. Others may be trustworthy, and cheap.

It is also quite possible nowadays, and increasingly common, to travel in China without the services of any agency.

Note that within China, agencies – including CITS – have nothing to do with visa extensions. Visit the police for these.

CITS Offices
Beijing, Beijing Tourist Building, tel: 6515-8562;
28 Jianguomenwai, China World Hotel, tel: 6607-1575/6608-7124; Tourism Hotline tel: 6513-0828.
Chengdu, 65, Sec 2, Renmin Nan Lu, tel: 667-5578.
Guilin, 41 Binjiang Lu, tel: 282-8017.
Guangzhou, near the main railway station at 179 Huangshi Si Lu, tel: 8666-6267.
Hangzhou, 1 Shihan Lu, tel: 515-2888, Ext 256.
Hong Kong, 6/F, Tower 2, South Seas Centre, 75 Mody Rd, Tsim Sha Tsui, Kowloon, tel: 2732-5888, fax: 2721-7454.
Kunming, 285 Huan Cheng Nan Lu, tel: 313-2895.

Nanjing, 202-1 N Zhong Shan Lu, tel: 342-8999.
Shanghai, Beijing Xi Lu 1277, tel: (021) 6321-7200.
Suzhou, 115 Shiquan Lu, tel: 522-3783.
Tianjin, 22 You Yi Lu, tel: 835-5309.
Wuhan, Rm 303, 1365 Zhongshan Dajie, Hankou, tel: 284-2331.
Xiamen, No. 2 Zhongshan Lu, tel: 203-1781 or 202-5277.
Xi'an, 48 (N) Changan Lu, tel: (029) 524-1864;
Bell Tower Hotel, tel: (029) 727-9200, ext 2842.

CNTA Offices Overseas
China National Tourist Office, London, 4 Glentworth St., London NW1, UK, tel: 935-9427, fax: 487-5842.
China National Tourist Office, New York, 350 Fifth Ave, Suite 6413, Empire State Bldg, New York, NY 10118, USA, tel: 760-9700, fax: 760-8809.
China National Tourist Office, Los Angeles, 333 West Broadway, Suite 201, Glendale, CA91204, USA, tel: 545-7505, fax: 545-7506.
China National Tourist Office, Sydney, Level 19, 44 Market St., Sydney, NSW 2000, Australia, tel: 299-4057, fax: 290-1958.
China National Tourist Office, Singapore, 1 Shenton Way, #7-05 Robina House, Singapore 068803, tel: 211-8681, fax: 221-9267.

American Express Travel Service Offices
Beijing, Room 2101, China World Trade Centre, Beijing 100004, tel: 6505-2888/2639 (Mon–Fri 9am–5pm, Sat 9am–noon).
Guangzhou, 339 Huan Shi Dong Lu, Guangzhou 510060, tel: 8331-1771 (Mon–Fri 9am–5pm, Sat 9am–noon).
Shanghai, 206 East Tower, Shanghai Centre, 1376 Nanjing Rd West, 200040, tel: 6279-8082 (Mon–Fri 9am–5pm, Sat 9am–noon).

Practical Tips

Emergencies

SECURITY & CRIME

There is still less crime in China than in many other countries, but as vigorous crime crackdowns by the government attest – over 1,000 executions in a two-month period in 1996 – crime is increasingly a problem, particularly in urban areas.

Take the same precautions applicable anywhere, on the street and on public transport and with valuables in hotels. Pickpockets and bag-slashers can be a problem, especially on crowded trains and buses, and at stations. Because of large numbers of migrant workers seeking employment, cities like Guangzhou have higher levels of crime than elsewhere. Nevertheless, in most towns and cities, one needn't worry.

The **Public Security Bureau** (Gongan Ju) is the ever-present police force responsible for *everything* – chasing murderers, quenching dissent, issuing visa extensions. They are usually friendly towards foreigners, even if the rules that they are strictly enforcing seem illogical at times. Also, they are usually able to resolve the problem with serious travel-related disputes – for example, with taxi drivers or hotels. To stay on their friendly side, don't try to travel in restricted areas or on an expired visa.

MEDICAL SERVICES

There is a big difference in China between urban and rural medical services. If travelling in the country-side, there may be no appropriate

medical services beyond primary health care, which is a success story in China. Some city hospitals have special sections for foreigners where English is spoken.

Many of the large hotels have their own doctors. Payment must be made on the spot for treatment, medicine and transport.

Beijing
Asia Emergency Assistance (AEA), Clinic, tel: 6462-9112
24-hours, tel: 6462-9100
Admin, tel: 6462-9199/9111
International Medical Centre, Beijing Lufthansa Ctr, 50 Liangmaqiau, tel: 6465-1561/62/63; fax: 6465-1961.
Emergency service 24 hours; vaccinations and dental services.
Beijing United Family Hospital, 2 Jiangjui Lu, tel: 6433-3960; fax: 6433-3963.
Family health care and gyneocological facilities; 24-hour pharmacy.
Sino-German Polyclinic, Landmark Tower, B-1, tel: 6501-1983.

Shanghai
Shanghai Emergency Centre, 68 Haining Lu, tel: 6324 4010.
Shanghai Medical Area Intl, 2606 Shartex Plaza, 88 Zunyi Road, tel: (021) 6295-0099 (24-hour).
Huashan Hospital, 12 Wulumuqi Zhonglu, tel: 6248-9999 ext 1921 and 6248-3986.
New Pioneer Intl, 2/F, 3/F Ge Ru Bldg, 910 Hen Shan Lu, tel: (021) 6469-7259, 6469-4884 and 6469-3898 (24-hour).

Guangzhou
Red Cross Hospital, emergencies, tel: 8444 6411, in English.
Guangzhou No. 1 People's Hospital, 602 Renmin Beilu, tel: 8333 3090.

When you're
bitten by the travel bug,
make sure you're protected.

Check into a British Airways Travel Clinic.

British Airways Travel Clinics provide travellers with:
- A complete vaccination service and essential travel health-care items
- Up-dated travel health information and advice

Call **01276 685040** for details of your nearest Travel Clinic.

New Insight Maps

Maps in Insight Guides are tailored to complement the text. But when you're on the road you sometimes need the big picture that only a large-scale map can provide. This new range of durable Insight Fleximaps has been designed to meet just that need.

Detailed, clear cartography
makes the comprehensive route and city maps easy to follow, highlights all the major tourist sites and provides valuable motoring information plus a full index.

Informative and easy to use
with additional text and photographs covering a destination's top 10 essential sites, plus useful addresses, facts about the destination and handy tips on getting around.

Laminated finish
allows you to mark your route on the map using a non-permanent marker pen, and wipe it off. It makes the maps more durable and easier to fold than traditional maps.

The first titles
cover many popular destinations. They include Algarve, Amsterdam, Bangkok, California, Cyprus, Dominican Republic, Florence, Hong Kong, Ireland, London, Mallorca, Paris, Prague, Rome, San Francisco, Sydney, Thailand, Tuscany, USA Southwest, Venice, and Vienna.

👁 INSIGHT GUIDES
The world's largest collection of visual travel guides

Provincial Hospital No. 1, Foreigners' Dept,
123 Huifu Xilu,
tel: 8777 7812.

Business Hours

Shops are open every day, including public holidays. Opening hours are usually from 8.30am or 9am–8pm. Government offices and banks are usually open Monday to Friday, 8.30am–5.30pm, with a lunch break from noon–1.30pm. Times are approximate; allow for local variations. In western China, for example, offices often open later.

Tipping

Officially, it is still illegal to accept tips in China. Moreover, for a long time, it was considered patronising. Tourists and visitors in recent years, however, have changed attitudes in areas like Guangzhou and Shanghai. It's also become the custom for travel groups to give a tip to the Chinese travel guides and bus drivers. If you are travelling with a group, ask the guide, who is responsible for the "official" contacts of the group, whether a tip is appropriate.

Tipping is still not common in most restaurants and hotels, although it is accepted in the top-class hotels and restaurants. Note that it is part of the ritual that any gift or tip will, at first, be firmly rejected.

Media

An English-language newspaper, the *China Daily*, is published in China, daily except Sunday. It is informative and sometimes even a bit bold, depending upon the climate at the moment. Often obtainable free from the big hotels, it contains television schedules and a diary of cultural events in Beijing. The sports section is good and informative. Unfortunately, same-day editions are available only in large cities; elsewhere, it'll be several days late. Overseas editions of the *China Daily* are published in

Hong Kong and the United States. Another English-language paper, the *Shanghai Star*, is available in Shanghai.

Most large hotels sell foreign-language newspapers and journals, including the *International Herald Tribune*, *The Times*, *Asian Wall Street Journal*, *Time*, *Newsweek* and the *Far Eastern Economic Review*.

The overseas edition of the party newspaper *Renmin Ribao* (*People's Daily*) is usually available in hotels.

Telephone, Telex & Fax

Telephone:
Domestic long-distance calls are cheap, international calls are expensive. Local calls in China, including in the hotels, are usually free of charge. International calls made from hotels typically have high surcharges added to China's already high IDD rates. Increasingly common in cities are card phones, with cards available in Y20, 50, 100 and 200. There are also street stalls where you can make calls, charging about Y20–30 a minute. China has also announced that the international rate is coming down to prepare for opening up to foreign competition.

Telex and fax:
Most of the big hotels have telex and fax facilities to help business people. Alternatively, central telegraph and post offices offer these services.

Telegrams:
Sending telegrams abroad is expensive. Express telegrams are double the price. There is usually a telegram counter at the hotel; other-

Important numbers

Police: 110
Ambulance: 120
Fire: 119
Traffic Accident: 122
Local directory assistance: 114
International directory assistance (English): 115

Domestic Area Codes

Add 0 to the codes below if dialling from within China:

Beijing	10
Chengdu	28
Chongqing	811
Guangzhou	20
Guilin	773
Hangzhou	571
Harbin	451
Jilin	432
Kunming	871
Luoyang	379
Nanjing	25
Shanghai	21
Shenyang	24
Shenzhen	755
Suzhou	512
Taiyuan	351
Tianjin	22
Urumqi	991
Wuhan	27
Wuxi	510
Xi'an	29
Xiamen	592
Xinxiang	373
Zhengzhou	371

wise, go to the central telegraph or post office.

Like many nations expanding their domestic telephone networks, China's telephone numbers can change without too much fanfare. If you hear an odd ringing sound on the line and can't get through, the number may have changed.

Country code for China:
dial **86**

Direct-dial international calls:
dial **00**, then the country code and telephone number.

Home country direct-dial:
dial **108**, then the country's international area code. For example, to call Britain, dial 108-44, then the domestic area code and number. For the United States and Canada, dial 108-1. (For AT&T, 108-11; MCI, 108-12; Sprint, 108-13.)

Getting Around

Orientation

All main cities can be reached by plane and train. In the regions along the big rivers, boats play an important part. The road network has been improved in recent years but is still very poor in many areas.

Road names and orientation

Street names are determined by the traditional checkerboard of Chinese urban design. The most important traffic arteries are divided into sectors and laid out in a grid typically based upon the compass points.

Suffixes are added to the road name to indicate north, south, east or west, and, additionally, to indicate the middle section. The middle section is called *zhong*; *nan* means south; *bei*, north; *dong*, east; and *xi*, west. A main road is *lu*, smaller is *dajie* or *jie*.

On arrival

There are exchange bureaux in the arrival halls of the airports, railway stations and harbours where you can change money. Chinese airlines provide buses which will take travellers from the airport, which is often a long way outside the city, to the airline offices in town. The fare is modest.

There are plenty of taxis readily available from airports and other points of entry. Be wary of non-official taxis outside of taxi ranks. Also, before setting off in a taxi, agree on a price for the journey, or ensure that the driver will use the meter.

Domestic Travel

See also *Getting There* (pages 325–7).

BY AIR

The following gives travel time from Beijing to other major domestic destinations:

Chengdu	2.35 hrs
Guangzhou	3.00 hrs
Guilin	2.35 hrs
Hangzhou	1.50 hrs
Nanjing	1.50 hrs
Shanghai	1.50 hrs
Xi'an	2.00 hrs

BY RAIL

The Chinese rail network covers 53,400 km (32,470 miles), of which 4,400 km (2,730 miles) are electrified. Average train speed is low, mainly due to poor construction. There is no first or second class on Chinese trains, but four categories or classes: *ruanwo* or soft-sleeper; *ruanzuo* or soft-seat; *yingwo* or hard-sleeper, and *yingzuo* or hard-seat. The soft-seat class is usually only available for short journeys. Long distance trains normally only have soft-sleeper or hard-sleeper facilities. The softsleeper class has 4-bed compartments with soft beds. It is to be recommended, particularly for long journeys. The hard-sleeper class has open, 6-bed compartments. The beds are not really hard, but are not very comfortable either. While you can reserve a place for the first three classes (you always buy a ticket with a place number), this is not essential for the lowest class.

There is always boiled water available on the trains. There are washrooms in the soft-sleeper and hard-sleeper classes. The toilets, regardless of class, are usually not very hygienic, and it is a good idea to bring your own toilet paper. There are dining cars on long-distance trains which can vary in quality. Trains are usually fully booked and

it is advisable to get a ticket well in advance, particularly during the main travel season. There are special ticket counters for foreigners at railway stations.The price depends on the class and the speed of the train; there are slow trains, fast trains, express trains and inter-city trains. Reservations can be made at ticket offices in the town centre or through travel agencies. Be on time, as trains tend to be punctual.

The following gives the travel time from Beijing to other major domestic destinations:

Chengdu	34 hrs
Guangzhou	33 hrs
Guilin	31 hrs
Nanjing	15 hrs
Shanghai	17 hrs
Xi'an	17 hrs

BY ROAD

Overland buses (*gongonqiche*) are the most important means of transport in many parts of China, especially where there is as yet no railway line. In most towns and settlements, there are main bus stations for overland buses. They are the cheapest means of transport, but are correspondingly slow. There are regular breaks during bus journeys; on those lasting several days you will usually find simple restaurants and overnight accommodation near the bus stations. Many overland buses have numbered seats and it is advisable to book a ticket and seat well in advance. Otherwise, just get on the bus early, grab a seat and keep it. Modern buses with air conditioning are frequently available in the tourist centres.

BY BOAT

There are regular ferry and boat connections between the large coastal cities in China. The same is true for some of the big rivers, particularly the Yangzi and the Pearl rivers (but not the Yellow River). Both the ocean liners and the inland river boats have several classes. You can find out the exact timetable from travel agents or the shipping agencies.

Town Transport

The visitor can choose between taxis, buses or bicycles for transport in cities. In Beijing, Hong Kong and Shanghai there is also the underground. Taxis are certainly the most comfortable form of transport, and can be hired for excursions.

Buses in Chinese towns are always overcrowded. The fare depends on distance, and should be paid to the conductor. Buses are usually easy to use, and timetables or town maps are available everywhere. In some Chinese cities such as Beijing, there are also mini-buses for certain routes.They are a bit more expensive but will stop at any point you want along the route. Drivers will pack in as many people as they can and you may end up standing or sitting next to the driver.

You can hire bicycles in many Chinese towns, either at the hotels or at special hiring shops. It is advisable to park the bike at guarded parking spaces for a small fee. China has bicycle thieves, and there is a fine for illegal parking.

Where to Stay

China's large cities have seen the sprouting of numerous new hotels, most of them at the top end of the market, and some of world-class calibre. Many belong to either international hotel chains, or to international marketing associations, and their management and staff have been trained abroad. Usually the prices in these hotels are in line with those in the West. Tour groups are usually accommodated in good tourist hotels.

Bookings at hotels in the middle and lower price ranges can be difficult, particularly during the main summer season in May, September and October, when they are hopelessly booked up. But if you have confirmed reservations, your room will be waiting, as hotels rarely overbook.

Worth mentioning are a few well-preserved hotels built by the former colonial powers in some cities. They include the Peace Hotel (*Heping*) in Shanghai, the People's Hotel (*Renmin Dasha*) in Xi'an and the Friendship Hotel (*Youyibinguan*) in Beijing. The interiors have been modernised, of course.

Luxury hotels abound in the largest cities. Rates at all but the cheapest hotels are subject to 10 to 15 percent service surcharge. Rates indicated are for standard rooms.

Beijing

tel code (10)
INTERNATIONAL CLASS
China World Hotel
1 Jianguomenwai Dajie
Tel: 6505-2266
Top of the line service and accommodation, well located for business. Health club with pool;

shopping plaza and business centre; a variety of Western and Asian restaurants.
Kempinski Hotel
(Beijing Lufthansa Ctr)
50 Liangmaqiao Lu
Tel: 6465-3388
Fax: 6465-3366
Shiny new five-star hotel; attached to Youyi Shopping City.
Palace Hotel
8 Jinyu Hutong Wangfujing
Tel: 6512-8899
Fax: 6512-9050
Centrally located for shopping and Imperial Palace sights. Restaurants and designer shopping.
Shangri-La Hotel
29 Zizhuyuan Rd
Tel: 6841-2211
Fax: 6841-8002
Top-notch accommodation with experienced staff and friendly surroundings. Located on the western edge of town, but shuttle buses take guests to the centre.

SUPERIOR CLASS
Hilton Hotel
1 Dongfong Lu
Dongsanhuanbei Lu
Tel: 6466-2288
Fax: 6464-3052
New 5-star hotel right off the airport expressway. Posh surroundings, good food.
Hotel New Otani
26 Jianguomenwai Dajie
Tel: 6512-5555
Fax: 6512-5346
Swimming pool and health club. Well located for business in the eastern part of the city.
Holiday Inn Crowne Plaza
48 Wangfujing Dajie Dengshikou
Tel: 6513-3388
Fax: 6513-2513
Located on a busy shopping street in central Beijing, close to the Imperial Palace and other sights. Health club and swimming pool.
Hotel Beijing-Toronto
3 Jianguomenwai Dajie
Tel: 6500-2266
Fax: 6500-2022
Friendly four-star lodging in eastern Beijing.

Peace Hotel
3 Jinyu Hutong Wangfujing
Tel: 6512-8833
Fax: 6512-6863
Unremarkable rooms, centrally located for shopping and the Imperial Palace. Lively nightlife in the neighbourhood.
Prime Hotel Beijing
2 Wangfujing Dajie
Tel: 6513-6666
Fax: 6513-4248
Relaxing atmosphere and de-luxe accommodation in a prime location.
Traders Hotel
(China World Trade Centre)
1 Jianguomenwai Dajie
Tel: 6505-2277
Fax: 6505-0818
Good solid service, food and accommodation. Well located for business in the east section of the city.

STANDARD CLASS
Beijing Bamboo Garden Hotel
24 Xiaoshiqiao Lane
Jiugulou Dajie
Tel: 6403-2229
Fax: 6401-2633
Modest but clean rooms opening onto a classical-style Chinese garden. Just one block from the Drum Tower.
Fragrant Hills Hotel
Fragrant Hills Park
Tel: 6259-1166
Fax: 6259-1762
Sunny modern getaway in the lush hills to the northwest of Beijing, near Summer Palace, but far from the city. Swimming pool, Chinese and Western restaurants.
Jianguo Hotel
5 Jianguomenwai Dajie
Tel: 6500-2233
Fax: 6500-2871
A favourite for long-term business travellers. Experienced staff and a pleasant atmosphere. Located in eastern Beijing. Good value.
Holiday Inn Lido Hotel
Jingtai Lu
Tel: 6437-6688
Fax: 6437-6237.
A village unto itself; swimming, tennis courts, business and shopping facilities. Near airport.

Novotel 88
Dengshikou Dajie
Tel: 6513-8822
Fax: 6513-9088
Clean, no frills, centrally located. A real bargain for Beijing.
Qianmen Hotel
175 Yongan Lu
Tel: 6301-6688
Fax: 6301-3883
Standard accommodation in old outer city, near Tiantan. Opera performances nightly.
Xin Qiao Hotel
2 Dong Jiaomin Xiang
Dongcheng District
Tel: 6513-3366
Fax: 6512-5126
Elegant old-style hotel located in the former Legation Quarter, close to Tiananmen Square. Peaceful and convenient to transportation.

BUDGET CLASS
Beijing Friendship Hotel
3 Baishiqiao Rd
Tel: 6849-8888
Fax: 6849-8866
An old-style, state-run hotel in the peaceful northwest corner of town. Located near the universities and the Summer Palace.
Ritan Hotel
1 Ritan Road
Jianguomenwai
Tel: 6512-5588
Fax: 6512-8671
Intimate little hotel located inside Ritan Park. Peaceful and reasonably-priced.

Guangzhou and Shenzhen

tel codes (20 and 755)
INTERNATIONAL CLASS
China Hotel
Liuhua Lu
Guangzhou
Tel: 8666-6888
Fax: 8667-7014
Five-star hotel; restaurants, electronic games arcade and bowling alley. The hotel is across the street from the Canton Trade Fair grounds.
Garden Hotel
368 Huangshi Donglu
Guangzhou
Tel: 8333-8989

Fax: 8335-0467
Five-star hotel located across the street from the largest Friendship Department Store.
White Swan Hotel
1 Shamian Nanlu
Tel: 8188-6968
Fax: 8186-1188
One of the finest hotels in China and a member of the Leading Hotels of the World network. The 843-room hotel on Shamian island has stunning views.

SUPERIOR CLASS
Dongfang Hotel
120 Liuhua Lu
Guangzhou
Tel: 8666-9900
Fax: 8666-2775
Centrally-located and convenient for businessmen, as the China Trade Fair grounds are just opposite.
Guangdong International Hotel
336 Huangshi Donglu
Guangzhou
Tel: 8331-1888
Fax: 8331-1666
The newest luxury-class hotel to open in Guangzhou. Has 14 food and drink outlets and a shopping arcade.
Holiday Inn City Centre Overseas Chinese Village
Huanshi Dong
28 Guangmin Lu
Tel: 8776 6999
Fax: 8775-3126
A 430-room hotel, which opened in 1990, known for its friendly service.
Landmark Hotel
2 Nanhu Lu
Shenzhen
Tel: 217-2288
Fax: 229-0473
A Cathay International hotel. The hotel has restaurants, coffee shop, bar and night club and health club with swimming pool.
Ramada Pearl Hotel
9 Mingyue Yilu
Tel: 8777-2988
Fax: 8776-7481
This 400-room hotel is located in the eastern part of the city.
Shangri-La
East Side
Railway Station Jianshe Lu
Shenzhen

Tel: 223-0888
Fax: 223-9878
Luxuriously appointed 553-room hotel, with extensive food and drink outlets.

STANDARD CLASS
Equatorial Hotel
931 Renmin Lu
Guangzhou
Tel: 8667-2888
Fax: 8667-2583
Comprehensive range of food and beverage outlets, business centre, health club and disco.
Overseas Chinese Hotel
90 Zhanqian Lu
Guangzhou
Tel: 8666-3488
Fax: 8666-3230
A 400-room hotel with two restaurants, a coffee house and disco.
Forum
67 Heping Lu
Shenzhen
Tel: 8558-6333
Fax: 8556-1700
Opened in 1990, the Forum is located just west of the railway station. A member of the Inter-Continental hotel and resorts chain.
Victory Hotel
54 Shamian Sijie
Guangzhou
Tel: 8186-2622
Fax: 8186-1062
Located on the former concession island of Shamian, near the old town. This was one of Guangzhou's top hotels in the 1930s.
Airlines Hotel
130 Shennan Dong Lu
Shenzhen
Tel: 223-7999
Fax: 233-7866
Recently redecorated, now clean and comfortable.
Century Plaza
Cunfeng Lu
Shenzhen
Tel: 8222-0888
Fax: 8223-4060
Luxury hotel situated in the hub of Shenzhen. Five restaurants, pool, and health and business centres.
Oriental Regent
Financial Centre Bldg
Shenan Zhonglu

Shenzhen
Tel: 8224-7000
Fax: 8224-7290
Centrally located, four-star hotel. Close to nightlife area.
Shenzhen Bay Hotel
Overseas Chinese Town
Shenzhen
Tel: 8660-0111
Fax: 8660-0139
Facing Deep Water Bay and a short walk from attractions like Splendid China, China Folk Culture Village and Windows of the World. This resort-style hotel on the beach offers a full range of recreational facilities.

BUDGET CLASS
Guangzhou Youth Hostel
2 Shamian Sijie
Guangzhou
Tel: 8188-4298
Cheap rooms can be found at this hostel, nicknamed the 'Black Duck', as it faces the luxury White Swan Hotel. A favourite with backpackers.

Guilin

tel code (773)
INTERNATIONAL CLASS
Lijiang Hotel
1 Shanhubeilu
Guilin
Tel: 22 2881
Fax: 22 2891
Centrally located, overlooking Cedar Lake and facing nearby Elephant

Guesthouses

Individual travellers may find accommodation in guesthouses in smaller towns off the tourist track. They usually have rooms with two or more beds, and often dormitories are available; there are usually shower and washing facilities, as well. Recommended as cheap accommodation for backpackers.

Some guesthouses or simple hotels refuse to take foreign guests, usually because of the rules of Chinese travel agencies or the local police, who often determine where foreigners may stay.

Trunk Hill. Big rooms, modern facilities, including sauna and gymnasium. The local roller-skating rink is around the corner, and Binjianglu, along the river, isespecially pretty at night.
Guilin Park Hotel
1 Luosi Hill, Guilin
Tel: 282 8899
Fax: 282 2296
On Guihu Lake, at the foot of Old Man Hill. Beautifully designed, with white walls, green tiles, Chinese pagoda-style roofs. Set in one of the most scenic parts of the city, with pool, Chinese and Western restaurants.

SUPERIOR CLASS
Guilin Osmanthus Hotel
451 Zhongshannanlu
Guilin
Tel: 383 4300
Fax: 383 5316
In the heart of the city on Peach Blossom River, a short walk from Elephant Trunk Hill, 1 km north of the railway station. Range of facilities, including water massage pond.

STANDARD CLASS
Guishan Hotel
Chuanshan Road
Guilin
Tel: 581 3388
Fax: 581 4851
Across the Li River from Elephant Trunk Hill with a good view of the port area at night. A short walk from Seven Star Park. The usual modern facilities in a less congested neighbourhood.

Shanghai

tel code (21)
INTERNATIONAL CLASS
Garden Hotel
58 Maoming Nanlu
Tel: 6415-1111
Fax: 6415-8866
A 33-storey tower that incorporates the former Cercle Sportif Français, injecting a little of the past into its modern facilities. Surrounded by a garden, the Garden is popular with Japanese, as it is managed by the Hotel Okura,

Hilton International
250 Hua Shan Road
Tel: 6248-0000
Fax: 6248-3868
Over 40 storeys tall, the Hilton makes an unforgettable first impression with its expansive marble lobby. Popular with both Europeans and Asians. Restaurants include the rooftop Sichuan Court, with fine views.

Holiday Inn Crowne Plaza
388 Pan Yu Road
Tel: 6280-8888
Fax: 6280-3353
Near the diplomatic neighbourhood, the Crowne Plaza follows the elegant design of the chain's top-end hotels everywhere. With full business and recreational facilities, several respected restaurants offer imaginative East-West menus.

Hyatt Regency
Lijuazui Road
Pudong Area
Tel: 5047-2288
Fax: 5049-1234
Newly opened in 1999.

JC Mandarin
1225 Nanjing Xilu
Tel: 6279-1888
Fax: 6279-1822
Conveniently located in the heart of Shanghai's shopping district on its most commercial avenue, within walking distance of the Bund and other sights. Facilities include indoor pool, gym, two tennis courts.

Portman Shangri-La
Shanghai Centre
1376 Nanjing Xilu
Tel: 6279-8888
Fax: 6279-8800
One of Shanghai's finest hotels, known not only for its central location, but also for its style – Chinese works of art adorn the lobby. Chamber music in the lobby each afternoon and evening. Part of the extensive Shanghai Centre, a complex with top restaurants, airline offices, and residential apartments.

Hotel Sofitel Hyland
505 Nanjing Dong Lu
Tel: 6351-5888
Fax: 6351-4088
Located right in the middle of downtown, this 34-storey hotel has

400 tastefully decorated rooms and comprehensive facilities.

SUPERIOR CLASS
Pacific Hotel
104 Nanjing Lu
Tel: 6327-6226
Fax: 6326-9620.
One of Shanghai's older establishments, the hotel is sagging and somewhat Gothic in ambiance. The granite structure is architecturally interesting: a gold-plated dome with a clock tower crowns the roof, and a classically-robust entrance leads into an art-deco lobby.

Peace Hotel
20 Nanjing Lu
Tel: 6321-1244
Fax: 6321-6888
Located on the Bund and a classic colonial retreat, one of the city's most famous landmarks. When it opened in the 1920s as the Cathay, it was *the* hotel in China. Somewhat run-down now, but comfortable, the Peace appeals to those who prefer nostalgia to generic creature comforts. Even if not staying here, drop by the bar in the evening to see the Old Jazz Band.

Xi'an

tel code (29)
INTERNATIONAL CLASS
Hyatt Regency Xian
158 Dongda Jie
Tel: 723-1234
Fax: 721-6799
Top of the line accommodation in an elegant setting. Conveniently located within the old city wall near the heart of the shopping district on Dong Dajie. Business centre, conference rooms, health club and various Western and Asian restaurants.

ANA Grand Castle Hotel
12 Xi Duan Huan Cheng Nan Lu
Tel: 723-1800
Fax: 723-1500
Spacious, modern, 5-star hotel located just outside the South Gate of the old city. The roof of the hotel is modelled after the Great Wild Goose Pagoda. Facilities include Western, Chinese and Japanese restaurants.

Grand New World Hotel
48 Lian Hu Lu
Tel: 721-6868
Fax: 721-9754
A cavernous hotel with friendly, efficient service. It is located just inside the western city wall and is a short walk from the night market and the Muslim quarters. The hotel also offers a Tang dynasty cultural show in its 1130-seat theatre.

Shangri-La Golden Flower
8 Changle Xi Lu
Tel: 323-2981
Fax: 323-5477
Located 3 km (2 miles) from the historic city centre in an unremarkable neighbourhood, this pleasant hotel also has apartments with kitchens.

Xi'an Garden Hotel
Tang Hua
4 Yan Yin Lu
Dayan Ta
Tel: 526-1111
Fax: 526-1998
Constructed in the style of a Chinese garden with lakes, willow trees, and pavilions, this popular hotel is located 6 km (4 miles) outside of the old city, right next to the Dayan Ta. It offers Western and Asian restaurants, and even a set dinner featuring Chinese herbal health cuisine.

SUPERIOR CLASS
Bell Tower Hotel
Southwest Corner of Bell Tower
Tel: 727-9200
Fax: 721-8767
Managed by Holiday Inn, this friendly, functional, three-star hotel is popular for being directly in the centre of town. Good solid service. It offers a business centre, a mini-mart, and a CYTS office.

People's Hotel (Renmin Dasha)
319 DongXin Jie
Tel: 721-5111
Fax: 721-8152
A large, sprawling Soviet-style hotel, it is dark and somewhat run-down, although the East Tower was renovated in the mid-1990s. Located near the city centre in its own compound, the hotel offers 600 rooms, over 20 restaurants, a business and commercial centre,

gym, shops, and an entertainment and recreation centre.

May First Hotel (Wu Yi Hotel)
351 Dongda Jie
Tel: 723 1844
Fax: 721 3824
A former budget traveller's paradise, this hotel was renovated in 1997, and is now a mid-range hotel with full facilities. Still popular with many travellers, it offers clean and comfortable rooms, and an excellent location right in the city centre.

Jie Fang Hotel
321 Jie Fang Road
Tel: 742 8946
Fax: 742 2617
Drab, no frills budget accommodation located right across from the railway station. It is also near the northeastern entrance to the old city wall. Offers standard rooms as well as triples and quads. Ticket booking and money changing services available.

What to Eat

Chinese cuisine

For Westerners, the single identifying symbol of Chinese cuisine is the use of chopsticks, which are practical as the food is cut into small pieces.

Only about 10 percent of China's land area is suitable for agriculture, so beef and dairy products are not widely used. In place of animal protein, soybeans have often been a primary source of protein.

Traditionally, food should not only be filling, but should also have a healing effect. A Chinese meal is based on balance, even the largest and most extravagant banquets.

There are roughly four main styles of Chinese cuisine (not taking into account the often completely different cooking and eating traditions of the national minorities):

Northern cuisine is centered around Beijing. In contrast to the south, where rice is preferred, noodle dishes predominate here. The main vegetable is Chinese cabbage: boiled, steamed, fried, preserved, with a variety of different spices. Special mention should be made of Peking Duck and the Mongolian hotpot, feasts not to be missed if in Beijing. **Haiyang**, from the eastern coastal areas around Shanghai, specialises in fish (particularly freshwater) and shellfish. There is a greater choice of vegetables here than in the north. **Cantonese**, the southern cuisine, is most familiar to Westerners, and the commonest in Chinese restaurants around the world. **Sichuan** cuisine is famous for its highly-spiced foods, good for keeping warm through the cold, damp Sichuan winters.

The Chinese tend to eat quite early; lunch is often served in

Chinese restaurants from 11am. (Hotels and restaurants for foreigners have, of course, adjusted to their preferences.) In the evenings, you won't easily find a meal after 8pm, though this is different in the south, where social life continues until the late evening.

Drinking Notes

In most hotel rooms there are thermos flasks with hot and cold water, and bags with green or black tea. A cup of hot tea, or just "white" tea (hot water), as the Chinese usually drink it, is the most effective way of quenching your thirst. At meal times, Chinese beer, which contains less alcohol than European beer, mineral water or lemonade (very sweet) are offered as well as the ubiquitous green tea.

While being in drunk in public is considered unacceptable in China, there is a surprisingly large choice of Chinese spirits on offer. The best-known are *maotai jiu*, a 55-percent spirit made of wheat and sorghum that, for centuries, has been produced in Maotai, in Guizhou Province, and *wuliangye jiu*, a spirit made from five different grains. You'll either take to it immediately or never. Chinese wine, both red and white, tends to be very sweet, tasting a bit like sherry. Wine for Western tastes is now also being produced.

Where to Eat

Chinese meals are best eaten in a group, with diners sharing a variety of dishes; Chinese restaurants are often not suited to individual diners.

The individual traveller is more likely to frequent one of the typical roadside eateries. Make sure the restaurant is clean and the food has been freshly-prepared and is hot. Bringing one's own chopsticks isn't considered an insult at all. Chinese restaurants are often not heated even during winter, so it is advisable to dress warmly.

Culture

CONCERTS

There are regular concerts of Western classical or traditional Chinese music in various cities. Indigenous or foreign songs and musical performances are often part of the programme. Dance performances are also common. In many areas – particularly in those of the national minorities – you can see performances of local dances and songs on the stage. Ballet is also performed. Young people are very keen on concerts by various pop stars, whether from the PR of China, Hong Kong or even Taiwan. You can find out about time and place of performances in each town from the hotel or through travel agencies.

OPERAS

There are more than 300 types of opera in China. You can attend performances of traditional opera in virtually every town. The most famous one is the Beijing Opera. Addresses of the opera and theatre are available from the hotel or from travel agencies. A visit to the Chinese opera is a relaxed affair and occasionally quite noisy. Normal day clothes are worn.

Beijing Opera
Liyuan Theatre, Qianmen Hotel, Yong'an Lu. Daily performances in a large theatre.
Gong Wangfu Huayuan. Small theatre in the former residence of Prince Gong, just north of Beihai Gongyuan (Park). Performances daily at 7.30pm.
Zheng Yi Ci Theatre. the only surviving Peking Opera Theatre, built entirely of wood. Re-opened in

1995 after extensive renovation. Tea and snacks come with the entrance fee, or you can pay extra and enjoy a Peking Duck dinner while you watch the opera. Perfomances nightly at 7.30pm. lel: 6303-3104 for reservations.

ACROBATICS

Acrobatics are popular throughout China. Almost every large town has its own troupe of acrobats, many of which tour the country. You can get details of time and place of performances locally. In big cities such as Beijing, Shanghai and Guangzhou, there are permanent performances. Acrobatics means a mixture of proper acrobatics, magic and animal acts, and of course clowns. Circus performances are similar.
Chaoyang Theatre
36 Dongsanhuan Beilu,
tel: 6507-2421.
Performances daily at 7.15pm.
Huaxia Cultural and Martial Arts Centre (National Children's Arts Theatre)
64 Donganmendajie,
tel: 6513-4115, (9am–8pm).

Festivals and holidays

Holidays such as National Day and International Labour Day are fixed on the modern calendar, but most traditional festivals and events are determined by the lunar calendar, which means the date varies a little from year to year.

January/February
The most important festival time is the Lunar New Year, or **Spring Festival**, which falls in late January or early February. Public buildings are festooned with coloured lights, people from all over China travel to reunite with families, debts are settled, and there is food consumed – lots of it. On the first days of the lunar year, Chinese visit family and friends. In recent years, a more relaxed atmosphere has brought the revival of old Spring Festival traditions, such as giving

hongbao – small, red envelopes containing money – to children and young adults. Temple fairs feature martial arts demonstrations, standup comedians, home-made toys and, of course, food.

Northerners, who have amazing resilience to the bitterly cold winters, partake with gusto in ice-sculpting competitions and winter swimming. The time and duration of the festivals depends on the weather. Both Beijing and Harbin are noted for their ice-sculpting festivals.

April
On the 12th day of the third lunar month, in the beginning of April, the Chinese honour their deceased ancestors by observing **Qingming**, sometimes referred to as the 'grave-sweeping' day. It is much less impressive nowadays, as people are cremated instead of being buried. Qingming is a time for remembering ancestors, but also for revelling on a warm spring day.

May/June
International Labour Day is a one-day public holiday. Following hot on its heels is **Youth Day**, a commemoration of the May 4th Movement of 1919, reflected by large editorials and government hoopla in the official press.
International Children's Day is celebrated in earnest on June 1, by letting classes out early and treating children to outings at public parks.

July/August
July 1 is the **Anniversary of the Communist Party**, which was founded in Shanghai in 1921. This means very little to the average citizen but plenty of fun for high-level party members.

The fifth day of the fifth lunar month – usually late July – brings the **Dragon Boat Festival**, marked by dragon boat races in many cities, sometimes involving teams from around the world. It commemorates the memory of Qu Yuan (340–278BC), a poet in the days of the Kingdom of Chu, who, rather than submit to political pressure, drowned himself in the Miluo river in Hunan. To prevent the fishes from eating his body, the people threw glutinous rice cakes into the river. Nowadays, these *zongzi* are simply eaten to mark the occasion.

August 1 is the **Anniversary of the People's Liberation Army**. Inaugurated in 1927 and formerly marked by enormous parades, it is now noted mainly in the media.

September/October

The **Mid-Autumn Festival** again depends on when the moon reaches its fullest, usually around mid-September. The shops do great business in 'moon cakes' – pastries filled with gooey sesame paste, red-bean and walnut filling. *Tang yuan*, glutinous rice flour balls with sweet fillings in sugar syrup, and *yue bing*, a cake baked specifically for this occasion, are eaten. In the tradition of poets, this is the time to drink a bit of wine and toast the moon.

Late September is normally the time when Chinese communities celebrate the memory of Confucius.

October 1 is the PRC's birthday, **National Day**, celebrated with a two-day public holiday. Government buildings, road intersections and hotels are decked out in lights and flower arrangements, and Sun Yatsen's portrait is displayed in Tiananmen Square. Tens of thousands turn out on the square for picture-taking and general merry-making.

November/December

November and December are quiet months in China, but **Christmas** is gaining momentum as a consumer's celebration. Christian churches hold special services that draw thousands of spectators. In Beijing, for example, it is trendy to exchange greeting cards and presents, while Santa Claus makes the odd shop appearance.

Shopping

What To Buy

Typically "Chinese" goods such as silk, jade and porcelain are still cheaper and of a better quality in Hong Kong than elsewhere. The choice varies – if you are lucky, the shelves are well stocked and you can find excellent and well-cut silk articles being sold cheaply. You will find good quality goods which are produced for export in the Friendship Stores (*Youyi Shangdian*) and in hotel shops.

Until recently, it was not usual to bargain and it is still not advisable in the state-owned shops and warehouses. But at the many souvenir stands, it is a good idea to bargain because of the greatly over-priced goods on offer. It is also worth comparing prices in the free markets (if you can read them) and watch how much Chinese customers pay.

When buying antiques, it is essential to check that the official red seal of the shop is on the product. Buying and exporting of antiques is only permitted with this official stamp.

It is worth looking for local products in the smaller towns or in the places where ethnic minorities live. These will be difficult to find anywhere else in China. The most usual articles are craft objects for everyday use or specially worked or embroidered garments.

Import & Export

Antiques that date from before 1795 may not be legally exported. Those that can be taken out of China must carry a small red seal or have one affixed by the Cultural Relics Bureau. All other antiques are the property of the Peoples' Republic of China and, without the seal, will be confiscated without compensation. Beware of fakes; producing new 'antiques' (and the seal) is a thriving industry.

You should not export, nor even buy, objects made from wild animals, especially from ivory. Most Western countries ban the import of ivory objects, and will confiscate them without compensation.

Shopping Areas

Department stores: In every town there is a department store selling products for everyday use, from toothpaste to bicycles. The big stores are state-owned institutions, but many small shops and street stalls – privately owned – have sprung up as well. Here you will often find products from Hong Kong.

Friendship stores: These stores usually offer a good selection of wares for export: silk fabric, craft articles, electronic devices, clothing and books. Often, there is a whole department offering both traditional and modern medical products and equipment. The Friendship Store in Beijing has an excellent food department. A visit to the antiques department in the Friendship Store in Shanghai is also worthwhile.

Some large Friendship Stores have a delivery section that will send purchases to one's home country. Shops and department stores generally open around 9am and close at 6pm or 7pm.

Markets: Food items such as fruit, vegetables, fish and meat are sold at markets. In the free markets, where prices are more flexible, and sometimes more expensive (off-setting higher quality and availability), there are often additional items, such as wicker baskets and clothes; tailors are sometimes found. In the big towns, numerous street traders offer their wares well into the evening; one can often find jeans or silk blouses from Hong Kong at such places.

At any market, try to watch how much the Chinese themselves pay.

BEIJING

Speciality Markets

Silk Alley (Xiushui Shichang) – on Xiushiu Jie and intersecting with Chang'an Lu about 800m east of the Friendship Store, has been growing in the past few years. As the name implies, vendors sell silk in all shapes and sizes – ties and boxer shorts, dresses and slinky nightgowns – at prices about half of those found in Hong Kong. This market has also recently become the place to buy goods that are made in China for export only. You can buy well known Western brands of clothing and footwear here at very low prices.

Just a few blocks away is **Yabaolu Market**, commonly known as the Russian market (open daily 9am–6pm) and on Ritan Lu, opposite Ritan Park. It is a huge clothing market specialising in cotton and wool garments, and also goose-down jackets.

A few blocks straight north of Yabaolu Market is the **Chaowai Flea Market** (open daily 10am–6pm), a favourite shopping ground for resident diplomats and journalists. The front building is filled with antique and classical-style furniture. In the rear building are curios: snuff bottles, ceramics and Mao memorabilia. **Hongqiao Farmers' Market**, on Tiantan Lu (open daily 7am–5.30pm), has the best collection of antique clocks and Mao statues, as well as freshwater pearls.

For traditional Chinese paintings, calligraphy supplies and rare books, poke around at **Liulichang** (open daily 9am–5.30pm), just west of Qianmen district. A bit further afield, but considered to be the most reliable source of antique porcelain in Beijing, is **Jingsong Market** (open daily 9am–6pm) located at East Third Ring Road at the Jingsong east intersection.

Tucked under the southeast corner of the Xizhimen overpass, the **Bird Market** (open daily 7.30am–sunset) has a wonderful array of feathered creatures. At least as important are the elegant handmade cages, ceramic feeders and other avian paraphernalia.

City Centre Shops

There are three lively shopping streets in the city centre that cater to local customers. **Wangfujing**, **Xidan** and **Dongdan**, which run perpendicular to Chang'an Lu, have mostly inexpensive local goods, with bargains in leather and furs.

At 192 Wangfujing Dajie, check out the **Jianhua Leather Goods Company** (open daily 8am–8.30pm). Further north, along the east side of Wangfujing, is the **Foreign Languages Bookstore**, run by the China News Agency. The first floor has a wide range of books on China.

All three streets are undergoing radical transformation, with more and more boutiques, watch stores and ice-cream shops replacing the old standbys. Xidan and Wangfujing are both undergoing massive rebuilding, which will expand the shopping greatly.

Among the most popular department stores for Chinese products is **Longfu Dasha** (No 95 Longfusi Jie, Chaoyang District; open daily 8.30am–8.30pm). This is the spot to buy China's most famous brands of household products – Flying Pigeon bicycles and Butterfly sewing machines.

One-stop Shopping

Capitalism's answer for one-stop shoppers is the glossy, new joint-venture shopping centres that draw China's *nouveau riche,* as well as tourists and mobs of window shoppers. Directly across the street from the Friendship Store is the **CIVIC-Yaohan** (No 22 Jianguomenwai Dajie, open daily 9am–9pm), a Japanese department store full of luxury, trendy imports.

The **Youyi Shopping City** in the Beijing Lufthansa Centre (No 52 Liangmaqiao Lu, Chaoyang District; open daily 9am–9pm) carries products with a broader price range. The city's best silk selection – sold by the yard – is offered at reasonable prices.

Stock up on all the beautiful things that China produces – traditional paper cuttings (cheap and easy to pack), jade carvings, kites and chopsticks – at the state-run **Friendship Store** (No 17 Jianguomenwai Dajie; open daily 9am–9pm).

GUANGZHOU

Guangzhou offers interesting shopping and good bargains. Among Chinese cities it is considered to have the widest range of goods, many of which are imported from other parts of the country.

Antiques

The largest private market for antiques is the **Daihe Lu Market**. Enter by the first lane on the right after entering Daihe Lu from Changshou Xilu. There are smaller antiques markets nearby; one at the middle lane of the Qingping Market and the other at the Jade Market. Avoid antiques that the vendor claims are over 100 years old. Even if not trying to rip you off (and most are), a genuine antique that is over a century old cannot be exported if it doesn't carry an official red-wax seal. Also, beware of fakes; new 'antiques' with the official seal are a thriving industry.

Despite the difficulties, there is still much to buy: *kam muk* (gilded sculptured wood panels), vintage watches, tiny embroidered shoes for Chinese women with bound feet, and beautiful Shiwan porcelain.

For serious collectors, antiques with authentic red-wax seals authorising export can be bought from government shops. Try the **Guangzhou Antique Shop** on Wende Beilu (Tel: 8333 0175; Fax: 8335 0085) for *kam muk*, calligraphy works, jewellery boxes, paintings, porcelain and silver jewellery.

Clothing and Textiles

Guangdong province is a major production centre for ready-to-wear clothes and shoes. The biggest variety is to be found at the government-owned **Friendship Stores**. These stores are your best bet for down jackets and cashmere sweaters and scarves. The **Bingfen Fashion Market** on Haizhu Square, the **Gong Lu Fashion Market** on Zhongshan Erlu in Dongshan District, the night market under the Quzhuang Overbridge, and the Xihu Lu night market are also good hunting grounds for apparel.

Handicrafts
Paper Cuts: The Renshou Temple in Foshan, previously famous for its paper cuts of scenes from the Cultural Revolution, has remained the major production centre for this delicate craft.
Bird cages: Antique cages cost from 100 to 700 yuan; newer ones can be bought at the **Bird Market**, located at the Dongfeng Lu entrance of Liuhua Park.
Seals: You can have your name engraved in Chinese characters on a seal, called a chop in colonial English, at the basement floor of the White Swan Hotel. The material used can be hard wood, soapstone, crystal or agate. The shop will also sell you the special red ink (*hong yau*) that goes with the seal.

Jade and Pearls
Buy from established shops like the **Jade Shop** (12–14 Zhongshan Wulu), **Baoli Yuqi Hang** (220 Zhongshan Silu), **Guangzhou Antique Shop** (696 Wende Lu), and the jewellery shops of the China, Garden and White Swan hotels.

Most of the pearls on sale in Guangzhou are saltwater southern pearls called *hepu*, cultured in silver-lipped oysters. The largest of these lustrous pearls can have a diameter of 1.2–1.6 cm. Recommended shops are: **Guangzhou Gold and Silver Jewellery Centre** (109 Dade Lu) and Sun Moon Hall (Equatorial Hotel, Renmin Beilu).

Mao Memorabilia
In celebration of Mao's 100th birthday in 1993, centennial souvenirs appeared, such as commemorative watches and musical cigarette lighters playing revolutionary ditties.

The Daihe Lu antiques market has a reasonable variety of Mao artifacts, while the Friendship Stores sell diamond-studded medals. For badges, the stamp market in People's Park has the best pieces. Prices can be steep.

SHANGHAI

Shanghai is one of China's commercial capitals, and the number of both foreign and domestic goods available to the consumer has skyrocketed in the last few years. The best streets to shop on are Nanjing Lu and Huaihai Lu. Nanjing Lu is mobbed by local and out-of-town Chinese shoppers on the weekends, while Huaihai Lu offers a more quaint, upscale experience that attracts foreigners and Shanghai's nouveau riche.

Department Stores and Malls
Shanghai is full of Western-style malls and department stores. The Dickson Centre, 400 Changle Lu, Tel: 6172 6888 and Maison Mode, 1312 Huaihai Zhong Lu, Tel: 6431 0100 offers high-level brand names like Ralph Lauren, Salvatore Ferragamo, Christian Dior, Nina Ricci, and Guy Laroche. The ritzy French-run Printemps, 939–947 Huaihai Zhong Lu, Tel: 6431 0118 also features upscale shopping and foreign name brands.

Middle- to high-level shopping can be found at the Hongqiao Friendship Shopping Centre, 6 Zunyi Lu, Tel: 6270 0000, and the huge Yaohan Department Store, 501 Zhangyang Lu, Pudong, Tel: 5830 1111, supposedly Asia's largest, which sell everything from groceries to clothing to furniture, both domestic and imported. The Japanese-run Isetan, 527 Huaihai Zhong Lu, Tel: 6375 1111; Nanjing Lu at Jiangning Lu is one of the most fashionable in Shanghai and has a good selection of mid- to upscale boutiques such as Isetan, Episode and Benetton. Jusco, 218 Tianmu Xi Lu, Tel: 6354 1110, a true mall in the American sense, also contains a large department

store and foreign boutiques.

On a more upscale, but still local, level is the Orient Shopping Centre, 8 Caoxi Bei Lu, Tel: 6407 1947, located in the bustling Gotham City-like area of Xujiahui. It sells everything from clothing to appliances.

Antiques
Antique goods and furniture markets, shops and warehouses are plentiful in Shanghai, but prices have greatly increased over the last few years. Antique buying is made interesting at the Fuyou Lu Sunday Market off Henan Lu. Hawkers gather their goods on the sidewalks of this tiny alley early in the morning. You must come before 9am to find the best goods. The daily Dongtai Lu Market located off Xizang Lu also has a good selection of antiques, but goods are presented in stalls rather then on the ground. The Haobao Building in Yuyuan Garden, 265 Fangbang Lu, Tel: 6355 9999, has an entire floor of booths selling antiques.

For antique furniture, there are several warehouses in town that include renovation in the sale of any piece. They are located at: 1970 Hongqiao Lu, Tel: 6242 8734, 1220 Hongmei Lu, Tel: 6436 1500 ext. 195, 9100 7152, 307 Shunchang Lu, Tel: 6320 3812, and 1430 Hongqiao Lu.

Arts and Crafts
The famous state-owned department store, the Friendship Store, 40 Beijing Dong Lu, Tel: 6329 4600, sells foreign and domestic goods, primarily Chinese arts and crafts and silk. You can watch Shanghai artisans create traditional arts and crafts at the Arts and Crafts Research Institute, 79 Fenyang Lu, Tel: 6437 0509.

Porcelain and other wares can be purchased at the Shanghai Jingdezhen Porcelain Store, 1175 Nanjing Xi Lu, Tel: 6253 3178, while tea and Yixing pots are plentiful at the Shanghai Huangshan Tea Company, 853 Huaihai Zhong Lu, Tel: 6545 4919.

Language

General

English is increasingly spoken in the People's Republic of China, but on the whole, you will still find it difficult to meet people away from the big hotels and business and tourist centres who speak English, not to mention German or French. It is therefore advisable – especially for individual travellers – to learn some Chinese. Some people joke that, apart from *meiyou* ("it doesn't exist"), the most common words in China are "change money?".

More than a billion people in China, and many other Chinese in Southeast Asia and the United States, speak Chinese. In the People's Republic of China, other languages in addition to Chinese – the language of the Han people, the original Chinese – are spoken in the regions where the national minorities are settled, including Tibetan, Mongolian, Zhuang or Uygur. But everywhere in the People's Republic today, standard Chinese, also called Mandarin, is more or less understood or spoken. Regardless of whether you are in Guangzhou or in Heilongjiang, in Tibet or in Xinjiang, you can get through with standard Chinese.

The Chinese language is divided into several groups of dialect. For instance, a native of Guangzhou or Hong Kong cannot understand someone from Beijing or vice versa, unless both speak standard Chinese. The different dialects have, however, the same grammar and vocabulary; but above all, the writing is the same. The pronunciation may differ, but the written symbols can be understood by all literate Chinese. Thus, a native of Guangzhou and a Beijing

citizen can understand each other by simply writing down the symbols.

Since the 1950s, all schools in the People's Republic of China teach standard Chinese or Mandarin – also called Putonghua or common language. It is also used on radio and television. Young Chinese people, particularly, know standard Chinese. Consequently, one can manage throughout the People's Republic – including in Guangzhou – by using standard Chinese. You will immediately notice the difference when you go from Guangzhou to Hong Kong: in Hong Kong, the official language amongst the Chinese is Cantonese.

The transcription of Chinese symbols: Standard Chinese is based on the pronunciation of the northern dialects, particularly the Beijing dialect. There is an officially approved roman writing of standard Chinese, called Hanyu Pinyin (the phonetic transcription of the language of the Han people). Pinyin is used throughout the People's Republic; many public transportation facilities show name places and street names both in symbols and in the romanized transcription.

Most modern dictionaries use the pinyin system. (Taiwan, however, usually uses the older Wade-Giles transliteration system.) This transcription may at first appear confusing if one doesn't see the words as they are pronounced. The city of Qingdao, for example, is pronounced *chingdow*. It would definitely be useful, particularly for individual travellers, to familiarise yourself a little with the pronunciation of pinyin. Even when asking for a place or street name, you need to know how it is pronounced, otherwise you won't be understood. This guide uses the pinyin system throughout for Chinese names and expressions.

The pronunciation of Chinese: The pronunciation of consonants is similar to those in English. b, p, d, t, g, k are all voiceless. p, t, k are aspirated, b, d, g are not aspirated. The i after the consonants ch, c, r,

sh, s, z, zh is not pronounced, it indicates that the preceding sound is lengthened.

Pinyin/English transcript/Sound
a/a/f**a**r
an/un/**on**
ang/ung/**ong**
ao/ou/l**ou**d
b/b/**b**ath
c/ts/ra**ts**
ch/ch/**ch**ange
d/d/**d**ay
e/er/d**ir**t
e (after i,u,y)/a/tr**a**m
ei/ay/m**ay**
en/en/b**un**
eng/eong/u**ng** has a nasal sound
er/or/hon**or**
f/f/**f**ast
g/g/**g**o
h/h/**h**ello
i/ee/k**ee**n
j/j/**j**eep
k/k/**c**ake
l/l/**l**ittle
m/m/**m**onth
n/n/**n**ame
o/o/b**o**nd
p/p/**tr**apped
q/ch/**ch**eer
r/r/**r**ight
s/s/me**ss**
sh/sh/**sh**ade
t/t/**t**on
u/oo/sh**oo**t
u (after j,q,x,y)/as **G**erman
u+/m**u+d**e
w/w/**w**ater
x/**sh**/**sh**eep
y/y/**y**ogi
z/ds/re**ds**
zh/dj/**j**ungle

It is often said that the Chinese language is monosyllabic. At first sight this may seem the case since, generally, each symbol is one word. However, in modern Chinese, most words are made up of two or three syllable symbols, sometimes more. Chinese generally lacks syllables, there are only 420 in Mandarin to represent all symbols in sounds or tones. The tones are used to differentiate – a specifically Chinese practice which often makes it very difficult for foreigners when first learning the Chinese language.

Each syllable has a specific sound. These sounds often represent different meanings. For instance, if one pronounces the syllable *mai* with a falling fourth sound (mài) it means to sell; if it is pronounced with a falling-rising third sound, mai, it means to buy. When one reads the symbols carefully this is always clearly shown. To show this again with the simple syllable ma:

First sound *ma* mother
second sound *má* hemp
third sound *ma* horse
fourth sound *mà* to complain

The Chinese language has four tones and a fifth, 'soundless' sound: The first tone is spoken high pitched and even, the second rising, the third falling and then rising, and the fourth sound falling. The individual tones are marked above the vowel in the syllable in the following way: First tone -, second tone ´, third tone, fourth tone `.

The Chinese sentence structure is simple: subject, predicate, object. The simplest way of forming a question is to add the question particle 'ma' to a sentence in ordinary word sequence. It is usually not possible to note from a Chinese word whether it is a noun, adjective or another form, singular or plural. This depends on the context.

The Chinese language is a language of symbols or pictures. Each symbol represents a one-syllable word. There are in total more than 47,000 symbols, though modern Chinese only use a part of these. For a daily paper, between 3,000 and 4,000 symbols are sufficient. Scholars know between 5,000 and 6,000. Many symbols used to be quite complicated. After 1949, several reforms in the written language were introduced in the People's Republic in order to simplify the written language. Today, the simplified symbols are used throughout the People's Republic, though in Hong Kong and Taiwan, the complex ones are still used.

Many Chinese words are composed of two or more symbols or single-syllable words.

HONG KONG

Getting Acquainted

Time Zones

The International Dateline puts Hong Kong ahead of most of the world: GMT +8 all year round.

Climate

The climate is (just) tropical and monsoonal. Two seasons dominate: one consistently humid, from March to September), and the other cool and dry (the northeast monsoon from October to February). But there can be great variations, notably between successive monsoons and during the typhoon season. If you are unlucky enough to be here when a full-scale typhoon sweeps in from the South China Sea, there is not much you can do except slink back to your hotel and have a typhoon party, which is what many Hong Kong residents do in their homes.

The dry monsoon season begins in late September, and brings three months of warm days and clear blue skies. Nights are cool, humidity low, and day-to-day temperature changes are slight. From December to early January it is still mainly sunny during the day and cool at night.

Beginning with Chinese New Year (mid-January to mid-February) spells of cold wind and dank mist become more frequent, and beaches are largely deserted. The rainy season arrives in earnest in mid-March, when temperatures rise, humidity thickens and trees turn green. Skies are grey and heavy and afternoon rainstorms are common. Though changeable, it generally stays cool enough to be agreeable to most visitors.

Mid-May to September is high summer, and also the unpredictable typhoon season. Punctuated by cloudbursts, there is intense tropical sunshine, and humidity averages over 80 percent; temperatures reach, but rarely exceed, 90–93°F (32–34°C).

Typhoons

Mid-May to September is the typhoon season. When a typhoon or severe tropical storm comes within a 640-km (400-mile) radius of Hong Kong, storm signal No. 1 is hoisted and is announced on radio, TV and in public places. The populace is quite blasé about a number one signal, which can remain aloft for days sometimes during beautiful pre-storm weather, or be quickly changed to the next important signal. Number 3 is the first real alert because it signifies that winds are reaching speeds of 22 to 33 knots with gusts up to 60 knots. At typhoon No. 8, everything shuts down. Although some buses and trains may still run, ferries cease operation and taxis usually charge a premium for driving during the storm. The highest signal, No. 10, indicates the storm will hit Hong Kong head on, with predictable damage to property and threat to life and limb. Never underestimate a typhoon.

To get a storm warning update, tel: 2835-1473.

Planning the Trip

What To Wear

In January and February you will need sweaters, heavy jackets or an overcoat. In March and April take adaptable, all-purpose outfits. Tropical summer (May–September) demands the lightest clothes, umbrellas (traditional local models are superb, raincoats a steamy wash-out) and some sort of protection against fanatical air-conditioning. The dry autumn (October–December) demands middle-weight clothes with a sweater for cool evenings.Shorts, sandals and haltertops are as popular locally as they are practical. A skirt for women or jacket and tie for men qualifies in the few hotel restaurants requiring formal dress.

Health

Standards of health and medicine in Hong Kong today compare well with the West, and aside from the obvious, travellers need take no particular precautions. Off the beaten track, things can be more problematic, but common sense should tell you the obvious pitfalls to avoid. The buzz of a hundred flies is one bad sign, as is food served tepid rather than steaming hot. A quick glance at the raw ingredients never hurts. Go where the locals seem to go, do as they do by rinsing chopsticks and bowls in hot tea, and drink hot tea or anything from a bottle without ice. Fruit, with the usual tropical caveat about avoiding pre-peeled items, is fine, but the cautious might stick to ice cream. In the end, though, getting sick results more from bad luck than from anything else.

Getting There

By Air

Hong Kong is a major international crossroads and is served by over 30 airlines, plus a dozen charter and cargo companies.The shiny new airport at Chek Lap Kok on Lantau island is pleasant and efficient, a complete little city in itself with lots of shops and restaurants. There are connections via the MTR and bus – the latter is cheaper but not as fast.

The new international airport in Macau has scheduled flights to Bangkok, Manila, Singapore and several cities within China. There is a helicopter service to Hong Kong.

By Sea

Hong Kong is linked by catamaran with Guangzhou, Huangpu (Guangzhou's commercial port), Wuzhou, Macau, and the delta cities of Lianhua Shan, Nansha, Shekou, Shunde, Zhongshan and Zhuhai. The catamarans have small canteens serving hot cup noodles and drinks. For information on schedules, tel: 2833-9300 or 2542-3428. Departures are from the Hong Kong–Macau Ferry Terminal at the Shun Tak Centre (200 Connaught Road). There are over 100 daily scheduled sailings (catamarans and jetfoils) each way between Hong Kong and Macau; journey time is 55 minutes. Three high-speed catamaran hydrofoils operate daily between Nansha and Hong Kong at 8.30am, 9.15am, 2pm from Hong Kong (1-hour trip), and 11.20am, 4pm and 5pm from Nansha. Tickets can be purchased from the China Ferry Terminal (tel: 2375-0537) in Kowloon.

By Rail

Four daily trains link Guangzhou with the Hunghom station in Hong Kong. Travelling time is 2 hours. In Hong Kong, tickets can be purchased through travel agents, hotels, CTS offices or at the lobby of the Hunghom railway station, tel: 2627-4400.

Money Matters

The Hong Kong dollar has a singular distinction: it is the world's last major currency issued by local private banks. The Hongkong and Shanghai Banking Corporation and the Standard Chartered have recently been joined by the Bank of China, the state bank, in issuing all the currency. The notes are emblazoned with grandly styled views of their headquarters, while the images of Queen Elizabeth II have been replaced by the Bauhinia, Hong Kong's new emblem. The Hong Kong dollar (HK$) is divided into 100 cents. There are seven standard bills: each bank uses a different motif, but all share similar colours: $1,000 (gold), $500 (brown), $100 (red), $50 (blue), $20 (orange) and – increasingly rarely – $10 (green). There is also a small and rarely seen one cent (1¢) note, slightly larger than a bus ticket. They are blank on one side and make great souvenirs. Coins include 10¢, 20¢, 50¢, $1, $2, $5 and $10.

Because it's a centre for international transactions, Hong Kong has banks of every description and there are no local restrictions on the import, export, purchase or sale of foreign currency. Anything from credit cards to cash can be handled although some merchants may try to add an extra percentage point or two to the price for the latter.

Traveller's Cheques (TCs) are sold by foreign exchange dealers and banks. European and Japanese TCs are as acceptable as US dollar cheques. Many small merchants prefer TCs to credit cards, so hold out for more than the going bank rate during any negotiations.

The currency in Macau is the pataca. It is pegged to the HK dollar and has similar value (there are approximately 8 patacas to the US dollar). Hong Kong dollars are widely accepted in Macau.

Practical Tips

Emergencies

The Hong Kong Police Force (HKPF) wear light green uniforms in summer, blue ones in winter, and carry handguns. Most officers can speak some English. In cases of theft they are efficient and will give what assistance they can. Consulates are usually quite helpful and sympathetic to victims. Sometimes hotels are reluctant to assist because of the bad publicity.

To complain about fraud, contact: HKPF Fraud Squad, Commercial Crimes, tel: 2860-2000.

If you find out about a fraudulent sale after you have departed Hong Kong, write to: the HKTA or the Consumer Council, 22/F, K Wah Centre, 191 Java Road, North Point, tel 2856-3113.

Emergency Services

In an emergency dial 999 and ask for the police, ambulance or fire department.

Medical Services

Hong Kong has modern chemists, or dispensaries as they are called here. The main pharmacies are Watson, Mannings, Colonial Dispensary and the Victoria Dispensary. There are also hundreds of Chinese medicine companies which accept prescriptions and usually stock both Western and Asian medicines. These should not be confused with traditional herbalists (with whom they sometimes share premises).

Hospitals

The most notable private hospitals (in descending price order) are:
Matilda
41 Mt Kellett Road
The Peak
tel: 2849-0111
Canossa
1 Old Peak Road
Mid Levels
tel: 2522-0181)
The Baptist Hospital
222 Waterloo Road
Kowloon
tel: 2337-4141
Hong Kong Adventist Hospital
40 Stubbs Road
Happy Valley
tel: 2574-6211
None are cheap, but all are comfortable and offer highest quality specialists and facilities.

Clinics

Clinics are a practical and economical alternative. The Adventist (*see above*) operates an expat-staff out-patient department Sunday to Friday noon, and also has a good dental clinic with 24-hour emergency service.
Anderson & Partners
tel: 2523-8166
Vio & Partners
tel: 2521-3302
Dr Oram & Partners
tel: 2525-1730
All have clinics on both sides of the harbour.

Private Doctors

Though many Chinese people still prefer traditional cures for minor ills, modern Western practices dominate the field, and most doctors did much of their training overseas. There are also numerous expatriate doctors and dentists. Private physicians' fees tend to be internationally scaled.

Acupuncturists

You will have to decide whether the needle treatment is for you. There are many clinics in Hong Kong, but few practitioners speak English or have the time to explain the treatment to visitors.

Public Holidays

- **January** New Year's Day
- **January–February** Chinese New Year
- **March/April** Ching Ming; Easter
- **May 1st** Labour Day
- **June** Tuen Ng (Dragon Boat Festival)
- **July 1st** SAR Establishment Day
- **October** Chung Yueng
- **August** Summer Bank Holiday (Last Monday)
- **December 25 & 26** Christmas Day, Boxing Day

Business Hours

Local banking hours are in the process of gradual extension, but 9am–4.30pm on weekdays, and 9am–noon Saturday are normal business hours for foreign exchange services. Exchange booths in tourist areas are open longer but the rates are less favourable. Check for any charges beforehand and count your notes carefully before leaving.

Post Offices: Monday–Saturday 8am–6pm, Sunday 8am–2pm, closed public holidays.

Tipping

Though a 10 percent gratuity is added to most hotel and restaurant bills, you are still expected to tip, but do not feel pressurised to do so if the service has not been good. Some of the smaller traditional Chinese restaurants do not add a service charge.

Postal Services

Hong Kong's postal services are reliable and usually efficient. Air letters normally take 4–5 days to Europe or Australia, 6–8 to most destinations in the United States and Canada. Surface packages can vary from 3 weeks to 3 months. The most complete and convenient facility is Hong Kong-side's General Post Office (tel: 2921-2222, followed by 2 for English language). Located just off the Star Ferry Concourse, the two-storey white building has a full range of services, including a philatelic window and a ground-floor General Delivery counter (Poste Restante, GPO, Hong Kong). Outside working hours the GPO's stamp machines and letter slots are open round-the-clock. For large and delicate items, there are reliable commercial packing and shipping firms.

Telecommunications

The international code for Hong Kong is 852 (for Macau it is 853). For local calls, coin and card-operated telephones charge HK$1 a call, and hotels usually institute a fee for calling from your room. Some old-fashioned corner shops and restaurants have a phone which the public can use for free. There are three residential phone books (Hong Kong, Kowloon and the New Territories), a Business Directory, plus the Yellow Pages.

International enquiries tel: 10013. Other enquiries/assistance tel: 1000 followed by 1 for English.

Information operators tel: 1081. They speak reasonable English although you may need to spell out words phonetically.

Time, temperature/weather forecasts tel: 18501.

Cheaper off-peak charges for international calls are in effect midnight–7am daily, plus from 1pm Saturday–Sunday. Most hotel rooms have IDD and you may also call abroad using public phones. Phone cards are available from Hong Kong Telecom shops and convenience stores. HK Telecom also operates international and other services from its main offices, tel: 2888-8888 for details.

E-MAIL

A number of cyber cafés operate in Hong Kong. Here are some of the best:

Xyberia Interactive

China Bear Mui Wo Centre
3 Ngan Wan Road
Mui Wo
Lantau Island
e-mail: sahr@xyberia.com
HK$40 per hour.

Cyber-X Multimedia Fun Pub Café
G/F Empress Plaza
17–19 Chatham Road
Kowloon
Tel: 2367-2399
Fax: 2367-9678
Daily 11am–2am
e-mail: webmaster@cyber-x.com.hk
HK$1 per minute.

Kublai's
3/F Capital Place
18 Luard Road
Wan Chai
Tel: 2529-9117
Daily 12.30am–10.30pm
e-mail: webmaster@kublais.com
www.kublais.com
HK$48 per half hour (but this can be used towards purchase of food and drink as well). All branches of the Pacific Coffee Company grant free access for the price of a cup of coffee (www.pacificcoffee.com).

Tourist Information

Hong Kong Tourist Association (www.hkta.org) is a bubbling fount of information, via its website, verbally or in the form of numerous brochures promoting everything from eating and shopping to hiking and horse races. Frontline HKTA staff seem genuinely interested in helping visitors. For brochures, maps or basic questions and answers, as well as souvenirs and gifts, the HKTA has walk-in Information & Gift Centres at the airport, at the Kowloon Star Ferry Concourse (weekdays 8am–6pm, weekends 9am–5pm), Jardine House basement (weekdays 9am–6pm, Saturday 9am–1pm) on Hong Kong Island. The centre at the airport stays open from 8am–10.30pm daily. For elusive addresses, directions and train or ferry schedules, there is also a telephone enquiries service: tel: 2807-6177 (weekdays 8am–6pm, weekends 9am–5pm). For serious queries or shopping

complaints,contact HKTA Headquarters on the 10th floor of Citicorp Centre in North Point. Overseas, the HKTA maintains offices in Auckland, Barcelona, Beijing, Chicago, Frankfurt, Johannesburg, London, New York, Osaka, Paris, Rome, Singapore, Sydney, Los Angeles, Seoul, Taipei, Toronto and Tokyo.

The Macau Government Tourist Office is at:
9 Largo do Senado
Macau
Tel: 315566
Fax: 510104
Website: www.macautourism.gov.mo

Media

The HKTA leaflet *Essentials* (updated monthly) is a good local information source. Many hotels offer this book free with their own name and logo printed on the cover. The two major English-language newspapers are the *South China Morning Post* and the *Hong Kong Standard*. Both maintain their own information websites. Handy sources of information, distributed free in hotels, bars and restaurants, include the monthly *Where* magazine and the rather more hard-hitting weekly *HK Magazine*, which is actually a newspaper and whose topical articles take an often satirical look at life in the SAR and offer an excellent insight into the city's zeitgeist.

Getting Around

Orientation

Modern, high-speed trains, frequent ferries, some valiant trams, a plethora of bus routes and fleets of taxis make getting around Hong Kong both easy and inexpensive. All public signs are written in both English and Chinese, and although Cantonese is the language spoken by 98 percent of the population – English is also widely used. It helps, however, to have an address or item written out in Chinese characters.

If you are going to be travelling around a lot, buy an Octopus stored-value card (HK$100) at one of the stations, which will save you fiddling with change each time you board. They can be used on all rail routes as well as some buses and ferries and the Airport Express link. You can even use them for calls at some phone boxes.

RAIL

Airport Express (AE)
The Airport Express links the SAR's new airport at Chek Lap Kok with Hong Kong Island in just over 20 minutes. There are three stops – at Tsing Yi, Kowloon, and Olympic stations – on the way. This is the fastest way into the city from the airport, the staff on board are especially accommodating, and numerous shuttle bus services operate out of the stations to nearby hotels and other important places. Double-decker buses (which are cheaper) also make the journey from the airport to most parts of the SAR.

Mass Transit Railway
Linked to the AE is the fully air-conditioned Mass Transit Railway, commonly called the MTR. The system has more than 40 stations, with four lines running overground, underground and beneath the harbour to Tsuen Wan in the western New Territories, along the north shore of Hong Kong island, around the Kowloon peninsula and out to Tung Chung on Lantau Island near the airport. It is the cheapest, easiest and most convenient way to get to most of the tourist areas in the SAR. Expect a crush during morning and evening peak hours.

Kowloon–Canton Railway
The old Kowloon–Canton Railway (KCR) is now a modern electrified commuter train. There are a dozen or so stops on this 51-km (32-mile) segment through Kowloon and the New Territories to the border at Lo Wu. The main railway station is in Hung Hom, Kowloon, which can be easily reached by bus or minibus; tel: 2602-7799 for details.

Light Railway
This above-ground railway runs between Tuen Muen and Yuen Long in the New Territories from 6am–11pm, although times vary for different stations.

BUS & MINIBUS

Three bus companies – Kowloon Motor Bus (tel: 2745-4466), Citybus (tel: 2873-0818) and New World First Bus (tel: 2136-8888) – run extensive inter-connected routes all over the SAR, while the Lantau Bus Company (tel: 2984-8361) has the monopoly on Lantau Island. Fares are cheap and the more modern vehicles are air-conditioned. Filling in the gaps and operating on some of the same routes as major bus companies are the fast and furious mini- and maxi-cabs – 16-seater cream-coloured minibuses which carry a red or green stripe respectively. These will stop more or less anywhere to pick up and let off passengers. The

destination and fare are displayed in the driver's cab in English and Chinese.

TAXIS

You will see three sorts of taxis in Hong Kong, coloured red, green or blue and each with its own strictly defined area of operation. All taxis can ply the route to and from the airport to their respective turf. Red taxis can go anywhere in Hong Kong except those parts of Lantau Island not covered by the road to the airport, and are mainly found in the urban areas. Some drivers are reluctant to go from Hong Kong island to Kowloon or vice versa; there are certain specific taxi ranks for these cross-harbour routes – check with your hotel or the tourist office.

Green taxis operate in the New Territories, while blue taxis are confined to Lantau. Taxis can be hailed anywhere, but will not stop on a yellow line. You will have to pay extra if you use a tunnel or have a lot of heavy baggage. A list of charges is displayed inside the taxi. Most have radios in the cab, so if you have trouble making yourself understood ask to speak to the despatcher.

Taxis in Macau are black with green roofs, and are slightly cheaper than in Hong Kong.

Complaints
If you have any trouble with a taxi, say you are overcharged or you have left your wallet in the back seat, contact the Hong Kong Police special taxi hotline tel: 2577-6866 or 2527-7177. (Don't forget to record the taxi number.) If a complaint is not resolved, you must be prepared to appear as a witness to the police prosecution. In most cases, the courts will push a tourist's case to the front of its judicial queues to make an example of the offender. However, if a constable is nearby, threaten to take your complaint directly to him – this usually makes obdurate drivers back down.

FERRIES

The Star Ferry

You can always tell the tourists from the residents on Hong Kong's most famous mode of transportation, the Star Ferry. Tourists are agog at the magnificent sight of the world's third busiest port – and one of the best natural harbours in the world – as the double-bowed, green and white, two-decker ferries weave their way across the water between Hong Kong and Tsim Sha Tsui. The residents are quite content to spend the 7-minute voyage with their noses tucked into their own newspapers or racing sheets. This inexpensive trip is one of the best travel bargains in the world. The ferry runs from 6.30am–11pm.

Inter-Island Ferries

There are more than 230 islands in Hong Kong, although only a handful are inhabited. Ferries link the main islands of Lantau, Cheung Chau and Lamma with Hong Kong island. At the Outlying Districts Ferry Pier in Central, you'll find double and triple-decker ferries – all with at least one air-conditioned deck – that regularly travel to the outlying islands. There is regular service – quite crowded at weekends and holidays – to Lantau, Cheung Chau and Lamma islands. The Hong Kong Tourist Association has a complete schedule of all available ferry services (tel: 2807-6177).

The Hong Kong & Yaumatei Ferry Company,s enquiry number is 2542-3081. The Polly Ferry Company operates daily services to stops (including Grass Island) along Tolo Harbour and – at weekends and on public holidays – a ferry to Ping Chau. These depart from Ma Liu Shui, near the University KCR station; tel: 2771-1630 for details.

TRAMS

The turn-of-the-century double-decker trams which rumble along Hong Kong island's north shore between Chai Wan and Western are one of the best and cheapest ways of taking in the sights. Avoid rush hour and go upstairs, preferably at the front for a cooling breeze and the best views. Trams run from 6am–1am.

The Peak Tram

Hong Kong's other tram is the century-old Peak Tram, which is actually a funicular railway up to The Peak. It is a regular commuter route as well as a favourite tourist attraction. The funicular rises 397 metres (1,305 ft) above sea level in about 10 minutes on a steep journey over 1,364 metres (4,500 ft) of track. It operates daily from 7am to midnight.

The Lower Peak Tram Station in Central District is on Garden Road. A free shuttle bus service operates between the Lower Station and the Star Ferry from 9am–7pm daily at 20-minute intervals. There are four intermediate stations before the Upper Peak Tram Station, nestled underneath the Peak Tower, a futuristic building containing a shopping and entertainment plaza. Tel: 2522-0922 for more details.

PRIVATE TRANSPORT

With the wide availability of public transport there is little reason to hire a car, but rental cars, with or without drivers, are available. Hotels, through their own transportation services, can usually handle requests for chauffeur-driven cars. Be warned that driving in Hong Kong is not for the timid.

Rickshaws

Hong Kong still has a small number of rickshaws that congregate around the Star Ferry concourse on Hong Kong Island. Tourists usually hire the rickshaws to pose for pictures. Rickshaw-pullers refuse to budge without a round of bartering, so the price extracted from visitors is usually higher than its official rate.

Where to Stay

Whether to stay on Hong Kong or Kowloon side is a long-standing debate. Money is not a factor: there are expensive and budget hotels on both sides (although the really cheap places are almost all in Kowloon), and access to shops and restaurants is good on both sides of the harbour. The MTR connects various parts of Kowloon and Hong Kong Island in minutes, as does the Star Ferry.

Despite certain Hong Kong advantages, most people end up in Kowloon's Tsim Sha Tsui District because it has more hotels. Hong Kong's Central District is considerably more restrained, because it is the business, financial and government centre. Though there are many good stores in Central, this part of the city is more geared to business than bargain basement shopping. Hong Kong's Causeway Bay, however, features a wide range of accommodation, late-night shopping and eating. And between Central and Causeway Bay is the entertainment district of Wan Chai, rife with honky-tonk local colour and just down the tram-line from Central or Causeway Bay.

Hong Kong

INTERNATIONAL CLASS
Conrad International
88 Queensway
Pacific Place
Tel: 2521-3838
Fax: 2521-3888
A European-style deluxe hotel. Understated elegance; spacious rooms and good location adjacent to Pacific Place shopping, Admiralty MTR and tramlines.
Grand Hyatt
1 Harbour Road
Wan Chai

Tel: 2588-1234
Fax: 2802-0677
One of the most expensive and glitzy hotels in Hong Kong, overlooking the harbour and only a couple of steps from the HK Convention and Exhibition Centre.

Island Shangri-La
Supreme Court Road
Pacific Place
Central
Tel: 2877-3838
Fax: 2521-8742
Elegant decor, helpful staff and beautiful, spacious rooms with stunning views of the harbour or Peak; adjacent to Hong Kong Park, Pacific Place shopping and Admiralty MTR.

Mandarin Oriental
5 Connaught Road
Central
Tel: 2522-0111
Fax: 2810-6190
Exceptional hotel, consistently rated among the world's best. Impeccable service and quality. Chic top-floor restaurant serves contemporary French food with Asian influences.

Renaissance Harbour View
1 Harbour Road
Wan Chai
Tel: 2802-8888
Fax: 2802-8833
A shade cheaper than the Grand Hyatt but enjoys same location overlooking the harbour; easy access to Kowloon from Wan Chai Pier. Superb recreation facilities.

Ritz-Carlton
3 Connaught Road
Central
Tel: 2877-6666
Fax: 2877-6778
Post-modernist exterior gives way to classy traditionalist interior. Facilities include outdoor pool and outstanding Italian and Japanese restaurants. Convenient location close to Central MTR, Star Ferry, and Admiralty and Central districts.

Hong Kong Hotel
3 Canton Road
Harbour City,
Tsim Sha Tsui
Tel: 2113-0088
Fax: 2113-0011
Many rooms with magnificent harbor views. Deluxe facilities

include an outdoor pool and 5 restaurants. Inside the enormous shopping complex stretching from Ocean Terminal up to the Gateway.

Kowloon Shangri-La
64 Mody Road
Tsim Sha Tsui East
Tel: 2721-2111
Fax: 2723-8686
Opulent grandeur and great harbour views; indoor swimming pool and highly rated restaurants. Across from Tsim Sha Tsui East waterfront with easy access to Central.

The Peninsula
Salisbury Road
Tsim Sha Tsui
Tel: 2366-6251
Fax: 2722-4170
Hong Kong's oldest and most prestigious hotel has been a byword for impeccable service since it opened in 1928. Extensively refurbished, with a gorgeous pool and spa overlooking the harbour. Eight top restaurants and superb location right next to Kowloon's shopping, restaurant and entertainment area.

The Regent
Salisbury Road
Tsim Sha Tsui
Tel: 2721-1211
Fax: 2739-4546
Elegant, with breathtaking views across Victoria Harbour; poolside spa with private rooms, the 1930s-style Club Shanghai night-club and top-notch restaurants. Superb location on the waterfront.

Sheraton Hong Kong Hotel and Towers
20 Nathan Road
Tsim Sha Tsui
Tel: 2369-1111
Fax: 2739-8707
Swish, newly-renovated property with full range of deluxe facilities, including an outdoor pool, five excellent restaurants.

SUPERIOR CLASS
Century Hong Kong Hotel
238 Jaffe Road
Wan Chai
Tel: 2598-8888
Fax: 2598-8866
Modern hotel with good facilities including outdoor pool, health club

and Lao Ching Hing, one of oldest and best Shanghai restaurants in town. Convenient for HK Exhibition and Convention Centre.

The Excelsior
281 Gloucester Road
Causeway Bay
Tel: 2894-8888
Fax: 2895-6459
Overlooking the colourful Causeway Bay typhoon shelter; efficient service and a pleasant environment. Close to shopping and commercial district and MTR.

Furama
1 Connaught Road
Central
Tel: 2525-5111
Fax: 2845-9339
Quietly plush business hotel. Good value considering its convenient location to Central MTR, Star Ferry, and Admiralty and Central district.

Grand Plaza
2 Kornhill Road
Quarry Bay
Tel: 2886-0011
Fax: 2886-1738
Modern business hotel with good facilities including golf, tennis courts, indoor pool and gym. Close to Tai Koo MTR.

Wharney Hotel
57–73 Lockhart Road
Wan Chai
Tel: 2861-1000
Fax: 2865-6023
Smart modern hotel with good facilities including indoor pool. Located in the heart of the commercial and nightlife district, close to HK Convention Centre.

The Kowloon Hotel
19–21 Nathan Road
Tsim Sha Tsui
Tel: 2369-8698
Fax: 2739-9811
Smart, modern business hotel tucked in the heart of Kowloon's commercial and entertainment district. Close to MTR.

Majestic
348 Nathan Road
Yau Ma Tei
Tel: 2781-1333
Fax: 2781-1773
Well-appointed business hotel. Close to Temple Street night market, shops, cinema and Jordan

MTR; also well-served by buses.

Marco Polo
Harbour City
Canton Road,
Tsim Sha Tsui
Tel: 2113-0888
Fax: 2113-0022
Elegant, Continental-style hotel in
the middle of Harbour City complex;
marginally cheaper than its sister-
property, the Hong Kong Hotel, but
lacking views and pool.

Nikko
72 Mody Road
Tsim Sha Tsui East
Tel: 2739-1111
Fax: 2311-3122
Japanese business hotel with
impeccable service and panoramic
harbour views. Outdoor pool and
good Cantonese, French and
Japanese restaurants. Convenient
location just across from Tsim Sha
Tsui East waterfront promenade.

Prince
Canton Road
Harbour City
Tsim Sha Tsui
Tel: 2113-1888
Fax: 2113-0066
Similar standard to Marco Polo;
outdoor pool; convenient for China
Ferry Terminal and Kowloon Park.

Regal Airport
Chek Lap Kok
Lantau
Tel: 2286-8888
Fax: 2286-8686
Five minutes by covered walkway
from the international airport, this
light and airy hotel makes the most
of its location with views over the
runway.

Macau

INTERNATIONAL CLASS
Westin Resort
1918 Entrada de Hac Sá
Coloane Island
Tel: 871111
Fax: 871122
Peaceful seclusion at the southeast
tip of Coloane Island. Eight-storey
resort hotel with 208 spacious
rooms each with private outdoor
terraces overlooking the beach.
Adjacent 18-hole golf course.

SUPERIOR CLASS
Hyatt Regency Macau
2 Estrada Almirante Marques
Esparteiro
Taipa Island
Tel: 831234
Fax: 830195
All mod cons, including an attractive
landscaped pool, tennis courts and
restaurant offering Macanese
cuisine in a relaxed setting,

Pousada de São Tiago
Avenida de Republica
Tel: 378111
Fax: 552170
Macau's most romantic hotel, an
elegant Portuguese-style inn built
within the walls of the 17th-century
Barra fort. Only 23 rooms so book
ahead.

Mandarin Oriental Macau
956–1110 Avenida de Amizade
Tel: 567888
Fax: 594589
Five-star comfort and facilities,
including the excellent Mezzaluna
restaurant and a casino. A new
resort area between the hotel and
the new Cultural Centre has added
a full range of resort-style facilities.

Pousada de São Tiago
Avenida de Republica
Tel: 378111
Fax: 552170
Macau's most romantic hotel, an
elegant Portuguese-style inn built
within the walls of the 17th-century
Barra fort. Only 23 rooms, so book
ahead.

STANDARD CLASS
Hotel Royal
2–4 Estrada de Vitoria
Tel: 552222
Fax: 563008
Value-for-money city-centre hotel
with indoor pool.

What to Eat

There are more than 5,000
restaurants listed in Hong Kong
telephone directories. Everywhere
you turn, there is a restaurant,
whether it's gourmet class, fast-
food or simply a clutch of tables
and chairs on a street corner.
Conversation invariably involves the
merits and demerits of restaurants,
the best dishes and what's in
season. Restaurants in Hong Kong
are places where people meet to
gossip, or gather for celebrations,
as well as cut deals, and wine and
dine important contacts. Be
adventurous: get out of your hotel
and sample some of the best
Chinese, Japanese, Korean,
Singaporean, Malayasian,
Indonesian, Filipino, Thai, Indian
and Vietnamese food in the world.

Over the centuries Macau has
developed a unique cuisine
blending influences from Portugal's
African and Indian colonies. For
many, one of the highlights of a visit
involves the sampling of signature
Macanese dishes such as African
chicken or spicy prawns. Portions
tend to be large and prices low.
More traditional Portuguese food is
also good, with excellent
Portuguese wine available at a
fraction of the price you'd pay
elsewhere in the region.

High Tea
High tea is an institution in Hong
Kong, and the best-known milieu for
the past half century has been the
colonnaded lobby of the Peninsula
Hotel. High tea there is a good
place to watch the world go by.
The Luk Yu Tea House located at
26–42 Stanley Street, Central,
Hong Kong, tel: 2523-5463 offers
high-tea in a classic Cantonese
atmosphere.

Culture

Hong Kong does not have a glittering reputation for the arts, performing or otherwise, but it is by no means a cultural desert. Broadway and West End shows pass through, to say nothing of renowned symphony orchestras and opera troupes. The action takes place at the Hong Kong Arts Centre, where, in addition to plays and shows, small film festivals are almost a monthly occurrence. Just across the street is the Hong Kong Academy for Performing Arts – both buildings are on Harbour Road in Wan Chai on Hong Kong Island. This is a superb venue, complete with an outdoor amphitheatre, for all kinds of performances. Across the harbour in Kowloon, just adjacent to the Star Ferry, is the Hong Kong Cultural Centre. Wing-shaped, it has three first class venues that can stage anything from grand opera to intimate performances. Rarely visited by tourists is the Ko Shan Theatre in Kowloon, an outdoor venue used for pop concerts, operas and variety shows. There are also local symphonic orchestras, such as the Hong Kong Philharmonic and the Hong Kong Chinese Music Orchestra, plus several amateur and professional theatres.

The Hong Kong Arts Festival, in January and February, features an intriguing programme of Western and Eastern art. Renowned orchestras, dance companies, drama groups, opera companies and jazz ensembles are invited to perform here alongside talented local artists. Traditional Chinese performance blends with Western cultural fare to create a truly Hong Kong extravaganza. Another annual arts affair, the Festival of Asian Arts (October and November), invites artists and performers from various regions to introduce indigenous art forms to Hong Kong audiences. Hong Kong is represented by groups which perform traditional Cantonese and Beijing opera, Cantonese drama, multi-regional Chinese folk dance and music. Also included are performances by the Hong Kong Philharmonic Orchestra and the Hong Kong Chinese Music Orchestra. Chinese operas, puppet shows and dancing take place regularly throughout the year, especially during festivals.

Shopping

Hong Kong has frequently been called a shopper's paradise and it is certainly true that Hong Kong people are insatiable shoppers. Shopping places range from colourful night markets to glitzy malls, multi-storey department stores to bustling narrow streets of antiques and bric-a-brac.

These days, Hong Kong may not be the shopping bargain basement it once was, but shopping will nonetheless prove one of the most compelling activities of any trip to the territory.

Where to Shop

The "prime" shopping centres are Central, Admiralty and Causeway Bay on Hong Kong island and Tsim Sha Tsui and Mong Kok in Kowloon. Shopping hours vary, but the good news is that shopping basically goes on till late seven days a week. Even during public holidays, shops are almost always open, except during the annual lunar new year holiday. As a guide, shops in Central close earlier, around 6pm, but the other main areas tend to stay open till 9.30pm, sometimes later.

Malls

Hong Kong has some of the world's most glitzy and glamorous shopping malls. These may not seem as colourful to tourists as outdoor markets, but they are certainly more comfortable than traipsing around the streets during the hot and humid summers.

The best-known shopping malls on Hong Kong Island are Landmark in Central, Pacific Place in Admiralty, Times Square in Causeway Bay, and City Plaza in

Taikoo Shing. In Kowloon, the linked Ocean Terminal and Harbour Centre complexes can keep you busy for a long time.

Bargaining

Contrary to popular belief, the practice of bargaining for goods in Hong Kong is very much on the way out. Price differences are usually so marginal that it is hardly worth the energy trying to bargain. Shopkeepers that are not used to bargaining will probably react rather impatiently to your efforts. If you settle by cash you may get a slightly better deal than by using credit cards. In many cases, shops will add an extra few percent to the price if you use credit cards.

What to Buy

Antiques and works of art

The network of antiques shops around Hollywood Road and Cat Street offers an extraordinary range of Asian antiquities and artworks at a wide range of prices. The CRC Department stores also stock many inexpensive antiques and handicrafts from mainland China.

Computers

Hong Kong is a major exporter of computers, components, and accessories and you will find the most up-to-date models at good prices. There are a number of arcades solely devoted to selling computers and accessories. The best are Star House in Tsim Sha Tsui near the Star Ferry, Windsor House in Causeway Bay, and Whampoa Gardens in Hung Hom, Kowloon.

Cameras and electronic goods

These are still good buys in Hong Kong, but it is in the camera shops where you have to beware of being ripped off. Most camera and electronics stores are in Causeway Bay, Tsim Sha Tsui, and Mong Kok. They seldom have price tags on the items, so bargain, compare prices, and beware.

Most resident expatriates prefer the camera stores in Stanley

Street, Central. There is not such a range there, but they are friendly, reasonably priced, and there are few reports of cheating.

With electronic goods, remember to check for correct voltage, adaptors etc. Hand-held electronic games are particularly advanced in Hong Kong and make great gifts for teenagers. Hong Kong also has some of the best prices in the world for compact discs.

Clothing

Hong Kong has a superb range of clothing to suit all ages, tastes and budgets. But although many visitors from South East Asia flock to Hong Kong for the latest names in international fashion, most Western visitors will find they get much better buys on the big names at home.

The factory outlets in Wan Chai, Tsim Sha Tsui, and Mong Kok, however, are extremely popular with tourists. These are essentially seconds and overruns from Hong Kong's export industry and are available at a fraction of the intended selling price overseas. The Chinese Products emporia such as the CRC Department Stores have excellent bargains on silks.

Custom Tailors

Having your own suit made to measure is still a popular luxury for visitors to Hong Kong. The territory has some of the legendary tailors of old Shanghai who have passed on their skills to the next generation. The speed and quality of craftsmanship and the range of fabrics are all excellent. It is no longer a sensational bargain, but still worthwhile. A few places continue to offer the 24-hour suit, but these are not usually the best. Expect your tailor to take about a week if you want a high-quality garment worth paying for.

There are plenty of tailors in Tsim Sha Tsui and a few in Wan Chai and Causeway Bay. The Shanghai Tang store in Central also offers a Shanghainese tailoring service for either Western- or Mandarin-style suits.

Jewellery

Hong Kong is the world's fourth largest exporter of jewellery, and there is a wide range of jewellery available in retail outlets. Because Hong Kong is a free port and there is no tax on the import or export of precious metals, prices are good. Particularly popular jewellery includes jade items (though you should avoid buying expensive items without expert advice) and bright yellow 24-kt gold, called *chuk kam* in Cantonese. Jewellery stores specialising in *chuk kam* are usually very crowded and the atmosphere resembles a betting shop more than an exclusive store. These items are sold by the weight of the gold only, so you pay no premium for the design. There are, of course, many fine jewellery stores selling gem set jewellery in a huge range of classical and stylish designs where you pay for the craftsmanship as well as the materials.

Another good buy in Hong Kong is pearls, which come in all shapes, sizes and colours. The practice of bargaining is much less common in jewellery stores now, but you can certainly try your luck by asking for a discount.

Leather Goods

Many shops stock a wide range of leather shoes, bags, wallets and luggage. There are top-quality, brand-name goods as well as very inexpensive wallets and bags from discount stores in the main shopping areas of Tsim Sha Tsui and Causeway Bay.

Watches

If not at a reputable outlet, and if the price is a bargain, it's a fake.

Sportswear

Hong Kong has many shops selling inexpensive sportswear. In Mong Kok there are several streets consisting of almost nothing but sports stores.

Macau

Macau is a good place to buy Chinese antiques and artifacts. The main street, Avenida Almeida Ribeiro, has a few antiques shops on both sides of the street as you walk from the Outer Harbour (near the Lisboa and Sintra hotels), and towards the Inner Harbour (near the floating casino).

Otherwise, Macau is rarely thought of as a shopping mart, except for its magnificently priced wines, brandies and ports, which are restricted upon return to Hong Kong. Though it is a duty-free port like Hong Kong, the array of goods available is not nearly so extensive. Some items, such as cameras or stereo systems, are more expensive in Macau because of the smaller number sold. And like Hong Kong, Macau is a clothing manufacturing centre, especially of knitwear, though whatever is displayed is apparently not very fashionable.

TAIWAN

Getting Acquainted

The Place

Taiwan comprises the main island of Taiwan, the Penghu Archipelago (known in the West as the Pescadores), which is made up of 64 islands, and 21 other islands scattered around the main island. Together, they make up about 36,000 sq. km (14,000 sq. miles), with the main island occupying 89 percent of that area. Situated just off the southeastern coast of mainland China, Taiwan is bisected by the Tropic of Cancer.

A central mountain range runs parallel to the length of the main island of Taiwan, dividing it into east and west halves. With the Pacific Ocean on the east, which is sculpted by a dramatic coastline, the high land levels off gradually on the western side. The terraced table lands and alluvial coastal plain, thus formed on the west coast, are home to about 80 percent of Taiwan's 22 million people.

Taiwan's highest mountain, Yu Shan, rises to a lofty 3,952 meters (12,966 ft).

Time Zones

Taiwan Standard Time is GMT +8 hours. There is no daylight savings time.

Climate

Taiwan has a tropical climate in the southern and western flatlands, and a subtropical climate in the north and mountainous regions. It is also subject to annual typhoons, which pass through between July and Oc-

tober. Most cause little more than strong winds and heavy rains.

Taiwan has two distinct seasons: hot (May–October), and cold (December–March). The island is excessively humid throughout the year and receives abundant rainfall, more in the east (uplands) than the west (lowlands). Snow falls on the summits of the Central Range in the cold season, while the lowlands remain frost-free.

The most pleasant times of the year for travel are March to May and September to November, especially in Taipei.

Etiquette

The Western handshake has today displaced the ancient custom of bowing with clasped hands, but the Chinese still shy away from boisterous greetings in public. A firm handshake, friendly smile, and slight nod of the head are the usual gestures of greeting.

In Chinese, a person's family surname precedes both given name and formal title. The majority of Chinese family names come from the "Old Hundred Names" (Lao Bai Hsing), first formulated over 3,000 years ago in feudal China. Among the most common are Li, Wang, Chen, Hwang, Chang, Yang, Liang and Sun.

During formal introductions, the Chinese usually exchange name cards – many people don't even listen to oral introductions, but wait to read the person's card. It is a good idea to have some personal name cards printed up before

Courtesy Titles

Some of the most common titles used in Chinese introductions are:

Hsien-sheng/Mr (as in Li hsien-sheng)
Tai-tai/Mrs (Li tai-tai)
Hsiao-jye/Miss (Li hsiao-jye)
Fu-ren/Madame (Li fu-ren)
Lao-ban/Boss (Li lao-ban)
Jing-Li/Manager (Li jing-li)

travelling anywhere in the Far East.

The Chinese term *ching-keh* literally means "inviting guests" and refers to the tradition of entertaining friends and associates with lavish generosity, usually at banquets. Inviting guests out for dinner and drinks is a delightful way to repay favours or to cultivate new business relationships. Apart from anything else, the moment the host has paid the hefty dinner bill, everyone at the table is obliged to return the favour in the near future. In the final analysis, it all balances out, and everyone takes turns earning the "big face" that comes with being a generous host.

When toasted at dinner parties, it is well-mannered to raise your wine cup with both hands: one holding it and the other touching the base. The host usually takes his seat opposite the guest-of-honour, with his back to the door and the guest-of-honour facing it.

Tea served at the end of a meal is your host's polite insinuation that the party is over and that it is time for you to leave. So don't overstay your welcome even though your host may insist. Out of courtesy, even though it is late and the host would love to call it a day, he will gently persuade his guest to stay longer. In this case, it is up to the guest to detect from the host's tone what's the best thing to do. But this requires skill and cultural sense.

The Chinese Zodiac

In the Chinese lunar calendar, which follows the cycles of the moon rather than the sun, each year is designated by its association with one of the twelve celestial animals, along with one of the Five Cosmic Elements. The animals, in order of sequence, are the Rat, Ox, Tiger, Rabbit, Dragon, Snake, Horse, Ram, Monkey, Chicken, Dog, and Pig. The Five Elements are metal, wood, earth, water, and fire. Since each of the animals is associated in turn with each of the Five Elements, a full cosmic cycle takes 60 years to complete.

The most popular aspect of the zodiac today is the description of basic personality traits according to which animal dominates the year of birth. Professional match-makers still refuse to introduce prospective marriage partners whose signs conflict, and businessmen often attribute financial failure to ill cosmology.

The Chinese continue to hold great faith in their age-old cosmology. Prior to births, weddings, funerals, major business contracts, grand openings of new buildings, and other important events, most Chinese in Taiwan still consult ancient almanacs, fortune-tellers and geomancers for advice regarding auspicious days.

The dates for weddings and funerals in Taiwan are always set according to ancient Chinese cosmology. Many Chinese even refuse to travel or embark on new business ventures without considering auspicious dates. Not to do so would invite disaster.

When a modern skyscraper goes up in Taiwan, the owners routinely consult a Chinese geomancer to determine the optimum position for the main entrance. Called *feng shui* (wind and water), geomancy is the branch of classical cosmology which helps humanity build dwellings in optimum harmony with the elements of the natural environment.

The Government

The Republic of China (ROC) on Taiwan, as the government officially refers to Taiwan, still marches to the battle cry of Dr Sun Yatsen, who established a governing system "of the people, by the people and for the people" early in the 20th century.

The government adopted a constitution based on those principles. It incorporates five branches of government called Yuan under a president. The executive Yuan resembles the cabinet of Western governments and includes ministries and other offices and departments. Law-making is the function of the Legislative Yuan. The Control Yuan has powers of consent, impeachment, censure and audit. Under the Judicial Yuan are the courts, Council of Grand Justices and other offices that uphold and interpret the law. Finally, the Examination Yuan supervises examinations and personnel.

In addition to the ROC government, the Taiwan Provincial Government and numerous county, city and ethnic minority groups have freely-elected representatives who participate in daily decision-making.

Planning the Trip

What to Wear

During the hot season, appropriate clothing should include light, loose cotton garments, casual sportswear, and comfortable walking shoes. Men usually need not wear jackets and ties, but if you are coming on business, it's best to bring them. Most modern offices are air-conditioned. You may also want to bring a lightweight jacket or dress if you are likely to attend formal banquets or receptions.

During the cold season, be sure to bring some comfortable woollens to help protect you from the bone-chilling, moisture-laden air of winter. Sweaters, woollen jackets and dresses, warm trousers and socks will all come in handy, especially in Taipei. During both seasons, bring some sort of rain-gear; thunderstorms can occur at any time.

Health

Effective cholera and yellow fever inoculation certificates are required for passengers who are coming from certain countries or have stayed more than five days in infected areas. Otherwise, health certificates are not normally required. It is very much recommended to have inoculations against Hepatitis A and in some cases Hepatitis B well in advance if travelling to remote areas.

Entry Regulations

Citizens of Australia, Austria, Belgium, Canada, France, Germany, Japan, Luxembourg, New Zealand, Netherlands, Portugal, Spain, Sweden, United Kingdom and the United States – with passports valid at least for six months and confirmed onward or return tickets – are allowed visa-free entry to Taiwan for a period of 14 days. It is **not** possible to extend the validity of such visas.

Foreigners applying for visitors' visas must hold valid passports, incoming and outgoing travel tickets (or a letter from your travel agent), three photos, and documents stating the purpose of the visit (except for sightseeing or transit) and the completed application form. Such visas are usually good for 60 days and may be extended twice for 60 days, for a total of six months' stay. Foreigners entering Taiwan on a visitor visa may not work without official authorisation.

Customs

Inbound Declaration: All inbound passengers must fill in a customs declaration form upon arrival.

All personal belongings such as clothing, jewellery, cosmetics, food and similar items may be brought into Taiwan free of duty. Items such as stereo equipments, TV sets and recorders, though also duty-free, must be declared on arrival. Each passenger is also permitted to bring in duty-free one bottle (1 litre/35 fl. ounces) of alcohol and one carton of tobacco (200 cigarettes, 25 cigars, or 450 grams/1 lb of pipe tobacco).

Although unlimited amounts of foreign currency may be brought into Taiwan, passengers who wish to take excess foreign currency out again must declare the full amount upon arrival. The unused balance may then be declared on the Outbound Passenger Declaration form upon departure.

Airport Tax

All outbound passengers must pay an exit airport tax of NT$300. You must present the receipt when checking in.

Getting There

Taiwan lies along one of the busiest air routes in Asia, and stopovers may be included on any round-the-world or regional air tickets at no extra cost. Many international airlines provide regular air service to Taiwan. Chinese travel a lot and it is a good idea to make flight reservations as early as possible. **Taipei:** a lot of the international air traffic to and from Taiwan goes through the **Chiang Kaishek International Airport** in Taoyuan, about 45 minutes' drive from downtown Taipei. This is one of the best-designed airports in Asia, fully-equipped with the latest technology. The second international airport is located at **Kaohsiung**.

Money Matters

Coins come in denominations of NT$1, 5, 10, 50 and 100. Bills come in units of NT$100, 500 and 1,000.

Major foreign currencies can be easily exchanged for the local currency at certain banks, hotels, some shops and all authorised money dealers. In smaller towns or in the countryside, it is almost impossible to change foreign currency into NT$. If travelling overland, change money before the trip. In smaller towns usually only the **Bank of Taiwan** changes foreign currency; the procedure is complicated, exhausting and time-consuming.

Important: Be sure to obtain receipts of all such transactions: you'll find they save you a lot of hassle with the bank, when you try to reconvert unused New Taiwan dollars on departure. Usually you will get US$ for your surplus NT$. The banks at CKS International Airport in Taipei are best. There is also a bank at Kaohsiung International Airport, but with irregular opening times.

Traveller's cheques are also widely accepted at most hotels and other tourist-oriented establishments. This also applies to major credit cards.

Practical Tips

Emergencies

The following telephone numbers are useful for visitors to Taiwan:
Fire tel: 119
Police tel: 110
Foreign Affairs, National Police tel: (02) 2396-9781.
Tourist Information Hotline tel: (02) 2717-3737 (8am–8pm)

Medical Services

Although medical treatment and dental work cost far less in Taipei than in any Western country, the quality of medical facilities and services is excellent and up-to-date.

Business Hours

Government business hours: 8.30am–12.30pm and 1.30–5.30pm, Monday to Friday; 8.30am–12.30pm Saturday.
Banks: 9am–3.30pm Monday to Friday; 9am–noon on Saturday.
Commercial business hours: 9am–5pm Monday to Friday; 9am–noon on Saturday.
Department stores and large shops: 10 or 11am–9 or 10pm Monday to Saturday. Many smaller shops and stalls keep longer hours and open on Sunday.

Tipping

Generally speaking, large tips are not expected in Taiwan, although small gratuities are always appreciated. Hotels and restaurants automatically add 10 percent service charge to bills, but this rarely gets distributed among the staff, so a small cash tip of 5 to 10 percent is always welcome in restaurants.
Taiwan taxi drivers do not get upset if you don't tip them, but it is customary to let them "keep the change" in small coins. Taxis still cost far less in Taipei than most places, but the cost of petrol and maintenance is high, so drivers appreciate even the smallest tips. The only places where heavy tips are routinely expected are in winehouses and dance-halls, where big tipping wins you "big face" and big favours from the ladies.

Media

Newspapers and Magazines

Two English-language newspapers are published daily: *China Post* (morning) and *China News* (afternoon). In addition to international, regional and local news, these newspapers carry financial news, entertainment sections, sports reports and guides to English-language TV and radio programmes. Most hotel news-stands carry both papers.
The Government Information Office publishes an illustrated monthly magazine in English, *Free China Review*, which features articles on Chinese culture, travel in Taiwan, and other aspects of life in the Republic of China. Beyond this, the only English periodicals published locally are devoted exclusively to industrial and financial news.
Foreign periodicals include *Time*, *Newsweek*, *Life*, and several fashion magazines, all of which are sold at English-language bookstores and hotel news-stands. All foreign publications brought into Taiwan are subject to official government censorship, so don't be surprised if you discover a page or two missing from your magazine.

Radio

International Community Radio Taipei (ICRT) broadcasts popular Western music and other programmes in English 24 hours a day, with international news reports on the hour. Tel: (02) 2861-2280 for details of broadcasts, on an island-wide frequency of FM 95.3. Chinese radio stations broadcast a wide variety of music, both Western and Chinese.

Television

There are four television stations which broadcast scheduled programmes throughout Taiwan: China Television Co. (CTV), Chinese Television System (CTS), Taiwan Television Entreprise (TTV), and People Broadcasting Corporation (PBC). All broadcast exclusively in Chinese, but frequently schedule English-language films and programmes from the West. Check the local English-language newspapers for details.

Postal Services

Taiwan has one of the fastest, most efficient postal services in the world. Mail is collected and delivered every day all year, and all incoming mail is sorted and distributed within 48 hours of arrival.
Taipei's **Central Post Office** is located at the North Gate intersection, close to the Taipei Railway Station. This is the best place to collect and post mail. It also provides inexpensive cartons and packing services for parcels. Post offices in town are open from 8am–6pm Monday to Friday, 8am–1pm Saturday.
Stamps may be purchased at the mail counter of any hotel, and letters dropped in any hotel or public mail box, of which there are many. Local mail goes in the green boxes, and international airmail into the red boxes.
Taiwan's decorative and commemorative postage stamps are highly prized in the world of philately. Chinese themes, such as landscape painting, porcelain and calligraphy, are often incorporated into the design of stamps.

Telephones

Local calls: may be made from any public pay telephone, of which there are many. Local calls currently cost NT$1 for three minutes, after which the line is automatically cut off. For further conversation, drop in another coin for local calls and dial again. Better, use a telephone-card, which currently costs NT$100, as most phones are card phones.

International calls: On private phones, the overseas operator may be reached on **100.** For directory assistance in English: tel: (02) 2311-6796. Direct-dialling is available from some phones, especially in hotels. International direct dialling rates are calculated every six seconds. Overseas phone calls may also be made at ITA **(International Telecommunications Adminstration)** offices. The main office in Taipei is open 24 hours, seven days a week, and is located at 28 Hangchou S. Rd, Sec. 1, Taipei, tel: (02) 2344-3780.

Fax: Fax-services are available 24-hours a day for Taiwan or overseas at the ITA main office. Hotels also provide fax services to guests, usually charging an additional fee.

Telegrams: Both international and domestic telegrams may be sent from the main ITA or branch offices, or from the mail counter of major international tourist hotels. ITA offers both Urgent (12 hours) and Ordinary (24 hours) telegram services.

Visitors who wish to register local cable addresses in Taiwan should do so at ITA's main office.

Telex: Services are available at the main office of ITA, and at major international tourist hotels.

Tourist Information

Service and information centres are located at both the Chiang Kaishek International Airport in Taoyuan, outside Taipei, and the Kaohsiung International Airport in Kaohsiung. Receptionists usually speak English, and can help with transport, accommodation, and other travel requirements.

There are two organisations in Taiwan which oversee and promote the tourism industry. The **Tourism Bureau,** a branch of the Ministry of Communications, is the official government organ responsible for

tourism in Taiwan, tel: (02) 2349-1635/6. The **Taiwan Visitors' Association** is a private organisation that promotes Taiwan tourism abroad and provides travel assistance to visitors in Taiwan, tel: (02) 2594-3261. Since neither of these organisations is blessed with a generous budget, the facilities are limited, but they do their best.

At the Sungshan Airport (domestic) in town, you'll find the **Travel Information Service Centre,** tel: (02) 2349-1580 (open 8am–8pm daily, including Sundays and holidays). This facility is designed primarily to provide information on foreign countries to the ever-growing volume of outbound Chinese travellers from Taiwan. However, in addition to audio-visual and printed information on 55 countries, the centre also offers a 25-minute audio-visual presentation on the most outstanding tourist attractions in Taiwan. You could also visit the centre to familiarise yourself with the culture and conditions of your next Asian destination.

Tourist Offices Abroad

Hong Kong: Room 904, 9/F Wingshan Tower, 173 Des Voeux Rd, Central. Tel: 2581-0933, fax: 2581-0262.
Japan: Taiwan Visitors' Association, A-9, 5/F Imperial Tower, Imperial Hotel, Uchisaiwai-cho 1-1-1, Chiyoda-ku, Tokyo 100. Tel: 3501-3591, fax: 3501-3586.
Singapore: Taiwan Visitors' Association, 5 Shenton Way, #14-07, UIC Building, Singapore 0106.
USA: 166 Geary St (Suite 1605), San Francisco, CA 94106. Tel: (415) 989-8677, fax: (415) 989-7242. Also at 1 World Trade Center (Suite 7963), New York, NY 10048. Tel: (212) 466-0691, fax: (212) 432-6436.

Electricity

Electricity in Taiwan is 110v (60 cycles). Remembers to bring an international adapter for plugs.

Getting Around

From the Airport

Taipei: The CKS International Airport is about 45 km (28 miles) southwest of Taipei. An airport bus connects the CKS International Airport with the Taipei Sungshan Airport (domestic), located north. The journey time is 40–60 minutes,and buses run every 10 to 20 minutes between 6.20am–10.30pm. From the Sungshan Airport bus terminal you are only 10–20 minutes (depending on traffic) by cab from most major downtown hotels.

A taxi from the CKS International Airport to downtown Taipei will cost at least NT$1200 at current prices. For the trip from Taipei to the CKS International Airport the drivers are allowed by law to add a 50 percent surcharge.
Kaohsiung: The easiest and best transport is a taxi to the downtown hotels. The airport, located to the south of Kaohsiung, is very close to the city centre.

Domestic Travel

BY AIR

Regular scheduled domestic air service in Taiwan is provided by the international flag-carrier China Airlines (CAL), by Far Eastern Air Transport (FAT) and many more domestic airlines. In total, eight domestic airlines serve Taiwan and its islands. Strict security measures are enforced on all domestic flights within Taiwan, and all foreign passengers need to show their passports prior to boarding.

For bookings and other information before arriving in

Taiwan, call a travel agent. For flight reservations and ticketing in Taiwan, it is best to go directly to an airline office; second-best is a travel agent.

BUSES

A special fleet of de-luxe express buses serves Taiwan's major towns and cities. Between Taipei and Kaohsiung there are frequent scheduled buses. By departure time, almost all buses are fully booked. Come early and wait in a long queue for a ticket, or bad news. The best way to purchase reserved bus tickets is to go directly to the appropriate bus company and buy them one or two days prior to departure. Most hotel travel desks and local travel agencies can make arrangements.

RAILWAY

The Taiwan Railway Administration maintains an extensive railroad network which runs around the island and connects all major cities and towns. Usually the trains are full, so if you don't want to stand a seat reservation is necessary. But without a travel agent, this is quite complicated and time-consuming.

The Railway Administration offers three types of services:

Fu Hsing (FH): air-conditioned, limited express; **Chu Kuang (CK):** first-class, air-conditioned, express; and **Tsu Chiang (TC):** air-conditioned, electrical multiple units.

Reservations for first-class express trains in Taiwan must be made at least one, but not more than two days prior to departure. But although you may purchase round-trip tickets in advance, reservations for return trips must be made upon arrival at your destination, also one to two days in advance. Even for local trains, it is highly advisable to purchase tickets at least several hours, and preferably a full day, in advance. In all cities and towns, advance train tick-

ets may be bought at the main station by lining up before the appropriate window. Most hotels and travel agencies will arrange advance train reservations.

Don't expect to see too much on a train ride. Most locals close the curtains to get some sleep, and they may complain if your window remains uncurtained.

CAR RENTALS

It's best to rely on public transport to get around Taiwanese cities and towns. Trying to drive yourself around a city is a needless risk and could spoil your day. But if you plan an extended tour on the North–South Expressway, which runs like a spinal column down the centre of the island, or plan to go along the northern coastline, then renting a car is ideal, for you'll see far more sights and enjoy the freedom to stop whenever you wish.

Before renting a self-drive car, it is usually best to ask your hotel for some suggestions. You could also book through an Avis, Budget or Hertz reservation centre before your trip to Taiwan.

If you like to splurge a bit and see the island in true comfort and convenience, the best way is by air-conditioned (or heated) limousines, driven by chauffeurs who also act as personal guides and interpreters. Any hotel travel desk or local travel agency can arrange this. The cost varies according to the type of car.

MOTORING ADVISORIES

Taiwan's roads are well maintained and give convenient access to all of Taiwan's scenic treasures. It's the drivers that are the problem. But with a bit of luck you should have no problems on the road if you bear in mind the following points:
• There are millions of motor scooters on the roads, and they constitute the single greatest hazard to car drivers.
• Steer clear of all military vehicles,

whose drivers are notorious for their careless driving. Regardless of circumstances, military vehicles always have the right of way, and they know it.
• Though roads down south are well marked, the instructions are often in Chinese, so look for route numbers instead of place names, and match them with those on your maps. Route numbers are also inscribed on the stone mileage indicators set along the roadsides.
• Stop and ask directions when in doubt. The further south you drive, the friendlier the people become,

Taxis

Taiwan is full of taxis. Stand on the kerb and wave your arm and within moments a taxi will glide to a halt and the door will automatically swing open.

All fares are calculated according to the meter. Drivers are allowed to charge for waiting time in traffic. If you wish to retain a taxi for a full day, or for a long, round-trip excursion, ask a hotel clerk to negotiate a set fee for the whole day or discount on the meter fare.

Taiwan taxi meters calculate both time and distance. From 11pm–6am, there is an additional 20 percent charge.

Small towns and villages have fixed rates. It is best to ask locals for the correct rate; even Taiwanese travellers have to do this if they don't want to be over-charged.

Note: Although Taiwan's taxi drivers are almost uniformly friendly and polite, they tend to drive like maniacs, weaving carelessly between buses and trucks, narrowly missing pedestrians, and screeching blindly around corners. This sort of driving is the rule rather than the exception in Taiwan. Should you get a particularly reckless driver; tell him to pull over immediately, pay the fare on the meter (with no tip), and hail another cab. There is never a shortage.

and someone is always there to help. Don't attempt to pronounce place names in the countryside, because often people there don't understand Mandarin, at least not when it is spoken by foreigners. Show them the Chinese characters.
• Always keep your tank at least a third full. In the more remote mountainous and coastal regions, petrol stations are few and far between, and often closed at night.

Travel in Taipei

RAPID TRANSIT SYSTEM

Construction of Taipei's Mass Rapid Transit System began in 1988. First finished was the Mucha–Sungshan Airport Line. It is one of six lines scheduled for Taipei, totalling 88 km (55 miles).

BUSES

One of the first things you'll notice in Taipei is the incredible number of public buses, which provide frequent and inexpensive means of transport to any point within or outside the city limits. However, it is advisable to avoid buses during heavy rush hours, which are between 7.30–9.30am and 5–7pm. There are two types of city buses: regular and air-conditioned, the latter costing slightly more. Tickets and tokens should be purchased in advance at the little kiosks at or close to all bus-stops.

City bus services run continously from about 6am–11.30pm. To signal the driver to stop, pull the bell cord. There are so many buses and bus routes within metropolitan Taipei that it is best to ask a hotel clerk or local aquaintance for directions. Some bus stops in Taipei have a computer-information machine, indicating in English which buses to take to your destination.

All buses are designated by code numbers, which indicate their routes and final destinations. Once you know the numbers, it is quite easy to get around.

Where to Stay

Hotels

Luxury Chinese hotels are renowned for attentive, gracious service, where visitors are treated as personal guests rather than anonymous patrons. However, Western travellers occasionally encounter frustrations. One reason is the ever-present language barrier: though uniformly trained in English, most Chinese hotel staff understand very little. Yet they'll avoid losing face by pretending to understand when they don't. Another reason is cultural: Chinese priorities often differ from a Westerner's, and what seems of vital importance to you, such as punctuality, may seem trivial to the Chinese.

Tourist hotels in Taiwan are ranked in two categories: International Tourist and Regular Tourist. The former offers greater luxury and more varied facilities, while the latter offers lower rates and simpler services.

Hotels in Taipei are extremely expensive. Single or twin rooms will cost from NT$4,000–9,000. In Kaohsiung, the cost per room is from NT$2,500–5,000. In other places, expect to pay between NT$1,000–4,000 per night.

TAIPEI (TEL CODE 02)

INTERNATIONAL CLASS
The Ambassador
63 Chungshan N. Road
Sec.
Tel: 2551-1111
Fax: 2561-7883
500 rooms; indoor swimming pool, golfing, banquet and convention facilities, roof-top bar lounge with

superb views, convenient access to shops, cocktail lounge.
Asiaworld Plaza Hotel
100 Tunhua N. Road
Tel: 2715-0077
Fax: 2713-4148
1057 rooms; 27 bars and restaurants, cinemas, theatre restaurant, fitness centre, underground parking, convention facilities, shopping mall with 500 boutiques.
Brother Hotel
255 Nanking E. Road
Sec. 3
Tel: 2712-3456
Fax: 2717-3344
268 rooms; excellent Cantonese dim-sum restaurant, roof-top lounge, well-maintained rooms.
Far Eastern Plaza Hotel Taipei
201 Tunhua S. Road
Sec. 2
Tel: 2378-8888
Fax: 2377-7777
422 rooms; two health clubs and swimming pools, shopping mall with 130 shops adjacent to the hotel.
Grand Formosa Regent Taipei
41 Chungshan N. Road
Sec. 2
Tel: 2523-8000
Fax: 2523-2828
546 rooms; 10 different restaurants, health spa and fitness centre, roof-top swimming pool.
Hilton International Taipei
38 Chunghsiao W. Road
Sec. 1
Tel: 2311-5151
Fax: 2331-9944
385 rooms; polished, professional service, award-winning restaurants; lively disco; sauna, roof garden, jacuzzi pools.
The Grand Hotel
1 Chungshan N. Road
Sec. 4
Tel: 2596-5565
Fax: 2594-8243
530 rooms. One of Taipei's architectural landmarks, with facilities including pool, health club and tennis courts.
Grand Hyatt Taipei
2 Sunghsou Road
Tel: 2720-1234
Fax: 2720-1111
872 rooms; next to the convention

centre, good parking, fitness centre with outdoor pool.
Howard Plaza Hotel
160 Jenai Road
Sec. 3
Tel: 2700-2323
Fax: 2700-0729
606 rooms; elegant decor, outdoor swimming pool, health centre, sauna, shopping mall.
Lai-Lai Sheraton
12 Chunghsiao E. Road
Sec. 1
Tel: 2321-5511
Fax: 2394-4240
703 rooms; facilities include disco, health-club, and several restaurants.
President Hotel
9 Tenhwei Street
Tel: 2595-1251
Fax: 2591-3677
421 rooms; popular among businessmen; access to nightlife area and highway.
The Ritz Taipei
155 Minchuan E. Road
Tel: 2597-1234
Fax: 2596-9222
200 rooms; small hotel with personalised service, good European food.
Hotel Royal Taipei
37-1 Chungshan N. Road
Sec. 2
Tel: 2542-3266
Fax: 2543-4897
203 rooms; sauna, health club, swimming pool, shopping arcade, in heart of the old business centre.
The Sherwood Taipei
111 Minsheng E. Road
Sec. 3
Tel: 2718-1188
Fax: 2713-0707
350 rooms; best hotel in Taiwan, health centre with indoor pool and jacuzzi, fitness centre and sauna, late check-out until 3pm, four restaurants and a bar, next to modern business and banking centre.

STANDARD CLASS
Fortuna Hotel
122 Chungshan N. Road
Sec. 2
Tel: 2563-1111
Fax: 2561-9777
302 rooms. In the heart of the

business district; health club, three restaurants.
Gloria
369 Linshen N. Road
Tel: 581-8111
Fax: 581-5811
250 rooms. Health club, business centre, free local calls. Good location in the centre of Taipei city.
Golden China Hotel
306 Sungchiang Road
Tel: 2521-5151
Fax: 2531-2914
250 rooms. In-hotel travel service, convenient for main railway station.
Imperial Inter-Continental Hotel
600 Linshen N. Road
Tel: 2596-5111
Fax: 2592-7506
224 rooms. Located in the busy "SoHo" area, facilities include five restaurants, fitness centre and business centre.
Taipei Miramar
420 Minchuan E. Road
Tel: 2505-3456
Fax: 2502-9173
584 rooms. Located close to the Martyrs' Shrine, with early check-in and three restaurants.
Rebar Holiday Inn Crown Plaza
32 Nanking E. Road
Sec. 5
Tel: 2763-5656
Fax: 2767-9347
300 rooms. Well-equipped hotel located downtown in the business and financial area.
Riverview
32 Nanking E. Road
Sec. 5
Tel: 2311-3131
Fax: 2361-3737
201 rooms. Situated on the Tan Shui river.

KAOHSIUNG (TEL CODE 07)

INTERNATIONAL CLASS
Ambassador Hotel
202 Minsheng 2nd Road
Tel: 211-5211
Fax: 281-1115, 281-1113
457 rooms. On the river in the central business district. Pool, health club, business centre.
Grand Hi-Lai Hotel
266 Chengkung 1st Road

Tel: 216-1766
Fax: 216-1966
450 rooms. Large hotel with many restaurants, executive club and shopping complex.
Grand Hotel
2 Yuanshan Road
Cheng-Ching Lake
Tel: 383-5911
Fax: 381-4889
108 rooms. Outside the business district; golf and tennis facilties, pool, fitness centre.
Hotel Holiday Garden
279 Liu Ho 2nd Road
Tel: 241-0123
Fax: 251-2000.
Recently renovated award-winning hotel with facilities including pool, spa, jacuzzi and nightclub.
Kingdom Hotel
32 Wufu 4th Road
Tel: 551-8211
Fax: 521-0403
312 rooms. Convenient for the harbour, breakfast buffet.
Linden Hotel Kaohsiung
33 Szuwei 3rd Road
Tel: 332-2000
Fax: 336-1600
400 rooms. Large hotel next to City Hall serving business and leisure travellers. Pool, health club, business centre with internet access.

STANDARD CLASS
Buckingham Hotel
394 Chihsien 2nd Road
Tel: 282-2151
Fax: 281-4540
200 rooms. Facilities include a dance club and karaoke pub.

ALISHAN (TEL CODE 05)

STANDARD CLASS
Alishan House
2 West Alishan
Shanglin Village
Wufeng Hsiang
Chiayi
Tel: 267-9811
Fax: 267-9596
60 rooms. Small hotel with elegant decor and gardens, perched high on the mountain.

HUALIEN (TEL CODE 038)

INTERNATIONAL CLASS
Chinatrust Hualien Hotel
2 Yungsing Road
Tel: 221-171
Fax: 221-185
221 rooms. Pool, fitness centre and in-house travel service.
Marshal Hotel
36 Kungyuan Road
Tel: 326-123
Fax: 326-140
303 rooms. Popular hotel with sea views.
Parkview Hotel
1-1 Lingyuan Road
Tel: 222-111
Fax: 226-999
343 rooms. Near the golf club and Taroko Gorge. Pool, tennis courts, health club.

KENTING (TEL CODE 08)

INTERNATIONAL CLASS
Caesar Park Hotel
6 Kenting Road
Hengchun Town
Pingtung Hsien
Tel: 886-1888
Fax: 886-1818
237 rooms. Resort hotel fronting Kenting's best beach. Tennis courts, golf, pool, games hall. Shuttle service to/from Kaohsiung.
Kenting Hotel
101 Park Road
Hengchun Town
Pingtung Hsien
Tel: 886-1370
Fax: 886-1377
250 rooms. Convenient for beaches and the area's best nightlife.

SUN MOON LAKE (TEL CODE 049)

INTERNATIONAL CLASS
Chinatrust Sun Moon Lake Hotel
23 Chungcheng Road
Nantou
Tel: 855-911
Fax: 855-268
116 rooms. Resort hotel with lakeview restaurant and private observatory. Shuttle service.

TAICHUNG (TEL CODE 04)

INTERNATIONAL CLASS
Evergreen Laurel Hotel
6 Taichung Kang Road
Sec. 2
Tel: 328-9988
Fax: 328-8642
254 rooms. Centrally located near Natural Science Museum. Excellent restaurants. Facilities include pool, squash courts, free local calls.
Landis Taichung Hotel
9 Taichung Kang Road
Sec. 2
Tel: 326-8008
Fax: 326-8060
200 rooms. Personalised service, complimentary city shuttle, four restaurants, health club, high-tech business centre.
National Hotel
257 Taichung Kang Rd
Sec. 1
Tel: 321-3111
Fax: 321-3124
404 rooms. Personalised service in garden setting. Pool, golf.
Plaza International Hotel
431 Taya Rd
Tel: 295-6789
Fax: 293-0099
305 rooms. Centrally located, with rooftop pool and gardens.

STANDARD CLASS
Marshal Hotel
58 Kuang Fu Rd
Tel: 226-7589
Fax: 226-2709
Soundproofed hotel in city centre near dance clubs, theatre and other nightlife.

TAINAN (TEL CODE 06)

INTERNATIONAL CLASS
Tainan Hotel
1 Chengkung Rd
Tel: 228-9101
Fax: 226-8502
152 rooms. Tastefully decorated with pool, business centre and limousine service.

STANDARD CLASS
Premier Hotel
128 Gong Yuen Rd
Tel: 225-2141
Recently renovated hotel in a central location. Complimentary breakfast buffet.

Youth Hostels

If you're willing to sleep in dormitories, eat in cafeterias, and travel exclusively by bus, then you can actually tour Taiwan for as little as US$100 per day by utilising facilities operated by the **China Youth Corps** (CYC). CYC operates a series of Youth Activity Centres and Youth Hostels around the island, and budget-minded travellers may use these facilities. Information and reservations for the hostels and activity centres can be arranged by writing or calling CYC headquarters at 219 Sungkiang Rd, Taipei, tel: (02) 2502-5858; fax: (02) 2501-1312. For an updated address list, contact the **ROC Tourism Bureau** offices overseas or the **Domestic Tourism Bureau** in Taiwan.

Due to the popularity of these facilities, those who wish to use them should make reservations well in advance. They are usually fully-booked from July to September, and January to February. If you have not made prior arrangements, then at least be sure to call ahead to your next intended stop to make sure that accommodation is available.

Rates for room and board vary at different centres, but on average three meals a day can be had for about NT$250 (1999 prices). The average price per night is NT$1,000 to 1,500. Most establishments also have private rooms at higher rates, and some have large bungalows for small groups.

Guesthouses

There are a number of guesthouses in the Taipei area whichprovide inexpensive accommodation. Weekly and monthly rates may be arranged as well. Ask the **Domestic Tourism Bureau** service centres for addresses and details.

What to Eat

Dining out remains the single greatest pleasure Taiwan holds for the traveller. Whether you opt for Chinese or Western cuisine, Japanese sushi or Korean barbecue, the restaurants of Taiwan have something tasty for every palate. Naturally, when in Taiwan, it's best to go for gourmet Chinese cuisine. But if you prefer Western food, there are plenty of places which will serve

Food for Thought

The best places to try the perfect Chinese cuisine are the hotel restaurants in Taipei and Kaohsiung. The Taipei Chinese Food Festival, held in August every year, demonstrates the skills of the hotels' master chefs. The second-best suggestion, at least for lunch, is to visit one of the many restaurants on the underground floors of the main department stores. Everything is freshly-cooked and the prices are quite low. If you see one place with no customers waiting, it may be better to go to another, where you have to queue.

Remember that Chinese restaurants cater to groups, never individuals. Four people at a table should be the minimum. And don't expect the food to be cheap.

Don't be afraid to experiment, either: it isn't easy when there's a language barrier, but most foreigners tend to end up with something safe like rice-and-chicken – which is one of the reasons why some gourmet Chinese restaurants don't take Western tourists seriously.

you a good meal with proper service. Be careful, though, because many of the so-called Western restaurants serve fare that looks and tastes like a careless melange of East and West.

When travelling down south, it's generally best to stick with Chinese food, as demand for Western cuisineis not yet sufficiently strong to support genuinely good Western restaurants.

TYPES OF CUISINE

Northern Style (Beijing, Mongolia). Recommended dishes: Beijing Duck, Lamb and Leek, Hot and Sour Soup, Celery in Mustard Sauce, Cold Shredded Chicken with Sauce, Sweet and Sour Yellow Fish, Steamed Vegetable Dumplings.
Southern Style (Cantonese). Recommended dishes: Roast Duck, Poached Chicken with Onions and Oil, Greens with Oyster Sauce, Steamed Whole Fish, Assorted *dim-sum*, Roast Pigeon, Cabbage with Cream.
Eastern/Coastal Style (Shanghai). Recommended dishes: West Lake Vinegar Fish, River Eel Sautéed with Leek, Braised Pork Haunch, Sautéed Sweet-Pea Shoots, Drunken Chicken, "Lionhead" meatballs, Braised Beef Loin.
Western/Central Style (Hunan, Szechuan). Recommended dishes: (Szechuan) Steamed Pomfret, Chicken "Duke of Bao", "Grandma's" Beancurd, Fragrant Egg-Sauce, Duck Smoked in Camphor and Tea, Twice-cooked Pork. (Hunan) Frog Legs in Chilli Sauce, Honey Ham, Beggar's Chicken, Minced Pigeon in Bamboo Cup, Steamed Whole Fish.
Taiwanese Food. Recommended dishes: Steamed Crab, Poached Squid, Fresh Poached Shrimp, Shrimp Rolls, Grilled Eel, Sashimi or raw fish, Grilled Clams, Turtle Soup.
Chinese Vegetarian Cuisine. Recommended Dishes: Try the various types of "beef", "pork" and "chicken" made entirely from various forms of soybean curd and/or different types of

mushrooms, as well as fresh and crispy vegetables.

CHOPSTICKS

The Chinese have been using two sticks to pick up a single grain of rice and one stick to carry two buckets of water since time began. Nothing ever appears on the Chinese banquet table that cannot be manipulated single-handedly with a simple pair of chopsticks. Today, as the popularity of Chinese cuisine spreads throughout the world, it is considered *de rigueur* to use chopsticks when eating Chinese food. And in Taiwan you'll find abundant opportunities to practise.

The Chinese only use forks and knives in the kitchen – and when eating Western food. Otherwise, they prefer to have everything prepared in the kitchen, so that the food is served in bite-sized pieces. Those who wield their chopsticks too slowly often miss the choicest morsels whenever a new dish appears on the table. However, for reasons of hygiene, some restaurants now serve so-called set menus with portions of everything on individual plates.

Chopsticks can also be used to select choice morsels from the best dishes for the guest-of-honour or just for a friend at the table. The polite way to do this is to turn the sticks around so that you use the clean blunt ends to serve food to others.

Last but not least, using chopsticks makes you a little more Chinese and a little less foreign in Chinese eyes, and this always improves the pleasure of travelling in Taiwan.

Culture

ART GALLERIES

These galleries exhibit works of art by established old masters and promising young artists. They display an impressive range of styles, from traditional Chinese landscape painting and calligraphy to contemporary Western abstracts and still-lifes. For further information contact:

Taipei Art Guild
8F, 218-2 Chunghsiao E. Road
Sec. 4
Tel: (02) 2773-6673.
Apollo Art Gallery
2F Apollo Bldg
218-6 Chunghsiao E. Road
Sec. 4
Tel: (02) 2781-9332.
Asia Art Centre
117 Chienkuo S. Road
Sec. 2
Tel: (02) 2754-1366.
Cave Gallery
B1, 138 Chunghsiao E. Road
Sec. 1
Tel: (02) 2396-1864.
Crown Centre
50 Lane 120, Tunhua N. Road
Tel: (02) 2717-1398.
East West Art Gallery
5/F, Rm 501
63 Chungching S. Road
Sec. 1
Tel: (02) 2314-8603.
Hsiung Shih Gallery
5/F, 16, Alley 33
Lane 216
Chunghsiao E. Road
Sec. 4
Tel: (02) 2772-1158.
Kander Arts and Antiquities Gallery
64 Chungching S. Road
Sec. 1
Tel: 2314-3210.
Lung-Men Art Gallery

3/F, 218-1 Chunghsiao E. Road
Sec. 4
Tel: (02) 2751-3170.
Ming Sheng Art Gallery
145 Chungshan N. Road
Sec. 1
Tel: (02) 2581-0858.
Taipei Fine Arts Museum
1818 Chungshan N. Road
Sec. 3
Tel: (02) 2595-7656.

CHINESE OPERA

Taiwan is one of the best places in the world to attend Chinese-style opera. From the bizarre melodies mouthed by magnificently-costumed performers to the exotic orchestral accompaniment, the astounding acrobatics and the martial arts displays of the performers, a night at the opera will prove entertaining and educational.

There is one place in Taipei where Beijing opera is performed regularly: **National Fu Hsing Dramatic Arts Academy,** 177 Neihu Rd, Sec. 2, tel: (02) 2796-2666.

For a taste of Beijing or Taiwan opera, try the television set – live performances are broadcast almost every day. In the back alleys of Taipei and outside the big city, keep your eyes open for the travelling opera companies that set up and perform for several days.

DANCE

There is a limited amount of traditional folk dancing in Taiwan, most performed by minority groups. Snippets of ethnic dances can be seen at the various tourism centres around the island.

The **Cloud Gate Dance Ensemble,** led by Lin Hwaimin, has spearheaded the movement. It combines both Chinese and Western techniques and ideas, choreographed to the music of contemporary Chinese performers. The group, internationally-acclaimed during world tours, holds regular performances in Taipei. Consult your hotel for the schedules of the Cloud Gate ensemble.

Handicrafts

The Taiwanese take great pride in things they can make with their hands: from lanterns and toys, handbags and baskets, bamboo and rattan crafts, rug and carpets, to knitwear and embroidery.

The **Handicraft Exhibition Hall** (daily, 9am–noon and 2–5pm except Mon and public holidays) displays a range of high quality items – more than 1,500, from all parts of Taiwan – some produced by cottage industry, others by factories. The hall is in Tsaotun, on the highway from Taichung to the Sun Moon Lake and the Hsitou Bamboo Forest.

While in Tsaotun, also call at the **Taiwan Provincial Handicraft Institute,** where there is a factory, kiln and research laboratory. In Taipei, a good place to do souvenir and gift shopping is at the **Chinese Handicraft Mart,** 1 Hsu Chou Street, tel: (02) 2321-7233.

MUSIC

Taiwan has produced numerous world-class musicians. Western music is regularly performed at various venues in Taipei by the **Taiwan Provincial Symphony Orchestra** and the **Taipei Municipal Symphony Orchestra.** Consult your hotel or information desk, or such organisations as the National Music Council and the Chinese Classical Music Association for information on scheduled performances. Traditional Chinese music has its roots in both special temple rituals and folk music.

Festivals and holidays

National holidays, which are of fairly recent origin, follow the Western calendar, but most festive dates still follow the lunar calendar and thus vary from year to year. Local festivals are known as *paipai* and are colourful celebrations held in honour of local city gods and deities.

January
Foundation Day: On 1 January 1912, Dr Sun Yatsen was inaugurated as the first President of the newly-founded Republic of China, and China officially switched from the lunar to the Gregorian calender. This occasion is celebrated annually in Taipei with parades, dragon and lion dances, traditional music, patriotic speeches, and, of course, lots of firecrackers.

Lunar New Year: Traditionally called the Spring Festival, the Lunar New Year remains the biggest celebration of the year. It is observed in various stages for a full month, from the 16th day of the 12th month, but offices and shops generally close for only a week around New Year's Day.

Many ancient customs are associated with the Lunar New Year: all outstanding debts must be paid off before New Year's Eve; failure to do so is a grave affront and an omen of bad luck for the coming year. Many Chinese businessmen keep running accounts in their favourite restaurants and clubs, paying their bills only once a year, just before New Year's Eve. Another custom is exchanging gifts, especially little red envelopes (hung-bao) stuffed with "lucky money". Everyone dresses up in new clothes at New Year – from hats down to shoes – which symbolises renewal and a fresh start for the coming year. People visit family and friends and spend a lot of money on entertainment. Local banks are often plagued with cash shortages. The dominant colour is red, which is universally regarded as auspicious among the Chinese; red flowers, red clothing, red streamers, red cakes and candies, as well as the ubiquitous red envelopes.

At the stroke of midnight on New Year's Eve, the entire island reverberates to the explosions of millions of firecrackers and rockets, as every temple and household in Taiwan lights the fuses which will frighten away evil spirits, ensuring an auspicious start to the New Year. The Chinese invented gunpowder for this purpose over

1,000 years ago, long before the West ever knew of it, and the fusilladesmake America's Fourth of July celebrations seem tame by comparison.

The stock phrase to offer your friends and acquaintances is kung-hsi-fa-tsai (pronounced goong-shee-fah-tsai), which means "I wish you happiness and prosperity".

February
The Lantern Festival: This festival, which falls on the first full moon of the Lunar New Year, marks the end of the Spring Festival. Celebrants appear at night in the streets, parks and temples of Taiwan carrying colourful lanterns with auspicious phrases inscribed on them. This is supposed to ensure against evil and illness in the coming year. The festival food is a sweet dumpling of glutinous rice-paste stuffed with bean or date paste and called yuan-hsiao. Major temples are excellent places to observe the Lantern Festival in full colour and pageantry. Prizes are awarded for the most beautiful and original lanterns.

March
Birthday of Kuanyin, Goddess of Mercy: Kuanyin is one of the most popular Buddhist deities in Taiwan, Korea and Japan. Known for her compassion and love for people, she is one of Taiwan's patron protective deities. Her birthday is celebrated with colorful paipai ceremonies in major temples.

April
Youth Day: Originally called Revolutionary Martyrs' Day, this commemorates the deaths of 72 young revolutionaries in China in 1911.

Tomb-Sweeping Day: Traditionally calculated as the 105th day after the Winter Solstice and called the Chingming (Clear and Bright) Festival, this isnow celebrated annually on 5 April, which coincides with the date of President Chiang Kaishek's death in 1975, making this both a traditional Chinese festival and a contemporary national holiday.

During this festival, entire families go out to their ancestral burial grounds to sweep accumulated dirt and debris from the tombs, place fresh flowers around the graves, and perhaps plant some new trees, flowers and bushes in the area.

Buddha's Bathing Festival: This day commemorates the birth of Sakyamuni (the historical Buddha) 2,500 years ago. The festival is marked in temples throughout the island with cleansing-of-Buddha ceremonies, during which all statues of Buddha are ritually washed while monks recite appropriate sutras. Many of the icons are then paraded through the streets to the beat of gongs and drums.

Birthday of Matsu, Goddess of the Sea: One of the biggest paipai of the year in Taiwan, this festival is dedicated to Matsu, Goddess of the Sea, patron saint of Taiwan, and guardian deity of the island's fishermen. It is celebrated with great fanfare in over 300 temples where Matsu is enshrined. The biggest festival takes place in central Taiwan, at the Peikang Temple near Chiayi. But you can also see it at the famous Lungshan (Dragon Mountain) Temple in Taipei. Sacrificial offerings of roast pig and boiled chickens, billows of smoke from incense and burning paper "money", undulating lion and dragon dances, colourful parades, and lavish feasting are some of the festivities dedicated to Matsu.

May
Dragon Boat Festival: One of China's most ancient festivals, this event commemorates the death of Chu-Yuan, an accomplished poet and upright minister who plunged to his death in a river about 2,500 years ago to protest against the corruption and misrule of his king, who had banished him from the court. According to the legend, upon hearing of his tragic death, the local people rowed their boats out on the river and dropped stuffed rice dumplings tightly wrapped in bamboo leaves into the water to

nourish his spirit, or distract animals from eating him. These dumplings, called *dzung-dze*, remain this festival's major food item.

The festival is celebrated with colourful dragon-boat races, which have become a major sporting event. Teams from all over the island, including several "foreigner teams" from the expatriate community, and from Singapore, compete for top honours in various divisions. The bows of the boats are carved into elaborate dragon-heads, and the crews row vigorously to the resounding beat of big drums placed at the back of each boat.

June
Birthday of Chenghuang, the City God: This *paipai* festival is celebrated with great pomp and ceremony at Taipei's city-god temple at 61 Tihua St, Sec. 1. The worship of city gods is a practice that has been recorded in China as far back as the early Xia dynasty (2200 BC). They are said to have the power to protect a city's inhabitants from both natural disasters and enemy intruders, and they also advise the Lord of Heaven and the King of Hell regarding appropriate rewards and punishments for the city's residents after death. No wonder the Chinese pay them such lavish homage.

Among the colourful and highly photogenic festivities are parades with icons of the City God held high upon pedestals, offerings of whole pigs and cows stretched on bamboo racks, processions of celebrants wearing stilts and colourful costumes, lion and dragon dances and lavish feasts.

July
Chinese Valentine's Day: Chinese Valentine's Day is derived from the legend of the herd boy (a star formation in the constellation Aquila, west of the Milky Way) and the spinning girl (the star Vega in the constellation Lyra, east of the Milky Way). They appear closest together on this night, and all the magpies on earth are said to ascend to the sky to form a bridge across the Milky Way so that the lovers may cross over for their brief once-a-year tryst. This is a festival for unmarried girls and for young lovers, who observe the occasion by exchanging gifts, strolling in moonlit parks, and praying for future matrimonial bliss.

August
Ghost Festival: The Chinese believe that on the first day of the 7th lunar month, the gates of hell swing open, permitting the ghosts of the dead to visit their earthly homes. In order to placate the spirits and discourage mischief, trays of food are set out before each house as offerings, and Buddhist priests are invited to bless these offerings and supplicate the spirits with prayer. Incense is burned and bundles of paper "clothing" and "money" are set alight for use by the spirits in the other world. These offerings are also meant to prevent the ghosts of criminals and spirits with no living relatives from entering one's home. Rites are held daily in Buddhist temples during the festival, which formally ends on the last day of the 7th month, when the spirits return to their underworld abode.

September
Confucius' Birthday: An official national holiday, celebrated as Teachers' Day, which commemorates the birth of the sage Confucius in 551 BC. Known as China's greatest teacher, Confucius continues to exert profound influence on culture and society in Taiwan. Elaborate traditional ceremonies are held every year on this day, at 6am at Taipei's Confucius Temple, complete with ancient musical instruments, formal court attire, ritual dances, and other Confucian rites.

Tickets to attend this ceremony must be arranged in advance through local tourism authorities.

October
Mid-Autumn Moon Festival: The Chinese celebrate the annual appearance of the harvest moon by going en masse to parks, hillsides, riverbanks and seashores to gaze at "The Lady in the Moon", nibble tasty snacks, and drink wine. According to the Chinese legend, Chang-Er, beautiful wife of the Tang emperor Ming-Huang, one day discovered a vial of the Elixir of Immortality specially prepared for her husband and decided to take a sip. But he caught her in the act, and in order to conceal the evidence, she swallowed the entire potion. It took instant effect and she immediately flew up from earth and landed on the moon. She's been there ever since, and on this night her beauty radiates at its best.

The festival is celebrated by exchanging gifts of moon cakes – large, round pastries stuffed with fruits and chopped nuts. Exchanging moon cakes also has patriotic overtones, because during the successful overthrow of the Mongol Yuan dynasty by the Chinese Ming, secret plans for the insurrection were concealed in the cakes and distributed to patriots throughout the empire.

Double-Ten National Day: "Double-Ten" refers to the 10th day of the 10th month, and commemorates the overthrow of the Manchu Qing dynasty, China's last, by revolutionaries on 10 October 1911. It is by far the most important national holiday, and is celebrated with massive military parades, aerial acrobatics by the air force's Thunder Tigers, commando-landing demonstrations, patriotic speeches, and displays of folk dancing, sword-fighting and martial arts. Most of the action takes place in the plaza in front of Taipei's Presidential Building.

Hotels and restaurants in Taipei remain packed throughout the week prior to Double-Ten day, as tens of thousands of Chinese from all over the world pour into town for the festivities. Tourists who visit Taiwan at this time should make early reservations for hotels and airlines.

Restoration Day: This national holiday celebrates the return of Taiwan to Chinese rule after the

defeat of Japan in 1945, thereby ending 55 years of Japanese occupation. It is marked with several major athletic events, including regional competitions in soccer and basketball for the Presidential Cup awards. Other festivities include lion and dragon dances and feasting at Taipei's many restaurants and hotels.
Birthday of Chiang Kaishek: A national holiday celebrated in Taiwan to commemorate the birth of the late President Chiang Kaishek, on 31 October 1887.

November
Birthday of Dr Sun Yatsen: Sun Yatsen, founder and first president of the Republic of China, is regarded as the George Washington of China by Chinese throughout the world, including the Communist mainland. This holiday celebrates his birth on 12 November 1866 and is marked with solemn patriotic ceremonies and speeches.

December
Constitution Day: This is an official national holiday which marks the day in 1947 on which the constitution of the Republic of China became effective, 25 December.

KOREA

Getting Acquainted

The Place

Occupying the southern section of the Korean peninsula, South Korea has an area of 98,500 sq. km. The country is bordered on the north by North Korea, on the east by the Yellow Sea (Bo Hai) and to the west and south by the Japan Sea, known to Koreans as the East Sea.

Local Time

Korean time is GMT +9 hours.

Climate

Korea's location in the mid-latitudes and East Asian Monsoon Belt means four distinct seasons. A spring thaw comes in mid-April and lasts little more than two months. In early spring northwesterly gusts bring swirls of dust from the Gobi Desert and a light rain. As summer approaches, humid southerlies vie for control and the spring drizzle becomes an occasional downpour.

July and August are the hottest, most humid months, especially in the inland basin around Taegu, where afternoon temperatures climb into the lower 30°s centigrade (around 90°F). Temperatures in Seoul are around 28°C (82°F). Autumn arrives in early October when the air currents shift back to the crisp northerlies. This climatic ideal intensifies by the end of November when the Siberian freeze whips down the peninsula in a cycle of three consecutive cold days followed by four milder days.

The northern inland region of North Korea has a mean winter

temperature of minus 20°C or minus 4°F. South Korea is milder, but still cold; Seoul's January mean is minus 5°C (23°F), while in the far south, Cheju-do's temperature mean for January is 4°C or 39°F.

The favourable months in Korea are April (10°C or 50°F in Seoul), May (16°C or 60°F), June and September just before and after the summer rains (19°C or 66°F) and October (12°C or 54°F). You may call 735-0365 in Korea for weather forecasts.

Korean Names

Korean surnames, most of which are a single syllable, are as easy to learn as they are to forget. The problem is that many Koreans share the same romanized surname (although some of the Chinese characters may be written differently). Referring to someone by his surname can only become confusing and futile after meeting many Koreans. To compound the problem, Korean wives retain their maiden names. Thus, it is best to learn the entire Korean name.

Korean surnames were derived from the Chinese during the early Three Kingdoms period. The most common surnames are Kim, Yi (Lee I, Rhee), and Pak (Park), followed by Choi, Chung, and Cho. Throughout the ages, surnames have dictated one's social position, a tradition still honoured only in reclusive villages. Whether *yangban* (aristocrat) or *pyongmin* (commoner), however, one's name was recorded in a family tree book, *chokbo*, which traced one's lineage back to the origin of the clan.

Planning the Trip

What To Wear

Influenced by climate and occasion, clothing in Korea follows function rather than style. Business suits are the proper mode, even in the summer, for metropolitan business activities. Otherwise, dress is casual. Mini-skirts and shorts are acceptable, although foreigners are advised to dress more conservatively. An umbrella, sunglasses, and rainy day footwear are practical accessories to pack.

Entry Regulations

Visas & Passports

Visitors to Korea must present a valid passport or travel document, and may stay for up to 15 days without a visa if they have confirmed out-bound tickets. Most European, and many Asian and South American countries have agreements that permit citizens to stay for longer without a visa. Canadian citizens can stay for 6 months. Note that any traveller holding a US, Canadian or Japanese visa is granted a 15-day, visa-free stopover, and Chinese group tours and nationals from CIS nations, Russia and Albania may enter Chejudo without a visa. For more information, consult your local Korean embassy before making travel plans.

Customs

You may bring in 200 cigarettes, (50 cigars or 250 grams of tobacco), one bottle (not over 1 litre) of liquor and two fluid ounces of perfume. Items for personal use (except certain exclusive goods such as vehicles, guns and musical instruments) may be brought in duty free, but visitors must leave with these items.

Korean antiques pre-dating 1910 should be checked and appraised by the Arts and Antiques Assessment Office and a permit should be secured. For five or fewer antiques, checking may be done at its Kimp'o Airport office (Tel: 02 662-0106). A limit of three kilograms of red ginseng with a sales receipt is acceptable.

There is a W9,000 international airport tax; domestic passengers pay W3,000.

Health

Except for those whose itineraries include cholera-infected areas, no certificate of vaccination is required.

Electricity

Outlets for both 110 and 220 volts are available, although most new hotels carry 220 volt outlets as standard.

Money Matters

The won comes in 1,000, 5,000 and 10,000 denomination notes and 10, 50, 100, and 500 won coins. Bank drafts for large amounts (normally drafts of W100,000) are available.

Changing Money

Procuring won outside Korea is virtually impossible. In the country, however, there are foreign exchange counters at the airport, major tourist hotels (which charge a few won per exchanged bill or travellers' cheque), major banks (some with branches in large hotels) and a few major department stores (such as Midopa and Lotte) in Seoul. The most viable currencies to carry in Korea are Japanese yen and US dollars, although other major foreign currencies can also be exchanged. Remember to retain all exchange receipts for reconversion on departure.

Credit Cards

American Express, Visa, JCB, MasterCard, and Diners Club cards are readily accepted in major hotels, department stores and restaurants as well as many tourist-oriented shops. There are 888 Automated Teller Machines (ATMs) sited at hotels, department stores and tourist attractions across the country which display instructions in English and dispense cash advances.

Getting There

BY AIR

Kimp'o International Airport, 24 km (15 miles) west of Seoul, is served from the United States by Korean Air, Japan Airlines, United Airlines, and Northwest Airlines among others. Carriers routed through Seoul include Cathay Pacific, China Airlines, Malaysian Airlines and Singapore Airlines. Kimp'o is due to become the domestic airport when the new international airport opens at Inchon in 2001.

Seoul can often be added as a stopover on northeast Asia air tickets at no extra cost. It is less than 13 hours from the US West Coast, 2½ hours from Tokyo, 3½ hours from Hong Kong, and 1½ hours from Beijing.

You can call Kimp'o Airport Information, (02) 660-2200.

Korea's second international airport is at Pusan, which runs a number of non-stop flights to major cities in Japan.

BY SEA

Ferries run from Pusan year-round between Shimonoseki and Hakata (Fukuoka) in Japan; and on most days of the week between Inch'on and the Chinese ports of Weihei, Qingdao and Tianjin (near Beijing).

Practical Tips

Emergencies

Police: 112
Fire: 119
Ambulance: 119
AEA International provides a 24-hour emergency service, acting as a link between patients and the Korean hospital for a fee. Tel: (02) 790-7561.

To recover lost possessions, including those left in taxis, contact the nearest police box or ask the hotel front desk clerk to help you do so. The Seoul Metropolitan Police Lost and Found Centre is at 102, Hong-ik-dong, Songdong. Tel: 299-1282; Fax: 298-1282.

Medical Services

Many kinds of medicines and health care goods – from bottled sweetened vitamin tonics to contraceptives – are available at local pharmacies.

Immunisations are administered at the International Clinic at Severance Hospital which uses disposable needles as a preventive measure, and at the Seoul Quarantine Office to the right of the USO compound in Kalwol-dong, Yongsan-gu.

Dentists and optometrists are generally reliable and their work is reasonably priced. Major hotels have house doctors.

Business Hours

Banks: Weekdays: 9.30am–4.30pm; Saturdays: 9.30am–1.30pm; Sunday & Public Holidays: Closed.
Embassies: Weekdays: 9am–5pm Saturdays, Sundays & Public Holidays: Closed.

Department Stores: All week and some public holidays: 10.30am–7.30pm.
Private Companies: Weekdays: 9am–6pm; Saturdays: 9am–1pm; Sundays & Public Holidays: Closed.
Government Offices: Weekdays March–October: 9am–6pm (5pm November–February) Saturdays: 9am–1pm; Sundays & Public Holidays: Closed.
Post Offices: Weekdays: 9am–6pm; Saturdays: 9am–1pm; Sundays & Public Holidays: Closed.
Private Companies tend to start earlier and close later.

Tipping

This western custom is expected only in businesses which cater primarily to westerners. A 10–15 percent service charge is automatically added to major hotel room and restaurant tabs (read the bill to make sure before tipping). Airport baggage porters are tipped generously at the exit door according to a set standard. Taxi drivers do not expect a tip unless they perform extra service. And unless requested, they may not return the change if it is small. Bellhops usually receive around W150 tip per bag.

Religious Services

There are numerous places of worship in Seoul catering to many different faiths. Details of service times are published in the Saturday edition of English language newspapers, and your hotel concierge will also be able to provide information.

Media

There are 10 national dailies, five economic dailies and three sports dailies, plus two English newspapers – *The Korea Herald* and *The Korea Times*, which carry international wire reports. *The Asian Wall Street Journal* and *Far Eastern Economic Review* are also circulated locally.

Weeklies, semi-weeklies, bi-weeklies, monthlies and bi-monthlies flood the bookstores. The most popular English language periodicals are the *Korea Economic Weekly* and the monthly *Korea Economic Report*. *Time* and *Newsweek* are prominently displayed in bookstores.

Major hotels carry satellite news services like BBC and CNN, as well as other channels like MTV and Star. AFKN broadcasts in English in Seoul on 1530 AM and 102.7 FM.

Post

The central post office is located on Chungmu Street across from the Chinese Embassy, a block east of Shinsegye Department Store. The Kwanghwamun post office branch is located near the corner of T'aep'yong-no and Chong-no. General post office hours are 9am to 6pm Monday to Saturday.

Aerograms cost W400 and postcards W350. A 10-gram airmail letter to Europe, North America or the Middle East is W480, and to southeast Asia, W450. Letters to the US and Europe take 5–7 days. You may make further enquiries at the Central Post Office (Tel: 752-0007), Kwanghwa-mun Post Office (Tel: 732-0007) or International Post Office (Tel: 777-0020).

Telephones

Using a public phone can be something of an endurance test in Korea. There are four different types: blue, grey, card phones and credit card phones. If you need to make a number of calls, stock up on small change and buy a phone card first.

Grey or blue phones can be used for both local (W50 for three minutes) or long distance calls (more, depending on the distance) but not international calls. Both phones take W10 and W100 coins, and grey will also accept W50 coins, but neither accepts W500 coins.

Phone cards (in denominations of W2,000, W3,000, W5,000 and W10,000) are sold at banks and convenience stores such as Lawsons and 7-Eleven. Card phones can be used for calls to anywhere in Korea or the rest of the world, as can credit card phones. International access codes are 001, 002 or 008, which should be followed by country code, area code and the number. International calls and collect calls can be made through the operator by dialling 007 99.

Other useful phone numbers:
Korea Directory Assistance
080 211-0114 (English speaking)
International Information 007 94
Tourist Information 1588-1717
Tourist Complaint Centre
(02) 735-0101
Exchange Rate Information
(02) 775-5550

INTERNET

Most hotel business centres can provide internet access, although it can be pricey. However the WWW has caught on in a big way here, and there are a number of Internet cafes such as Cyberia (Tel: (02) 3785-3860) in Itaewon around the corner from the Hamilton Hotel. Closer to the centre of town, the Net House (Tel: 725-4417) is at 1/F 111 Chunghak-dong, Chongno-gu, near the Kwanghwamun Gate and charges W2,000 for the first 30 minutes, and W1,000 for each additional half hour. Free internet access is available in the Tourist Information Centre (TIC) at the Korean National Tourism Organisation (KNTO) 10, Ta-dong, Chung-ku, Seoul. Tel: 02-729-9600; Fax: 757-5997.

Tourist Information

A wide range of tourist information and related services are readily available at the TIC of the KNTO, which has an information counter, reservation and ticketing desk, tourism exhibition hall, book and souvenir shop and a small theatre. It also has a comprehensive library. The TIC is open daily from 9am to 6pm.

There are also information counters at Kimp'o, Kimhae, and Cheju International Airports. They provide you with city maps, brochures and useful information on tours, shopping, dining and accommodation.
Seoul: Kim'po Airport
Terminal 1, Tel: (02) 665-0088/6
Terminal 2, Tel: (02) 665-0986.
Pusan: Kimhae Airport,
Tel: (051) 973-1100/2800.
Cheju: Cheju Airport,
Tel: (064) 42-0032.

Other information centres in Seoul are: (prefix 02)
Itaewon
Tel: 794-2490.
Myongdong
Tel: 757-0088.
Seoul Railway Station
Tel: 392-7811.
Seoul Express Bus Terminal
Tel: 537-9198.
Toksugung
Tel; 756-0045.

The KNTO also provides assistance in English, Chinese and Japanese by phone via any of the following numbers:
In Seoul: 757-0086.
Outside Seoul: 080-757-2000 (toll-free).
Nationwide: 1587-1717.
Guided Bus Tours: Seoul city tours and excursions outside the capital are conducted by numerous commercial tour guide agencies. Some agencies with English and Japanese speaking guides are:
Bosuk Tours, Tel; 595-2900.
Chung-ang Express, Tel: 266-3350.
Dongbu Express, Tel: 754-6044.
Global Tours Ltd, Tel: 776-3153.
Grace World Travel, Tel: 332-8946.
Hanjin Travel Service, Tel: 726-5540.
Kim's Travel, Tel: 323-3361.
Korea Travel Bureau, Tel: 778-0150.
Root Travel, Tel: 572-5367.
Seoul Travel Service, Tel: 753-8585.
Star Travel, Tel: 564-1232.
Two organisations which plan tours particularly for resident foreigners and which also welcome outsiders are:

Public Holidays

- **1–2 January** New Year's Day
- **Jan/Feb** Lunar New Year (Sollal)
- **1 March** Samiljol (Independence Day)
- **5 April** Arbor Day
- **mid-April** Han-sik-il (visiting ancestors' graves)
- **5 May** Children's Day
- **mid-May** Buddha's Birthday
- **6 June** Memorial Day
- **17 July** Constitution Day
- **15 August** Liberation Day
- **Sept/Oct** Ch'usok (the Korean equivalent of the American Thanksgiving festival)
- **3 October** National Foundation Day (also called Tan'gun Day)
- **25 December** Christmas Day

The Royal Asiatic Society (RAS), Christian Building, 6th Floor, Room 611, Chong-no 5-ka. Tel: 763-9483. The USO (**United States Service Organisation**), 104 Kalwol-dong, Yongsan-ku. Tel: 792-3028.

KTB Tours: The Korea Travel Bureau offers tours to the Panmunjom area, the Folk Village, Kyongju, Pusan, and around Seoul by day and night. Reservation counters can be found at several main hotels.

Tours to Panmunjom itself have been suspended due to an unresolved incident which resulted in the death of a South Korean officer in 1998. In the meantime it's still possible to take a peek at the demilitarised zone, as well as an invasion tunnel dug beneath the border by the north. The trip, including lunch and a "briefing", takes eight hours, and children under 10 years of age are not admitted. Travellers are advised to wear suitable clothes and must carry a passport at all times.
Both Root Travel and Kim's Travel organise special Veterans' tours, taking in the DMZ and other historic sites from the war years.

Getting Around

From The Airport

The best way into town from Kimpo is aboard the Korean Air Limousine (KAL) bus, which is inexpensive, reasonably quick (about one hour), comfortable, and stops at the major hotels. There's a phone and free water on board, and the uniformed driver will help you with your luggage. Tickets (W5,000) are available from KAL counters inside the terminal, and the stops are prominently signposted outside. Buses run every 15-20 minutes. Call (02) 667-0386/7 for information.

KAL runs four lines into the city, the first to City Hall, the second to Mount Namsan, the third south of the Han River to Kangnam-gu and the fourth to Chamsil. If you are in doubt about which one to take, tell the KAL clerk the name of your hotel.

A cheaper option is to take the Airport Express Bus, which runs every 12 minutes. #600 runs to Lotte World via the Express Bus Terminal, #601 terminates at Hung-injimun Gate, and #1002 goes via the Holiday Inn to City Hall. Tickets cost W1,100.

Subway Line 5 runs out to the airport. Tickets are W500 but it's a long haul into town. A taxi is the most expensive option into town, costing around W25,000.

Domestic Travel

BY AIR

Two airlines, Korean Air and Asiana Airlines conduct all air travel within Korea. Daily flights from Seoul to Cheju-do (65 minutes), Pusan (60 minutes), and Kwangju (50 minutes) are available on both domestic carriers. Flights from Seoul to Taegu (40 minutes), Yosu (60 minutes), Sokch'o (40 minutes), Chinju (60 minutes), and Ulsan (50 minutes), are available only on Korean Air. Tickets are available at major hotels and tourist and travel agencies. Security at the airport is tight; passengers and baggage are checked, and cameras, knives, and certain other articles are withheld during the flight. Tourist passports are necessary.

BY SEA

Numerous ferries and fishing boats make regular connections between the coasts and the outlying islands. The schedules change frequently and operators will cancel trips at any time if the weather gets bad. Travel arrangements should be made with travel agents and time should be allowed for last-minute changes if you travel during the monsoon season.

Several routes on the south coast in the Hallyo Waterway may be travelled either by ferry or by hydrofoil. Although the hydrofoil is faster, it is small and cramped. If time allows, the ferry is by far the more pleasant mode of transport and it allows passengers to take in some scenery. There's not much of a view from the hydrofoil and those prone to seasickness should definitely avoid it. You may call any of the following ferry terminals for further details.
Pusan,
Tel: (051) 466-0518 international,
Tel: (051) 463-0605 domestic.
Cheju, Tel: (064) 751-1901/5.
Hongdo, Tel: (0631) 274-3977.
Kunsan, Tel: (0654) 42-0115.
Inch'on, Tel: (032) 884-4247.
Masan, Tel: (0551) 45-0116.
Mokp'o, Tel: (0631) 244-9915.
P'ohang, Tel: (0562) 42-5111/3.
Sogwipo, Tel: (064) 32-0220.
Ullungdo, Tel: (0566) 791-4811.
Wando, Tel: (0633) 54-3294/5.
Yosu, Tel: (0662) 63-0116.

BY RAIL

The introduction of the locomotive to Korea was not without political motives. Several foreign powers, including Russia, Japan, France, and the United States, bid hard for the contract, which was eventually awarded to an American, James R. Morse. Soon after initiating construction, Morse, beset with financial difficulties, was forced to pass the project to the Japanese. The Korean government directed Japan to complete the line in the standard gauge system Morse used rather than import narrow-gauge rails in from Japan. The first railroad, which linked Seoul to Inch'on, was opened in September 1899. Other major lines were laid by the Japanese, including lines originating in Mokp'o, Masan, and Pusan to Seoul and to Sinuiju in North Korea, which linked with the Trans-Siberian Railway. At one time, a serious traveller could take the train from Pusan to Paris. The railway suffered considerable damage during various wars, but since 1953 the railway system in South Korea has been steadily modernized to accommodate tourists comfortably.

Today three kinds of service are available in Korea's efficient and fast inter-city train system: the super-express Saemaul-ho, fast, comfortable and air-conditioned and which usually has a dining car; the limited express Tong-il-ho and the express Mugunghwa-ho, which may also have a dining car and sleeper facilities. All trains have comfortable seats with plenty of legroom and may also have private compartments for families. If you are planning to travel on a weekend or public holiday, it's advisable to book at least two weeks in advance. A special hotline for foreign travellers has been set up in Seoul: 02 392-7811, and there are also special ticket counters for overseas visitors at some stations. The KNTO TIC in Seoul (Tel (02) 753-9870) operates a ticket sales outlet.

BY ROAD

Inter-city Buses: Nine expressways cut across the farmlands and mountains of Korea: the Kyungjin (Seoul-Inch'on); Yongdong (Yongin-Kangnung); Tonghae (Kangnung-P'ohang); Kuma (Taegu-Masan); Kyongbu (Seoul-Pusan); Namhae (Masan-Kwangju); Honam (Kwangju-Taejon); the Chungbu (Seoul-Taejon); and the '88 Olympic (Taegu-Kwangju) Expressways.

There are four kinds of inter-city buses: the *Udeung kosok*, which is the most comfortable and includes a public phone and probably a VCR; the *Kosok* express bus; the *Chikhaeng* (first class local and direct route); and the *Wanhaeng* (round about with frequent stops). Because of the high rate of occupancy, it is advisable to buy bus tickets in advance for a reserved seat. Listed below are eight main bus stations in Seoul and their more popular destinations (check Seoul map for locations):

Kangnam Bus Terminal: Located across the Han River in Banpo-dong; provides the only express bus service to cities out of Seoul. Tel: 591-3402, 535-4151.

Tongbu Bus Terminal: In Majang-dong; several metres away from city bus #41 stop; service to Ch'unch'on, Sorak, Sokch'o, Yangyang, Yongmun-sa, Kangnung, Yoju, Chungju, Kwangju, Wonju, Andong. Tel: 279-4160.

Nambu Bus Terminal: In south Yongsan along the main road; service to Kanghwa-do, Kosam, Taech'on Beach, Puyo, Kongju, Chonju, Songni-san, Ch'ongju, Taejon. Tel: 521-8550.

Sinchon Bus Terminal: Service to Kanghwa-do: 6am-8pm; trip takes 1 hour 15 minutes. Tel: 324-0611.

Dong Seoul Bus Terminal: Located beside Kangbyon Subway station on the Han River; services to east and south of Seoul. Tel: 458-4851.

Sangbong Bus Terminal: Located in Sangbong-dong and covers northern region, including Uijongbu and Tongduchon. Tel: 435-2122.

Seoul Sobu Bus Terminal: In Pulang-dong (northern Sodaemun-gu); service to Haengju-sansong, Uijongbu. Tel: 356-3517.

Public Transport

The majority of people living in Seoul depend on public transport. The subway is efficient and foreign user-friendly, the bus system less adapted to non-Korean speakers but still workable, while taxis seem to swarm everywhere.

CITY BUSES

During less hectic commuting hours, getting around on the local city bus can be interesting, quick and cheap. The driver usually turns up his radio so all may listen to the local baseball game, a melodrama, or to the latest rock'n roll or classical hits. Confucian ethics generally prevail on board the bus: students offer their seats to mothers toting babies and to the elderly, and out of mutual consideration, those seated relieve those standing of their schoolbooks and shopping bags. Smoking is prohibited.

Buses run frequently from 5am to around 11.45pm daily. Tokens are available at most stops for W500. You can pay in cash but drivers won't have the time – or the inclination – to wrestle with change.

In addition to the regular city buses, there are express buses, which follow similar routes but with fewer stops and for a somewhat higher fare (W1,000). These are designed for commuter use and generally make few stops downtown.

A word of caution: beware of pickpockets on the bus and at crowded bus stops.

Destinations are written on the side of the bus in *han'gul* and on street signs at the bus stops. Route maps for the entire system are virtually non-existent and change so frequently that it is impossible to keep track. The routes are mapped out on a panel inside the bus, but destinations are again written only in *han'gul*. The best way to get around the matter is with directions from a hotel concierge or a business partner. Two rules of thumb: when the bus comes, run to where it stops and leap on; at the other end, get to the exit before the bus stops and jump off just as fast.

TAXIS

Taxis fill in the gaps left by the bus and subway networks, or are a handy alternative when you don't feel like braving the crowds any more. Cabs cluster outside hotels and in ranks in busy city areas, and in Seoul may also be requested by phone (02 3431-5100). Some drivers may be hazy when it comes to knowledge of English, and more surprisingly the geography of their home town, so it's best to have clear instructions written in hang'ul – and if possible a map too – before you board.

There are two types of taxi – regular and deluxe. The latter are more comfortable and thus more expensive. Cabs may be hailed to the curbside and are sometimes shared with other passengers bound in the same direction. Each passenger pays only for the distance he travels (two or more travelling as one party pay as one passenger). This taxi-sharing system is called *hapsong*.

Fares for regular cabs begin at W1,300 for the first 2 kilometers (1¼ miles) with W100 for each additional 210 meters. The meter also runs on time when movement is slower than 15 kilometers per hour and W100 is charged for every 60 seconds in addition to the basic fare. Between midnight and 4am fares are automatically increased by 20%.

The deluxe 'mobam' taxis – distinguished by their black and yellow livery – cost W3,000 for the first three kilometers and W200 for each additional 250 meters or each 60 seconds if the speed drops below 15 kilometers per hour. Receipts and in-car phones are available and there is no late-night surcharge.

US military ID holders may also use Army-Air Force Exchange taxis, which charge slightly higher rates in dollars.

SUBWAY

Roomy, inexpensive, colour-coded, prominently signed in English and hang'ul, Seoul's subway system – first opened in August 1974 – is the most convenient form of public transport for visitors. Five lines are in full day-to-day operation, Line 6 is under construction and Lines 7 and 8 are in partial operation. Note that the circular Line 2 is under repair where it crosses the Han River between Tangsan and Hapchong stations. The subway also hooks up with the Korean National Railway. From Seoul Railway Station, it goes to six major destinations: Chongnyang-ni Train Station and Songbuk district to the north, and, to Inch'on (39 km west), Suwon (41.5 km south), Chamsil and Kuro. One-way tickets cost a basic W500, although you can buy stored value tickets for up to W10,000. The computer chip fare cards you will see locals using are only available to Korean bank account holders. Trains run from 5am to midnight at three minute intervals during rush hours, and six minute intervals at other times. Smoking is prohibited in the cars. The following are points of interest within walking distance of each subway stop within the city walls:

City Hall (T'aepyong-no): City Hall, Toksu Place, British Embassy, major hotels, banks, department stores, Seoul Tourist Information Centre.

Chonggak (Chong-no): Posin-gak (city bell tower), bookstores (with foreign language sections), Korean National Tourism Corporation, Ch'ogye-sa (Buddhist Temple), Communications Memorial Centre, Seoul Immigration Office, Kyongbok Palace, National Museum, Folk Museum, Embassies of USA, Japan, and Canada, Sejong Cultural Centre, Yi Sun-sin statue at Kwanghwa-mun Intersection.

Chong-no 3-ka: Pagoda Park and shopping arcade, Chongmyo (Royal Confucian Shrine), Insa-dong (Mary's Alley antique shops, art galleries, etc).

Chong-no 5-ka: East Gate marketplace, herb shops.

Tongdae-mun: Tongdae-mun (East Gate), Seoul Baseball Stadium.

Car rental

Foreigners are advised to avoid driving in Korea. The accident rate is one of the highest in the world and, in a legal dispute, foreigners tend to come off worse unless accompanied or supported by a local. It's best to take on a chauffeur with your rental car, which costs around W150,000 inclusive for a ten-hour day. Hertz and Avis are represented by local companies Kumho (Tel: 02 798-1515) and VIP (Tel: 02 838-0015).

Where to Stay

Hotels

Many international hotel chains have properties in Korea, vying for business with accommodation that ranges from five-star to the most basic homestays. Suffice it to say that there is something for all budgets and tastes in the accommodation stakes. Naturally, the best hotels are in the capital.

SEOUL (TEL CODE 02)

INTERNATIONAL CLASS
Grand Hyatt
747-7 Hannam-dong, Yongsan-ku
Tel: 797-1234; Fax: 798-6953
Apart from all the joys of the "Hyatt touch" (the swimming pool becomes an ice rink in winter!) the reputation of JJ's nightclub here has assumed legendary proportions.
Hilton International
395 Namdaemunno 5-ga, Chung-ku
Tel: 753-7788; Fax: 754-2510
A mainstream conference hotel, but one which still retains an intimate and friendly atmosphere.
Inter-Continental
159-8 Samsung-dong, Kangnam-ku
Tel: 555-5656; Fax: 559-7990
A business-oriented hotels on Seoul's "Wall Street".
Lotte
1 Sogong-dong, Chung-ku
Tel: 771-1000; Fax: 752-3758
Located in the heart of the city centre, and ideal for those with retail therapy on their mind.
Lotte World
40-1 Chamsil-dong, Songp'a-ku
Tel: 419-7000; Fax: 417-3655
Right next to Korea's answer to Disneyland, this is a family fun hotel, rather than an executive's boutique haven.

Radisson Seoul Plaza
23 T'aepyongno 2-ga, Chung-ku
Tel: 771-2200; Fax: 755-8897
Smart, fashionable and excellently
located for exploring the centre of
Seoul.

Ritz Carlton
602 Yeoksam-dong, Kangnam-ku
Tel: 3451-8000; Fax: 3451-8188
Discreet, tasteful and head and
shoulders above many of its
competitors south of the river when
it comes to service and facilities.

Seoul Renaissance
676 Yeoksam-dong, Kangnam-ku
Tel: 555-0501; Fax: 553-8118
A smart hotel, with the airy,
spacious top-floor Club Horizon,
which serves one of the best
breakfasts in Seoul.

Sheraton Walker Hill
Kwangjang-dong, Songdong-ku
Tel: 453-0121; Fax: 452-6867
Dame Fortune rules at this Mecca
for gamblers, which infuses the
entire hotel with an aura of
excitement.

Shilla
202 Changch'ung-dong 2-ga
Chung-ku
Tel: 230-3111, Fax: 233-5073
The grande dame of Seoul
accommodation, with an especially
picturesque sculpture garden.

Swiss Grand
201-1 Hong-un-dong, Seodaemun-ku
Tel: 3216-5656; Fax: 3216-7799
A very swish hideaway at the foot of
Mount Paengnyonsan.

Westin Chosun
87-1 Sogong-dong, Chung-ku
Tel: 771-0500; Fax: 752-1443
Patrons return time and again to
sample the charm of this downtown
five-star anchored by the
rumbustious Irish bar O'Kims.

SUPERIOR CLASS
Crown
34-69 Itaewon-dong, Yongsan-ku
Tel: 797-4111; Fax: 796-1010
170 rooms (13 Korean-style).
Nightclub and sauna.

Hamilton
119-25 Itaewon-dong, Yongsan-ku
Tel: 794-0171/9; Fax: 795-0457
139 rooms (one Korean-style).
This has a nightclub and outdoor
swimming pool.

Holiday Inn Seoul
169-1 Tohwa-dong, Map'o-ku
Tel: 717-9441
Fax: 715-9441
367 (four Korean-style) rooms.
Health club, sauna and nightclub.

Novotel Ambassador
603 Yeoksam-dong, Kangnam-ku
Tel: 567-1101
Fax: 564-4573.
336 (six Korean-style) rooms.
Indoor pool, cocktail bar, health
club and sauna.

Novotel Ambassador Toksan
1030-1 Toksan 4-dong, Kumchon-ku
tel: 838-1101
Fax: 854-4799
239 rooms (five Korean-style).
Health club, sauna and cocktail bar.

Ramada Olympia
108-2 P'yongch'ang-dong
Chongro-ku
Tel: 396-6600
Fax: 396-6633
270 rooms (four Korean-style).
Indoor and outdoor pools, health
club, sauna, theatre, restaurant and
cocktail lounge.

Sofitel Ambassador
186-54 Changch'ung-dong 2-ga
Chung-ku
Tel: 275-1101
Fax: 272-0773
432 rooms (six Korean-style).
Cocktail lounge, health club, indoor
pool, sauna.

STANDARD CLASS
Airport
11-21 Konghang-dong, Kangsoku
Tel: 662-1113
Fax: 663-3355
55 rooms (ten Korean-style).

BUDGET CLASS
Central
227-1 Changsa-dong, Chongro-ku
Tel: 265-4121
Fax: 265-6139
72 rooms (eight Korean-style).
Cocktail lounge, nightclub and sauna.

PUSAN (TEL CODE 051)

INTERNATIONAL CLASS
Hyatt Regency Pusan
1405-16 Chung-dong, Haeundae-ku
Tel: 743-1234

Fax: 743-1250
363 rooms (27 Korean-style).
Cocktail lounge, health club, sauna,
indoor pool, tennis court, hot spring
bath, nightclub.

Westin Chosun Beach
737 Ui-dong, Haeundae-ku
Tel: 742-7411
Fax: 742-1313
305 rooms (ten Korean-style).
Cocktail lounge, health club, sauna,
indoor pool, hot spring bath.

SUPERIOR CLASS
Commodore
743-80 Yongju-dong, Chung-ku
Tel: 466-9101
Fax: 462-9101
326 rooms (Ten Korean-style).
Cocktail lounge, health club, sauna,
indoor pool, nightclub.

Empire
398-14 Deochon 3-dong, Puk-ku
Tel: 337-8811
Fax: 337-8820
50 rooms (ten Korean style)

STANDARD CLASS
Dong Bang
210-82 Onch'on 1-dong, Tongae-ku
Tel: 552-9511
Fax: 552-9274
42 rooms (16 Korean-style). Sauna
and hot spring bath.

BUDGET CLASS
Hillside
743-33 Yongju 1-dong, Chung-ku
Tel: 464-0567
Fax: 464-1214
40 rooms (15 Korean-style). Sauna.

TAEGU (TEL CODE 053)

SUPERIOR CLASS
Crown
330-6 Shinch'on-dong, Tong-ku
Tel: 755-3001
Fax: 755-3367
56 rooms (14 Korean-style).
Cocktail lounge and sauna.

Grand
563-1 Pomo-dong, Susang-ku
Tel: 742-0001
Fax: 756-7164
109 rooms (20 Korean-style).
Health Club, sauna and nightclub.

STANDARD CLASS
Hilltop
3408-35 Taemyong-dong, Nam-ku
Tel: 651-2001
Fax: 651-2006
52 rooms (16 Korean-style).
Cocktail lounge.

BUDGET CLASS
Emerald
459-7 Pokyo-dong, Puk-ku
Tel: 951-3031
Fax: 951-3035
36 rooms (nine Korean-style).

INCH'ON (TEL CODE 032)

SUPERIOR CLASS
New Star
29 Shinheung-dong 3-ga, Chung-ku
Tel: 883-9841
Fax: 882-8307
50 rooms (five Korean-style).
Cocktail lounge and nightclub.
Songdo Beach
812 Tongch'un-dong, Nam-ku
Tel: 865-1311
Fax: 865-1325
192 rooms (20 Korean-style). Health
club, sauna and cocktail lounge.

STANDARD CLASS
Pupyong
181 Kalsan-dong, Pupyong-ku
Tel: 504-8181
Fax: 504-8182
31 rooms (Four Korean-style).
Sauna and cocktail lounge.

BUDGET CLASS
Soobong
618-2 Tohwa-dong, Nam-ku
Tel: 868-6611
Fax: 868-4333
30 rooms (six Korean-style).
Cocktail lounge and sauna.

TAEJON (TEL CODE 042)

SUPERIOR CLASS
Chateau Grace
72-5 Yongjon-dong,
Tong-ku
Tel: 634-5600
Fax: 634-5608
102 rooms (37 Korean-style).
Sauna and nightclub.

Riviera Yousong
445-5 Pongmyong-dong, Yuosong-ku
Tel: 823-2111
Fax: 822-5250
216 rooms (43 Korean-style). Health
club, sauna, hot spring baths,
indoor and outdoor pools, nightclub.

STANDARD CLASS
Family
460-3 Taehung 2-dong, Chung-ku
Tel: 255-4083
Fax: 255-4089
32 rooms (8 Korean-style). Nightclub.

BUDGET CLASS
Hanil
296-6 Yongun-dong, Tong-ku
Tel: 283-4401
Fax: 282-7203
30 rooms (14 Korean-style). Sauna

KWANGJU (TEL CODE 062)

SUPERIOR CLASS
Grand
212 Pullo-dong, Tong-ku
Tel: 224-6111
Fax: 224-8933
65 rooms (23 Korean-style). Sauna,
cocktail lounge and nightclub.
Mudungsan Spa
9-2 Chisan-dong, Tong-ku
Tel: 226-0026
Fax: 226-0020
110 rooms (35 Korean-style). Health
club, sauna, tennis court, hot spring
baths, cocktail lounge and nightclub.

STANDARD CLASS
Riverside
72-1 Honam-dong, Tong-ku
Tel: 223-9111
Fax: 223-9112
35 rooms (11 Korean-style).
Cocktail lounge and nightclub.

KYONGGI-DO

SUPERIOR CLASS
Miranda
408-1 Anhung-ri, Ichon-gun, Ichon
Tel: (0336) 33-2001
Fax: 33-2030
165 rooms (84 Korean-style). Health
club, indoor and outdoor pools,
sauna, hot spring baths, nightclub.

Rasung
846-3 Wonkok-dong, Ansan
Tel: (0345) 80-6161
Fax: 80-6190
84 rooms (40 Korean-style). Sauna,
cocktail lounge and nightclub.

STANDARD CLASS
Pyongtaek
62-10 Pyongtaek-dong, Pyongt'aek
Tel: (0333) 54-3331
Fax: 54-2231
46 rooms (Nine Korean-style).
Sauna and cocktail lounge.

KANGWON-DO

SUPERIOR CLASS
Chuncon Sejong
San1 Pongul-dong, Ch'unch'on
Tel: (0361) 52-1191
Fax: 54-3347
65 rooms (24 Korean-style).
Cocktail lounge.
Sorak Park
24-3 Sorak-dong, Sokch'o
Tel: (0392) 34-7711
Fax: 34-7732
121 rooms (36 Korean-style).
Casino, cocktail lounge, nightclub,
sauna and health club.

STANDARD CLASS
Imperial
San 84-2, Chumunjin-ri,
Chumunjin-up, Kangnung
Tel: (0391) 1950/4
Fax: 661-1955
52 rooms (18 Korean-style). Tennis
court.

BUDGET CLASS
Royal
395-12 Upsang-ri,
Hoengsong-up, Hoensong-gun
Tel: (0372) 343-6601
Fax: 343-5221
35 rooms (16 Korean-style). Sauna,
cocktail lounge and nightclub.

CH'UNGCH'ONGBUK-DO

SUPERIOR CLASS
Songnisan
198 Sanae-ri
Naesokri-myon, Poun-gun
Tel: (0433) 42-5281

Fax: 42-5281
132 rooms (88 Korean-style).
Cocktail lounge and outdoor pool.

STANDARD CLASS
Chongju
844 Pokdae-dong, Ch'ongju
Tel: (0431) 64-2181
Fax: 66-8215
70 rooms (19 Korean-style).
Cocktail lounge and nightclub.

BUDGET CLASS
Jinyang
1831 Pongmyong-dong, Ch'ongju
Tel: (0431) 67-1121
Fax: 63-9532
36 rooms (five Korean-style).
Cocktail lounge

CH'UNGCH'ONGNAM-DO

SUPERIOR CLASS
Jeil
228-6 Onch'on-dong, Onyang
Tel: (0418) 44-6111
Fax: 42-6100
143 rooms (73 Korean-style). Sauna,
hot spring baths and cocktail bar.

STANDARD CLASS
Hoseo
82-12 Onch'on-dong, Onyang
Tel: (0418) 43-5500
Fax: 43-5509
51 rooms (25 Korean-style). Sauna.

BUDGET CLASS
Kongju
139-1 Sansong-dong, Kongju
Tel: (0416) 855-4023
Fax: 855-4028
32 rooms (17 Korean-style). Sauna.

CHOLLABUK-DO

SUPERIOR CLASS
Core
627-3 Seonosong-dong
Tokchin-ku, Chonju
Tel: (0652) 85-1100
Fax: 85-5707
110 rooms (27 Korean-style). Sauna,
cocktail lounge and nightclub.
Naejangsan
71-14 Naejang-dong, Chonju
Tel: (0681) 535-4131

Fax: 31-5665
104 rooms (54 Korean-style). Sauna,
cocktail lounge and nightclub.

BUDGET CLASS
Iksan
54-7 Chung-ang-dong, Iksan
Tel: (0653) 263-1260
Fax: 851-2040
38 rooms (12 Korean-style).

CHOLLANAM-DO

SUPERIOR CLASS
Chirisan Plaza
32-1 Hwangjon
Masan-myon, Kurye-gun
Tel: (0664) 782-2171
Fax: 782-3675
101 rooms (57 Korean-style).
Sauna, cocktail lounge and
nightclub.

STANDARD CLASS
Yosu Park
979-1 Kwanmun-dong, Yosu
Tel: (0662) 63-2334
Fax: 63-2338
40 rooms (19 Korean-style). Sauna,
cocktail lounge and nightclub.

BUDGET CLASS
Paekche
10-13 Sangnak-dong1-ga, Mokp'o
Tel: (0631) 42-4411
Fax: 42-955
38 rooms (13 Korean-style).
Cocktail lounge.

KYONGSANGBUK-DO

INTERNATIONAL CLASS
Hyundae
477-2 Shinp'yong-dong, Kyongju
Tel: (0561) 748-2233
Fax: 748-8234
429 rooms (12 Korean-style).
Indoor and outdoor pools, health
club, tennis court, hot spring baths.

SUPERIOR CLASS
Andong Park
324 Unboung-dong, Andong
Tel: (0571) 859-1500
Fax: 57-5445
41 rooms (15 Korean-style).
Cocktail lounge.

Cignus
145-21 Yongheung-dong
P'ohang
Tel: (0562) 75-2000
Fax: 75-2218
112 rooms (16 Korean-style).
Sauan, hot spring baths, health
club, cocktail lounge and nightclub.

STANDARD CLASS
Kyongju
645 Shinp'yong-dong, Kyongju
Tel: (0561) 745-7123
Fax: 745-7129
50 rooms (14 Korean-style).
Cocktail lounge and sauna.

BUDGET CLASS
Donghae Beach
68-1 Namho-ri
Namjong-myon, Yongdok-gun
Tel: (0564) 33-6611
Fax: 33-6611
47 rooms (27 Korean-style).

KYONGSANGNAM-DO

INTERNATIONAL CLASS
International
97-4 Chung-ang-dong, Changwon
Tel: (0551) 281-1001
Fax: 284-2000
121 rooms (18 Korean-style). Sauna,
cocktail lounge and nightclub.

SUPERIOR CLASS
Kimhae
827-4 Puwon-dong, Kimhae
Tel: (0525) 35-0101
Fax: 34-4717
41 rooms (five Korean-style). Sauna.

STANDARD CLASS
Masan Arirang
229-17 Sokchon-dong, Masan
Tel: (0551) 94-2211
Fax: 294-2111
57 rooms (22 Korean-style).
Cocktail lounge and nightclub.

CHEJU-DO (TEL CODE 064)

INTERNATIONAL CLASS
Cheju Grand
263-15 Yon-dong, Cheju city
Tel: 747-5000
Fax: 742-3150

517 rooms (30 Korean-style). Casino, cocktail lounge, health club, outdoor pool, nightclub, sauna.

Cheju Hyatt Regency
3039-1 Saekdal-dong, Sogwip'o
Tel: 733-1234
Fax: 732-2039
224 rooms (25 Korean-style). Casino, cocktail lounge, health club, indoor and outdoor pools, tennis court, nightclub, sauna.

Shilla
3039-3 Saekdal-dong, Sogwip'o
Tel: 738-4466
Fax: 735-5415
427 rooms (ten Korean-style). Casino, cocktail lounge, health club, indoor and outdoor pools, tennis court, nightclub, sauna.

SUPERIOR CLASS
Cheju KAL
1691-9 2-do1-dong, Cheju city
Tel: 724-2001
Fax: 720-6515
282 rooms (ten Korean-style). Casino, cocktail lounge, health club, indoor pool, nightclub, sauna.

Cheju Pearl
277-2 Yon-dong, Cheju city
Tel:742-8871
Fax: 742-1221
88 rooms (28 Korean-style). Cocktail lounge.

STANDARD CLASS
Grace
261-23 Yon-dong, Cheju city
Tel: 742-0066
Fax: 743-7111
61 rooms (12 Korean-style). Cocktail lounge and sauna.

BUDGET CLASS
Milano
273-43 Yon-dong, Cheju city
Tel: 742-0088
Fax: 742-7705
72 rooms (27 Korean-style). Cocktail lounge.

Youth Hostels

A chain of youth hostels has been established in many of the provinces, and hostels are open to international members. The charge for one night ranges from W5,000–W10,000.

Reservations or further information can be obtained from the Korea Youth Hostel Association, Tel: 02 725-3031. Below is a selective list of youth hostels in Korea.

Seoul
Olympic Parktel
88, Pang-i-dong,
Songp'a-gu.
Tel: 02 410-2114.

Pusan
Dongsong Youth Hostel
41, 1-ga, Posu-dong,
Chung-gu.
Tel: (051) 743-8466.

Kangwon-do
Naksan Youth Hostel
Chun jin-ri,
Konbyun-myun,
Yangyang-gun.
Tel: (0396) 672-3416.

Ch'ungch'ongpuk-do
Umsong
47-1, Ch'agok-ri,
Saengguk-myon,
Umsong-gun.
Tel: (0446) 877-7802.

Ch'ungch'ongnam-do
Samjung Puyo
105-1, Kukyo-ri,
Puyo-up,
Puyo-kun.
Tel: (0463) 835-3102.

Kyongsangbuk-do
Kyongju Youth Hostel
470-2, Ch'unghyo-dong,
Kyongju.
Tel: (0561) 742-1771.

Home Stay

The Korea Labo Corp arranges home-stays or *minbak* for foreigners with Korean families who may speak English, Japanese, Chinese, Spanish, French or German. If you want to take part in this program, you should contact Labo at least two weeks in advance with details of where you want to stay, when and for how long. Rates start at US$30 per person per night, which includes breakfast, however a four-

week stay costs only US$500. Labo will then find a family and send you some information about them and arrange a rendezvous. For more information Tel: 02 817-4625, Fax: 02 813-7047.

Inns

Yogwan: While many *yogwans* nowadays have western-style beds and other amenities, quite a few are still homey yet respectable inns, providing a mattress (*yo*), quilt (*ibul*) and a hard pillow (*pyogae*) filled with wheat husks. They provide inexpensive home-cooked Korean meals. In chilly weather, the room is heated by *ondol* underfloor heating. Some inns will serve meals in your room for an extra fee. Nightly prices range from W10,000 to W50,000, which must be paid on arrival. More details can be found at the KNTO website www.knto.or.kr
Yoinsuk: The *yoinsuk*, another type of Korean inn, offers lodging in a private compound and isn't as consistently clean, convenient, nor as appealing as the *yogwan*. But the room rates are usually lower and accommodation is native all the way.
Boarding House (*Hasuk Chip*). The *hasuk chip* has its place among students, working bachelors, and itinerants. Rooms are rented by the month, usually to long-term residents. Rent includes very simple home-cooked meals.
Rented Rooms (*Setbang*). For the working foreigner, the *setbang* – a rented room in a local home – is yet another option. Except for the fact that he happens to share the same roof with others, the tenant is generally on his own.

What to Eat

Below is a list of the types of restaurants you are likely to encounter in Korea.

Barbecue meat restaurants (*Pul Koki Jip*). Beef (*so-koki*) and pork (*toechi-koki*) and short rib (*kal bi*) are marinated in soy sauce, sesame oil, garlic, green onions, and toasted sesame seeds, then char-broiled.

Raw fish restaurants (*Saengson Hoe Jip*). Fresh raw fish is served sliced with a soy sauce (*kan-chang*) or red pepper sauce (*cho-chang*). Other kinds of fish dishes such as *maeun t'ang* (hot pepper soup of fish, soybean curd, egg, and vegetables) are served.

Ginseng Chicken Dish restaurants (*Samgyae T'ang Jip*). Chicken stuffed with rice, white ginseng, and dried oriental dates are steamed and served hot. Deep-fried chicken and other chicken dishes are also served.

Dumplings restaurants (*Mandoo Jip*). Meat, vegetables, and sometimes soybean curd are stuffed into a dumpling and steamed, fried or boiled in a broth. Chinese-style cookie pastries baked in the restaurant fill the display window.

Noodles restaurants (*Poonsik Jip*). Noodle dishes are the speciality but so are easily prepared rice dishes. Some of the popular dishes are *Momil kooksoo* – buckwheat noodles served with a sweet radish sauce; *Naengmyon* – cold potato flour or buckwheat flour noodles topped with sliced meat, vegetables, a boiled egg, and a pepper relish sauce and rice; *K'ong kooksoo* – wheat noodles in fresh soymilk; *Odaeng kooksoo* – wheat noodles topped with oriental fishcake in a broth; *Ramyon* –

instant noodles in instant broth; *Udong* – long, wide wheat noodles with onions, fried soybean curd, red pepper powder, and egg; *Pipim-pap* – rice topped with parboiled fern bracken, bluebell root, soysprouts, spinach, and a sunny-side-up egg, accompanied by a bowl of broth; and *Chap Chae* – rice vermicelli stir-fried with vegetables and meat slices.

Steamed rice restaurants (*Paekpan Jip*). A bowl of rice is served with a variety of *kimch'i*, *namul* (parboiled vegetables), fish, and soup (usually made of soybean paste) – the basic Korean meal. Other simple dishes, such as *naengmyon* and *pipim-pap* are often on the menu.

Dog Meat Soup restaurants (*Posin T'ang Jip*). *Posin-hada* means to build up one's strength. Thus, to the people, dog meat soup, *Posin t'ang*, is considered to be a delicacy. Other popular Korean dishes include: *Sinsullo* – chopped vegetables, meat, quail egg, fish balls, and gingko nuts in a brazier; *Sollong t'ang* – rice in a beef and bone stew; and *Pindaettok* – the Korean bean flour and egg pancake filled with different combinations of vegetables and meat.

Chinese Shantung restaurants are as popular as Korean restaurants. They are designated by a red or green door plaque draped with a red strip of cloth. Homemade wheat noodles with various sauces make for a slurpy meal. *Tchajangmyon* is a popular order consisting of pork, seafood, and vegetable tidbits stir-fried in a sweet-sour black bean sauce, and topped with a boiled egg. Larger Chinese restaurants have a more varied menu that includes delicacies such as sweet-sour fried fish and meat.

Japanese restaurants complete with *sushi* (laver-covered rice rolls), *sashimi* (raw fish), and *tempura* (deep-fried battered fish and vegetables) bars are all over Seoul, and are even more common in the southern part of Pusan.

Drinking Notes

Water: potable water is available in hotels. In establishments for locals, *bori ch'a* (roasted barley boiled in water), distinguished by its light brown colour, is served instead. Another popular water substitute is *sungnyung*, tea boiled from browned rice gathered from the bottom of a rice pot. It is also quite safe to drink water which spring from certain mountain sites at temples in the countryside. Unboiled tap water is never advised for drinking. Bottled water can be purchased for from supermarkets or convenience stores.

Tearooms (Tabang)

Tabang (or *tasil*) is one of the most common signs in any Korean town. Koreans go to the *tabang* for everything but tea (in fact, the tea is free) or coffee. It is where businessmen strike deals, where students practice English with "native speakers", where friends gather to gossip, joke, and listen to music, and where lovers tryst. A cup of thin coffee is but a token to hours of socialising.

The *tabang* has become a vital institution in contemporary Korean culture; a meeting hall outside the home and office for young and old, male and female. And with ten million souls in the capital alone, there is always room for one more tearoom to open above, below, or next to all the others.

Pubs

The common bar or pub is usually a small, simple café which serves liquor and beer. *Anju* (hors d'oevres) are served at an additional cost in most places. The cheapest liquor is soju (sweet potato wine).

Beer (*maekchu*) comes either bottled (*pyong*) or as a draft (*saeng*). *Anju* are pricey but are nevertheless customarily ordered.

Culture

Korea's cultural history is vividly displayed in numerous museums (municipal and national) and cultural centres. Drama theatres and libraries present more contemporary perspectives.

Concerts

National Classical Music Institute. Just past Tower Hotel on the slopes of Namsan is the school where many of the nation's finest classical musicians of different genres, including Royal Court musicians, practice and teach their art. Performances are given in the concert hall. Check the entertainment section of newspapers for engagements. Tel: 02-274-1151.
Open Music Hall. Periodic Korean and western concerts are given here on the western slopes of Namsan near the Central National Library.
Sejong Cultural Centre. 81-3, Sejongno, Chongno-gu. Tel: 02-399-1514 Opened in 1978, the Sejong Cultural Centre holds foreign and Korean classical and contemporary concerts and dramatic plays.
Seoul Arts Centre. Tel: 02 580-1234. Located at the foot of Mount Umyonsan in Soch'o-dong this centre is made up of a concert hall, calligraphy hall, gallery, library, opera house and outdoor performance areas. It is also the home of the National Centre for Korean Traditional Performing Arts.

Theatres

Drama Centre. The Drama Centre (Tel: 02-778-0261) is off Namsan

Street, at 8-19, Yejang-dong, Chung-gu. Everything from P'ansori to Shakespeare is performed. Check the newspapers for current performances.
Korea House. Situated on the slopes of Namsan off Toegyero. Korea House stages free folk dance performances at 3pm on Saturday and Sunday. Art displays decorate the rooms and Korea-related books are sold in the bookshop. A Korean restaurant overlooks an oriental garden. Tel: 266-9101.
Space Centre. Housed in an architectural artpiece near the Secret Garden of Ch'angdok Palace (219, Wonso-dong, Chongno-gu), the Space Centre (Tel: 02-763-0771) stages a variety of shows from classical kayakum (Korean zither) solos to Dixieland jazz to drama. The Centre also publishes a cultural magazine called Space.

Other Modern Drama Theatres in Seoul:
Madang Cecil Theatre 3-7, Chong-dong, Chung-gu Tel: (02) 737-8836.
Elcanto Art Theatre 50, Myong-dong 1-ga, Chung-gu Tel: (02) 776-8035.
Mun Ye Theatre 130-47, Tongsung-dong Chongno-gu Tel: (02) 744-0686.
National Theatre San 14-67, Changch'ung-dong 2-ga Chung-gu Tel: (02) 274-1173.
Silhum Theatre 609-1, Shinsa-dong, Kangnam-ku. Tel: (02) 515-7661.

Cinema

Giant painted billboards of kungfu duels, infernal disasters, love, and despair draw thousands of people to Korea's commercial theatres. Foreign films, including an occasional American film, are also screened, usually with Korean subtitles. The Centre Culturél Français, located on the right side of Kyongbok Palace, just past the Hyundai Modern Art Gallery and Andre Kim's boutique, is a multi-

media oasis where one can browse through a modern art gallery, sit and view French cultural videotapes or watch a classic French film subtitled in English in a small theatre downstairs. The CCF shows a variety of films from 12 noon–6pm daily except Sundays.
Films undergo government censorship and sometimes are edited if too long to allow impressarios to squeeze in a maximum number of showings. During cold months, underfloor hot water pipes provide some warmth in the theatre. Check the entertainment section of The Korea Times or The Korea Herald for current engagements.
Foreign films are not dubbed, but have subtitles in hang'ul, so overseas visitors can enjoy them too. Shows usually run continuously from about 11am each day.

Libraries

Royal Asiatic Society (RAS)
The RAS is the Korean chapter of an international British association. Its office is in the Christian Centre Building (136-46 Yunjidong, Chongno-gu. Tel: 763-9483) near Chongno 5-ka. There you'll find English translations of most books written locally about Korea and a complete collection of their magazine, Transactions, which contains Korea-related articles that have been written by lecturing members since 1900. Visitors are welcome to sign up for tours conducted by the RAS and by an affiliate, the Korea Art Club.

Korean Research Centre
The Korean Research Centre is located in Socho-dong (Tel: 535-3130). The Centre publishes cultural research articles in Korea with some translations in English but also provides a quiet library of old and recent Korea-related books written by foreign explorers, diplomats, and expatriates. Some current periodicals written in other languages are available. The Centre is open weekdays from 9am–5pm.

United States Information Service

USIS (Tel: 397-4114) offers a library for public viewing and study. Passport identification is needed. Art gallery hours are 8.30am–5pm weekdays and library hours are 9.30am–6pm weekdays.

UNESCO Library

Back issues of the *Korea Journal* and the *Courier*, as well as Korean cultural magazines are available, the latter in English, French, and Spanish. The Library is also stocked with other reference publications.

Ewha, Sogang, Yonsei, and other universities also invite foreigners to use their libraries.

Bookstores

Reading material in English or European languages can be tricky to locate in Seoul but there are several places where titles can be regularly found. The major hotels have bookstores which carry periodicals although they are usually late in coming and are unduly expensive. For the latest issues (also at high prices), the most reliable bookstore is in the basement of the Kyobo Building which is near the American Embassy on Taepyong-ro 2-ga. The Youngpoon Book Store, on Namdaemunro by Chonggak subway station also has a respectable foreign language selection.

   Used books and magazines can be found in Myong-dong just across from the Chinese Embassy. There are several small shops here overflowing with books and old magazines which are sold for much less than their original cost. You can also trade in your own used paperbacks or bargain for lower prices, particularly if you purchase several books at a time.

Shopping

Seoul

Places to shop in Seoul include:
Antiques: Ahyon-dong, Insa-dong, Chun-gang Sijang (Central market), It'aewon
Brassware: It'aewon
Boutique goods: Myong-dong, Idae-ap
Calligraphy paint brushes – Insa-dong, Kyonji-dong
Korean costumes: Tongdae-mun Sijang, and most other marketplaces
Korean cushions and blankets: Insa-dong, marketplaces
Korean herbal medicine: Chong-no 5-ka, Chong-no 6-ka
Name seals (custom-made name seals in stylistic characters carved of hard wood, stone): along the busy streets
Oriental paper: Insa-dong, Kyonji-dong
Silk Brocade: Tongdae-mun Sijang (2nd floor), Chong-no 2-ka, Myong-dong (K'o Silk Shop)
Custom-tailored men's suits: hotels, Myong-dong
Sweatsuits and athletic shoes and gear: It'aewon, Namdae-mun Sijang (across the Tokyu Hotel)
Topaz, "smokey topaz", amethyst, jade: underground arcades

Shopping Centres

Major Seoul shopping centres outside central city hotels are:
Lotte Shopping Centre
1, Sogong-dong, Chung-gu
Tel: 771-2500.
Metro-Midopa Department Store,
Store 123, Namdaemun 2-ga, Chung-gu
Tel: 754-2222.
New Core Shopping Centre
70-2, Chamwon-dong, Soch'o-gu
Tel: 530-5000.

Saerona Department Store
1-2, Namch'ang-dong, Chung-gu.
Tel: 778-8171.
Shinsegae
52-2, Ch'ungmuro 1-ga, Chung-gu
Tel: 754-1234.

Underground Arcades

Specialty shops can be found in underground shopping malls. Don't let the price tags deter you from bargaining. The larger more centrally located arcades are: Namdaemun Arcade, Myong-dong Arcade, Sogong Arcade, Hangram Arcade, Ulchi-ro Arcade, Lotte Centre 1st Avenue Arcade, Arcade Bando-Chosun.

Marketplaces

Seoul marketplaces run on for block after block. Anyone who has anything to sell is out there – from the button merchant to the antique dealer to the rice cake *ajumoni*, including *chige* (A-frame) bicycle and Kiamaster delivery men and haggling shoppers. The distinguishing feature of Korean markets, however, is that shops with the same goods tend to group together, and even set up their goods in the same way. Merchants say they are not hurt by competition caused by the close proximity; instead, the area becomes known for specialising in, say, second-hand books, sinks or antiques. Most things can be found at all the markets.

Regional Arts & Crafts

Korea's unique arts and crafts and the towns which traditionally produce the best of particular products are:
Bamboo craft: Tamyang
Brassware: Ansong, Taegu
Hemp cloth: Hansan, Andong
Lacquerware: Wonju
Oriental paper: Chonju
Pottery: Inch'on
Porcelain: Ansong
Ruchecraft: Kanghwa City
Silk: Ch'unch'on, Kanghwa City

Language

Survival Korean

Korean han'gul is romanised in two ways: by the Ministry of Education system and by the McCune-Reischauer system, an internationally recognised romanisation scheme. Both romanisations are used in literature, maps, and signs, which can confuse those unacquainted with the language. Thus, learning the Korean alphabet, which is simple, would prove most beneficial, especially for the lone traveller.

Provided below are commonly used questions and statements romanised according to the McCunne-Reischauer system. No matter what village, town or city in Korea you visit, you should be able to survive with the following common questions and statements.

Useful Phrases

airport/konghang
subway/cho-hach'ol
taxi/taeksi
Seoul train station/Seoul yok
express bus terminal/Kosok t'ominal
ticket office/p'yo p'a-nun kos-i
entrance/ipku
exit/ch'ulku
public bathhouse or private bathroom/mogyokt'ang
restroom/hwajang-sil
restaurant/sik-tang, umsik-chom
tea or coffee house/tabang
bank/unbaeng
hotel/hotel
a good Korean inn/cho-un yogwan
post office/uch'e-guk
post box/kyongch'al-so
embassy/daesa-kwan
International.../...Kukche-Chonsin...
...telecommunication office/

chonhwakuk
dry cleaners/saet'ak-so
public telephone/kongchung-chonhwa
department store/paekhwa-jom
duty free shop/myonse-p'um-jom
marketplace/sijang
souvenir shop/t'osang-p'um-jom

Useful Questions & Sentences

How many kilometers is it from here?/Yogi-so myot kilo im-nikka?
How long does it take to go there?/Olmana kollimnikka?
It takes 30 minutes/1 hour/Samship-pun/han si-gan kollimnida
Please call a taxi for me/Taeksi jom pullo ju-seyo
Just a moment please/Cham-kkan man kitari-seyo
Please go straight/Ttok paro ka-seyo
Please stop here/Sewo ju-seyo

Numbers

The following is a list of basic numbers and their Korean pronunciation:
1/Il
2/Ee
3/Sam
4/Sa
5/O
6/Yuk
7/Ch'il
8/P'al
9/Ku
10/Ship
11/Ship-il
20/Ee-ship
30/Sam-ship
40/Sa-ship
50/O-ship
60/Yuk-ship
70/Ch'il-ship
80/P'al-ship
90/Ku-ship
100/Paek
200/Ee-paek
300/Sam-paek
567/O-paek yuk-ship ch'il
1,000/Ch'on
2,000/Ee-ch'on
4,075/Sa-ch'on ch'il-ship o
10,000/Man
13,900/Man Sam-ch'on ku-baek

What is this place called?/Yogi-nun odi imnikka?
Hello (to get the attention of a waiter, sales clerk, etc)/Yobo-sey
I will have coffee (or) please give me some coffee/K'op'i-rul chu-seyo
May I have more beer?/Maekchu to ju-seyo?
May I have the bill?/Kaesanso-rul chu-seyo?
Do you have amethyst?/Chasujong iss-umnikka? (see index-glossary for other items)
Please show me another one/Tarun kos-ul poyo ju-seyo
How much does it cost; what is the price?/Olma imnikka?
Can you give me a discount?/Tisukauntu rul hal-su iss-umnikka?
It's too expensive/Nomu pissamnida
Thank you/Kamsa-hamnida
I will buy this/Ee Kos-ul sa kess-umnida
Good-bye (said to somebody not departing)/Annyŏng-hi ke-seyo
Good-bye (said to somebody who is also departing)/Annyŏng-hi ka-seyo
Can you speak English?/Yong-o halsu-issum-nikka?
Do you understand me?/Ee hae ha-seyo?
Please bring me some.../...chom katta ju-seyo
...beer/maekchu...
...cold drinking water/naeng su...
...hot water (for bathing)/ttugo-un mul...
...barley tea/pori ch'a...
...Korean food/Han chong sik...
Good morning/Good afternoon/Good evening/Annyŏng ha-simnikka
Excuse me/Sille-hamnida
I am sorry/Mian-hamnida
You are welcome/Ch'onman-eyo
Yes/Ne
No/Anio
(Something, someone is) good/Cho ssumnida
(Something, someone is) bad/Nappumnida

Korean Langauge Schools

Korean language courses are offered at a few institutes in Seoul

in two or three-month terms.
Student visas can be arranged.
Among the prominent schools are:
Language Teaching Research Centre
16-17, T'aep'yong-no
1-ka, Chong-dong
Chong-no ku
Tel: 737-4641
Yonsei University
Korean Language Institute
Taek 134
Sinch'on-dong
Sodaemun-ku
Tel: 392-6405
Ewha Womans University
Tel: 362-6151
Yongsan Education Centre
(University of Maryland Programme)
Tel: 7904-3194, 7904-6708

JAPAN

Getting Acquainted

The Place

Japan is made up of four main islands – Honshu, Hokkaido, Kyushu and Shikoku – and several thousand smaller ones that stretch nearly 3,000 km (1,900 miles) in the temperate and sub-tropical zones, between 20° and 45° latitude. The total land area is 377,435 sq. km (145,728 sq. miles), 85 percent of which is mountainous. The country is divided into four different climatic and cultural zones by mountain ranges: the Japan Sea and Pacific Ocean on the northeast half, and the Japan Sea and Inland Sea on the southwest half. The famed Mount Fuji, seen on clear days from many places in and around Tokyo, is the country's highest mountain at 3,776 metres (12,388 ft). The population of Japan is about 130 million.

Local Time

Japanese time is GMT +9 hours, and there is no seasonal adjustment.

Climate

"Japan has four seasons" is a phrase you will hear often, though it is still not clear why the Japanese feel that it is a feature unique to their country. The climate in Tokyo can be a bit of everything, and in recent years, the manifestation of the "four seasons" has not been all that clear, but generally in spring most of Japan is pleasant until May. In June begins the rainy season

which should last about a month, but often longer. The summers are hot and sticky through to September. The typhoons usually come through in August and September. Autumn begins in late September and lasts through mid-November and is cool and pleasant. The winter lasts from mid-November to the end of February or beginning of March.

Government

Form: Parliamentary Democracy
Head of State: Emperor Akihito
(born December 23, 1933, took office January 7, 1989)
   While the emperor's actual power is less than that of, say, the queen of England, his social, cultural and political influence is much stronger than intended by the allied powers who, during the occupation of Japan following World War II, "guided" the

People

Population density: 326 persons per square kilometre
Life expectancy at birth: 76 for males; 82 for females
   Life expectancy has been steadily rising for the last three decades, and the "greying" of Japan is becoming a major social concern. In 1985, only 10.3 percent of the population was 65 or older; in the year 2020 it is expected to reach 25 percent.
   Retirement age for salaried employees, stable at 55 during most of the post-war era, is now gradually being raised to 60 by many major companies. Private and national pension plans are provided, covering 99 percent of the country's working population. However, the economic downturn in Japan during the 1990s, which lasted into the 21st century, has restructured the "life-time" employment expectation of workers. Moreover, the cost of providing pensions is expected to create considerable economic problems as the population ages.

drafting of Japan's present constitution.

Although Article 1 of that document states the the "Emperor shall be the symbol of the State," and that he derives his position from the will of the people, the exact powers of the emperor are not specifically defined. Still, he has no control or influence over national or international policy of the Japanese government, and his public speeches are carefully scripted by the Imperial Household Agency, which administers the imperial family.

Prime Minister: (President of majority party in Lower House; there has been a Liberal Democratic Party (LDP) Prime Minister since 1955, except for the period from 1993 to 1996.

Customs and Culture

At work and in most formal situations, the Japanese may seem a very reticent and reserved people, lacking in spontaneity or personality. There are books and theories explaining this behaviour, but it only provides one side of the picture. Japanese (especially men) can become extremely raucous when drinking and often let out their real opinions and feelings after a few drinks. The next morning in the office, all is forgotten. Intentionally.

On the crowded trains you will find yourself being pushed and bumped around. You do not need to be polite here; just push along with everyone else. It is often said that "the Japanese are only polite with their shoes off," which means that they are polite and courteous with people they know well and would be indoors with (where shoes are almost always removed).

The Japanese distinguish between inside and outside the home. Inside the entrance to all homes (and some restaurants) is an area for removing shoes. You then step up into the living area, wearing slippers or in your stockinged feet. (Slippers are never worn on *tatami* mats, however, only socks and bare feet.) Taking shoes off keeps the house clean, besides being more relaxing, and it also increases the amount of usable space, since you can sit on the floor without worrying about getting dirty. The toilet, however, is one area of the house that is considered "dirty," so separate slippers are provided there.

The custom of bowing has, in many cases, become something of a conditioned reflex. Foreigners, in general, are not expected to bow, and this is especially evident if a Japanese person first reaches out to shake hands.

As to punctuality and keeping appointments, the Japanese have a reputation for not being very punctual. At several of the famous "meeting places" (in Tokyo, for example, in front of Ginza's Sony Building or at the Hachiko entrance to Shibuya Station) you can observe people waiting, often for an hour or more, for someone. After several apologies and explanations, everything is forgotten and forgiven.

The way the Japanese usually speak and express themselves gives a very good picture of their culture. Direct statements of fact are most often avoided as this implies that the speaker has a superior knowledge, and this is considered impolite. Therefore, much "beating around the bush" is done which often leads to misunderstandings and seems like a waste of time to foreigners, but this must be taken into consideration when in Japan.

In their own language, the Japanese are expert at reading between the lines and interpreting deft nuances of words and tone.

In any case, whatever happens, foreigners are usually forgiven for any breach of etiquette. Japanese behaviour in general is situational, and the Japanese themselves often don't know the right thing to do in any given situation. "It all depends on the situation," remarks the smart alec, but it's often fun for everyone involved when one of "us" makes a slip. Sometimes it actually does help to break the ice and put everyone in a more relaxed mood.

Planning the Trip

Entry Regulations

Visas and passports

A proper visa is necessary for foreigners living in Japan and engaged in business or study. Passengers with confirmed departure reservations can obtain a stopover pass for up to 72 hours.

Visitors from the following countries are not required to obtain a visa prior to arrival in Japan, provided they do not intend to stay for more than 90 days nor receive remuneration in Japan: Argentina, Belgium, Canada, Chile, Colombia, Costa Rica, Cyprus, Denmark, Finland, Greece, Holland, Iceland, Israel, Italy, Luxembourg, Malaysia, Norway, Portugal, Singapore, Spain, Sweden, Turkey, United States.

Visitors from the following countries may reside in Japan for up to 6 months providing they are not earning an income: Austria, Germany, Ireland, Liechtenstein, Mexico, Switzerland and the U.K.

Extension of Stay

Foreigners wishing to extend their stay in Japan must report, in person, to the Immigration Bureau two weeks before their visa expires. Present your passport, a statement with the reasons why you want an extension of stay, and documents certifying the reasons. The fee is ¥4,000.

Electricity

The power supply is 100 volts AC. Eastern cities in Japan, including Tokyo, run on 50 cycles, while those in the west such as Kyoto, Osaka and Nagoya, use 60 cycles.

Immigration Information

Tel: (03) 3213-8523 or 3213-8527. Open Monday–Friday 9.30am–noon, 1–4pm.

Customs

Japan strictly bans the import and use of narcotic drugs, firearms and ammunition. If caught in possession of any of these, the offender will not face the death penalty, but can expect no leniency. Many a foreigner is still sitting in a Japanese prison, long forgotten by everyone but himself.

You can bring in any currency, personal ornaments and other valuables into Japan, but there is an official limit of ¥5 million that can be taken out.

You are also allowed to bring with you into Japan, free of tax, three 760 ml (25 fl oz) bottles of spirits, 400 cigarettes and 100 cigars or 500 g of tobacco, and 50 g (2 fl oz) of perfume.

Health

In general, levels of hygiene are very high, and it is very unlikely that you will become ill as a result of eating or drinking something. The tap water, though heavily chlorinated, is potable. Most food is of a high standard. However, because the Japanese place so much emphasis on presentation and how food looks, there is wide use of chemical fertilisers in Japan, and therefore it is not recommended to eat the peel of fruits and some vegetables.

Toilets

Apart from major hotels and some train stations, most toilets in Japan are of the Asian squatting type, which takes some getting used to, but are supposed to be the most hygienic (no part of your body actually touches them) and physiologically best. In Tokyo and other major cities, they are slowly being replaced with Western-style toilets in many establishments. By law, every coffee shop and restaurant etc. must have its own toilet, or access to one in the same building. Toilets in train stations and other large places are often dirty and smelly.

Money Matters

The unit of currency is the yen (indicated as ¥), and the coins are ¥1, ¥5, ¥10, ¥50, ¥100 and ¥500. Notes are ¥1,000, ¥5,000 and ¥10,000. Japanese shops, services, and merchants are legally forbidden to accept foreign currencies. You can buy yen at foreign exchange banks and other authorised money changers on presentation of your passport. At the international airports at Narita and Osaka, the banks are open 24 hours. Traveller's cheques are useful only at banks and major hotels. Elsewhere, they are virtually worthless. Many banks in the large cities will issue international Travellers' cheques.

Major credit cards are accepted at establishments in and around Tokyo and Osaka/Kyoto, and there is no surcharge for their use. Unfortunately, acceptance is sporadic. Even at establishments displaying acceptance of Visa or MasterCard, for example, it is often quite difficult for a merchant to get approval for a credit card issued by a non-Japanese bank. If they refuse your card, don't get testy. Carry lots of cash instead, just in case.

Banks

Despite the wide use of computers and on-line systems, Japanese banks are often slow and inefficient in many fields. Especially when transferring money in or out of the country, you can expect the process to take a long time and to be costly. Also, small neighbourhood branches are often not able to process any international transactions. In order to send money out of the country, or cash foreign cheques, you will find it much easier to go to a major branch, where someone *may* be able to speak English and usually understand what you want to do. (An exception is Citibank, which has aggressively shaken up the way banks in Japan do business. If you are a Citibank customer elsewhere, your chances in Japan are much, much better.)

Banks are open Monday to Friday between 9am and 3pm for normal banking. Cash dispensers (ATMs) are few and far between, located usually only at bank branches and with restricted hours; most only "speak" Japanese, too. Moreover, most cash dispensers can't be used for cash advances on cards not issued by a Japanese bank. Even if there is a logo for Visa or MasterCard, it's for a Japanese bank-issued card only. In short, don't plan on cash advances from an ATM – you'll be caught short.

Useful Addresses

TOURIST OFFICES

Tourists may write to or contact any of the following offices of the Japan National Travel Organisation for assistance:

JNTO Overseas Offices

Australia: Level 33, The Chifley Tower, 2 Chifley Square, Sydney, NSW 2000
Tel: (02) 9232-4522
Fax: (02) 9232-1494.
Canada: 165 University Ave, Toronto, Ont. M5H 3B8
Tel: (416) 366-7140
Fax: (416) 366-4530.
France: 4-8, rue Sainte-Anne, 75001 Paris
Tel: (01) 42-96-20-29
Fax: (01) 40-20-92-79.
Germany: Kaiserstrasse 11, 60311 Frankfurt/M
Tel: (069) 20353
Fax: (069) 284281
e-mail: info@jntofra.rhein-main.com
Hong Kong: Suite 3704-05, 37/F, Dorset House, Taikoo Place, Quarry Bay
Tel: 2968-5688
Fax: 2968-1722.
Switzerland: 13 rue de Berne, 1201 Geneva
Tel: (022) 731-81-40
Fax: (022) 738-13-14.
United Kingdom: Heathcoat House, 20 Savile Row, London W1X 1AE.

Tel: (0171) 734-9638
Fax: (0171) 734-4290
e-mail: jntolon@dircon.co.uk
United States
New York: One Rockefeller Plaza, Suite 1250, New York, NY 10111. Tel: (212) 757-5640
Fax: (212) 307-6754
e-mail: jntonyc@interport.net.
Chicago: 401 North Michigan Ave., Suite 770, Chicago, IL 60611
Tel: (312) 222-0874
Fax: (312) 222-0876
e-mail: jntochi@aol.com
San Francisco: 360 Post St, Suite 601, San Francisco, CA 94108
Tel: (415) 989-7140
Fax: (415) 398-5461
e-mail: sfjnto@aol.com
Los Angeles: 624 South Grand Ave, Suite 1611, Los Angeles, CA 90017
Tel: (213) 623-1952
Fax: (213) 623-6301
e-mail: hideki.tomioka@sit.com

Domestic Offices of JNTO
If you have a message or questions, send e-mail to: jnto@jnto.go.jp. It may take some time until you get the answer.

Tourist Information Centres
Tokyo: Tokyo International Forum, 3-5-1 Marunouchi, Chiyoda-ku, Tokyo 100. (Located between Yurakucho and Tokyo stations.)
Tel: (03) 3201-3331. Open from 9am–5pm on weekdays, 9am–noon Saturday, closed Sundays and national holidays.
Narita TIC: Airport Terminal Bldg, Narita, Chiba Pref. 282
Tel: (0475) 32-8711 or (0476) 34-6251.
Kyoto Office (TIC): 1st fl., Kyoto Tower Bldg, Higashi-Shiokojicho, Shimogyo-ku, Kyoto 600
Tel: (075) 371-5649. Open from 9am–5pm weekdays, 9am–noon Saturday, closed on Sunday and national holidays.

   Japan Travel-Phone is a nationwide toll-free service offering travel-related information and language assistance. If within Tokyo or Kyoto, call the respective TIC offices. You will be connected to an English-speaking travel officer. Note that they will *not* book reservations, but simply offer information. Weekdays 9am–5pm, Saturday, 9am–noon. Numbers are toll-free:
Tokyo: (0120) 44-4800, (0088) 22-4800, or (03) 3201-3331 (toll).
Eastern Japan: (0088) 22-2800 or (0120) 222-800.
Western Japan: (0088) 22-4800 or (0120) 444-800.

   The **Teletourist Service** offers recorded information in English on events currently taking place that might be of interest to travellers. Tel: (03) 3201-2911.

TRAVEL AGENCIES

The following agencies, listed by the JNTO, offer travel services for foreign travellers:
Japan Travel Bureau (JTB), Int'l Travel Division, 5-5-2 Kiba, Koto-ku, Tokyo 135. Tel: (03) 5620-9411, Fax: 5620-9502. Internet (English): web2.jtb.co.jp/eng/index.html
Kinki Nippon Tourist Co., Kanda-Matsunaga-cho, Chiyoda-ku, Tokyo 101. Tel: (03) 3255-6535, Fax: 3251-1113. Internet (English): www.knt.co.jp/kokusai/top.htm www.kintetsu.com/index.html
Nippon Travel Agency, Shimbashi Ekimae Bldg., 2-20-15 Shimbashi, Minato-ku, Tokyo 105. Tel: (03) 3572-8716, Fax: 3574-9610. Internet (English): www.nta.co.jp/nippon/kokusai2.htm
JTB Traveland, Kotsukosha Ikebukuro Bldg., 1-13-6 Higashi-Ikebukuro, Toshima-ku, Tokyo 170. Tel: (03) 3983-9444, Fax: 3983-5148.
Japan Gray Line, Pelican Bldg., 3-3-3 Nishi-Shimbashi, Minato-ku, Tokyo 105. Tel: (03) 3433-4831, Fax: 3433-4807
Toppan Travel Service, Towa-Hamamatsucho Bldg. 7F, 2-6-2 Hamamatsucho, Minato-ku, Tokyo 104. Tel: (03) 5403-2500, Fax: 5403-2504
Okinawa Tourist Service, 1-2-3 Matsuo, Naha, Okinawa 900
Tel: (098) 862-1111, Fax: 861-7965

Practical Tips

Emergencies

Emergency Numbers
Police (crime and accidents): 110
Fire and ambulance: 119
Police info in English: (03) 3501-0110
Emergency calls can be made from any phone without using coins or prepaid telephone cards.

Japan Hotline, information and help about everything, in English, 10am–4pm weekdays. Tel: (03) 3586-0110.
   For **hospital information**, call (03) 5285-8181 in Tokyo (English, Chinese, Korean, Thai and Spanish spoken).

Medical Services
Try to remember that you are in Japan and must be prepared to adapt to the Japanese system. Although some doctors may speak English, the receptionist and nursing staff will not, so it is advisable to bring along a Japanese friend or someone else who can speak both languages. Most hospitals and clinics do not have appointment systems, so you have to be prepared to wait your turn, however frustrating that may be. Here is a list of hospitals and clinics in Tokyo where you would have no problem in being understood or treated. They all have different hours and systems.

Hospital Hotline (English): in Tokyo, Tel: (03) 3212-2323.
Tell-Tokyo English Lifeline: in Tokyo, Tel: (03) 3968-4099.

Prescriptions: Pharmacies do not dispense prescription drugs. Prescriptions (in Japanese only) must be taken to a doctor or hospital for filling. Call one of the two above numbers for assistance.

Hospitals in Tokyo
International Catholic Hospital (Seibo Byoin)
2-5-1 Nakaochiai, Shinjuku-ku
Tel: (03) 3951-1111
Open Monday–Saturday 8–11am.
Closed Sunday and 3rd Saturday.
Red Cross Medical Centre (Nisseki)
4-1-22 Hiroo, Shibuya-ku
Tel: (03) 3400-1311
Open Monday–Friday 8.30–11am;
Saturday 8.30–10.30am. Closed Sunday.
St Luke's International Hospital (Seiroka Byoin)
10-1 Akashicho, Chuo-ku
Tel: (03) 3541-5151
Open Monday–Saturday 8.30–11am
Closed Sunday.
International Clinic
1-5-9 Azabudai, Minato-ku
Tel: (03) 3582-2646
Open Monday–Friday 9am–noon, 2.30–5pm; Saturday 9am–noon. Closed Sunday.
Tokyo Adventist Hospital (Tokyo Eisei Byoin)
3-17-3 Amanuma, Suginami-ku
Tel: (03) 3392-6151
Open Monday-Saturday, 8.30–11am
Toho Fujin Women's Clinic
5-3-10 Kiba, Koto-ku
Tel: (03) 3630-0303
Open Monday–Saturday 1–5pm.
Closed Sunday.

Business Hours

Officially, business is done on a 9am to 5pm basis, but this is in theory only. The Japanese will often do overtime till 8 or 9pm. In general, **government** offices are open from 8.30 or 9am to 4 or 5pm Monday to Friday, and from 9am to noon on the 1st and 3rd Saturday of the month. **Main post offices** are open 9am to 7pm Monday to Friday, 9am to 5pm on Saturday, and 9am to noon on Sunday and holidays. **Branch post offices** are open 9am to 5pm Monday to Friday. **Department stores** are open daily from 10am to 7.30 or 8pm, except

that they tend to close the store only twice or three times a month, which varies with each store. **Restaurants** are open for lunch from 11.30am to 2pm and for dinner from 5 to 9 or 10pm. **Major companies** and **offices** are open from 9am to 5pm Monday to Friday. Some are also open on Saturday mornings. Most **small shops** open between 9 and 11am and close between 6 and 8pm.

Tipping

No tipping remains the rule in Japan, except for unusual or exceptional services. Porters at large stations and airports charge a flat rate of around ¥300 per piece of luggage. Taxi drivers don't expect any tips, nor do hotel staff.

Post

There are nearly 30,000 post offices in Japan, and in a small country like this, that means they are easily found. In addition to postal services, post offices offer savings services; in fact, the post office is Japan's largest holder of personal savings. Postal service and delivery is highly efficient and fast, but expensive for both international and domestic post.

Local post offices are open Monday–Friday, 9am–5pm; some are open Saturday mornings. Larger central post offices are open Monday–Friday, 9am–7pm, and Saturday, 9am–noon. For late owls, there's a 24-hour window at the **Tokyo Central Post Office**, on the Marunouchi side of Tokyo Station. For 24-hour, 365-day international mail services, there's a special **Tokyo International Post Office** (kokusai yubin kyoku), also near Tokyo Station for foreign mail only, 2-3-3 Otemachi, Chiyoda-ku.

International express mail: Larger post offices offer EMS services; for some reason, the isolated post offices outside of the major cities of Tokyo and Osaka may require that an account be opened, though it's just a formality. If language is

proving to be a problem in getting a package sent via EMS, this could be the reason.
International parcel post: foreign parcel post cannot exceed 20 kg per package to any international destination. For heavier packages or those that exceed certain size or content restrictions (which vary by country), a commercial courier service must be used.

Postal information (English) in Tokyo: (03) 3241-4877.

Telephones

To use the public telephones, which come in a variety of colours and abilities, just insert a ¥10 coin and dial the number desired. ¥10 for three minutes. Yellow and green phones accept ¥100 coins, which make them more convenient for long-distance calls, but no change is returned for unused portions.

Most common are the green phones, all taking prepaid telephone cards and some taking only prepaid cards, no coins. Telephone cards can be obtained at any Nippon Telegraph and Telephone (NTT) office, KDD office, many stores, or through special vending machines near phones.

Domestic calls, expensive over 60 km distant, are as much as 40 percent cheaper at night and on weekends and holidays.

Telephone Codes

Japan's country code: 81
Domestic area codes:
Fukuoka: 092
Hiroshima: 082
Kagoshima: 099
Kyoto: 075
Nagasaki: 0958
Nagoya: 052
Naha: 098
Osaka: 06
Sapporo: 011
Sendai: 022
Tokyo: 03
Yokohama: 045

NTT Information, domestic telephone directory information, in English. 9am–5pm weekdays.

Tokyo: Tel: (03) 5295-1010
Narita: Tel: (0476) 28-1010
Yokohama: Tel: (045) 322-1010
Hiroshima: Tel: (082) 262-1010
City Source, free English telephone directory from NTT. Tel: (03) 5256-3141, fax: (03) 5256-3148. Osaka, Tel: (06) 571-7866, fax: (06) 571-4185.
Japan Hotline (NTT/KDD), broad-based, hard-to-find phone numbers. Tel: (03) 3586-0110. Monday–Friday, 10am–4pm.

TOLL-FREE NUMBERS

Domestic telephone numbers that begin with "0120" or "0088" are toll-free, or "free-dial", calls.

INTERNATIONAL

Foreign companies such as AT&T and call-back companies have been revolutionising international phone service in Japan. Western-style hotels, of course, usually offer the standard IDD capabilities. Elsewhere, the situation is changing so quickly that it's best to ask around for the current conditions.

International calls can be made only from specially-marked – in English and Japanese – green telephones; look for an IDD sticker on the phone or booth. Increasingly, dark-gray card phones are appearing in hotels, public places, and at airports. They have analog and digital computer connections, with small screens displaying operating instructions in both Japanese and English.

To make a **person-to-person, reverse charge/collect,** or **credit-card** call from anywhere in Japan through KDD, the dominant international telecom company, simply dial 0051.

KDD Information, international telephone information, in English: 0057 (toll free).

TELEPHONE CARDS

The Japanese love prepaid cards, and telephone cards – not coins – are the primary form of payment for public telephones. These cards come in a number of different denominations and are for sale just about everywhere, including from vending machines. Companies and groups have customised cards printed for promotion and gifts. Collecting telephone cards is a big thing in Japan.

There are actually two types of prepaid cards available: NTT (domestic) and KDD (international). The cards are slightly different sizes and can only be used in the appropriate phone.

Note: touts on the street, usually illegal immigrants overstaying their visas, will try to hustle cards at large discounts. These are definitely counterfeit and may not work in phones. This is a persistent problem around Ueno Park and Ueno Station.

INTERNET AND E-MAIL

If carrying a laptop or PDA and you already have an ISP in your home country, check to see if they have a local phone number in Japan to make a connection; many do.

Telephone costs are high everywhere in Japan, and thus surfing the internet comes at a price if making a toll call.

For those who must have their own connection in Japan while travelling, **Global OnLine** offers a modified account that costs around ¥500 per month for 5 hours, with additional per-minute costs after 5 hours. Local access numbers throughout Japan. In English, Tel: (03) 5334-1720, Fax: 5334-1711. e-mail: sales@gol.com

An account may be set up from anywhere using their Web site: http://home.gol.com/index_e.html

Newspapers

Readers of English are blessed with four English-language daily newspapers published by Japanese

media: *The Japan Times, Mainichi Daily News, Asahi Evening News,* and *The Daily Yomiuri.*

Travellers should read one or more for their coverage of local news, features, and events, and for the advertisements that can yield deals. Monday's edition of *The Japan Times* is the place to find help-wanted ads, half of them for English teachers (and a few for French or German) and the rest for everyone else. Papers can be purchased at most newsstand kiosks on the street and in train and subway stations. Also found frequently at kiosks is the *International Herald-Tribune* and *The Asian Wall Street Journal.* Other foreign newspapers can be found at most hotels and at the larger bookstores.

Public Holidays

1 January: *Ganjitsu* (New Year's Day)
15 January: *Seijin no Hi* (Coming-of-Age Day)
11 February: *Kenkoku Kinen no Hi* (National Foundation Day)
21 March: *Shumbun no Hi* (Vernal Equinox Day)
29 April: *Midori no Hi* (Greenery Day)
3 May: *Kempo Kinembi* (Constitution Memorial Day)
4 May: *Kokumin no Kyujitsu* (bank holiday)
5 May: *Kodomo no Hi* (Children's Day)
15 September: *Keiro no Hi* (Respect-for-the-Aged Day)
23 September: *Shubun no Hi* (Autumnal Equinox Day)
10 October: *Taiiku no Hi* (Sports Day)
3 November: *Bunka no Hi* (Culture Day)
23 November: *Kinro Kansha no Hi* (Labour Thanksgiving Day)
23 December: *Tenno Tanjobi* (Emperor's Birthday)
25 December: *Kokumin no Kyujitsu* (bank holiday)
If a holiday falls on a Sunday, the following Monday will be a "substitute holiday".

Getting Around

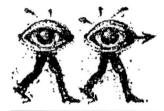

On Arrival

FROM NARITA AIRPORT

A taxi to downtown Tokyo from Narita costs between ¥20,000 and ¥30,000, depending on destination and traffic. Most people prefer either the bus or train, a tenth of the price of a taxi. Either way, it's 2–3 hours by road.

Bus

A regular limousine bus service runs between Narita and TCAT (Tokyo City Air Terminal) in downtown Tokyo, to Tokyo and Shinjuku Stations, and to most major hotels in Tokyo. Tickets (around ¥3,000) are bought at the airport after clearing immigration and customs. There are several routes depending on destination. Buses are boarded outside the terminal at the curb, and will accept any amount of luggage at no extra charge. The buses leave every 20 minutes or so, taking two to three hours to arrive at the hotel. There are also buses to Yokohama and Haneda, the domestic airport.

Trains

There are two train alternatives into Tokyo: the Keisei Skyliner and the JR Narita Express. Both are twice as fast as by taxi or bus, but not as convenient, as once at a station, you'll have to make arrangements for transport around the city. (While the city's subway system is all-encompassing, if carrying more than one small bag, or unless of considerable stamina, forget getting around or getting to the hotel by train or subway, especially during the humid and hot months of summer. You've been warned...)

In terms of connections, the Narita Express is more convenient, stopping at JR Stations in Chiba, Tokyo (Station), Shinjuku, Ikebukuro, Yokohama and Ofuna. The Skyliner stops just at Ueno Station and nearby Nippori. Both take about an hour to reach Tokyo and neither have restrictions on luggage.

The Narita Express costs about ¥3,000 for regular class and tickets must be bought in advance. The Skyliner costs around ¥2,000 and tickets can be bought in advance or at the Station for the next train.

The Skyliner is far more comfortable than the Narita Express (unless travelling in first class, which is a delight). Narita Express's regular seats are small with almost no leg room: usually you sit facing another seat, knee to knee, in groups of four. When travelling with families, the Japanese prefer this style. But for the arriving traveller trying to shake jet lag, or exhausted from last-minute sightseeing before leaving Japan, this arrangement leaves a lot to be desired, especially for the price and especially when the train is overcrowded. (JR permits standing passengers when trains are full, making them even fuller.)

The Keisei Skyliner, on the other hand, is never overbooked or crowded, and the seats are quite comfortable with lots of leg room. Considering the difference in price, the Skyliner is far and away the better deal, both in price and in comfort. If one isn't carrying a lot of luggage, a connection can be made at Ueno Station to JR trains or the subway. Or there's the taxi.

Domestic air connections

If making a domestic air connection, you must take the taxi, bus or train into Tokyo and make the connection at Haneda Airport. No domestic flights are made out of Narita. The limousine bus will take you directly from Narita to Haneda, as will a very expensive taxi.

Baggage delivery

Most residents of Japan take advantage of Japan's fast and reliable delivery network. After clearing immigration and customs, take your luggage to the ABC counter in the main terminal (there are several). Often a line indicates the counter. For about ¥1,500 per bag, ABC will deliver the bag by the following day wherever you are. If carrying more than a couple of bags, seriously consider this alternative.

FROM HANEDA AIRPORT

If you are coming into Haneda Airport, then a taxi to the town centre will cost about ¥5,000 to ¥6,000 and takes about 30–40 minutes. Provided your luggage is light, you can take the Monorail to Hamamatsucho Station on the JR Yamanote Line. The trip takes about 17 minutes.

FROM KANSAI AIRPORT

The Kansai International Airport (KIX) has replaced Osaka Airport (Itami) as the international air terminus for the Kansai region. It was also intended to relieve the overcrowding at Narita Airport, which has restricted operating hours. However, some domestic flights still fly from Itami, possibly necessitating an inconvenient connection from international to domestic flights. The second largest and the first 24-hour-operation airport in Japan, Kansai International Airport, opened in 1994. It is located southeast of Osaka Bay, 5 km off the coast and about 60 km from JR Shin-Osaka Station for *shinkansen* (bullet train) connections. KIX, constructed on an artificial island in Osaka Bay and one of the world's most expensive – ¥2,600 departure tax – is architecturally impressive and extremely functional. All international and domestic connections at KIX are made at the same terminal in a matter of minutes. (Note: Make sure to confirm that domestic flight connections are from KIX and not

Itami-Osaka Airport.) Despite being on an island, getting to and from KIX is relatively easy: two railways, two expressways, some 10 limousine bus lines, and four high-speed ferries connect the island to every point in the Kansai.

For travel information, the **Kansai Tourist Information Centre** is located in the arrival lobby (1st Fl.) and is open daily from 9am to 9pm. For handling currency exchange, there are 10 banks at the airport, with one or more open from 6am to 11pm. Japan Rail Passes can be exchanged either at the JR West Information Counter in the International Arrivals Lobby (1st Fl, open daily, 8am to 9pm), at the TIS-Travel Service Centre (open daily, 10am to 6pm), or at the green-coloured Midori-no-madoguchi Reservations Ticket Office (open daily, 5.30am to 12 midnight) of JR Kansai Airport Station.

TO/FROM OSAKA

Train

JR (Japan Railway) Haruka Express, with reserved seating, runs between KIX and Osaka's Tennoji Station (29 min) and Shin Osaka Station (45 min), where you catch the *shinkansen*, or bullet train. The JR Kuko-Kaisoku connects KIX with Osaka's Tennoji Station (45 min) and Namba Station's Osaka City Air Terminal (O-CAT), which offers express baggage check-in (60 min).

For **JR train information** tel: (0724) 56-6242.

Nankai Railroad also connects KIX with Osaka's Namba Station. Three trains make the run.

For **Nankai train information** tel: (0724) 56-6203.

Bus

There are a number of deluxe buses between KIX and various Osaka hotels and rail stations. These take about an hour, on a good day, and are a bit cheaper than the train.

For bus information call Keihan Bus Co. tel: (07240 55-2500.

Ferry

Two high-speed ferries connect KIX with Osaka's Tenpozan port (40 min). For ferry information tel: (06) 575-1321.

TO/FROM KYOTO

Train

JR Haruka Express, reserved seats, connects Kyoto Station with KIX (75 min). For JR train information tel: (075) 351-4004.

Bus

A Keihan bus leaves from Uji, south of Kyoto, for KIX and takes about 2 hours. For bus Keihan bus information call tel: (0724) 55-2500.

TO/FROM NARA

Bus

A bus runs from KIX to Nara JR Station (95 min). For bus information call Keihan Bus Co. tel: 0724-55-2500.

TO/FROM KOBE

Bus

Connect by bus from KIX to Kobe's Sannomiya Station (90 min). For bus information call Keihan Bus Co. tel: (0724) 55-2500.

Ferry

The Kobe Jet Shuttle is the best and fastest way to get to or from Kobe. The Jet Shuttle runs between KIX and the Kobe City Air Terminal (K-CAT) on Port Island (30 min), where free bus service is provided to Kobe's Sannomiya Station. For Jet Shuttle information tel: (078) 306-2411.

TO/FROM SOUTHERN ISLANDS

Ferries

Two high-speed ferries connect KIX with Awaji and Shikoku islands: To Tsuna and Sumoto on Awaji Island (40 min), for information tel: (0799)

24-3333. To Tokushima on Shikoku Island (82 min), for information tel: (06) 575-2101.

Public Transport

RAIL

JR Train Information, in English, information only, no reservations, 10am–6pm weekdays. Tel: (03) 3423-0111.

Japan has one of the most efficient and extensive rail networks in the world. Rail service is provided by **Japan Railways (JR)** and several regional private lines. The trains on important routes run every few minutes. Trains – such as JR's *shinkansen*, sometimes called the bullet train, which travels at speeds of up to 275 kph (170 mph) – offer alternatives to air and long-distance bus travel. Between Tokyo and Kyoto, travel times are the same for both air and shinkansen. The train, however, is from city centre to city centre; air, from airport to airport.

The **subway** systems in Japan are clean, safe, and convenient. Subways are faster than congested road transportation. However, Japanese trains are notorious for being crowded, especially during morning and evening rush hours. Trains and subways are sometimes packed to more than three times their specified capacity (and during holiday periods the bullet train is packed to standing room only), though it actually feels like more.

All subway stations post a timetable. Regular service is Monday to Saturday. The Sunday and holiday schedule has slightly fewer runs. Trains run until around after midnight, so be sure to check the time of the last train. All subway and train stations have a route map with fares for each stop near the ticket machines. However, it is not always in English. Your present location is indicated with a red mark.

The fares are regulated on a station-to-station basis, so if you cannot determine the fare required, just purchase the cheapest ticket available. You can pay the difference, if needed, at the exit gate upon arrival at your destination. The ticket machine will dispense the ticket and give the correct change.

A child's ticket is half fare. Most ticket machines accept coins only, although some will take ¥1,000 notes or prepaid cards. There is usually a machine that gives change or sells prepaid cards nearby.

Transport cost savings can be made by buying a *teiki* (train pass), valid for one, three or six months. Major subway and train stations issue passes. Another way to save on train fares is to buy a *kaisuken*, a series of 11 tickets between two destinations for the price of 10. Lastly, one-day tickets good on either subway lines or JR trains are available.

Station arrivals are announced in Japanese inside the trains but are often difficult to understand. There is usually a map of the stops on the line and connecting lines above the train doors. The names of the stations are usually written in both Japanese and English.

Timetables and subway maps in Japanese can be obtained at most stations. Subway maps in English are available in various English-language publications and at some major train and subway stations.

DISCOUNT TICKETS

In the major cities, there are special tickets that allow unlimited travel for one day. If doing a lot of sightseeing, the savings are considerable. They can be purchased at ticket windows and sometimes at special ticket machines, often marked in English.

Tokyo

Tokyo Free Kippu: One-day pass for JR trains, Toei trains, Toei buses, and TRTA (Eidan) subways. All may be used as often as possible (except JR express trains). Approx. ¥1,500.

Tokunai Free Kippu: Unlimited-use, one-day pass in Tokyo for use only on JR trains (except JR express

trains) running within the 23 wards of Tokyo. Approx. ¥800.

Toei Economy Pass: Unlimited-use, one-day pass for Toei trains, buses and subways within Tokyo on any day within a 6-month period. Approx. ¥700.

TRTA (Eidan) Subways: Unlimited-use, one-day open ticket for all TRTA (Eidan) subways. You can take all TRTA (Eidan) subways. Approximately ¥700.

Kyoto

Unlimited-use, one-day bus and subway ticket that can be used on all city buses and subways in the Kyoto area. Approx. ¥1,200; 2-days, ¥2,000.

Osaka

Unlimited-use, one-day pass for buses and subway. Approx. ¥900.

JR TRAIN DISCOUNTS

If you've not purchased a Japan Rail Pass or don't qualify, JR offers a number of special fare discounts. Amongst them:

Discount round-trip: a 20-percent discount to destinations more than 600 km distant, one-way.

Japan Rail Pass

Japan's rail services are unsurpassed in the world. Remarkably efficient, they go nearly everywhere, even to the remotest neck of the woods.

Foreign travellers in Japan should consider purchasing a Japan Rail Pass. The pass allows for virtually unlimited travel on the national JR network, including the *shinkansen*, or bullet trains. Passes cannot be purchased within Japan and you must be travelling in Japan under the visa entry status of "temporary visitor".

Once in Japan, the pass must initially be validated at a JR Travel Centre (which are everywhere in Japan). Once it is validated,

Shuyuken tickets: excursion tickets with a savings of around 20 percent for direct travel between a starting point and a designated area in which unlimited travel can be made. Valid on all JR trains and bus lines.

Package tours: discount lodging as well as discounted rail and bus travel. Packages may be purchased at JR Travel Centres, at the Green Window (*midori no madoguchi*) or leading travel agents.

Orange Card: a prepaid card with discounts for travel on JR trains. Cards come in several denominations and are used to buy JR tickets from vending machines for distances of less than 100 km.

Full Moon Green Pass: senior-citizen discount for couples. Available for a husband and wife whose total age is over 88 years. Good for a Green Car (first-class) and B-type sleeping car berth on any JR line except the JR bus line. Extra charges for other services. Prices start at ¥80,000 for 5 days.

Seishun 18 Kippu: a coupon good for five days' travel, each section used for one day's unlimited train travel. Good for ordinary JR trains, rapid JR trains, and the JR ferryboat between Miyajimaguchi and Miyajima Island. Passengers may get on and off as many times as

reservations can be made at any so-called Green Window (*midori no madoguchi*) at major stations.

While trains are not especially cheap in Japan (long-distance fares equal air fares), the pass represents a great deal. A 7-day pass costs around ¥30,000 – less than the round-trip fare from Narita Airport to Kyoto via Tokyo.

	regular	first-class
7-day:	¥30,000	¥40,000
14-day:	¥50,000	¥65,000
21-day:	¥60,000	¥80,000

Prices are approximate.

Children aged 6 to 11 travel at half the above prices.

they want at any JR station and at the JR ferry terminal within the same date. The price is approximately ¥12,000 both for adults and children. It may be shared by several people, provided they travel together and do not split the coupon.

Private Transport

Driving in Japan is a headache. Roads are narrow and crowded, signs confusing, and rental cars and petrol are expensive. Expressway tolls are very costly, as are bridge tolls. If at all possible, consider flying or taking the train.

Taxis

Taxis are the most comfortable way of getting around, but also the most expensive. The basic fare in Tokyo is ¥650 for the flag drop. A short trip can easily cost ¥3,000 to ¥5,000. Once again, no tipping is expected or required. Taxis are readily available on almost every street corner, major hotel and railway station. A red light in the front window is illuminated if the taxi is available.

- Don't touch the door when getting in or out of a taxi. The doors on taxis are operated by the driver with a remote lever. Get out, walk away and forget the door. Try opening or closing the door and you'll get a scowl from the driver.
- Most taxi drivers speak only Japanese, so it can be helpful to have your destination written in Japanese.
- Don't be surprised if an available taxi ignores you late at night; the driver is looking for a *sarariman* – and a nice, tidy fare – on his way back to the suburbs.

Where to Stay

Hotels

There are hotels everywhere, but unfortunately few of them are up to international standards. Those that are reflect it in their price. However, convenience is a very pricey commodity here, so you are often paying for the location more than the service or luxury. Below is a brief listing of major hotels in alphabetical order. Please note that the rankings are according to prices of single or twin rooms. In most hotels and all *ryokan*, you are provided with a *yukata* robe, toothbrush, razor, shower cap, etc.

Many hotels offer only twin beds, which are the most popular arrangement in Japan. Rooms for smokers may have a thick stench of stale smoke.

Finally, hotel rooms are quite compact. Even a ¥20,000 room in a deluxe hotel can be snug. So-called business hotels, generally found in the moderate and budget categories (and a few in the expensive category), have rooms that are not just snug, but cramped. Expect submarine-style spaciousness.

Western-style hotels offer rooms whose rates may vary from ¥8,000 to ¥30,000. There are hotels which also provide Japanese-style guest rooms and landscaped gardens. Others have restaurants serving Continental food as well as local *sukiyaki*, *sushi* and *tempura*.

Ryokan (Japanese-style inns) exude an atmosphere of traditional Japanese living. They charge an average of ¥9,000 per person, depending on the type of bath facilities offered.

There are about 80,000 *ryokan* in Japan, of which 2,000 are

members of the Japan Ryokan Association (JRA), who ensure that a high standard of service is maintained. Guests sleep in rooms covered with *tatami* (straw) mats, on *futon*. The baths are communal, though there are usually separate baths for men and women. Morning and evening meals are served in the guest's room.

Minshuku are bed-and-breakfast lodgings without the frills (toiletries and *yukata* gowns etc). Rates are from ¥5,000 up. The Japan National Tourist Organisation (JNTO) lists some 230 minshuku for overseas visitors.

Japanese Inn Group offers the foreign traveller recommendations and bookings for traditional Japanese inns, usually with traditional *tatami* floors, *futon* beds, *yukata*, and *furo*, the Japanese-style bath. The Japanese Inn Group consists of about 90 reasonable *ryokan*, hotels, *minshuku* (family-run accommodation) and pensions located throughout Japan. Most of member facilities are small, family-run Japanese-style accommodation with home-town atmosphere and affordable rates (per person between ¥4,000-6,000), with meals extra.

Head office: c/o Sawanoya Ryokan, 2-3-11 Yanaka, Taito-ku, Tokyo 110. Tel: (03) 3822-2251 Fax: (03) 3822-2252.

Kyoto office: c/o Hiraiwa Ryokan, 314 Hayao-ho, Kaminokuchi-agaru, Ninomiya-cho-dori, Shimogyo-ku, Kyoto 600. Tel: (075) 351-6748 Fax: (075) 351-6969.

Japan Minshuku Centre Booking office, B1, Tokyo Kotsu Kaikan Bldg, 2-10-1, Yurakucho, Tokyo. Tel: (03) 3216-6556 (English spoken). 10am–6pm, Monday–Saturday. Average fee: ¥6,000–¥13,000 per person with 2 meals. Reservation by phone is basically not accepted. Reservation for high tourist season (July–August, April 29–May 5, December 25–January 4, weekends) can only be accepted for more than 2 persons per room.

Tokyo

tel code (03)
INTERNATIONAL CLASS
Akasaka Prince Hotel
1-2 Kioicho
Chiyoda-ku
Tel: 3234-1111
One of the Prince chain. Very
modern and efficient, and great
views from every room.
Century Hyatt Tokyo
2-7-2 Nishi Shinjuku
Shinjuku-ku
Tel: 3349-0111
One of the buildings amidst all the
skyscrapers of Shinjuku. Japanese-
style Hyatt service and accomm-
odation. Health facilities and disco.
Crowne Plaza Metropolitan
1-6-1 Nishi-Ikebukuro
Toshima-ku
Tel: 3980-1111
Three minutes from Ikebukuro
Station's west exit, Ikebukuro's
finest hotel.
Hotel Okura
2-10-4 Toranomon
Minato-ku
Tel: 3582-0111
Officially rated the 2nd-best hotel in
the world. Health facilities, excellent
restaurants and executive salon.
Hotel New Otani
4-1 Kioicho
Chiyoda-ku
Tel: 3265-1111
The largest hotel in Asia. Health
facilities, a 400-year-old Japanese
garden, and very good location.
Keio Plaza Hotel
2-2-1 Nishi Shinjuku
Shinjuku-ku
Tel: 3344-0111
A 45-storey skyscraper on the west
side of Shinjuku. Near the Tokyo
Metropolitan Government Office
towers. Health facilities and
executive salon.
New Takanawa Prince Hotel
3-13-1 Takanawa
Minato-ku
Tel: 3442-1111
Addition to the Takanawa Prince. All
of the rooms have private
balconies. Pool (summer only).
Roppongi Prince Hotel
3-2-7 Roppongi
Minato-ku

Tel: 3587-1111
A few minutes from Roppongi
Station. Outdoor heated pool.
Palace Hotel
1-1-1 Marunouchi
Chiyoda-ku
Tel: 3211-5211
Old but quiet and peaceful
surroundings overlooking the
Imperial Palace moats and gardens.
Royal Park Hotel
2-1-1 Nihombashi
Kakigaracho
Chuo-ku
Tel: 3667-1111
Next door to the Tokyo City Air
Terminal. Indoor swimming pool,
fitness club, Japanese garden and
executive floors. Convenient to
many different locations.
Tokyo Hilton International
6-6-2 Nishi Shinjuku
Shinjuku-ku
Tel: 3344-5111
Completed in 1984 and following in
the tradition of the former Hilton.
Health facilities and executive salon.
Tokyo Prince Hotel
3-3-1 Shibakoen
Minato-ku
Tel: 3432-1111
Another of the Prince chain. Located
next to Zojo-ji temple. Pleasant
outdoor garden restaurant, which is
very popular in summer. Pool
(summer only).

SUPERIOR CLASS
Asakusa View Hotel
3-17-1 Nishiasakusa
Taito-ku
Tel: 3842-2111
Good location for sightseeing and
shopping in downtown Asakusa.
There is always something
happening in the area.
Fairmont Hotel
2-1-17 Kudan Minami
Chiyoda-ku
Tel: 3262-1151
Old British style. About six minutes
from Kudanshita Station, right in
front of the Imperial Palace moat.
Ginza Dai-Ichi Hotel
8-13-1 Ginza
Chuo-ku
Tel: 3542-5311
Conveniently located, less than five
minutes from Shimbashi Station.

Haneda Tokyu Hotel
2-8-6 Haneda Kuko, Ota-ku
Tel: 3747-0311
Right next to Haneda Airport.
Shuttle service between the hotel
and the airport.
Hillport Hotel
23-19 Sakuragaokacho
Shibuya-ku
Tel: 3462-5171
A three-minute walk from Shibuya
Station. Excellent access to
restaurants, department stores and
theatres.
Hilltop Hotel
1-1 Surugadai
Kanda
Chiyoda-ku
Tel: 3293-2311.
Five minutes from Ochanomizu
Station. This very pleasant hotel is
an old favourite of writers and
artists. Excellent food and service.
Hotel Grand Palace
1-1-1 Iidabashi
Chiyoda-ku
Tel: 3264-1111
Downtown location. Ten minutes by
car to Tokyo Station and Tokyo City
Terminal.
Mitsui Urban Hotel
8-6-15 Ginza
Chuo-ku
Tel: 3572-4131
Great location.
President Hotel
2-2-3 Minami Aoyama
Minato-ku
Tel: 3497-0111
Located near the Crown Prince's
residence and the Roppongi and
Aoyama areas.
Shiba Park Hotel
1-5-10 Shibakoen
Minato-ku
Tel: 3433-4141
Quiet and cozy, away from all the
noise and bustle.
Sunshine City Prince Hotel
3-1-5 Higashi-Ikebukuro
Toshima-ku
Tel: 3988-1111
A modern hotel located in the
Sunshine City complex.
Yaesu Fujiya Hotel
2-9-1 Yaesu
Chuo-ku
Tel: 3273-2111
One minute from Tokyo Station.

STANDARD CLASS
Taisho Central Hotel
1-27-7 Takadanobaba
Shinjuku-ku
Tel: 3232-0101
Just one minute from
Takadanobaba Station on the JR
Yamanote Line.
Dai-ichi Inn Ikebukuro
1-42-8 Higashi Ikebukuro
Toshima-ku
Tel: 3986-1221
Good for shopping and business.

Kanto Region

Nara (tel code 0742)
SUPERIOR CLASS
Nara Hotel & Annex
Tel: 26-3300
Fax: 23-5252
Nara's top hotel, with excellent
facilities.
Nara Green Hotel
Tel: 26-7815
Upmarket business hotel situated
near Kintetsu Nara railway station.

STANDARD CLASS
Fujita Nara
Tel: 23-8111
Pleasant hotel on the west side of
town close to Nara railway station.
Offers reduced room rates in low-
season.
Ryokan Hakuhoh
Tel: 26-7891
Central location and good value
rooms.

BUDGET CLASS
Seishonen Kaikan Youth Hostel,
Tel: 22-5540
Just about the cheapest place to
stay in Nara. Friendly staff.

Kyoto

tel code (075)
INTERNATIONAL CLASS
Fujita Hotel Kyoto
Tel: 222-1511
Fax: 256-4561
Central location, a few minutes
from Marutamachi station.
Hiiragiya (Ryokan)
Tel: 221-1136
Fax: 221-1139
Also well positioned; pre-book.

Miyako Hotel
Tel: 771-7111
Fax: 751-2490
Beautifully situated in the hills to
the east of the city, with verdant
gardens.
Tawaraya (Ryokan)
Tel: 211-5566
Over 300 years old. Reservations
are essential.

SUPERIOR CLASS
Holiday Inn Kyoto
Tel: 721-3131
Fax: 781-6178
Comfortable hotel with free shuttle
bus from Kyoto station.
Kyoto Century Hotel
Tel: 351-0111
Fax: 343-3721
Well-equipped and close to the
railway station.
Kyoto Hotel
Tel: 211-5111
Fax: 221-7770
Impressive new hotel, large and
central.

STANDARD CLASS
Kyoto Central Inn
Tel: 211-1666
Comfortable business-style hotel
close to Kawaramachi station.
Ryokan Hiraiwa
Tel: 351-6748
Functional tatami rooms; facilities
include air-con, TV and laundry.
Uemura (Ryokan)
Tel: 561-0377
Very attractive small ryokan with
just 3 rooms, situated close to the
Kiyomizu-Dera temple.

BUDGET CLASS
Tani House Annexe
Tel: 211-5637
Popular budget choice. En-suite
bathrooms and air-con are available
in some rooms. A 20-minute bus
ride from Kyoto station.

Hokkaido

Sapporo (tel code 011)
INTERNATIONAL CLASS
Keio Plaza Hotel Sapporo
7-2 Nishi Kita 5 Chuou
Tel: 271-0111
Fax: 221-5450

Near the railway station, this is one
of Sapporo s premier hotels. Full
five-star facilities.
Hotel New Otani Sapporo
1-1 Nishi 2-W, Chuo-Ku
Tel: 222-1111
Fax: 222-1111
Also close to the station with top
quality facilities.

SUPERIOR CLASS
KKR Sapporo
Tel: 231-6711
Popularity makes advance booking
essential. Good value spacious
rooms.
Hotel Sapporo Garden Palace
Tel: 261-5311
Located near the botanical gardens
and the railway station in a quiet
part of town.

STANDARD CLASS
Yugiri Ryokan
Tel: 716-5482
Very popular ryokan located close
to the university.

BUDGET CLASS
Sapporo International Inn Nada,
Tel: 551-5882
Close to the entertainment area of
Susukino, and very popular with
younger travellers.

Osaka

tel code (06)
INTERNATIONAL CLASS
ANA-Sheraton Hotel Osaka
Tel: 347-1112
Fax: 348-9208
One of the region's premier luxury
hotels, with full five-star facilities.
Located close to Osaka station.
Hankyu International
Tel: 377-2100
Fax: 377-3628
In the north of the city close to
Hankyu-Umeda station, this is the
most expensive hotel in town.

SUPERIOR CLASS
Holiday Inn Nankai Osaka
Tel: 213-8281
Fax: 213-8640
A popular choice close to the
Namba subway station in a lively
part of town.

Hotel Nikko Osaka
Tel: 244-1111
Fax: 245-2432
Close to Shinsaibashi subway station,
Osaka Hilton
Tel: 347-7111
Fax: 347-7001
Located opposite Osaka railway station in the Umeda area.

STANDARD CLASS
Ark Hotel Osaka
Tel: 252-5111
By Nagahoribashi subway station.
Hotel California
Tel: 243-0333
Decent-sized rooms. Good location near Shinsaibashi station in the Minami area.

The South

Hiroshima (tel code 082)
INTERNATIONAL CLASS
Granvia Hiroshima
Tel: 262-1111
Fax: 262-4050
Business hotel situated behind the railway station.

SUPERIOR CLASS
ANA Hotel Hiroshima
Tel: 241-1111
Fax: 241-9123
Centrally located and good for the summer with its roof-top garden.
Hiroshima Green Hotel
Tel: 248-3939
Pleasant hotel located close to the Peace Memorial Park.

STANDARD CLASS
Minshuku Ikedaya
Tel: 231-3329
Located in a quiet part of town on the far side of the Peace Park, the Ikedaya has spacious rooms and helpful staff.

Fukuoka (tel code 092)
INTERNATIONAL CLASS
Hotel Clio Court
Tel: 472-1111
Luxury hotel with excellent facilities, located right next to Hakata station.
Hotel Centraza Hakata
Tel: 461-0111
Opposite the Clio Court.

Underneath is Gourmet City, with two floors of restaurants offering cuisine from all over the world.

SUPERIOR CLASS
ANA Hotel Hakata
Tel: 471-7111
Fax: 472-7707
Located close to the main Hakata railway station, this is an excellent hotel.
Mitsui Urban Hotel
Tel: 451-5111
Well-equipped but with small rooms (as implied by its name).

Nagasaki (tel code 0958)
INTERNATIONAL CLASS
Nagasaki Tokyu Hotel
Tel: 25-1501
Down by Glover Garden in the southern area of the city.
Nagasaki Washington Hotel
Tel: 28-1211
Fax: 25-8023
Business hotel near the entertainment area and Chinatown.

SUPERIOR CLASS
Harbour Inn Nagasaki
Tel: 27-1111
Modern, comfortable business hotel.
Nagasaki Grand Hotel,
Tel: 23-1234
Fax: 22-1793
Located near the central entertainment and business areas. Good facilities and a popular beer garden.

STANDARD CLASS
Nishiki-so (ryokan)
Tel: 26-6371
An attractive old building with great views near Maruyama-Koen Park and the entertainment district.
Fukumoto (ryokan)
Tel: 21-0478. Another popular ryokan with a central location.

BUDGET CLASS
Nagasaki Youth Hostel
Tel: 23-5032
Close to the main railway station, this is one of three youth hostels in the city offering basic accommodation.

What to Eat

The Basics

Japan is a gourmet's paradise, and the eclectic diversity of possibilities are seemingly infinite. For a broad-brush survey of Japanese cuisine, see the Cuisine chapter on pages 263–265. But since you've come so far, be bold and try anything that you come across, and stay away from the Western fast-food joints, increasingly common in Japan.

In general, don't expect to escape from most decent restaurants for less than ¥5,000 per person, excluding drinks. On average, a night on the upscale side of town can cost ¥10,000 to ¥15,000. Stick to (Japanese) fast-food and street stands, and to convenience stores, to stay on the cheap side.

Below is a brief guide to the mainstays of Japanese cuisine.

SUSHI

Thin slices of only the choicest parts of the freshest fish, served on a bed of specially-prepared vinegared rice, with a dab of wasabi (green horse radish) in between.

SUKIYAKI

Thinly-sliced beef, sauteed for just a few seconds in a hot pan in front of you. A broth is added, and the beef is lightly simmered. Vegetables are added after the beef is cooked. Shabu-shabu is prepared in a similar way, but the broth is different. For sukiyaki, the broth is soy-based, thick and slightly sweet, while for shabu-shabu the broth is a clear stock, only lightly seasoned.

TEMPURA

Mostly fish and vegetables dipped in batter and then deep-fried for a short time. It should be eaten hot. Tempura is dipped into a soy-based sauce mixed with ginger and radish.

SOBA

These are buckwheat noodles, served in hot or cold soup, often with vegetables and/or meat. **Udon** are thick white noodles served in the same way as soba.

RAMAN

Popular Chinese noodles served in a similar way to soba and udon.

Culture

Theatres and Concerts

Bunkamura
2-24-1 Dogenzaka,
Shibuya-ku 150
Tel: Info: (03) 3477 3244,
tickets: (03) 3477 9999.
Hibiya Kokaido (public hall)
1-3 Hibiya-koen, Chiyoda-ku
Tel: (03) 3591-6388.
Kabuki-za (kabuki)
4-12-15 Ginza, Chuo-ku
Tel: (03) 3541-3131.
Kinokuniya Hall (Japanese drama)
3-17-7 Shinjuku, Shinjuku-ku
Tel: (03) 3354-0141.
Kokuritsu Gekijo (contemporary Japanese drama)
4-1 Hayatocho, Chiyoda-ku
Tel: (03) 3265-7411.
Kosei Nenkin Hall
5-3-1 Shinjuku, Shinjuku-ku
Tel: (03) 3356-1111.
Meijiza (historical Japanese drama)
2-31-1 Hamacho, Nihombashi, Chuo-ku
Tel: (03) 3660-3939.
National Theatre Nogakudo (noh)
4-18-1 Sendagaya, Shibuya-ku
Tel: (03) 3423-1331.
NHK Hall (classical)
2-1 Jinan, Shibuya-ku
Tel: (03) 3465-1111.
Nihon Budokan
2-3 Kitanomaru Koen, Chiyoda-ku
Tel: (03) 3216-0781.
Nissei Gekijo
1-1-1 Yurakucho, Chiyoda-ku
Tel: (03) 3503-3111.
Shibuya Kokaido
1-1 Udagawacho, Shibuya-ku
Tel: (03) 3463-5001.
Suehirotei (rakugo)
3-6-12 Shinjuku, Shinjuku-ku
Tel: (03) 3351-2974.
Sunshine Gekijo (Japanese versions of Broadway hits)
Sunshine City Bunka Kaikan,

3-1-4 Higashi-Ikebukuro, Toshima-ku
Tel: (03) 3987-5281.
Suntory Hall (classical)
1-13-1 Akasaka, Minato-ku
Tel: (03) 3505-1001.
Teikoku Gekijo (Imperial Theatre)
3-1-1 Marunouchi, Chiyoda-ku
Tel: (03) 3213-7221.
The Tokyo Globe (Shakespeare/opera)
3-1-2 Hyakunincho, Shinjuku-ku
Tel: (03) 3360-1151.
Tokyo Bunka Kaikan (classical/opera)
5-45 Ueno Park, Taito-ku
Tel: (03) 3828-2111.
Tokyo Dome (Big Egg)
1-3 Koraku, Bunkyo-ku
Tel: (03) 3811-2111.
Tokyo Takarazuka Gekijo (female revue)
1-1-3 Yurakucho, Chiyoda-ku
Tel: (03) 3591-1711.

Festivals

Festivals, or *matsuri* seem to be happening at any given time somewhere in Tokyo, and indeed have been an important part of Japanese life for hundreds of years. Many of the festivals have their roots in the long history of Japan's agricultural society. In today's ever modernising Japan, they are one of the few occasions when the Japanese can dress up and live a nostalgic past. Below is a short list of the main national holidays and the most important festivals. For information on upcoming events going on during any particular week or month, please consult TIC or any of the tourist publications.

JANUARY

The first **sumo** tournament of the year, **Hatsu-basho**, is held for 15 days at Tokyo's **Kokugikan** in mid January.

FEBRUARY

On the 3rd is **Setsubun**, the traditional bean throwing ceremony that is meant to purify the home of evil. Roasted beans are scattered from the inside of the house to the outside while people shout, "*Oni wa soto*" (Devils, go out!), and from the outside of the home to the inside while "*Fuku wa uchi*" (good luck, come in) is shouted. The same ceremony is also held at temples and shrines.

MARCH

On the 3rd is **Hina Matsuri** (Girl's Day), a festival for little girls. Small *Hina* dolls, representing imperial court figures, are displayed at home and in several public places.

APRIL

From early to mid April is **O-hanami** (cherry-blossom viewing), one of the important spring rites. People picnic, drink *sake* and sing songs under the pink blossoms.

On the 8th is **Hana Matsuri** (Birthday of Buddha), when commemorative services are held at various temples such as **Gokoku-ji**, **Senso-ji**, **Zojo-ji** and **Hommon-ji**.

MAY

In mid May, the **Natsu-basho** (summer *sumo* tournament) is held for fifteen days at the **Kokugikan**.

On the 3rd Saturday and Sunday, the **Sanja Matsuri** is held. This is one of the big Edo festivals honouring the three fishermen who found the image of Kannon in the river. The **Asakusa-jinja (Senso-ji)** is a great place to go at this time to see the dancing, music and many portable shrines.

JUNE

On the second Sunday is **Torigoe Jinja Taisai**, a night-time festival, when the biggest and heaviest portable shrine in Tokyo is carried through the streets by lantern light. It all happens at the **Torigoe Shrine**. From the 10th to the 16th is

Sanno Sai, another big Edo festival featuring a *gyoretsu* (people parading in traditional costumes) on Saturday at the **Hie Shrine**.

JULY

From the 6th to the 8th is the **Asagao Ichi** (Morning Glory Fair), when over 100 merchants set up stalls selling the morning flower at **Iriya Kishibojin**.

On the 7th is the **Tanabata Matsuri**, a festival celebrating the only day of the year when, according to the legend, the Weaver Princess (Vega) and her lover the Cowherder (Altair) can cross the Milky Way to meet. People write their wishes on coloured paper, hang them on bamboo branches, and then float them down a river the next day.

On the 9th and 10th is the **Hozuki Ichi** (Ground Cherry Fair) at **Senso-ji** from early morning to midnight. A visit to this temple on the 10th is meant to be equal to

46,000 visits at other times.

On the last Saturday of July, the **Sumida-gawa Hanabi Taikai** (Sumida River Fireworks) is held. This is the biggest fireworks display in Tokyo, and the best place to watch the display is between the **Kototoi** and **Shirahige bridges**, or at the **Komagata Bridge**.

AUGUST

Between the 13th and the 16th is the **Obon** festival, when people return to their home towns to clean up the graves and offer prayers to the souls of departed ancestors. The traditional **Bon Odori** folk dances are held all over Japan around this time.

OCTOBER

From mid to late October is chrysanthemum viewing time. Flower displays are dotted around the cities.

Visiting Imperial Villas in Kyoto

Any visit to an Imperial residence in Tokyo or Kyoto is an honour and a privilege. Only the grounds of Tokyo's **Imperial Palace** are opened to the public on January 2 and December 23, Emperor Akihito's birthday, a national holiday (*Tenno Tanjobi*). The Imperial Palace and villas in Kyoto are open by appointment only through the Imperial Household Agency.

To see the **Kyoto Imperial Palace, Shugaku-in Imperial Villa**, or **Katsura Imperial Villa** in Kyoto, apply for permission at the Imperial Household Agency office on the Palace grounds in Kyoto. Admission to the Palace and villas is free. For palace tours, you must apply – with passport – 30 minutes before tour times: 10am and 2pm weekdays and Saturday morning. (The palace is closed on Sundays and national holidays.) While the palace is open on Saturday mornings, the agency office is closed, so you need to apply on

weekdays. Only overseas visitors can apply and visit on the same day. Japanese must apply months in advance or wait for the week in April and October when the palace is open to the general public – a good time to avoid visiting. Palace tours begin at Seisho gate in the middle of the western wall and take about an hour. Most, but not all, tours are conducted in English, but an English-language pamphlet is provided. You must also apply to the same office for visits to either of the imperial villas; this can normally be done a few days before your intended visit. Some restrictions on children apply, so check with the Imperial Household Agency office before your visit. Hotels can be helpful in pre-planning any visit.

Imperial Household Agency, Kyoto Palace – Kyoto Gosho, 3 Kyoto Gyoen, Kamigyo-Ku, Kyoto 602. Tel: (075) 211-1215. Office hours 9am to 4.30pm weekdays.

NOVEMBER

The 15th is *Shichi-Go-San* (Seven-Five-Three), a ceremony for 5-year-old boys and 3- and 7-year-old girls. The children usually dress up in *kimono* or Sunday best and are taken to visit a shrine.

DECEMBER

The 14th is *Gishi Sai*, a memorial service for the famous 47 Ronin who, on this day in 1702, avenged the death of their master and later committed ritual suicide. They are buried at the **Sengaku-ji** where the service is held.

On the 31st at the stroke of midnight, every temple bell throughout the country begins to toll. The bells toll 108 times representing the 108 evil human passions. This is called *Joya no Kane*, and the general public is allowed to strike the bells at various temples.

Tokyo Art Galleries

There are art galleries all over the Ginza area and other parts of Tokyo, but below are four well-known ones that almost always hold interesting shows.

Kaneko Art Gallery
Mitsunari Bldg, 3-7-13 Kyobashi, Chuo-ku
Tel: (03) 3564-0455.
11am–6.30pm daily. Closed Sundays and public holidays.
Maruzen Gallery
2-3-10 Nihombashi, Chuo-ku
Tel: (03) 3272-7211.
10am–6.30pm daily. Closed Sundays.
Nichido Gallery
7-4-12 Ginza, Chuo-ku
Tel: (03) 3571-2553.
10am–7.30pm daily.
Parco Gallery
Parco Part 1, Udagawacho, Shibuya-ku
Tel: (03) 3477-5781.
10am–8.30pm daily.

Shopping

Shopping Areas

Japan is a very expensive place to shop, but there are still bargains to be had if you look hard enough. The quality of Japanese products is well known, and there are some items which can only be bought in Japan. Certain areas promote only certain kinds of merchandise, which means that some domestic travel is involved for the serious shopper.

The following is a guide to the main shopping attractions in cities and other areas throughout Japan.

IN AND AROUND TOKYO

Akihabara: The electronic jungle of the world featuring hundreds of discount stores.
Aoyama: High-class fashion boutiques.
Asakusa: Traditional Japanese toys, souvenirs, workmen's clothes, etc.
Ginza: The most expensive shopping centre. Several major department stores are located here, such as Hankyu, Matsuya, Matsuzakaya, Mitsukoshi, Printemps, Seibu and Wako, and exclusive boutiques. Also some traditional Japanese goods stores.
Harajuku: Another fashion area, though mostly geared to the young, which makes shopping relatively cheap. Several antique shops, and Kiddyland for the kids.
Hibiya: Mostly antique shops, jewellery shops, and art galleries.
Kanda and **Jimbocho:** Many second-hand bookstores.
Nihombashi: A good place to pick up traditional craft work. Two of Japan's oldest department stores, Mitsukoshi and Takashi-maya.

Roppongi: Several antiques shops in the area, the Axis design building which features interior design as its main theme, and Seibu's Wave building which specialises in audio-visual equipment.
Shibuya: A good place to begin with, Shibuya has a little bit of everything. Tokyu Hands is a must to visit; probably the most complete do-it-yourself department store in the world. Also here are the Seibu, Tokyu and Marui departments stores, the Parco "fashion buildings" besides the hundreds of small boutiques geared to young shoppers.
Shinjuku: Several big camera and electronic discount stores such as Yodobashi and Sakuraya. Also, Isetan and Marui department stores.
Ueno: Ameyoko is good for cheap food, cosmetics, clothing and toys. One of the few open markets in Tokyo. The shops in the back streets sell traditional Japanese goods.

Antiques

In most of the shops listed here, the staff speak English and are helpful. Watch out for badly restored pieces that have been given a quick coat of glossy lacquer and sold at steep prices.
Antique Gallery Kikori
Hanae Mori Building, B1, 3-6-1 Kita Aoyama, Minato-ku
Tel: (03) 3407-9363
Small but interesting selection of *tansu* and other items.
Antique Gallery Meguro
Stork Building, 2nd Fl, 2-24-18 Kamiosaki, Shinagawa-ku
Tel: (03) 3493-1971
Antiques market of sorts covering 740 sq. metres (885 sq. yards) that houses several small antiques shops.
Edo Antiques
2-21-12 Akasaka, Minato-ku
Tel: (03) 3584-5280
Large selection of *tansu* and *hibachi*.
Harumi Antiques
9-6-14 Akasaka, Minato-ku
Tel: (03) 3403-1043
Mostly *tansu* that have been

restored, but some unrestored pieces can be purchased.

Japan Old Folkcraft and Antique Centre (Tokyo Komingu Kotto-kan)
3-9-5 Minami Ikebukuro, Toshima-ku
Tel: (03) 3980-8228
Thirty-five dealers occupying 600 sq. metres (718 sq. yards) and displaying various antique items.

Oriental Bazaar
5-9-13 Jingæmae, Shibuya-ku
Tel: (03) 3400-3933
Apart from antiques, it is also a nice place to browse and pick up traditional Japanese toys, paper (*washi*), *kimono*, etc.

Ceramics

Besides workshops, department stores are the best places for Japanese ceramics offered at reasonable prices. On back streets, small shops also sell ceramics but prices are higher.

Iscryu Shoten
3-8-2 Ningyocho, Nihombashi Chuo-ku
Tel: (03) 3661-4820
Closed Sundays and holidays.

Saga Toen
2-13-13 Nishi Azabu, Minato-ku
Tel: (03) 3400-3682.

Tachikichi & Co. Ltd
6-13 Ginza, Chuo-ku
Tel: (03) 3571-2924.

Department Stores

Daimaru
1-9-1 Marunouchi, Chiyoda-ku
Tel: (03) 3212-8011
Closed Thursdays.

Isetan
3-14-1 Shinjuku, Shinjuku-ku
Tel: (03) 3352-1111
Closed Wednesdays.

Marui
3-30-16 Shinjuku, Shinjuku-ku
Tel: (03) 3354-0101
10.30am–7.30pm.

Matsuya
1-4-1 Hanakawado, Taito-ku
Tel: (03) 3842-1111
Closed Thursdays.

Matsuzakaya
3-29-5 Ueno, Taito-ku
Tel: (03) 3832-1111.

Mitsukoshi
1-7-4 Muromachi, Nihom-bashi, Chuo-ku

Tel: (03) 3241-3311
Closed Mondays.

Printemps
3-2-1 Ginza, Chuo-ku
Tel: (03) 3567-0077
10am–7pm. Closed Wednesdays.

Seibu (Main Store)
1-28-1 Minami Ikebukuro Toshima-ku
Tel: (03) 3981-0111
Closed Thursdays.

Sogo
1-11-1 Yurakucho, Chiyoda-ku
Tel: (03) 3284-6711
Closed Tuesdays.

Takashimaya
2-4-1 Nihombashi, Chuo-ku
Tel: (03) 3211-4111
Closed Wednesdays.

Tokyu
2-24-1 Dogenzaka, Shibuya-ku
Tel: (03) 3477-3111
Closed Thursdays.

Japanese Paper (Washi)

Haibara
2-7-6 Nihombashi, Chuo-ku
Tel: (03) 3272-3801
Closed Sundays and holidays.

Isetasu
2-18-9 Yanaka, Taito-ku
Tel: (03) 3823-1453.

Kurodaya
1-2-11 Asakusa, Taito-ku
Tel: (03) 3845-3830
Closed Mondays.

Kyækyodo
5-7-4 Ginza, Chuo-ku
Tel: (03) 3571-4429.

Ozu Shoten
2-6-3 Nihombashi Honcho, Chuo-ku
Tel: (03) 3663-8788
Closed on Sundays.

Washikobo
1-8-10 Nishi Azabu, Minato-ku
Tel: (03) 3405-1841
Closed Sundays and public holidays.

Kimonos (antique)

These shops specialise in antique *kimono*, *obi*, traditional blue and white textiles, *furoshiki*, *hanten*, etc. Prices from ¥1,000 up.

Flea markets (see list under *Flea Markets*) also sell them, and you can usually pick up very beautiful old *kimono* and *obi* in good condition.

Ayahata
2-21-2 Akasaka, Minato-ku
Tel: (03) 3582-9969
Closed Sundays and public holidays.

Hayashi Kimono
International Arcade, 1-7 Uchisaiwaicho, Chiyoda-ku
Tel: (03) 3581-9826.

Ikeda
5-22-11 Shiroganedai, Minato-ku
Tel: (03) 3445-1269
Closed Sundays.

Konjaku Nishimura
Hanae Mori Building, B1, 3-6-1 Kita Aoyama, Minato-ku
Tel: (03) 3498-1759
Closed Thursdays.

Lacquerware (Shikki)

Bushi
Axis Building, B1 5-17-1 Roppongi, Minato-ku
Tel: (03) 3587-0317
Closed Mondays.

Heiando
3-10-11 Nihombashi, Chuo-ku
Tel: (03) 3272-2871
Closed Sundays and public holidays.

Inachu Japan
1-5-2 Akasaka, Minato-ku
Tel: (03) 3582-4451.

Kuroeya
Kuroeya Kokubu Building, 2nd Floor, 1-2-6 Nihombashi, Chuo-ku
Tel: (03) 3271-3356
Closed Saturdays, Sundays and public holidays.

Musical Instruments

Bachi Ei Gakkiten (*Shamisen*)
2-10-11 Ningyocho, Nihombashi, Chuo-ku
Tel: (03) 3666-7263
Closed Sundays and holidays.

Kikuya Shamisen Ten (*Shamisen*)
3-45-11 Yushima, Bunkyo-ku
Tel: (03) 3831-4733
Closed Sundays and holidays.

Tsurukawa Gakki Honten (*Koto*)
1-12-11 Kyobashi, Chuo-ku
Tel: (03) 3561-1872
Closed Sundays and holidays.

Ishida Biwa Ten (*Biwa*)
3-8-4 Toranomon, Minato-ku
Tel: (03) 3431-6548
Closed Sundays and holidays.

Miyamoto Unosuke Shoten
(*drums*), 6-1-15 Asakusa, Taito-ku
Tel: (03) 3874-4131
Closed Sundays and public
holidays.

Paper Lanterns
Hanato
2-25-6 Asakusa, Taito-ku
Tel: (03) 3841-6411
10am–9pm. Closed 2nd and 4th
Tuesdays.
Kashiwaya
2-3-13 Shintomi, Chuo-ku
Tel: (03) 3551-1362
Closed Sundays.

Umbrellas (Kasa)
Hasegawa Hakimonoten
2-4-4 Ueno, Taito-ku
Tel: (03) 3831-3933
Closed Sundays.
Iidaya
1-31-1 Asakusa, Taito-ku
Tel: (03) 3841-3644.

Woodblock Print (Ukiyo-e)
Asakusa Okuramae Shobo
3-10-12 Kuramae, Taito-ku
Tel: (03) 3866-5894
Closed on Sundays, but will stay
open for appointments. Specialist
on books and prints on *Edo* and
sumo.
Hara Shobo
2-3 Jimbocho, Kanda, Chiyoda-ku
Tel: (03) 3261-7444
All types of prints old and new, from
the highest quality to a "bargain
drawer." English is spoken here.
Matsushita Associates, Inc.
6-3-12 Minami Aoyama, Shibuya-ku
Tel: (03) 3407-4966
Closed Sundays.
Oya Shobo
1-1 Kanda, Jimbocho, Chiyoda-ku
Tel: (03) 3291-0062
Closed Sundays.
Sakai Kokodo Gallery
1-2-14 Yura-kucho, Chiyoda-ku
Tel: (03) 3591-4678.

Language

General

The visitor will have few language
problems within the confines of
airports and the major Western-
style hotels, but outside these the
going can get tough for those who
are unescorted. Quite apart from
being unable to communicate
verbally, the hapless visitor will also
have the disconcerting experience
of being almost totally illiterate.

The written language is made up
of three different sets of
characters: two simple home-grown
syllabaries, *hiragana* and *katakana*,
consisting of 46 characters each;
and the much more formidable
Chinese ideograms, *kanji*.
Knowledge of just under two
thousand of these is necessary to
read a daily newspaper.

While the expenditure of the
enormous effort required to
memorise this number of kanji (it
takes the Japanese most of their
school career to do so) is clearly
unjustifiable for those with only a
passing interest in the language, a
few hours spent learning the two
syllabaries (on the plane trip to
Japan, for example) would not be
time completely wasted for those
who can afford it.

Hiragana can be useful for
identifying which station your train
has stopped at; the platforms are
plastered with hiragana versions of
the station name so that children
who have not yet learned kanji can
see where they are. Station names
are usually (but not always) posted
in roman script (*romanji*) as well,
but not always as obviously.
Katakana is useful in that it is used
to transliterate foreign words.
Western-style restaurants often
simply list the foreign names for the

dishes on their menus in katakana.
Pronunciation: With its small
number of simple and unvarying
vowel sounds, the pronunciation of
Japanese should be easy for those
who speak Western languages,
which are rich in vowel sounds.
Japanese has nothing like the
dreaded tonal system of Chinese to
frustrate the student.

Vowels have but one sound,
much like Spanish. Don't be sloppy
with their pronunciations.
a – between fat and the u in but
e – like the e in egg
i – like the i in ink
o – like the o in orange
u – like the u in butcher

When they occur in the middle of
words, i and u are often almost
silent. For example, *Takeshita* is
really pronounced *Takesh'ta* while
sukiyaki sounds more like *s'kiyaki*.

In spite of the seemingly simple
pronunciation of Japanese, a lot of
foreigners manage to mangle the
language into a form which is
almost impossible for the native
speaker to understand. It is mainly
intonation that is responsible for
this. It would be fallacious to claim
that the Japanese language has no
rise and fall in pitch – just listen to
a group of schoolgirls conversing on
the train to confirm this – but it is
certainly "flatter" in character than
Western languages.

It is important to avoid stressing
syllables within words; whereas an
English speaker would naturally
stress either the second or third
syllable of *Hiroshima*, for example,
in Japanese the four syllables
should be stressed equally. Another
problem lies in long (actually
double) vowel sounds. These are
often indicated by a line above the
vowel, or simply by a double vowel,
e.g. *Iidabashi*. To pronounce these
long vowels properly, it is simply
necessary to give the vowel sound
double length.

GREETINGS

Good morning/*Ohayo gozaimasu*
Hello (afternoon)/*Konnichi-wa*
Good evening/*Komban-wa*

Good night/*Oyasumi nasai*
Goodbye/*Sayonara* (*Shitsure shimasu* for formal occasions)
How do you do?/*Hajime mashite?*
How are you?/*Ogenki desu ka?*
My name is.../*...to moshimasu*
I'm American/*Amerika-jin desu*
I'm British/*Igirisu-jin desu*
I'm Australian/*Osturaraia-jin desu*
I'm Canadian/*Kanada-jin desu*

ASKING FOR DIRECTIONS

Excuse me, where is the **toilet**?/ *Sumimasen.* **Toire** *wa doko desu ka?*
Excuse me, is there a **post office** near here?/*Sumimasen. Kono chikaku ni,* **yubin-kyoku** *wa arimasu ka?*
bakery/*pan-ya*
greengrocer's/*yao-ya*
stationery shop/*bumbogu-ya*
pharmacy/*kusuri-ya*
barber shop/*toko-ya*
bookshop/*hon-ya*
supermarket/*supa-maketto*
department store/*depato*
restaurant/*restoran*
hotel/*hoteru*
station/*eki*
taxi stand/*takushii noriba*
bank/*ginko*
hospital/*byoin*
police station/*koban*

OUT SHOPPING

This one/*Kore*
That one (near the other person)/ *Sore*
That one (near neither of you)/*Are*
Do you have...?/*...(wa) arimasu ka?*
Could you show me that one please?/*Sore o misete kudasai?*
How much is it?/*Ikura desu ka?*
Do you accept (credit) cards?/ *(Kurjitto) kado tsukaemasu ka?*
I'll take this./*Kore o kudasai.*

BOARDING THE TRAIN

Ticket (office)/*kippu (uriba)*
reserved seat/*shitei seki*
unreserved seat/*jiyuseki*

first-class car/*guriin (green) sha*
Which platform does the train for Nagoya leave from?/*Nagoya yuki wa namban sen desu ka?*
Thank you (very much)/*(Domo) arigato gozaimasu* (informally, *domo* is enough)
Don't mention it./*Doitashimashite*
Thanks for the meal./*Gochisosama deshita.*
Here you are./*Dozo*
After you./*Dozo*
Sure, go ahead./*Dozo* (in answer to "May I...?")

DAYS/TIME

(On) Sunday/*Nichi-yobi (ni)*
(Next) Monday/*(Raishu no) Getsu-yobi*
(Last) Tuesday/*(Senshu no) Ka-yobi*
(Every) Wednesday/*(Maishu) Sui-yobi*
(This) Thursday/*(Konshu no) Moku-yobi*
Friday/*Kin-yobi*
Saturday/*Do-yobi*
Yesterday/*kino*
Today/*kyo*
This morning/*kesa*
This evening/*konya*
Tomorrow/*ashita*
What time is it?/*Nan-ji desu ka?*

NUMBERS

Counting is very complicated in Japanese! Counting up to ten on their fingers, the Japanese will go: *ichi, ni, san, shi (yon), go, roku, shichi* (or *nana*), *hachi, ku* (or *kyu*), *ju*. If they are counting bottles, they will go: *ip-pon, ni-hon, sam-bon, yon-hon, go-hon*... Pieces of paper and oranges are counted differently, as are goats and coins. (Depending on what is being counted, the suffix will change.) You will be fairly safe with the numbers below that don't need suffixes:

one/*hitotsu*
two/*futatsu*
three/*mittsu*
four/*yottsu*
five/*itsutsu*
six/*muttsu*

seven/*nanatsu*
eight/*yattsu*
nine/*kokonotsu*
ten/*to*

If you want five of something, simply point at it and say, *Itsutsu kudasai*. Or, when in doubt, just count with your fingers, or write the number down. Both will work just fine in Japan.

ART & PHOTO CREDITS

Picture Spreads

INSIGHT GUIDE
East asia

Cartographic Editor **Zoë Goodwin**
Production **Stuart A. Everitt**
Design Consultants
Carlotta Junger, Graham Mitchener
Picture Research **Hilary Genin**

TAIWAN

Numbers in italics refer to photographs

KOREA

*Numbers in italics refer
to photographs*

The Insight Approach

The book you are holding is part of the world's largest range of guidebooks. Its purpose is to help you have the most valuable travel experience possible, and we try to achieve this by providing not only information about countries, regions and cities but also genuine insight into their history, culture, institutions and people.

Since the first Insight Guide – to Bali – was published in 1970, the series has been dedicated to the proposition that, with insight into a country's people and culture, visitors can both enhance their own experience and be accepted more easily by their hosts. Now, in a world where ethnic hostilities and nationalist conflicts are all too common, such attempts to increase understanding between peoples are more important than ever.

Insight Guides:
Essentials for understanding

Because a nation's past holds the key to its present, each Insight Guide kicks off with lively history chapters. These are followed by magazine-style essays on culture and daily life. This essential background information gives readers the necessary context for using the main Places section, with its comprehensive run-down on things worth seeing and doing.

Finally, a listings section contains all the information you'll need on travel, hotels, restaurants and opening times.

As far as possible, we rely on local writers and specialists to ensure that information is authoritative. The pictures, for which Insight Guides have become so celebrated, are just as important. Our photojournalistic approach aims not only to illustrate a destination but also to communicate visually and directly to readers life as it is lived by the locals. The series has grown to almost 200 titles.

Compact Guides:
The "great little guides"

As invaluable as such background information is, it isn't always fun to carry an Insight Guide through a crowded souk or up a church tower. Could we, readers asked, distil the key reference material into a slim volume for on-the-spot use?

Our response was to design Compact Guides as an entirely new series, with original text carefully cross-referenced to detailed maps and more than 200 photographs. In essence, they're miniature encyclopedias, concise and comprehensive, displaying reliable and up-to-date information in an accessible way. There are almost 100 titles.

Pocket Guides:
A local host in book form

However wide-ranging the information in a book, human beings still value the personal touch. Our editors are often asked the same questions. Where do *you* go to eat? What do *you* think is the best beach? What would *you* recommend if I have only three days? We invited our local correspondents to act as "substitute hosts" by revealing their preferred walks and trips, listing the restaurants they go to and structuring a visit into a series of timed itineraries.

The result: our Pocket Guides, complete with full-size fold-out maps. These 100-plus titles help readers plan a trip precisely, particularly if their time is short.

Exploring with Insight:
A valuable travel experience

In conjunction with co-publishers all over the world, we print in up to 10 languages, from German to Chinese, from Danish to Russian. But our aim remains simple: to enhance your travel experience by combining our expertise in guidebook publishing with the on-the-spot knowledge of our correspondents.

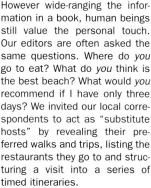

66 I was first drawn to the Insight Guides by the excellent "Nepal" volume. I can think of no book which so effectively captures the essence of a country. Out of these pages leaped the Nepal I know – the captivating charm of a people and their culture. I've since discovered and enjoyed the entire Insight Guide series. Each volume deals with a country in the same sensitive depth, which is nowhere more evident than in the superb photography. 99

Sir Edmund Hillary

The World of Insight Guides

400 books in three complementary series cover every major destination in every continent.